Financial Accounting

Financial Accounting

An introduction

Aidan Berry

Head of the Department of Finance and Accountancy
The University of Brighton, UK

CHAPMAN & HALL

London · Glasgow · New York · Tokyo · Melbourne · Madras

Published by Chapman & Hall, 2-6 Boundary Row, London SE1 8HN, UK

Chapman & Hall, 2-6 Boundary Row, London SE1 8HN, UK

Blackie Academic & Professional, Wester Cleddens Road, Bishopbriggs, Glasgow G64 2NZ, UK

Chapman & Hall Inc., One Penn Plaza, 41st Floor, NY 10119, USA

Chapman & Hall Japan, Thomson Publishing Japan, Hirakawacho Nemoto Building, 6F, 1-7-11 Hirakawa-cho, Chiyoda-ku, Tokyo 102, Japan

Chapman & Hall Australia, Thomas Nelson Australia, 102 Dodds Street, South Melbourne, Victoria 3205, Australia

Chapman & Hall India, R. Seshadri, 32 Second Main Road, CIT East, Madras 600 035, India

First edition 1993
Reprinted 1994

© 1993 Aidan Berry

Typeset in 10/11½ Times by Best-set Typesetters Ltd., Hong Kong
Printed in England by Clays Ltd, St Ives plc

ISBN   0 412 49250 4

A catalogue record for this book is available from the British Library

Library of Congress Cataloging-in-Publication Data
Berry, Aidan.
       Financial accounting: an introduction/Aidan Berry
         p. cm.
       Includes bibliographical references and index.
       ISBN 0-412-49250-4 (alk. paper)
        1. Accounting. I. Title.
HF5635.B524 1993
657-dc20
                                  92-38133
                                       CIP

Contents

Preface   x
Acknowledgements   xii

1   Introduction   1
     What is accounting?   1
     For what purpose is it used?   3
     Who uses accounting information?   4
     The conceptual framework   14
     Limitations of accounting information   17
     Some criticisms of the conceptual framework   20
     Summary   21
     References   22
     Further reading   23
     Review questions   23
     Problems for discussion and analysis   23

2   Accounting and organizations   25
     Alternative approaches to the objectives of financial reporting   25
     Type of organization   31
     Effects of organizational size   39
     Summary   43
     References   43
     Further reading   44
     Review questions   44
     Problems for discussion and analysis   44

3   Wealth and the measurement of profit   46
     Income, wealth and profit   46
     Cost-based measurements   52
     Value-based measurements   54
     Comparing the methods of measurement   55
     Conclusion   58
     Summary   60
     References   60
     Further reading   60
     Review questions   61
     Problems for discussion and analysis   61

4   Measurement of wealth and the balance sheet   63
     The measurement of wealth   63

Importance of balance sheets 65
Assets 66
Fixed and current assets 68
Liabilities 70
Owners' equity 71
The balance sheet equation 72
Determinants of the balance sheet format 77
Suggested balance sheet format 81
Summary 84
References 84
Further reading 84
Review questions 85
Problems for discussion and analysis 85

5 The profit and loss account 89
Importance of profit and loss accounts 89
Revenue 90
Expenses 94
The profit and loss account 98
Determinants of the format of the profit and loss account
    and its uses 102
Summary 104
References 106
Further reading 106
Review questions 106
Problems for discussion and analysis 107

6 Introduction to the worksheet 110
Basic double-entry book-keeping 111
Single-entry errors 116
Incorrect double-entry 116
Addition, subtraction and transposition errors 117
Summary 120
Review questions 125
Problems for discussion and analysis 125

7 Accrual accounting 129
Debtors and prepayments 129
Bad debts 132
Provisions for doubtful debts 133
Creditors and accruals 136
Prior year adjustments, extraordinary and exceptional items 143
Other liabilities 144
Summary 147
References 147
Further reading 147
Review questions 147
Problems for discussion and analysis 148

8 Stocks and work in progress 150
Stocks and work in progress 150

The nature of the business and stock valuation	152
The determination of the cost of stocks sold	154
Valuation of stocks	157
Long-term contracts	166
Disclosure requirements for stock and work in progress	167
Summary	169
References	170
Further reading	170
Review questions	170
Problems for discussion and analysis	171
9 Fixed assets and depreciation	**175**
Review of fixed and current assets	175
Depreciation	180
Methods of depreciation	185
Revaluation of fixed assets	189
Sale of fixed assets	191
Summary	194
References	195
Further reading	195
Review questions	195
Problems for discussion and analysis	196
10 Investments and intangible assets	**199**
Investments	199
Intangible assets	204
Research and development expenditure	209
Goodwill	212
Goodwill and consolidated accounts	213
Summary	218
References	219
Further reading	219
Review questions	219
Problems for discussion and analysis	219
11 Financing and business structures	**222**
Short-term finance	223
Medium-term finance	226
Long-term finance	229
Equity finance	232
Issue of shares	234
Financing structures and financial risk	236
Summary	240
References	240
Further reading	240
Review questions	240
Problems for discussion and analysis	240
12 Final accounts and organization structures	**243**
The traditional approach	243
End-of-period adjustments	246

Final accounts   248
Forms of organization   249
The sole proprietorship   250
Partnerships   250
Limited companies   256
Summary   260
References   263
Further reading   263
Review questions   263
Problems for discussion and analysis   264

13   Alternative financial statements   266
Funds flow and cash flow statements   266
The cash flow statement   268
Preparing a cash flow statement from final accounts   277
The statement of value added   285
Other statements and reports   288
References   289
Further reading   289
Review questions   289
Problems for discussion and analysis   290

14   Financial statement analysis   293
User groups   293
Context for financial statement analysis   297
Sources of information   299
The common needs explained   302
Techniques of analysis   306
Trend analysis   309
Common size statements   311
Ratio analysis   315
Summary   322
Further reading   324
Review questions   324
Problems for discussion and analysis   325

15   Income concepts and valuation   328
Economists' income measures   328
Net present value   329
Ex-ante income   330
Ex-post income   332
Economic measures and accounting income   336
Evaluation of the historic cost model   337
Summary   340
References   341
Further reading   341
Review questions   341
Problems for discussion and analysis   342

16   **Price level changes**   **343**
     Review of accounting for changing prices   343
     Current purchasing power accounting   344
     Arguments in favour of the CPP model   352
     Arguments against the CPP model   353
     CPP profit as a useful measure   354
     Summary   356
     References   356
     Further reading   356
     Review questions   357
     Problems for discussion and analysis   357

17   **Replacement cost accounting**   **358**
     Replacement cost accounting   359
     Arguments in favour of the replacement cost model   367
     Arguments against the replacement cost model   368
     Replacement cost profit as a useful measure   369
     Deprival value   370
     Summary   371
     References   374
     Further reading   375
     Review questions   375
     Problems for discussion and analysis   375

Index   **377**

Preface

The introductory textbooks in the area of financial accounting that are currently available can be broadly categorized as technical, theoretical and IT oriented. The first category is largely based on an exposition of double entry book-keeping and is weak on the context of accounting and on accounting theory. By contrast, the second category largely ignores the regulatory framework in the form of Accounting Standards and Companies Act legislation. Books in the third category are predominantly concerned with using computers to teach double entry book-keeping. Many of these texts are written in a style that students find difficult to read and understand. This book takes a somewhat different approach from those currently on the market. It provides a context for accounting, an introduction to the theory underlying accounting and at the same time provides the student with the basic tools of financial accounting and financial analysis.

The book has been written specifically with the needs of first year accounting students in mind. It builds from definitions through to a clear understanding of accounting statements, their uses and their limitations. Unlike other books in this field the examples and case studies have been tailor made for the student's needs rather than being simply an amalgamation of material. Thus the text is illustrated, where appropriate, with examples from the accounts of well known companies. Where appropriate reference is made to recent research in the field of financial accounting, but care has been taken to ensure that when this is done the research is likely to be written in a way that is comprehensible to a student with little or no background in the subject.

The text is broadly based round the needs of users of accounting information; this provides a structure for examining some of the alternative approaches to income measurement and valuation. From this base the student is then introduced to the components of financial statements through a careful examination of the definitions of assets, liabilities, revenue and expenses. The basic format used is that of a worksheet. This allows students to build their own accounting models using the various spreadsheet packages currently available. The author has deliberately avoided the trap of building computer-based spreadsheet models for students to work with. This results from a belief that the learning process is related to the exercise of building the spreadsheet model, as this encompasses the basic logic and understanding underpinning double entry principles. This is based on the premise that the use of spreadsheets *per se* does not provide this understanding, instead spreadsheet use is viewed as more appropriate to a later stage of development for which there is a pre-requisite knowledge of the building blocks which the adopted approach provides.

The adopted approach is to look initially at a simple cash-based business and then to build from this solid foundation to a more sophisticated model based upon accrual accounting principles. This allows the basic relationships between the items in the balance sheet and profit and loss account to be easily understood before the complications associated with depreciation, bad debts etc. are introduced. The regulatory framework and accounting standards are built where appropriate into the text, in order that they can be seen and understood in context. This approach has been used successfully with students on accounting degrees and other degrees in the business area at both the Universities of Brighton and Kingston.

Chapters are included on the accounts of different types of entity and the reasons for the differences are explained in terms of the needs of the potential users and the regulatory framework. A chapter on alternative financial statements, including the value added statement and the cash flow statement, is also included. From this firm foundation the student is introduced to the problems of financial analysis and the way in which the approach to this differs between various user groups. The limitations of financial statements prepared for external purposes are examined both in the context of external and of internal users. Finally some of the problems associated with income theory and alternative accounting models are introduced and discussed.

Unlike many other texts, this book uses examples from both manufacturing and service sector organizations to illustrate concepts, and wherever appropriate illustrates these concepts through real-world case studies. The examples provided in the chapters are cumulative and are intended to consolidate previous learning as well as introduce new concepts and techniques. Similarly the problems at the end of each chapter provide a vehicle for the consolidation of knowledge as well as the application of the points made within the particular chapter.

Finally, and perhaps most importantly, the text has been written with a strong emphasis on readability whilst at the same time providing the springboard for further studies in the area of financial accounting.

Acknowledgements

The ideas underlying the approach adopted in this book have evolved over a considerable number of years of teaching undergraduates and are informed by the author's own experience of accounting courses as an undergraduate. They have been refined as a result of discussions with colleagues and feedback from students and I would therefore wish to thank those people for their contribution to the final product. Some special thanks are due to Peter Perks and Peter Seneque who provided inspiration at various times through the process of developing my ideas. I also wish to acknowledge the contribution of the University of Brighton in providing me with the time to write the text and the material support to keep body and soul together. Finally, I should acknowledge the patience and support of my wife Gill, who looked after my social needs and stopped me becoming a computer addict and a recluse during the period of writing.

Introduction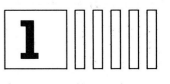

This chapter provides a broad introduction to accounting, to accounting theory, and to the users of accounting information. The conceptual framework, put forward by the Financial Accounting Standards Board in the United States, will be considered in some detail. We shall then look at some of the criticisms levelled at the conceptual framework. Prior to that, however, it is worth dwelling briefly on the role of accounting in our society.

Accounting and accountants have played a more visible role in the regulation of our society in the past decade. We have seen accounting information used to justify the closing of coal mines, sparking off the miners strike of the mid 1980s. It played a central role in the debate about value for money in the public sector, which has emerged throughout the 1980s. More recently, we have seen finance and accounting taking on a new importance as the government moves the health service towards self-management. In the private sector, the start of the 1990s saw major public companies such as Polly Peck and the Maxwell group getting into serious trouble. This will raise more issues and questions about the role of accounting, and accountants, in the regulation and control of the private sector. The 1980s and 1990s have also seen increasing public awareness and debate around environmental issues such as pollution control etc. Accountants are currently debating the role that accounting and accountants may play in this area in the future.

From this, you can see that accounting has a major role in society. It is not always a high profile role, nor is it always perceived as a glamorous role as can be verified from the way in which it has been portrayed in the Monty Python television comedy series and other comedy shows. However, its scope and its effects, are becoming more and more pervasive. We therefore need to understand what it is.

What is accounting?

The *Concise Oxford Dictionary* defines accounting as 'the process or art of keeping and verifying accounts'. As you will see as you progress through this book, there are many areas of debate within accounting which make the use of the word art in the definition above very apposite. However, the definition leads us to the question of what is meant by accounts. If you were to look up the word 'account' in *Roget's Thesaurus* you would be directed to words such as report and narration. Further investigation would reveal that accounting is also referred to as commercial arithmetic, double-entry book-keeping etc. These alternatives imply totally different things, a report being something that conveys information for a particular purpose, whereas commercial arithmetic implies a mechanical exercise following agreed rules or principles.

In practice, although accounting is normally seen as a series of figures, which may give the impression that it is only a form of commercial arithmetic, these are, in fact, merely a convenient way of summarizing and reporting information that would be indigestible in narrative form. For example, if you were asked to provide a report giving details of the value of everything you own, it would be simpler to use figures to represent the value rather than words. On the other hand, there are certain things that do not lend themselves to summaries in numerical terms. An example may be the value of good health, the value of lead-free petrol, or even the value of a qualification such as a degree.

Apart from being concerned with what can and what should be reported – which we shall consider in Chapter 2 – other issues need to be considered. For example, can the information be reported in a numerical format, and is that the best format? We also need to consider whom the report is for and what it is to be used for. For instance, you may give a totally different account of your car's capabilities to a prospective buyer than you would to your mechanic. So, we can see that the question of defining accounting has many facets, e.g. what do you report, how do you report, who do you report to, and for what purpose do you report. We shall look at some of these issues in more detail later in this chapter. Prior to that, in order to get a better idea of what accountants think accounting is, we shall look at some of the definitions contained in the accounting literature.

A definition that is commonly quoted in accounting texts, and this one is no exception, is that produced by the American Institute of Certified and Public Accountants (AICPA) in 1941:

> Accounting '. . . is the art of recording, classifying, and summarizing, in a significant manner and in terms of money, transactions and events which are in part at least, of a financial character, and interpreting the results thereof.'

This definition implies that accounting has a number of components – some technical (such as recording of data), some more analytical (such as interpreting the results) and some that beg further questions (such as 'in a significant manner': significant to whom and for what?).

Let us consider another definition offered by the same professional accounting body:

> Accounting '. . . is the collection, measurement, recording, classification and communication of economic data relating to an enterprise, for purposes of reporting, decision making and control.'

This gives us a clue to the fact that accounting is closely related to other disciplines (we are recording economic data), and it also gives us some clue as to the uses of accounting information, i.e. for reporting on what has happened and, as an aid to decision-making and control of the enterprise.

Another part of the same document sees accounting as:

'. . . a discipline which provides financial and other information essential to the efficient conduct and evaluation of the activities of any organization.'

This suggests that the role of accounting information within an organization is at the very core of running a successful organization. Thus, accounting can be seen as a multi-faceted activity which not only records and classifies information but also provides an input to the decision-making processes of enterprises.

The latter point is brought out more clearly in a later definition provided by the American Accounting Principles Board in 1970 (APB No. 4)

'Accounting is a service activity. Its function is to provide quantitative information, primarily financial in nature, about economic entities that is intended to be useful in making economic decisions, in making reasoned choices among alternative courses of action.'

The fact that it was described as a service activity reinforces the point made earlier, which was that in order to understand the usefulness of accounting we need to know who uses it and what they use it for.

For what purpose is it used?

This question can be answered at two levels at least: that of the individual and that of the enterprise. If we take the level of the individual first, we could say that the individual could use accounting information to help control the level of expenditure, to assist in planning future levels of expenditure, to help raise additional finance (e.g. hire-purchase, mortgages, etc.) and to decide the best way to spend their money. Thus we see that at the level of the individual, accounting can have three functions, i.e. planning, controlling and decision support.

At the level of the enterprise, it is used to control the activities of the organization, to plan future activities, to assist in raising finance and to report upon the activities and success of the enterprise to interested parties. You will note that the major difference between the two is that in the case of an enterprise, apart from its uses in planning, controlling and decision-making which are all internal activities or functions, accounting

---

The important points made in these definitions are that:	KEY CONCEPT 1.1
☐ accounting is about quantitative information; ☐ the information is likely to be financial; ☐ it should be useful for making decisions.	**ACCOUNTING**

also has what we could describe as an external function, i.e. that of providing information to people outside the enterprise. The latter function is usually met through the medium of annual accounts or financial reports and is generally referred to as **financial accounting**.

The external users may use the information contained in the financial report as part of their decision process, or to evaluate what management has done with the money invested in the business. Apart from meeting the needs of external users, the system that produces the financial accounting reports also meets some of the needs of internal users. For example, they need to know the results of the implementation of their plans over the last year. This requires information on actual outcomes which can then be evaluated against the projected outcomes. The reasons for differences can then be identified so that appropriate actions can be taken.

This, of course, is only one of a number of needs that management have. Their other needs are met through other reports based upon information provided by the internal accounting system. This internal accounting system, which may be additional to the system which underpins the financial reporting system, is often referred to as the **management accounting function**. The major difference between the two forms of accounting is that management accounting is primarily directed towards providing information of specific use to managers, whereas financial accounting information, which is often less detailed, has many users apart from managers. This leads us on to the second question which we posed regarding the users of accounting information.

Who uses accounting information?

Whether accounting information relates to the activities of an individual or to a business enterprise, its users can be placed in two broad categories:

☐ those inside the enterprise – the managers or, in the case of a small business, the owner (internal users);
☐ those outside the enterprise – these would include banks, the government, tax authorities, etc. (external users).

Internal users

The major internal user is the management of an enterprise. For a small enterprise this is likely to be the owner or, in the case of a partnership, a small number of individuals. However, many businesses are much larger and these may be owned by numerous individuals, or groups of individuals, as is the case with large enterprises such as Lohnro or British Airways. In many cases, the major investors are companies which are themselves owned by others, as is the case with major financial institutions such as pension funds.

In a situation such as British Airways Plc, it is extremely unlikely that the actual owners would, or could, take an active part in the day-to-day running of the enterprise. Consider the chaos if all the 295 970 people

Extract from British Airways Plc *Annual Report & Accounts 1990–91.* CASE 1.1

SHAREHOLDERS
As at 10 May 1991 there were 295 970 shareholders. An analysis is given below.

SHAREHOLDER INFORMATION

Size of shareholding	Percentage of shareholders	Percentage of shares	Classification of shareholding	Percentage of shareholders	Percentage of shares
1–1 000	96.45	9.59	Individuals	98.48	12.53
1 001–5 000	2.97	2.50	Nominee companies	0.78	70.74
5 001–10 000	0.25	0.71	Insurance companies	0.03	8.54
10 001–50 000	0.16	1.50	Banks	0.20	1.95
50 001–100 000	0.04	1.11	Pension Funds	0.03	1.25
100 001–250 000	0.05	3.43	Other corporate holders	0.48	4.99
250 001–500 000	0.03	4.45			
500 001–750 000	0.01	3.03			
750 001–1 000 000	0.01	3.06			
Over 1 000 000	0.03	70.62			
	100.00	100.00		100.00	100.00

The following have holdings in the Company in excess of three per cent of the total shares issued:	*Percentage shareholding*
Templeton Investment Management Limited	5.04
Capital International Limited (1.72 per cent is in ADR form and contained in the ADR figure below)	4.34
Delaware Management (all in ADR form and contained in the ADR figure below)	3.98
Prudential Corporation Group	3.96
Abu Dhabi Investment Authority	3.03

Morgan Guaranty Trust Company of New York, the Company's ADR Depositary, has a non-beneficial interest in 21.05 per cent of the shares in the name of Guaranty Nominees Limited. British Airways is not aware of any other interest in its shares of three per cent or more.

Commentary

The extract from the 1990–91 annual report of British Airways Plc reproduced above shows the major investors are not individuals. In fact in this case the vast majority of the shares are in the hands of nominee companies. These are companies that are holding shares on behalf of third parties.

who hold shares in British Airways tried to take an active part in the day-to-day running of that business. Instead, these owners or shareholders delegate the authority to handle the day-to-day running to a group of directors and managers.

The directors and managers are involved in the day-to-day decision-making and are the equivalent of the owners of a small business in terms of their information needs. These needs are normally met through unpublished reports of various kinds. These are generally based on information provided through both the financial and management accounting systems. The exact nature of these reports will vary from enterprise to enterprise. For example, an airline may require information about the profitability of each of its routes, whereas for a hotel chain the information required is more likely to be about the profitability of each of the individual hotels.

The form of report will also vary depending on the purpose of the report. For example, if management wish to control what is going on, it will need a report on the past transactions and performance, probably measured against some predetermined standard. For planning purposes, however, a forecast of what is likely to happen in the future will be more important. These different forms of reports and ways of grouping information are normally referred to under the generic heading of **management accounting**.

At this point it is worth summarizing the different types of management accounting reports we have alluded to in order to provide some idea of the potential scope for accounting and accountants within organizations. To do this, we need to make some broad generalizations about the needs of managers, and to categorize those needs in some meaningful way. In practice, of course, there is a certain amount of overlap between these categories but we need not concern ourselves with these here.

- ☐ **Stewardship**. What is often referred to as the stewardship function is in fact simply the need to protect the enterprise's possessions (normally referred to as assets) from theft, fraud, etc.
- ☐ **Planning**. The need to plan activities so that finance can be raised, marketing and promotional campaigns can be set up and staffing plans can be made. This is the planning function.
- ☐ **Control**. The need to control the activities of the enterprise which may include setting targets, ensuring that there is enough capacity and stock, etc. It will also include identifying where targets have and have not been met so that the reasons for the failure to achieve the targets can be identified. This is referred to as the control function.
- ☐ **Decision-making**. The need to make specific decisions (should we make the component ourselves or buy it in? how much will it cost to make a particular product? how much money will we need in order to run the enterprise? etc.). This is the decision support function.

A moment's reflection will lead you to the conclusion that the area covered by management accounting is vast in its own right. We shall therefore leave it to be covered elsewhere, and turn to the needs of the external users for whom financial accounting is one of the main sources of information.

External Users

In order to establish the information needs of external users, we first need to establish who the external users are. Fortunately there have been many reports which have done just that. Good examples of such reports are *The Corporate Report* published by the Institute of Chartered Accountants in England and Wales and in the US the report of the Trueblood Com-

Financial accounting can broadly be thought of as that part of the accounting system that tries to meet the needs of the various external user groups. This, it does, by means of an **annual report** which usually takes the form of a **balance sheet** and **profit and loss account** as a minimum.

KEY CONCEPT 1.2

FINANCIAL ACCOUNTING

mittee. The list below, taken from *The Corporate Report*, includes most of the accepted users of external financial reports.

- [ ] the owner/s (shareholders in a company);
- [ ] those who lend the enterprise money (e.g. bankers);
- [ ] those who supply the enterprise with goods or services (suppliers);
- [ ] those who buy the enterprise's goods or services (customers);
- [ ] the employees of the enterprise;
- [ ] the government;
- [ ] the general public.

These groups are normally provided with information by means of published annual reports which are the product of financial accounting. In order to decide the extent to which annual reports meet the needs of these users and to understand more fully the importance of accounting, we shall briefly discuss the needs of the external users listed above.

Owners/shareholders

As we have said, in the case of a small enterprise the owners are likely to be actively engaged in the day-to-day operations of the enterprise. In these small enterprises therefore the owners' needs will often be met by the management accounting information and reports, if these exist. As the enterprise grows, however, it is likely that the owners will become divorced from the immediate routine operations of the enterprise and will therefore not have access to the management accounting information, which in any case may be too detailed for their requirements. This is the case for many medium size companies and most if not all of the companies quoted on the stock exchange.

In all these cases the owner needs to know:

- [ ] whether the enterprise has done as well as it should have;
- [ ] whether the managers have looked after and made good use of the resources of the enterprise.

In order to evaluate how well the enterprise has done and whether resources have been adequately utilized, there is a need to be able to compare the results of one enterprise with the results of others. Information of this type is normally based on past results and under certain conditions it could be met by financial accounts.

Owners also need to know:

- [ ] how the enterprise is going to fare in the future.

Financial accounting is unlikely to provide this information for a variety of reasons, in particular because it is largely, if not exclusively, based on the past and takes no account of future uncertainties. Past results may be taken into account as one piece of information, amongst many, when trying to predict the future. However, in a changing world, it is unlikely that these results will be repeated as conditions will be different.

Although these are limitations on the usefulness of the information contained in annual reports, the annual reports are often the only form of report available to an owner who is not involved in the day-to-day activities of the business. Therefore, owners have to base their decisions on this information despite its inadequacies. Thus, for example, a shareholder, who is after all a part owner, may use the accounting information contained in the annual report to decide whether to sell his or her shares in the business. This may be done by comparing the results of that business with those of another business. In practice, the involvement of the shareholder in this process of making comparisons is, in the case of a quoted company, likely to be fairly indirect. This is because most of the information contained in the annual reports will already have been looked at by the owner's professional advisers, who may be accountants, stockbrokers or financial analysts. The investor is therefore likely to make the decision based on the professional advice they receive rather than relying upon their own interpretation of the information contained in annual reports. This is not to say that they will rely exclusively on expert information, or that they will not use the information provided in the annual reports for their decision. The reality is likely to be a mixture, the balance of which will depend on the degree of financial sophistication of the shareholder, or owner, i.e. the less sophisticated they are in financial terms the more they will rely on their external advisers. We shall return to the question of the sophistication of individual shareholders later in this chapter.

Lenders

People and organizations only lend money in order to earn a return on that money. They are therefore interested in seeing that an enterprise is making sufficient profit to provide them with their return, which is usually in the form of interest. This information is normally provided indirectly through the profit and loss account. They are also interested in ensuring that the enterprise will be able to repay the money it has borrowed; thus they need to ascertain what the enterprise owns and what the enterprise owes. This information is normally provided in the balance sheet.

In practice, research (Berry *et al.*, 1987 and 1993) has shown that UK bankers use a mixture of different approaches to arrive at the lending decision. The choice of approach is related to the size of the enterprise. In the case of smaller enterprises, the 'gone concern' or security based approach, which emphasizes the availability of assets for repayment in the event of the business failing, predominates and the emphasis is clearly on the balance sheet. However, with very large businesses the approach adopted is more likely to be the 'going concern' approach where the emphasis is more clearly focused on the present and future profitability of the enterprise. The importance of published accounting information to this group cannot be over-emphasized; nearly 100 per cent of respondents to a recent survey (Berry *et al.*, 1987) said that these reports were 'very important' and 'always used' in making a lending decision.

Suppliers

Goods and services can either be supplied on the basis that they are paid for when they are supplied, or on the basis that they are paid for at some agreed date in the future. In both cases the supplier will be interested to know whether the enterprise is likely to stay in business and whether it is likely to expand or contract. Both of these needs relate to the future and, as such, can never be adequately met by information in the annual report as this relates to the past.

Suppliers who have not been paid immediately will also be interested in assessing the likelihood of getting paid. This need is partially met, as the balance sheet shows what is owned and what is owed and also gives an indication of the liquidity of the assets. The reason that we are tentative about the use of the balance sheet in this way is that often the information is many months out of date by the time it is made public. In addition it is normally only published annually except for those companies quoted on the stock exchange who publish an interim report giving summarized information part way through the year.

Customers

Like suppliers, customers are interested in an enterprise's ability to survive and therefore to carry on supplying them with services. For example, if you are a frequent business traveller you need to be sure that the travel agency that does your booking is not likely to go out of business. The importance of this has increased with the acceptance of the idea of a global market and the recent opening up of Eastern Europe. The customers in this situation will need to see that the enterprise is profitable, that it owns enough to pay what it owes, that it is likely to remain in business and that it will provide a service efficiently and on time. Some of these needs are met, at least partially, by the profit and loss account and the balance sheet.

The employees

Employees depend on the survival of the enterprise for their wages and, as such, are interested in whether the enterprise is likely to survive. In the long term, an enterprise needs to make a profit in order to survive. The profit and loss account may assist the employee in making an assessment of the future viability of the company.

The employee may also be interested in seeing how well the enterprise is doing compared to other similar enterprises for the purposes of wage negotiations. As we shall see later in the book, the published accounts are only useful for this purpose if certain conditions are met. The accounts can also be used internally for wage negotiations, i.e. without comparisons being made, as information about a company's ability to pay and level of profitability can be obtained from the accounts. As is the case with private shareholders, there is some evidence that many members of this user group do not have the level of sophistication required to understand the contents of the financial accounts.

The government
The government uses accounting information for a number of purposes, the most obvious of which is the levying of taxes. For this purpose it needs to know how much profit has been made. This information is provided in the profit and loss account. The government also uses accounting information to produce industry statistics for the purposes of regulation etc. A recent example of regulation that stemmed from an examination of financial information along with other information has been the requirement for changes in the tenancy arrangements of the major breweries.

It should also be borne in mind that, in certain cases, the role of the government combines the function of owner (for example, British Coal), customer (the electricity boards) and a public watchdog (environmental protection boards). Equally, it can have any one of these and other roles such as regulatory roles etc. For all these purposes, the government uses accounting information.

The general public
The general public may require many different types of information about enterprises in both the public and private sector. Much of this information is not supplied directly by financial accounts. For example, the public might be interested in the level of noise pollution resulting from a particular activity, such as more frequent flights. This information is not at present provided by accounting reports; however, accounting reports may be useful in informing the public of the ability of an enterprise to absorb the additional costs of providing noise level controls. On the other hand, certain information provided in financial accounts may be of more direct relevance, e.g. the profitability or otherwise of nationalized industries. The ways in which nationalized industries use the annual reports to provide both financial and other information of interest to the public is illustrated in Case 1.2 taken from the annual report of British Coal.

Having looked at the users and their needs, the question is, how does this help us in deciding what information to report and how to report that information, or in deciding between alternative accounting treatments of a particular transaction? Unfortunately, *The Corporate Report* was published at a time when there was great debate around what was colloquially known as 'inflation accounting' and that debate almost completely overshadowed the report. Thus, there was little further action to develop the thinking contained in that report. However, the thinking behind *The Corporate Report*'s rejection of the idea that a general purpose financial statement could serve the needs of all users probably influenced Professor Macve when compiling his report for the ASC on the need for a conceptual framework. In his report published in 1981 Professor Macve concluded: 'It is unlikely that an agreed conceptual framework can be found that will give explicit guidance on what is appropriate in preparing financial statements.'

The following extracts from the 1991 *Annual Report of British Coal Corporation* show some examples of reporting on environmental and other issues of general interest to the public. Some of these will have direct impacts on the financial results, while for others the impacts may be more subtle.

Review of the year

Coal production and the environment

Policy
Following its adoption of a framework policy on the environment in 1990 British Coal has developed more detailed environment policies and guidelines dealing with deep mines, opencast, coal products and the use of coal. The objective is to achieve a balance between business aims and the need to respond positively to developing public environmental aspirations. This response is being directed to improving the quality of the environment in the communities in which we operate, as well as the wider world.

The deep mine environment
Following the visual survey conducted by the Groundwork Foundation last year a number of sites were selected as being suitable for visual improvement. Projects are now underway and extensive planting and screening schemes have been completed at a number of collieries.

British Coal's partnerships with environmental organisations continue. Several projects with Groundwork Trusts are currently being supported including the New Community Initiative in the North East and work involving the restoration of Bold Moss tip in the North West. Local nature conservation trusts are also benefiting from British Coal support: one example is the work in South Wales with the Glamorgan Wildlife Trust which is creating a new wetland habitat from old spoil tips and washery lagoons.

The key to the success of the Environmental Policy is what is done at local level. British Coal is training staff in a wide range of environmental issues, raising awareness, providing expertise, and promoting standards and policies.

To seek to ensure that environmental objectives are achieved, all operating sites will be subjected to a systematic and regular audit. Trained staff will investigate sites to check that activities comply with the environmental policy and make appropriate recommendations for action. The audits will provide a comprehensive picture of the improvements being achieved. Independent consultants will supplement the internal system.

Mining subsidence
A number of important developments took place during the year in the field of mining subsidence. Following the Government's 1988

CASE 1.2

NON-FINANCIAL INFORMATION

Continued over page

Continued from previous page consultation paper on new coal mining subsidence legislation, a new Department of Energy leaflet, 'Claimants' Rights: A Guide for House-holders' was issued in May 1990. This reflected British Coal's willing-ness to anticipate new legislation by adopting a unified approach, giving claimants the benefits of those aspects of previous legislation which are most advantageous to them.

On January 1 1991, British Coal introduced a new arbitration scheme, administered by the Chartered Institute of Arbitrators, as a quick, inexpensive and relatively informal means of resolving any disagree-ment between householders and the Corporation on subsidence claims. Organisational changes were made in early 1991 to ensure consistency in the treatment of claims in different areas.

The Coal Mining Subsidence Bill, which provides for the consolida-tion of the existing Acts governing coal mining subsidence, the enact-ment of various voluntary undertakings on the part of British Coal and a number of new provisions, was published at the end of January 1991.

During the year, 8315 new claims were received and 11 755 were resolved.

Proposed mine at Hawkhurst Moor
In February 1991 the Secretary of State for the Environment informed British Coal of his decision on its application to construct a new deep mine at Hawkhurst Moor to exploit reserves in the Warwickshire thick coal seam to the West of Coventry. While acknowledging that British Coal's proposal related to an important low cost energy resource, which it was in the national interest to develop, the Secretary of State accepted the recommendation of the Inquiry Inspector that there would be local environmental disadvantages and accordingly refused planning permission.

The opencast environment
British Coal Opencast has continued to respond positively to the national concern for nature and the local environment. The Opencast entry at the National Garden Festival, Gateshead, a half-acre nature reserve created from a derelict industrial site, was awarded the Festival Gold Medal and an award for the Best Educational Exhibit.

Nature conservation work has included support for the World Wide Fund for Nature and local Conservation Trusts in England, Scotland and Wales. Short wave radios provided for a badger protection group in Shropshire are helping in their work against badger baiting.

Research projects are looking at ways of increasing the population of bumblebees both during and after mining, and techniques have been developed to re-introduce earthworms on restored sites to benefit soil structure and to provide a food source for badgers and other creatures.

A new nature reserve on restored opencast land was opened at Park Slip, Glamorgan, while in Yorkshire, a species-rich meadow in the path of a road development was moved by volunteers using specialised Opencast equipment and advice. In the agricultural world, a Derbyshire farmer won a national award for his first crops produced on fields following restoration.

Opencast mining continues to remove unsightly industrial dereliction – 16 000 acres have been transformed over the last 20 years – returning the land to a variety of uses, including wooded areas to form part of the new planned Community Forests. In other schemes a length of canal near Chesterfield is to be restored. In Shropshire, buildings of archeological interest are being rebuilt at the Ironbridge Gorge Museum. In Derbyshire, opencast mining is the key element in an ambitious plan to relocate the 400 villagers of Arkwright, whose present homes are threatened by gas from old mineral workings, to a new village nearby.

Safety and health

Safety

There have been reductions in both the number and rates of accidents in 1990/91 in all accident categories compared with the previous year.

There were 11 fatal accidents during the year, seven fewer than the previous year. It was the second lowest number of fatalities in a single year (in 1987/88 there were nine).

Two seminars were held with representatives of senior mining management in June 1990, highlighting the 'human error' aspects of accidents.

Accidents in British Coal Mines

	Number of casualties		Casualties per 100 000 manshifts	
	1990/91	1989/90	**1990/91**	1989/90
Fatal	**11**	18	**0.05**	0.09
Major injury	**492**	597	**2.48**	2.53
Total fatal and major injury	**503**	615	**2.53**	2.62
Other accidents involving over 3 days absence	**3948**	4778	**22.14**	24.65
Total	**4451**	5393	**24.67**	27.27

To help prevent fires in mines, a working group with representatives from British Coal, Her Majesty's Inspectorate of Mines and the trade unions is looking at further ways of limiting the risk.

British Coal gave extensive written and oral evidence to the inquiry by the Select Committee on Energy into Safety in Coal Mines during the year. It welcomed the Committee's conclusion in its report that 'British Coal can be proud of its safety record compared with those of coal industries abroad.' British Coal's full response to the report was in preparation at the end of the year.

Continued over page

<table>
<tr><td>Continued from previous page</td><td>

Health

The downward trend in pneumoconiosis continued. Of the total number of men X-rayed in the 12 month period ending December 1990, only two cases were recorded. As in the previous year, no cases of Progressive Massive Fibrosis were recorded.

Constant vigilance by Medical Service and Dust Suppression Engineers remains essential if the low prevalence of pneumoconiosis is to be maintained. To this end a warning system has been implemented to detect when younger men show early signs of dust retention on their X-rays.

Routine audiometric screening was introduced on a pilot basis at collieries in most coalfields to ascertain the logistical problems of introducing it company-wide.

To raise health awareness among employees, Medical Service continues to run Health Workshops at collieries and other locations.

</td></tr>
</table>

Despite this initial rejection of the idea of a conceptual framework, the UK has gone down many similar avenues to the USA in identifying users and the qualitative characteristics of information. Where the thinking diverged was that *The Corporate Report*, having rejected the idea of a single general purpose financial statement, proposed that six further statements should be provided in addition to the normal statements. We shall be looking in more detail at one of these, i.e. the value added statement, in Chapter 13. In fact, in 1991 the UK did finally follow the US lead and issued an exposure draft on the objectives of financial statements and the qualitative characteristics of information. This, although taking a somewhat broader perspective, generally follows the same lines as the US conceptual framework which we consider in more detail below.

In the United States, the work of the Trueblood Committee was taken up virtually straightaway by the Financial Accounting Standards Board (FASB) which embarked on a programme to produce a conceptual framework for accounting. This is based on the decision usefulness approach, which is one of a number of alternative approaches that have been suggested. Details of the others can be found in the further readings identified at the end of this chapter.

The conceptual framework

The FASB, in 1978, published Statement of Financial Accounting Concepts No. 1 (SFAC 1) which states that financial reporting is not an end in itself. It is intended to provide useful information for making business and economic decisions concerning the allocation of scarce resources in the economy. The statement, which sees financial reporting in a broader sense than that identified in the earlier definitions which we quoted, includes three objectives of financial reporting. These are as follows:

Objective 1

Financial reporting should provide information that is useful to present and future investors and creditors and other users in making rational investment, credit and similar decisions. The information should be comprehensible to those who have a reasonable understanding of business and economic activities and are willing to study the information with reasonable diligence.

Two points here are worthy of note. The first is the selection of only two user groups from those identified in the earlier Trueblood Report which was the starting point for this standard. The reason put forward to support this is that a number of other users have common needs with these two groups. We shall explore this further in Chapter 14. The other point worthy of note is that the users have to have a reasonable level of sophistication. We shall return to a discussion of this point later in this chapter.

Objective 2

Financial reporting should provide information to help present and potential investors and creditors and other users in assessing the amounts, timing, and uncertainty of prospective cash receipts from dividends or interest and the proceeds from the sale, redemption, or maturity of securities or loans. Since investors' and creditors' cash flows are related to enterprise cash flows, financial reporting should provide information to help present and potential investors and creditors and other users, assess the amounts, timing, and uncertainty of prospective net cash inflows to the related enterprise.

Although this objective is about future cash flows the statement is clear that the user should derive these by looking at past profits, from these forecast future profits, and then convert these into future cash flows. This implies that in order to be useful any measure of the past must be helpful in predicting the future. We shall return to this point and examine its implications in more detail in Chapter 15.

Objective 3

Financial reporting should provide information about the economic resources of an enterprise, the claims to those resources (obligations of the enterprise to transfer resources to other entities and owners' equity) and the effects of transactions, events, and other circumstances that change its resources and claims to those resources.

This, in effect, includes the traditional stewardship role of accounting, i.e. reporting on what the enterprise owns and what it owes and how that has changed during the period.

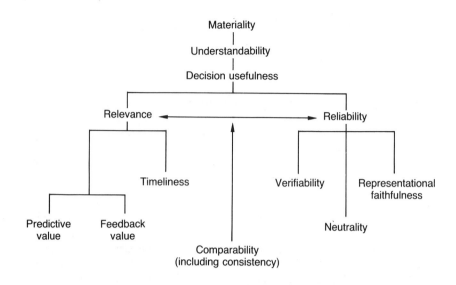

Figure 1.1 Qualitative characteristics of information. (Adapted from Underdown and Taylor (1985), p. 98.)

From the starting point of this statement of objectives the FASB has moved on to define the qualitative characteristics of information. These characteristics, it is argued, will assist in making choices when two or more alternative approaches to the solution of an accounting problem exist. The qualitative characteristics are set out in Statement of Financial Accounting Concepts No. 2 (SFAC 2) which also identifies a hierarchy of characteristics.

The most important characteristic is identified as understandability. If the user cannot understand the information then it cannot be used in making decisions. The others are decision usefulness, relevance, reliability, neutrality, verifiability, representational faithfulness, comparability, timeliness, completeness, consistency and materiality. Some of these qualitative characteristics are in conflict with each other. This is best summed up by the diagram in Figure 1.1.

Figure 1.1, which is the author's adaptation of the original, suggests that the characteristic of materiality should be considered first. If the information is material, i.e. it must be information that could make a difference if the user was given it, then we should consider understandability and decision usefulness which are primary characteristics. There is then a trade-off between relevance and reliability. In order to be relevant information must be timely, i.e. not out of date, and it must either have predictive value, i.e. be useful for predicting future events, or feedback value. On the other hand, it also needs to be reliable and for this it must be capable of independent verification which will take time, even if this is possible. It must be neutral, i.e. free from bias, and it must represent the economic events it is trying to portray faithfully. In order to be useful, it must also be comparable with other information as this will help the decision-maker in forming judgements.

As we have pointed out, the UK has not yet gone down the same line as the US by adopting a conceptual framework based on decision usefulness although it is clearly moving in that direction. Instead, it has largely continued without any theoretical basis, preferring to base its decisions around some fairly loose concepts contained in Statement of Standard Accounting Practice No. 2 (SSAP 2), which we shall discuss as we progress through the book. SSAP 2 was issued by the Accounting Standards Steering Committee (ASSC), which later became the Accounting Standards Committee (ASC) and is currently known as the Accounting Standards Board (ASB). The ASSC was set up in response to criticism of the accounting profession in the 1960s. Its role was seen as providing guidance on best practice. In many ways it has been reactive rather than proactive and what it has done to date is largely to formalize the somewhat *ad hoc* system for choosing between alternative solutions that has always characterized the British response to accounting problems. This has led to a situation where statements of standard accounting practice (SSAPs) have had to be revised or replaced when the approach adopted in that standard becomes unacceptable.

This revision and replacement could be taken to imply that some sort of framework is needed – whether that is the conceptual framework of the FASB or one of the other approaches to an accounting theory is open to debate. A number of alternatives have been suggested, including relating accounting theory directly to theories in economics and behavioural science – see, for example, Edwards and Bell (1961). Others have tried to build theories around a process of identifying postulates and principles for accounting, e.g. Moonitz (1961). All of these approaches have been attempts to move away from the previous system, which was based largely, if not entirely, on empirical observation and pragmatism to a system based on a sound theoretical base. This raises the question, what is an accounting theory and how do we choose between alternative theories?

In 1966 the American Accounting Association defined accounting theory as 'a cohesive set of hypothetical, conceptual and pragmatic principles forming a general frame of reference for a field of study'. Underdown and Taylor (1985) suggest that a good theory has to have the following characteristics. It must have explanatory or predictive powers; it must be capable of being tested; it must be logically consistent; it must be consistent with other theories in related areas; and it should provide a focus for guiding research into problems. The question of whether the conceptual framework meets these criteria will be discussed in more detail later. Prior to that, however, we need to look at the limitations of accounting information in order to provide a context for that discussion.

Limitations of accounting information

First, and perhaps most importantly, it has to be stressed that accounting is only one of a number of sources of information available to decision-makers. It may be the case that other sources of information are just as important, if not more so, than the information contained in the accounts. To give you a flavour of what we are talking about, the research with bankers referred to earlier showed that in certain cases a banker's personal interview with a client is as important as financial information. This is because accounting generally only reports on financial items, i.e. those that can be expressed in financial (monetary) terms, whereas the information bankers are trying to derive from the interview is more qualitative, such as an impression of the ability of the applicant to run a successful business. It could also be the case that the information which accounting provides is only of secondary importance, as might be the case where the business is a cash business, e.g. a fast-food outlet or market trader, and the information reflected in the published accounts may not be a precise indication of the true turnover of the business. A good example of information other than financial which may be useful to external users is that provided in the 1990–91 Annual Report of British Airways Plc reproduced in Case 1.3.

Even given the role of accounting information in relation to other information, we also have to bear in mind that in general financial accounting information relates to the past and the decisions that need to be taken relate to the future. Thus, unless the past is a reasonable predictor of the future, the information may have limited value for this purpose. In the real world, because of the impacts of such things as changes in technology, new innovations, changing tastes and inflation, the past is unlikely to be a good predictor of the future.

Apart from these problems, there is also the question of what is and what is not included in the financial accounts. For instance, some items which, it is generally agreed, should be included in financial reports are often difficult to measure with any accuracy and thus the figures become more subjective. For example, how do we decide on a figure to represent something that is only half complete? An example of this problem is a half finished hotel in Spain or Mauritius. In the case of Mauritius, the problem is exacerbated by the fact that the main access is by air and the present capacity of the airport is exceeded by currently completed and nearly completed hotels. Another example is the problem of deciding how long something is going to last. For example, a motor vehicle clearly loses value the older it gets and we might decide that a vehicle ceases to be useful to the business after four or five years. The time period is, to some extent, an arbitrary decision as there are many older vehicles that still serve a useful purpose. Most, if not all, of London Transport's Routemaster buses are over twenty years old. Indeed some even older vehicles have been made into tourist attractions in their own right, for example the Orient Express.

In addition to the problems of deciding how long things will last or what stage of completion they have reached, there are certain items which are not only difficult to quantify in terms of their value but about which there are still doubts relating to their inclusion in financial reports. For example, the value of a football club is dependent on its ability to attract supporters; this in turn is dependent on its ability to succeed which is dependent on the abilities of the players etc. However, it is doubtful that an objective value could be placed on a player as this value will vary with the player's fitness, form, etc. Having said that Spurs football club included their players in their accounts for 1989 at a figure of £7.8 million. Similar issues are at the root of the debate about the exclusion or

The relative importance of financial information in relation to other information will vary from organization to organization. The financial information also has to be looked at in the context of other information. In this regard it is interesting to see that the operating statistics provided in the 1990–91 Annual Report of British Airways Plc contain a lot of information about other performance measures as well as the financial performance measures.

CASE 1.3

IMPORTANCE OF NON-FINANCIAL INFORMATION

OPERATING STATISTICS
For the five years ended 31 March 1991

SCHEDULED SERVICES	1987	1988	1989	1990	1991
Traffic and capacity					
Revenue passenger km (RPK) (m)	41 356	49 123	57 795	61 915	64 734
Available seat km (ASK) (m)	61 722	69 970	82 984	86 601	92 399
Passenger load factor (%)	67.0	70.2	69.6	71.5	70.1
Cargo tonne km (m)	1 444	1 793	2 249	2 400	2 463
Total revenue tonne km (RTK) (m)	5 267	6 345	7 636	8 290	8 641
Total available tonne km (ATK) (m)	8 141	9 427	11 404	12 035	12 929
Overall load factor (%)	64.7	67.3	67.0	68.9	66.8
Passengers carried (000)	17 276	20 169	22 578	23 671	24 243
Tonnes of cargo carried (000)	291	361	459	498	506
Financial					
Revenue per RPK (p)	6.00	5.82	5.96	6.37	6.27
Revenue per ASK (p)	4.02	4.08	4.15	4.55	4.39
Net operating expenditure per ASK (p)	3.73	3.74	3.75	4.11	4.21
Break-even passenger load factor (%)	62.1	64.4	62.9	64.5	67.2
Revenue per RTK (p)	52.1	49.6	49.6	52.2	51.3
Revenue per ATK (p)	33.73	33.36	33.22	35.98	34.29
Net operating expenditure per ATK (p)	31.51	30.84	30.30	32.77	33.00
Break-even overall load factor (%)	60.4	62.2	61.1	62.8	64.3
Average fuel price (US cents/US gallon)	58.36	63.78	60.22	69.72	89.72
Operations					
Punctuality (% within 15 minutes)	81	80	72	72	73
Regularity (%)	99.2	99.2	99.0	98.9	98.7
Unduplicated route km (000)	555	692	677	685	665

TOTAL AIRLINE OPERATIONS
including Caledonian Airways Ltd

	1987	1988	1989	1990	1991
Total revenue tonne km (m)	5 784	6 895	8 002	8 627	8 979
Total available tonne km (m)	8 751	10 083	11 868	12 445	13 351
Passengers carried (000)	20 041	23 230	24 603	25 238	25 587
Aircraft in service at year end	164	197	211	224	230
Aircraft utilisation (average hours per aircraft per annum)	2 801	2 891	2 886	2 787	2 663
Revenue flights (000)	217	234	269	274	271
Revenue aircraft km flown (m)	282	312	364	375	389
Net operating expenditure per ATK (p)	30.9	30.4	30.0	32.4	32.7
Average airline staff employed (see Note below)	39 498	42 709	48 760	50 320	52 809
ATKs per employee (000)	221.6	236.1	243.4	247.3	252.8
RTKs per employee (000)	146.4	161.4	164.1	171.4	170.0

Note: The actual number of airline staff employed at 1 April 1991 was 51 695

inclusion on a balance sheet of the value of brands which we shall consider in Chapter 10.

In addition to the questions raised above, there are many environmental factors which need to be taken into account but which cannot be adequately included in accounts, although they may be quantifiable in money terms. Examples are the potential market for the product, the impact of the European Community (EC), quotas, tariff restrictions and environmental issues. Some commentators argue that if these were to be included in the annual reports of a business it could lead to a loss of competitive advantage. Others suggest that compared to the damage that non-reporting could – and indeed has – caused to the environment the loss of competitive advantage is not the main issue.

Finally, we have to deal with the fact that accounting information is expressed in monetary terms and assumes that the monetary unit is stable over time. This is patently not the case, and although there has been much discussion on the problems of accounting in times of changing prices, no agreed solution has yet been found. We shall return to this theme in Chapters 15 to 17.

We can conclude from the discussion above that, whilst it is clear that accounting provides some information that is useful to decision-makers, it has to be borne in mind that:

□ the information is only a part of that which is necessary to make 'effective' decisions;
□ accountancy is as yet an inexact science and depends on a number of judgements, estimates, etc.;
□ the end result of the accounting process can only be as good as the inputs and in times of rising prices some of these inputs are of dubious value;
□ accounting systems can be counterproductive, e.g. the maximization of a division's profit (such as the bars in a hotel) may not always ensure the maximization of enterprise profit.

With these limitations in mind, we shall now move our discussion to some of the main criticisms levelled at the conceptual framework.

Some criticisms of the conceptual framework

The fact that the conceptual framework is limited to only two users and the extent to which the assumption that the information that these users need is adequate for the other users has never been tested. Similarly, the assumption that the identified users will be sufficiently sophisticated to understand the contents of the financial reports is open to question. In the UK there has been a reasonable amount of empirical research into the users of accounting information and their views on the importance of that accounting information. For example, Lee and Tweedie looked at private shareholders in 1976, and in 1981 they looked at institutional investors; Berry *et al.* (1987 and 1993) covered bankers; Arnold and Moizer (1984) looked at investment analysts. However, of these studies, only the research by Lee and Tweedie (1976) with private shareholders specifically addressed the question of whether the accounts were understood, and they found that the level of understanding was not very high. Similar results can be found in the work of Hussey (1975) and Sherer *et al.* (1981) with employees which found that the extent of their understanding was not particularly high. Thus, although there is not a lot of empirical research, the indications are that the level of sophistication needed by users is higher than that exhibited by some user groups. Therefore, the second assumption underpinning the conceptual framework has yet to be rigorously tested.

In terms of the second objective, it is clear that an underlying assumption is that the past is not only useful for evaluation of results to date, but that it also provides a useful reference point for predicting the future. In this case there has been considerable research and the major conclusions of the studies, e.g. Watts and Leftwich (1973), is that past accounting profits are not good predictors of future profits. Some more positive results have been found when using accounting numbers to predict corporate failure, e.g. Altman (1968) and Taffler (1983). However, there is considerable criticism and disquiet with this work mainly directed at the fact that there is no theory to explain why a combination of certain numbers should be useful in failure prediction. Thus the basic assumption underlying the second objective that the past is useful as a predictor of the future is also still unproven.

On a more general level, some of the criticisms of the conceptual framework question the adoption of a decision-usefulness approach and suggest other approaches would be more relevant. These are outside the scope of this book but references to them can be found in the further reading at the end of the chapter. Countering some of these criticisms, the supporters of the conceptual framework would argue that it provides a framework for standard setters to work within, that it should make standards more internally consistent than they are currently, and finally that it helps to reduce the impact of personal bias and political pressures on standard setters. Thus, the debate about the conceptual framework and the need for such a conceptual framework is likely to continue for some years. However, in the opinion of the author it has produced a major step forward even if its main impact has been to open and widen the debate. We shall leave our consideration of that debate here and summarize our discussion before moving on to consider the impacts of different types and sizes of organization, and other factors on what is reported.

Summary

In this chapter, we have tried to give a flavour of what accounting is, and the debate around users and the fundamental objectives of financial accounting. We have looked at the conceptual framework and some of the criticisms surrounding it. We have indicated that accounting will only be useful if it is used knowledgeably and if its limitations are understood. We have identified the fact that there are a number of alternative theories suggested and that approaches other than the decision-usefulness approach, which is the one adopted by the conceptual framework, have also been suggested. Readers who are interested in pursuing these areas will find some useful references in the further reading at the end of this chapter.

Before moving on you should work through the review questions and problems to ensure that you have understood the main points of this chapter.

References

Altman, E. (September 1968) Financial ratios, discriminant analysis and the prediction of corporate bankruptcy. *Journal of Finance*.

American Institute of Certified Public Accountants (AICPA) (1975) *Report of the Study group on the Objectives of Financial Statements* (Trueblood Report).

Arnold, J. and Moizer, P. (Autumn 1984) A survey of the methods used by UK investment analysts to appraise investments in ordinary shares. *Accounting and Business Research*.

Accounting Standards Board (ASB) (1991) *Exposure Draft Statement of Principles: the Objective of Financial Statements and the Qualitative Characteristics of Information*. Accounting Standards Board, London.

Accounting Standards Committee (ASC) (1975) *The Corporate Report*, Institute of Chartered Accountants in England and Wales.

Berry, A., Citron, D. and Jarvis, R. (1987) *The Information Needs of Bankers Dealing with Large and Small Companies*, Certified Accountants Research Report 7, Certified Accountants Publications, London.

Berry, A.J., Faulkner, S., Hughes, M. and Jarvis, N. (1993) *Bank Lending: Beyond the theory*, Chapman & Hall, London.

Edwards, E.O. and Bell, P.W. (1961) *The Theory and Measurement of Business* Accounting Concepts No. 1 (SFAC 1) *Objectives of Financial Reporting by Business Enterprises*.

Financial Accounting Standards Board (FASB) (1980) Statement of Financial Accounting Concepts No. 2 (SFAC 2) *Qualitative Characteristics of Accounting Information*.

Hussey, R. (1975) *Who Reads Employee Reports*, Touche Ross.

Lee, T.A. and Tweedie, D.P. (1976) *The Private Shareholder and the Corporate Report*, ICAEW.

Lee, T.A. and Tweedie, D.P. (1981) *Institutional Use and Understanding of Corporate Financial Information*, ICAEW.

Macve, R. (1981) *A Conceptual Framework for Financial Accounting and Reporting*, ICAEW.

Moonitz, M. (1961) *The Basic Postulates of Accounting*, AICPA.

Statement of Standard Accounting Practice No. 2, (1971) *Disclosure of Accounting Policies*, Accounting Standards Committee.

Sherer, M. *et al.* (1981) *An Empirical Investigation of Disclosure Usage and Usefulness of Corporate Accounting Information*, Managerial Finance.

Taffler, R.J. (Autumn 1983) The assessment of company solvency and performance using a statistical model. *Accounting and Business Research* 295–308.

Underdown, B. and Taylor, P. (1985) *Accounting Theory and Policy Making*, Heinemann.

Watts, R. and Leftwich, R. (1973) The time series of annual accounting earnings. *Journal of Accounting Research*.

Further reading

A fuller discussion of accounting in its wider context can be found in *Financial Accounting*, Chapters 1–3, by J. Arnold, T. Hope and A.J. Southwood (Prentice Hall, 1985).

For a discussion of accounting theories and approaches to accounting theory read B. Underdown and P. Taylor, *Accounting Theory and Policy Making* (Heinemann, 1985).

An interesting comment and criticism of the ASB's proposed adoption of the same approach as the US can be found in M. Page, 'The ASB's proposed objective of financial statements: marching in step backwards? A review essay', *British Accounting Review*, Vol. 24, No. 1, March 1992.

A fuller discussion on environmental issues and accounting can be found in R. Gray's article in *Accounting Organisations and Society*, July 1992, Vol. 17, No. 5.

Review questions

1. For what purposes is accounting information used:

    (a) by the individual?
    (b) by the enterprise?

2. Who are the users of accounting information and which accounting reports do they normally use?

3. What are the needs of internal users? Can you identify any other needs of internal users? If so, can you suggest how these would be met?

4. What are the limitations of accounting information?

5. Examples were given for certain of the limitations. Can you give examples of your own?

6. What are the major determinants of a useful accounting system?

7. What are qualitative characteristics of information and what use are they?

8. What criticisms can be levelled at the conceptual framework?

9. What are the ingredients of a good theory?

Problems for discussion and analysis

1. It was pointed out that accounting information is only a part of the input to the decision-making process. In order to expand your understanding of the role of accounting information, for the situation outlined below:

    (a) identify the accounting information that would be relevant, and
    (b) identify any other information that would be relevant.

    Bed & Co. run a small provincial hotel catering mainly for commercial travellers and other business people. The existing business is reasonably profitable but because of the location there is little chance of expanding the trade. The owners believe there are opportunities to be taken in the home delivery food market which would utilize their existing surplus capacity for food production. The owners have little knowledge of the market but feel that there is money to be made and that it would be complementary to their existing business.

2. Sloth was left some money in a will and decided that he should give up his job and go in to business for himself. Whilst the lawyers were still sorting out the estate he started looking round for a suitable business. After a short while he identified a small bed and breakfast business that he felt was worth investing in. He was still uncertain how much he had inherited but thought it was probably between £100 000 and £120 000. The business was for sale for £180 000 so assuming that he could finance the remainder of the purchase price he engaged an accountant to check over the books of the existing business and report back to him. As proof of his good faith he deposited with the business agents the sum of £3000 which he had in savings.

The report from the accountant confirmed his initial impression that the business was worth investing in so he paid the accountant's modest fee of £500. At this stage he discussed his plans more fully with his bank manager who was duly impressed with the professional approach he had taken.

His bank manager pointed out that Sloth had no business experience and as such was a high risk from the bank's point of view. However, in view of their long-standing relationship the bank was prepared to take a chance and the manager indicated that the bank would lend Sloth 40% of the purchase price.

On the basis of this Sloth signed a conditional agreement to buy the business. A short while after this he received a letter from the lawyers stating that his inheritance amounted to only £90 000. He could not raise the additional finance to purchase the business so withdrew from the agreement, recovered his £3000 deposit and purchased the lease on the food concession at a local tourist attraction for £60 000 and employed somebody to run and manage it for him.

You are required to discuss the point at which, in your opinion, the accounting process should begin, giving reasons for your point of view. You should pay particular attention to the dual needs of Sloth as an owner and as a manager.

Accounting and organizations 2 ||||||

In Chapter 1, we discussed the users of accounting information and their needs. We also looked at the FASB's conceptual framework in which the objectives of financial reporting were set out. As we indicated in Chapter 1, a user-needs framework is one approach to the definition of the objectives of financial reporting. Some alternative approaches that we shall discuss in this chapter are that the producers of financial reports decide on the objectives or that the accounting profession decide on the objectives. We shall use the analysis of Cyert and Ijiri (1974) as a framework for discussing the ways in which these alternatives fit and interact with each other. From here, we shall move on to discuss the impacts of different types of organization and of organizational size on financial reporting. Through this discussion we shall identify some of the boundaries and limits of financial reporting. Our discussion of different types of organization will necessarily be limited by the space available and the fact that this is an introductory text. However, the examples chosen are intended to provide the reader with a broader perspective on what accounting reports should and do contain.

Alternative approaches to the objectives of financial reporting

We shall commence with a brief recap of the user-needs, oriented approach described in Chapter 1. As we said, in Chapter 1, parallel work on a user-needs oriented approach took place in the UK and the USA in the early 1970s. However, it developed in different ways in the two countries with the USA adopting the approach of narrowing the user groups down to two broad categories, i.e. owners and creditors, and assuming that if these groups' needs were met, then the majority of the needs of the other groups would be met. From this base, the FASB issued Statement of Financial Accounting Concepts No. 1. This set out the objectives of financial reporting in terms of meeting the needs of the particular user groups identified.

In the UK, the path followed in the early 1970s was very similar to that of the USA, involving the identification of user groups and their needs. This, however, led to a situation where the conceptual framework was initially rejected as the way forward on the basis that it was felt that a single general purpose financial statement could not meet the needs of all the user groups identified in *The Corporate Report*. The approach suggested in that report was one of producing different statements which were more user-specific than the balance sheet and profit and loss account. An example of one such statement is the value added statement which we discuss in Chapter 13. However, as we have seen, in 1991 the Accounting Standards Board decided to follow the US lead and issued an exposure draft on objectives and qualitative characteristics of information. The approach differs slightly from that adopted in the USA because more users are included, although the emphasis is clearly on investors and potential investors.

The fact that the two countries followed somewhat different paths from very similar starting points would at first sight appear to be surprising. However, part of the explanation may be that, in both cases, although user needs were identified, these were perceived needs, not actual needs. In other words, they were largely the accounting profession's perception of what accounting information users would require in order to enable them to make decisions. This perception and, to some extent, its translation into objectives was influenced by other factors. One of these would have been the accounting profession's perception of what the producers of accounts would supply. Another would have been, what the accounting profession in its role as auditor of annual accounts would be willing to verify.

The result of such a process, almost by definition, must be a compromise between the perceived needs and objectives of the three groups involved, i.e. the users, the producers and the accounting profession. It is argued, that these three groups have different perspectives on what the objectives of financial reporting should be. These different perspectives lead to areas where there are conflicts of interest between the groups, and it is only in the area where there are no conflicts of interest that consensus is achieved. Cyert and Ijiri (1974) considered the interaction between these three groups and Figure 2.1 illustrates their analysis.

The diagram describes the situation where there are conflicts of interest. We shall explain what each of the areas mean starting with the users and working anti-clockwise.

User needs

In Area 1, users would like to have the information but the firms are not prepared to provide it, nor is the accounting profession prepared to audit that information. An example of this type of information is forecasts of future profits or cash flows. It is clear that if users are trying to make decisions relating to the future, i.e. to invest or withdraw investment from this particular business, then forecast information would be helpful. Research with bankers in the UK (Berry *et al.*, 1987) showed that 62% of those surveyed considered this type of information very important. However, that research also showed that the use of such information was less than would be commensurate with its importance rating. The discrepancy between the two was explained by the fact that either the information was not available or the banker was not given access to the information, i.e. the producers were reluctant either to provide the infor-

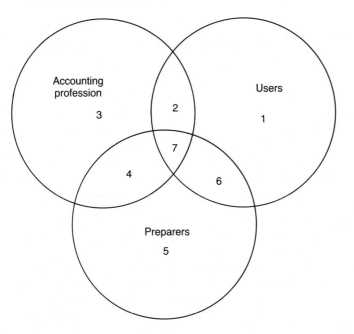

Figure 2.1 Conflict of interests and consensus between users and preparers of accounting information and the accounting profession.

mation or to disclose that information for reasons relating to competition and confidentiality. However, even if the producers were not reluctant to provide such information, it is extremely doubtful that the accounting profession would be happy to authenticate the information or even comment upon its validity.

In Area 2, once again, the firms are reluctant to provide the information that the users require. However, the difference is that here, if the information was provided, the accounting profession would be happy to audit that information. Information of this type would tend to be objective factual information that could be independently verified. This is because the accounting profession, in its role as auditors, prefers to deal with objective verifiable information rather than subjective information that is difficult to substantiate. An example could have been the profits made by supplying goods to South Africa during the period when sanctions were in place. Here, some user groups would have been interested in the information, and the information was factual as many British products were available in South Africa throughout the period of the sanctions. However, the producers of financial accounts would have been reluctant to disclose such information due to the pressures that had been put upon those firms who had maintained investments in and ties with South Africa.

The accounting profession

Area 2 would also include information that the accounting profession perceives to be important and that users require but which producers are reluctant to disclose. In many cases, this conflict can be resolved through the accounting profession influencing legislators or, more directly, through the mechanism of the issue of accounting standards. The accounting standards cover both the areas of and the levels of disclosure that have to be met in audited accounts. They are effectively mandatory, and if preparers do not follow them the accounting profession can, and does, bring that to the attention of the users of accounts through a qualification contained in the audit report. An audit report is included in the annual accounts of every company but is not required for sole traders.

The mechanism for the issue of these accounting standards in fact goes some way to solving conflicts of interest. This is because it involves consultation with users and preparers of accounts. This consultation process is normally followed by the issue of an exposure draft which is discussed and commented upon by interested parties and results, in most cases, in the issue of an accounting standard. The final version of the accounting standard takes into account the views expressed during the process. Although some of the conflicts can be resolved in this way, there are other conflicts which cannot be resolved so easily. This is where the FASB hopes that the conceptual framework will prove useful by providing a benchmark against which opposing views can be tested.

Area 3 describes information that the accounting profession would be happy to deal with via an audit, but which the users have no interest in, and the preparers are not willing to provide. It would include any factual information that can be objectively verified. This may include information that the accounting profession feels should be disclosed on the grounds of accountability, or information that the profession thinks the users would find useful. The problem with the latter position is that it cannot be easily tested as users are not in a position to judge the usefulness of something until they know what it is and what it can do. For example, early mankind could not judge how useful the wheel would be until it existed. In fact, many of the things we take for granted today were probably seen as crackpot, useless inventions at some time in the past. The same problem arises with financial information, in that until you have it you cannot identify what it is and what it can be used for. This was the 'Catch 22' in the employment legislation that gave worker representatives access to 'confidential' information. If management refused to provide the information on the grounds of confidentiality, the worker representatives had to show that it would be useful in negotiations. However, until they had access to the information they could not show how it could be useful in collective bargaining. This put them in a position from which it was almost impossible to win, and in fact very few cases that went before industrial tribunals were successful.

Area 4 contains information that both the preparers and the accounting profession are happy to provide, but the users do not want. The same problem as that described above can arise with some of the information that would be contained in this area. An example of this is the detailed breakdown of the figures contained in the annual accounts into their component parts. This information is, of course, readily available from the producers of the annual accounts and would already have been verified by the auditors as part of the process of verifying the figures included in the annual accounts.

The producers

Apart from the information contained in Area 4 which we have described above, producers of accounts would also be willing to provide some information that the users want but the accounting profession is not happy to verify. This is shown as Area 6. Some of this information is provided through other means, e.g. press releases and advertising, and some is provided directly with the annual accounts. A good example of the latter is the information contained in the chairman's statement which is provided with the annual report of quoted public companies. Other examples are five-year forecasts, reports of activities, etc., some examples of which are contained in the cases in this and other chapters of this book.

Area 5 relates to information that the firms will provide but which the users do not want nor is the accounting profession willing to audit. Examples of this type of information may be information about activities that show the management in a good light or boost their standing with the owners and potential investors. In fact, some of this information will be provided in the annual report, even though it is not required by the users and the accounting profession would be reluctant to verify it. Such information would be included in the parts of the company's annual report that are not subject to audit.

The feasible area

Area 7 is the feasible area for agreed disclosure. Here, there is no conflict of interest between the three parties on the provision of information. This area is, of course, continually shifting as the parties influence one another, and the individual circles shift towards or away from each other. This causes the feasible area to enlarge and contract. Some examples of the way in which this process works can be found in recent history. The examples we have chosen as illustrations are ones which we shall be discussing in more detail later in this book.

In the 1970s and the 1980s, the accounting profession sought to introduce a form of price level accounting. However, there was strong resistance to this from the preparers of information, who, of course, include some accountants. This group was, in the main, opposed to the provision of this information and disputed its relevance and costs openly. The question of whether the users wanted the information was unclear despite the existence of empirical research by Carsberg et al. and Berry et al. The reasons for the lack of clarity are, in some part, to do with resistance to change from a known, albeit flawed, system to one whose merits were unknown and about which there were deep differences of opinion within the accounting profession. In the end, the resistance from the preparers, which took the form of refusal to abide by the provisions of the accounting standard, led to a climb-down by the accounting profession. This is, in fact, an example of something that should have been in Area 7 or, at the very least, in Area 2, but for the reasons outlined above, amongst others, ended up in Area 3.

Another example that occurred in the late 1980s and early 1990s, was the debate around the inclusion of a value for brand names, such as Pepsi Cola or Milky Way, in accounts. In this case, the pressure for inclusion came from the producers who were willing to provide the information. The users, it can be assumed, would have been interested in the information as it told them more about their investment. However, the accounting profession was opposed to the inclusion of brands in the annual accounts because of the subjective valuations involved. This can be viewed as something that started in Area 5. The producers then sought to influence the users into accepting that this was useful information, so shifting it to Area 6. However, the accounting profession's resistance prevented it moving to Area 7.

Although Figure 2.1 gives the impression that the boundaries between the needs and objectives of the groups are clear cut, the cases described above illustrate that this is not the case. In reality the boundaries are fuzzy, and the processes involved in any change from the status quo involve competing pressures from, and often within, the interest groups. What the model does do, is to provide us with three possible starting points for identifying accounting objectives. The first is to start with user needs and then see if the other groups can be shifted to accommodate these needs. This, or to be more exact a proxy version of it, is what underlies the FASB statement of objectives which we discussed in Chapter 1. As we have said, this approach has, to date, been based upon the perceived needs of users rather than being derived from actual needs. This, in itself, would not be a problem if the perceived needs were then subject to empirical confirmation. Unfortunately, this is not the case for a number of reasons.

An alternative approach to the derivation of objectives of accounting would be to take the interests of the accounting profession and move the other circles towards these. It could be argued that the process whereby accounting disclosure in the UK is largely based on Accounting Standards set by the accounting profession, indicates that this process is already happening. However, as we shall see, many contentious issues are avoided as are areas where the amount of subjectivity leaves the accounting profession open to criticism and perhaps in the final analysis to litigation.

The third alternative is to approach the establishment of objectives from the point of view of the preparers and move the others to that point of view. There is once again evidence that this already happens to some extent, if only in a reactive way. A case in point was where the FASB issued a statement on the subject of foreign currency translation and then had to withdraw it and issue another statement taking a diametrically opposite position. This was due, in the main, to pressure from the preparers of accounts who did not like the outcomes from the first method in terms of their effect on the reported profit.

Thus, we can see that, although the analysis depicted in Figure 2.1 above provides a starting point, the reality is more difficult as accounting disclosure is, in the end, related more to the relative strengths of the groups involved than to any absolute. It does, however, serve as a useful springboard for a discussion of some of the other factors affecting what is reported by organizations and the ways in which the type and size of organization can affect it. In addition, it helps us to put the conceptual framework into a wider perspective.

Type of organization

The type of organization involved can have a profound effect on what the financial accounts contain. The reasons for this may be related to legislation, to organizational objectives, to ownership or whatever. We shall therefore provide a brief summary of the main types of organization, their characteristics, and the ways in which these may influence what is reported.

Sole proprietorships

This is where a person decides to start up in business on their own. It may take the form of trading in goods – a common example is the corner shop type of business – or selling services such as hairdressing or plumbing. The business is accounted for as a separate entity from the owner, although it is not recognized as such for tax purposes. Nor, in fact, does the law recognize the business as separate from the owner. Therefore, if the business fails the owner has to pay all the debts incurred by it and failure to do so would make the owner liable to be declared bankrupt. The sole proprietor or sole trader is not subject to any formal control over what is reported in the business accounts.

Partnerships

Partnerships occur where two or more people go into business together. They are more regulated than sole proprietorships as they are subject to the provisions of the Partnership Act of 1890 and to case law. They are similar to sole traders in that the partners are liable for the debts of the partnership and the business is not a separate legal entity. They are also similar in that they are not subject to regulation in terms of what and how they report. However, the nature of partnerships does mean that there are areas of difference in their accounting and reporting when compared to sole traders. These are covered in some detail in Chapter 12 of this book.

Companies

Unlike the two types of organization described above, a company is a separate legal entity from its owners. It is also a separate accounting entity. However, in the case of a company, what it reports and the way in which it reports is governed by legislation in the form of the Companies Acts and by the Accounting Standards. Conformity with the legislation and standards is ensured through the requirement that all companies, irrespective of size or type have to produce accounts annually and these annual accounts have to be audited. If the accounts do not conform with the legislation or the standards, the auditor will issue a qualified audit report stating that fact. Most companies enjoy limited liability, which means that the liability of the owners is limited to what they contributed in the case of a company limited by shares, or what they guaranteed in the case of a company limited by guarantee. Companies also differ from sole traders and partnerships in that they are recognized as separate taxable entities and are subject to corporation tax. The legal requirements regarding the format of company accounts are covered in Chapter 12 and an example of the profit and loss account and balance sheet of a company is shown in Case 2.1.

Nationalized industries

Although, some of the remaining nationalized industries are very similar to large companies, they are subject to different legislation and different pressures. They often have to meet two objectives, one being related to profitability and the other to providing a social good. British Rail is a good example of a nationalized industry where there are conflicts between making profits and closing down lines which provide a vital link for rural communities. In the 1980s, many of these nationalized industries were privatized and are now known as publicly owned companies. This is, of course, paradoxical as before they became publicly owned through privatization they were in fact owned by the public and reported to the public through the elected representatives. One of the results of privatization has been that the controls on these, mainly monopolistic, industries have had to take on new forms. An example of this is OFTEL, which is the public watchdog on the telecommunications industry and which provides part of the regulatory framework in which British Telecom has to work. The remaining nationalized industries are subject to additional disclosure requirements laid down by the government including the provision of information on a current cost basis as well as the traditional historic cost basis used in most accounts. We shall be discussing these various forms of accounting in Chapter 3 and again in Chapters 15 to 17. Apart from the effects of those regulations at a more basic level there are differences in the format of accounts. These are illustrated and explained in Case 2.2.

Local authorities

These organizations, like the nationalized industries, are ultimately responsible to the public. This responsibility takes two forms in terms of reporting mechanisms, one being via central government and the other being directly to the local community. As central government is where the majority of the funding of local authorities comes from, the government has, in the past decade, exercised considerable control over the amount of funds and how those funds were spent. This was done through mechanisms such as rate capping, which provided limits beyond which local authorities should not spend, and if they did, they were subject to financial penalties. For local authorities, therefore, one of the major influences on the accounting and reporting structures is the need to report in a form that shows that the local authority has complied with the

Commentary

The profit and loss account and the balance sheet of Bentalls Plc for 1992 are shown below. As can be seen the profit and loss account arrives at a figure for Profit on Ordinary Activities before Tax and the tax is deducted to arrive at a profit after tax. By contrast, in the case of partnerships and sole traders there would be no profit before and after tax as, unlike companies, they are not separate taxable entities. It is also worth noting the emphasis is on profit and how much of that profit can be attributed to each share.

As regards the balance sheet, the part which is of particular interest in terms of our discussion of different types of organization is the section entitled Capital and Reserves. Here you can see that there is a distinction between share capital and the other reserves and the total of these is referred to as Shareholders' Funds.

CASE 2.1

**FINANCIAL
STATEMENTS**

Bentalls PLC

Profit and Loss Account
for the year ending 1 February 1992

	Note	1992 £'000	£'000	1991 (53 weeks) £'000	£'000
Turnover	2	**70 997**			70 727
Cost of Sales		**44 763**			43 851
Gross Profit			**26 234**		26 876
Selling and distribution		**21 523**		20 445	
Administrative expenses		**2 895**		3 107	
			24 418		23 552
Operating Profit	3		**1 816**		3 324
Interest receivable		**34**		107	
Interest payable	6	**(2 874)**		(1 952)	
Interest capitalised	11	**2 453**		1 844	
			(387)		(1)
Profit on Ordinary Activities before Taxation			**1 429**		3 323
Tax on profit on ordinary activities	7		**499**		1 289
Profit on Ordinary Activities after Taxation			**930**		2 034
Extraordinary items	8		**–**		(1 419)
Profit available for Appropriation			**930**		615
Dividends	9		**1 617**		1 617
(Loss) Retained			**(687)**		(1 002)
Earnings per Ordinary Share	10		**2.21p**		4.87p

Continued over page

Continued from previous page

Balance Sheet
1 February 1992

	Note	1992 £'000	1992 £'000	1991 £'000	1991 £'000
Fixed Assets					
Investment in property	11		35 108		33 500
Other tangible fixed assets	12		52 382		51 603
			87 490		85 103
Current Assets					
Stocks		11 160		9 290	
Debtors	14	11 843		10 613	
Cash at bank and in hand	15	923		3 911	
		23 926		23 814	
Creditors – Amounts Falling Due Within One Year					
Bank overdraft	18	1 564		–	
Unsecured loan stock	17	30		30	
Trade creditors		7 019		8 437	
Sundry creditors	16	7 639		8 189	
		16 252		16 656	
Net Current Assets			7 674		7 158
Total Assets Less Current Liabilities			95 164		92 261
Creditors – Amounts Falling Due after More Than One Year					
Creditors	17	1 339		1 930	
Bank loan	18	22 000		18 000	
		23 339		19 930	
Provisions for Liabilities and Charges	19	2 169		1 867	
			25 508		21 797
			69 656		70 464
Capital and Reserves Called up Share Capital	20		4 294		4 273
Reserves	21				
Share premium account		188		130	
Revaluation reserve		49 531		49 531	
Profit and loss account		15 643		16 530	
Total Reserves			65 362		66 191
Shareholders' Funds			69 656		70 464

The Financial Statements were approved by the Board of Directors on 22 April 1992.

L. Edward Bentall
J.B. Ryan

Commentary

The balance sheet of British Coal Corporation at 31 March 1991 is reproduced below. If you compare it with the balance sheet of Bentalls Plc shown in Case 2.1 above, you will see that the only area of difference is that there is no share capital in British Coal Corporation. Instead the enterprise is financed by loans from the government provided under the Coal Industry Acts. There are in fact probably more similarities than differences between the focus of financial reporting for private companies and that of nationalized industries as both emphasize profit.

British Coal Corporation
Consolidated Balance Sheet
at 30 March 1991

	Note	1991		£ million 1990
Fixed assets				
Tangible assets	14	**1570**		1397
Investments	15	**24**		28
		1594		1425
Current assets				
Stocks	16	**656**		649
Debtors	17	**3748**		5422
Cash at bank and in hand		**16**		3
		4420		6074
Creditors – amounts falling due within one year	18	**(1283)**		(1631)
Net current assets			**3137**	4443
Total assets less current liabilities			**4731**	5868
Creditors – amounts falling due after more than one year	18	**(704)**		(847)
Provisions for liabilities and charges	19	**(2802)**	**(3506)**	(3052) (3899)
			1225	1969
Loans and reserves				
Loans under the Coal Industry Acts	20	**1147**		1969
Profit and loss account	21	**78**	**1225**	– 1969
			1225	1969

Debtors include amounts falling due after more than one year of £2591 m (1990 £3021 m).

J.N. Clarke Chairman
M.H. Butler Finance Director

legislation and directives of central government. Local authorities also provide reports and accounts to the local electorate. The form of these accounts is quite different from those of a company and indeed differs, to some extent, from one local authority to another. However, the form and the content of the accounting information is partially standardized and regulated by CIPFA, the professional accounting body for public sector accountants.

Building societies

These were originally set up as organizations that were 'owned' by the people saving with the building society and they were run for the mutual benefit of the members. They were, until the mid 1980s, not supposed to make profits. They have always been subject to fairly tight regulation covering what they could and could not do. However, the Building Societies Act of 1986 has changed some of this and the building societies are now competing, in certain areas, with the commercial banks who are themselves subject to a different regulatory environment. This has led to some blurring of the distinctiveness of the building society as an organizational type, as has the choice of some of the large building societies, e.g. the Abbey National, to change themselves into public quoted companies. An example of the type of report provided by a building society is provided in Case 2.3.

Other provident societies

This is really a catch-all heading that would include any non-government organization that does not have as its main objective the making of profit. It would include organizations such as private medical insurers, which are set up for the mutual benefit of the members, e.g. BUPA, and many local cooperatives and similar organizations. They are subject to different regulation from companies. Most of the differences reflect the different organizational goals of these organizations which are not primarily concerned with wealth or profit maximizing. Some examples of the financial reports of these organizations are given in Cases 2.4 and 2.5.

An interesting contrast is provided by the accounts of a retail co-operative where the actual operation does not differ markedly from that of Bentalls which is also a high street retailer. However, although the fact that they are in the same type of business gives some areas of similarity, the focus is very different. In the case of the cooperative, although many of the headings used are those prescribed for all companies, e.g. gross profit, their importance is played down, as is made clear in the commentary on Case 2.5.

There are, of course, many other organizations that exist and are subject to different legislation and reporting requirements which we do not have the space to include here. These include, charities, the health service and its component parts, schools and universities. However, the selection described above gives an indication of the effects of different types of organization on what is reported and for whom those reports are provided. It also shows that the model used in Figure 2.1 only relates to

Commentary

The balance sheet of the Brittania Building Society at 31 December 1990 is reproduced below. As you can see, this is very different from the two previous examples in terms of the assets held, the format of the balance sheet and the forms of finance used. In contrast to Bentalls, there is no share capital. Instead, the enterprise is funded, in the main, by deposits from individuals who are also the members of the building society.

**Britannia
Society Balance Sheet**
at 31 December 1990

	Notes	1990 £000	1989 £000
Assets			
Liquid Assets	10	1 262 405	960 509
Commercial Assets			
Advances secured on Residential Property	11	5 701 479	5 015 203
Other Advances secured on Land	12	316 190	206 232
Other Commercial Assets	14	35 336	9 220
		6 053 005	5 230 655
Fixed Assets			
Tangible Assets	17	114 561	94 387
Other Assets	18	6 420	5 650
Total Assets		7 436 391	6 291 201
Liabilities and Reserves			
Shares, Deposits and Loans			
Retail Funds and Deposits	19	5 192 047	4 775 205
Non-Retail Funds and Deposits	20	1 425 372	1 089 991
		6 617 419	5 865 196
Other Liabilities	21	412 264	119 902
Provisions for Liabilities and Charges	22	1 019	2 612
Subordinated Debt	23	51 472	–
Total Liabilities		7 082 174	5 987 710
Total Reserves	24	354 217	303 491
Total Liabilities and Reserves		7 436 391	6 291 201

Approved by the Board of Directors on 30 January 1991.

J.L. Hill, Chairman
F.M. Shaw, Managing Director
T.J. Bayley, Finance Director

CASE 2.4	Commentary

FINANCIAL STATEMENTS OF A PROVIDENT SOCIETY

This case shows the balance sheet and revenue accounts of Friends Provident. This is a provident society which has as its main activity the provision of insurance. Of particular interest is the fact that there is no profit and loss account, instead there are Revenue Accounts. Also, because it is a provident society, there are no shareholders and therefore no share capital is shown on the balance sheet.

Friends Provident
Revenue Accounts
for the year ended 31 December 1991

Office 1991 £m	1990 £m (Note 19)		Notes	Group 1991 £m	1990 £m
5053	4586	Funds at 1 January	1(b)	6659	6329
		Income			
816	631	Premiums	1(g), 5	1201	1011
412	410	Investment income	6	555	554
1228	1041			1756	1565
		Expenditure			
603	495	Claims and surrenders	1(g), 7	941	747
85	73	Commission		116	112
89	79	Expenses		139	127
33	32	Taxation	8	43	41
810	679			1239	1027
418	362	*Net income*		517	538
330	113	Transfer from reserve	1(e)	343	123
3	(8)	Fund adjustments	9	97	(331)
751	467	*Net addition to Funds*		957	330
5804	5053	Funds at 31 December		7616	6659

Balance Sheets
as at 31 December 1991

Office 1991 £m	1990 £m		Notes	Group 1991 £m	1990 £m
5804	5053	*Long-Term Funds*	1(c)	7616	6659
		Represented by: *Investments*	1(d)		
1326	1203	United Kingdom government		1355	1226
397	239	Other quoted fixed interest		842	616
88	89	Mortgages and loans		368	332

3238	2425	Quoted ordinary and convertible		**4021**	3003	Continued from previous page
59	54	Unit trusts		**224**	196	
849	842	Property		**1024**	1043	
23	19	Unquoted: fixed interest		**66**	33	
27	21	ordinary		**34**	28	
137	91	Subsidiaries	l(m),2	**–**	–	
6144	4983			**7934**	6477	
648	660	*Less Reserve*	l(e)	**747**	720	
5496	4323			**7187**	5757	
308	730	*Current assets less liabilities*	3	**429**	902	
5804	5053			**7616**	6659	

certain types of organization and that it is most relevant to companies. These we shall discuss, in a little more detail, under the heading of the effects of organizational size.

Effects of organizational size

In general, it is true to say that the larger and more complex the organization the more complex will be its accounting needs internally and externally. However, in addition to the effects of complexity there are also different financial accounting requirements in terms of what is reported and how it is reported that are related to size. For example, some accounting standards, which are the guidance on financial reporting issued by the accounting profession, do not apply to small companies. A case in point is Financial Reporting Standard 1, Cash Flow Statements, which we shall be discussing in detail in Chapter 13. Other accounting standards allow different levels of disclosure and differences in the precision of calculation required dependent upon the size of the organization. An example is contained in the accounting standard SSAP 21 on leasing and hire-purchase transactions. Others are framed in such a way that they can only apply to certain companies. For example, the recommended treatment of rights issues in SSAP 3 on the disclosure of earnings per share could not be applied to any company that does not have a stock market price.

From the examples, it is clear that the size of the organization does have an effect on what it reports and how it reports. At a more fundamental level, it is often the case in very small organizations, whether they are companies or any other organizational form, that the main objective in the production of accounts is to ensure that tax is minimized rather than a concern with what should be reported. At the other end of the size spectrum, the concern is more likely to be with how something is reported and what the stock market's reaction will be. Thus, at this level,

CASE 2.5

COOPERATIVE SOCIETY FINANCIAL STATEMENTS

Commentary

The Revenue Account and the Balance Sheet of Brighton Cooperative Society for 1992 are reproduced below. You will see that the Revenue Account replaces the profit and loss account used by Bentalls. Although there are areas of similarity in so far as the Sales, Cost of Sales and Gross Profit are shown, from that point on the statements differ dramatically. In the case of Bentalls, as we saw in Case 2.1, the focus is clearly on profit. By comparison the Brighton Cooperative Society Revenue Account adopts the term surplus rather than profit. Thus, instead of a heading Profit before Taxation we find the heading Surplus for the year before Taxation. This difference in wording reflects a difference in the philosophy of a cooperative and a profit-oriented company.

In the balance sheet the differences are not quite so stark and in fact on the surface the two balance sheets look very similar. However, this is only on the surface as in fact, although in both cases the term share capital is used, this represents different things in the case of a co-operative society as compared to a public company.

Brighton Cooperative Society
Group Revenue Account
Year ended 18 January 1992

	Note		1992		1991
			£'000		£'000
Turnover			**103 834**		98 099
Less Value Added Tax			**6 473**		5 474
Sales			**97 361**		92 625
Cost of sales			**74 960**		72 379
Gross Profit			**22 401**		20 246
Expenses	1		**19 983**		17 515
Trading Surplus			**2 418**		2 731
Share of profits-Associated Society		**229**		276	
Interest received	2	**539**		435	
Non-trade property income	3	**152**		121	
			920		832
			3 338		3 563
Interest payable	4		**1 832**		1 847
			1 506		1 716
Exceptional items	5		**208**		24
Surplus for year before Distributions			**1 714**		1 740
Share interest		**88**		86	
Dividend stamps		**372**		292	

	Note	1992	1991	
Co-op Party Grant proposed		**5**	5	Continued from previous page
Donations		**2**	3	
		467	386	
Surplus for year before Taxation		**1 247**	1 354	
Taxation	6	**(220)**	258	
Transfer to Reserve	13	**1 467**	1 096	

Group Balance Sheet
as at 18 January 1992

	Note	1992 £'000		1991 £'000	
Fixed Assets					
Tangible assets	7	**30 831**		27 329	
Investments	8	**1 083**		937	
		31 914		28 266	
Current Assets					
Stocks		**6 695**		6 257	
Debtors and prepayments	9	**1 161**		1 124	
Investments	8	**1 291**		2 095	
Cash at bank and in hand		**849**		1 526	
		9 996		11 002	
Current Liabilities					
Amounts falling due within one year:					
Creditors	10	**8 988**		8 270	
Loans	11	**7 134**		6 476	
		16 122		14 746	
Net Current Liabilities			**(6 126)**		(3 744)
Total Assets less Current Liabilities			**25 788**		24 522
Long Term Liabilities					
Amounts falling due after more than one year:					
Creditors	10	**313**		358	
Loans	11	**9 003**		8 879	
Deferred Taxation	6	**–**		220	
		9 316		9 457	
Net Assets		**16 472**		15 065	
Financed by:					
Share capital	12	**1 937**		1 914	
Revenue reserve	13	**14 535**		13 151	
		16 472		15 065	

| CASE 2.6 | Commentary |

RECONCILIATION OF PROFIT UNDER DIFFERENT ACCOUNTING RULES

Reproduced below is an extract from British Airways 1990–91 Annual report. The statement reconciles the profit as reported in the UK profit and loss account with what that profit would be if generally accepted US accounting principles had been used. The effect of this is that, had US principles been adopted, then the reported profit would have been £137 million as compared to £95 million using UK rules and recommendations. This helps to illustrate that accounting is not an exact science and that there is a need to understand the assumptions underlying the accounts in order to understand the accounts.

British Airways Plc
Net Income under US GAAP
For the year ended 31 March 1991

			Group	
	1991 £m	1990 £m	**1991** $m	1990 $m
Income attributable to shareholders as reported in the consolidated statements of income	**95**	246	**165**	406
Estimated adjustments:				
Depreciation				
Goodwill	**(9)**	(9)	**(15)**	(15)
Fleet	**35**	50	**61**	83
Property	**2**		**3**	
Pension costs	**56**	70	**97**	115
Other income/(charges)				
Exchange gains/(losses)				
Arising on translation of cost of aircraft	**(25)**		**(43)**	
Relating to revaluation of forward exchange contracts	**3**	(2)	**5**	(3)
Arising on translation of investments	**2**	(1)	**3**	(2)
Surplus on disposal of tangible fixed assets and investments				
Arising on disposal of revalued aircraft	**19**	17	**33**	28
Arising on sale and leaseback transactions	**(10)**	(50)	**(17)**	(82)
Deferred taxation	**(31)**	(70)	**(54)**	(116)
	42	5	**73**	8
Estimated net income as adjusted to accord with US GAAP	**137**	251	**238**	414

the concern is more likely to be with the effect a new accounting standard or policy will have on reported profits, or the effect a revaluation, or the inclusion of brands, would have on the market price of the company's shares.

In terms of legislation, the 1985 Companies Act allows certain exemptions for small and medium size companies in respect of the accounting information they file at Companies House. This legislation allows small companies, as defined by the Companies Act, to file modified accounts which do not need to contain a directors' report or a profit and loss account. In addition, the information required in the notes to the accounts is limited. For medium size companies the modifications only affect the content of the profit and loss account. It should be pointed out that, although companies can take advantage of this legislation in relation to the accounts filed at Companies House, they still have to produce full accounts for their shareholders. Despite the fact that in the mid 1980s there was pressure to abolish the requirement for small companies to produce annual audited accounts, the requirement was kept. However, it may well be that at some time in the future the requirement will be abolished for very small companies.

At the other end of the size spectrum, publicly quoted companies' annual accounts have to comply with the stock exchange regulations in addition to the accounting standards and company legislation. For some multinationals, this could involve having to produce different sets of accounts to comply with legislation and regulations in other countries where their shares are traded on the stock market. An example of the sort of reconciliation that companies in this position include in their annual report is provided in Case 2.6.

Summary

We have tried in this chapter to introduce some alternative approaches to the derivation of a set of objectives for financial reporting. We have shown through our discussion of different types of organization that the model illustrated in Figure 2.1 is limited in its application. We have also seen that the actual process of introducing new disclosure, whether on a volunteered basis or as a requirement, is not as clear-cut as the diagram would make it appear. Through our discussion of different types of organization and the effects of organizational size, we have given a flavour of the diversity of objectives, regulations, etc., that cover financial reporting. We shall now leave the question of regulation and return to it in more detail in Chapter 12.

References

Accounting Standards Board (ASB) (1991) *Exposure Draft Statement of Principles: the Objective of Financial Statements and the Qualitative Characteristics of Information*. Accounting Standards Board, London.

Accounting Standards Committee (ASC) (1975) *The Corporate Report*. Institute of Chartered Accountants in England and Wales.

Berry, A., Citron, D. and Jarvis, R. (1987) *The Information Needs of Bankers Dealing with Large and Small Companies*, Certified Accountants Research Report 7, Certified Accountants Publications, London.

Carsberg, B. and Page, M. *et al.* (1984) *Current Cost Accounting, the Benefits and Costs*, ICAEW, Prentice Hall International.

Cyert, R.M. and Ijiri, Y. (1974) Problems of Implementing the Trueblood Objectives Report. *Journal of Accounting Research*, Supplement.

Financial Reporting Standard No. 1 (1991) *Cash Flow Statements*, Accounting Standards Board.

Statement of Financial Accounting Concepts No. 1 (1978) *Objectives of Financial Reporting by Business Enterprises*, Financial Accounting Standards Board (FASB).

Statement of Standard Accounting Practice No. 3 (1972) *Earning per Share*, Accounting Standards Committee.

Statement of Standard Accounting Practice No. 21 (1984) *Accounting for Leases and Hire-Purchase Agreements*, Accounting Standards Committee.

Further reading

For a discussion of and approaches to accounting theory read either of the two books, B. Underdown and P. Taylor, *Accounting Theory and Policy Making* (Heinemann, 1985), Chapters 1, 2 and 6, and R. Laughlin and R. Gray, *Financial Accounting: Method and Meaning* (Van Nostrand Reinhold (International), London, 1988), Chapter 11.

More detailed information on financial reports in the public sector can be found in D. Henley, C. Holtham, A. Likierman and J. Perrin, *Public Sector Accounting and Financial Control* (Van Nostrand Reinhold, 1990).

Review questions

1. Why should there be conflicts of interest between preparers, users and the accounting profession?

2. Why would the accounting profession be reluctant to have forecasts included in annual accounts?

3. What are the characteristics of a sole proprietorship?

4. How does a company differ from a sole proprietorship?

5. Why does the type of organization affect the financial accounts produced?

6. How does an organization's size affect the content of its annual accounts?

Problems for discussion and analysis

1. The Cyert and Ijiri model does not include the government, the stock exchange or any other regulatory body. How do you think these bodies fit in?

2. A company produces a balance sheet and profit and loss account as part of its annual accounts. In the chapter, it was pointed out that there were organizations that did not have profit or wealth maximization as their prime objective.

In the case of a charity such as Save the Children, what do you think it should report and who do you think the users of such a report might be?

3. The analysis put forward by Cyert and Ijiri is mainly applicable to commercial organizations. Discuss how it would differ for a local authority and a health authority.

3 Wealth and the measurement of profit

In Chapter 1 we established that there are a number of different users of accounting information, each of whom needs different information for different purposes. However, there are some items of information that are required by most users. At a general level these relate to what an enterprise owns and what it owes, and to how it has performed or is performing – in other words, to a measure of performance. The former information, i.e. that about what an enterprise owns and what it owes, could be termed the worth of the enterprise or its wealth. This measure of wealth or worth relates to a point in time. The other information required is about the way in which the enterprise performed over a period of time. This performance during a period can be measured as a change in wealth over time. Thus if you increase your wealth you have performed better, in financial terms, than someone whose wealth has decreased over the same period of time. This measurement of changes in wealth over time is referred to in accounting terminology as profit measurement. In this chapter we shall consider some of the ways in which accountants can measure wealth and profit and we shall discuss some of the merits of the alternatives available. We shall also examine, in some detail, the way in which the choice of a measurement system affects the resultant profit and wealth measures. To do this we need to start by defining profit and wealth as these two concepts are directly linked.

Income, wealth and profit

A definition of profit that is widely accepted by accountants is based around the definition of an individual's income put forward by the economist Sir John Hicks (1946). This definition can be illustrated diagrammatically as in Figure 3.1.

KEY CONCEPT 3.1

HICKS' DEFINITION OF INCOME

Income is that amount which an individual can consume and still be as well off at the end of the period as he or she was at the start of the period.

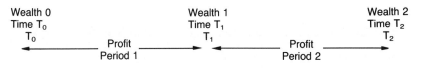

Figure 3.1 Hicks' definition of income.

We can see from Figure 3.1 that we can arrive at the profit for period 1 by measuring wealth at the start of the period, i.e. at time T_0, and subtracting that figure from our measurement at the end of the period, i.e. T_1. Similarly the profit for period 2 can be measured by subtracting the wealth at time T_1 from the wealth at the end of period 2, i.e. at time T_2.

It should be clear from Figure 3.1 that wealth is static and represents a stock at a particular point in time. Thus Wealth 0 is the stock of wealth at time T_0, Wealth 1 is the stock of wealth at time T_1 and Wealth 2 is the stock of wealth at time T_2.

If we look at the way in which profit is depicted in Figure 3.1 it is also apparent that profit is a flow over time, i.e. to measure the profit earned over a period of time it is necessary to measure the stock of wealth at the start and end of that period.

A relationship exists between income, or profit, and wealth. The definition above suggests that income can be derived by measuring wealth at two different points in time and the difference between the two figures is the income or profit. An alternative view proposed by other economists suggests that if you first measure income then you can derive wealth. This implies that the relationship is, to some extent, circular, as depicted in Figure 3.2. The different views expounded by various economists really relate to how you break in to the circle.

KEY CONCEPT 3.2

INCOME

Figure 3.2 Alternative view of income and wealth.

Wealth is a static measure and represents a stock at a particular point in time. This stock can change over time. Thus the wealth measured at the start of a period will not necessarily be equal to the wealth measured at the end of the period. The difference between the two is the profit or loss for that period of time.

KEY CONCEPT 3.3

WEALTH

KEY CONCEPT 3.4	Profit represents the difference between the wealth at the start and at the end of the period. Unlike wealth, which is essentially a static measure, profit is a measure of flow which summarizes activity over a period.
PROFIT	

To summarize, we have shown that we can express the profit for the first period, i.e. from time T_0 to time T_1, as:

$$\text{Profit Period 1} = \text{Wealth 1} - \text{Wealth 0}$$

Similarly we can express the profit for the second period, i.e. from time T_1 to time T_2, as:

$$\text{Profit Period 2} = \text{Wealth 2} - \text{Wealth 1}$$

We have also established that the profit is derived by measuring the wealth of an individual, or an enterprise, at two points in time. This, on the face of it, is reasonably straightforward but let us now look in more detail at what we are trying to measure and how we are to measure it.

We shall start by examining the case of an individual because this is simpler and more in line with your own experience. The underlying arguments and principles are just the same for an enterprise but the degree of complexity increases in the latter case. Let us suppose that we asked an individual to measure his or her wealth, i.e. the sum of his or her possessions less what is owed.

Example 3.1
Alex came up with the following lists of items owned and told us that he owed nothing:

At the start of the year T_0	**At the end of the year T_1**
A new Ford Fiesta 1.0 L	A one-year old Fiesta 1.0 L
Three new suits	Three suits
Five shirts	Five shirts
Four sweatshirts	Five sweatshirts
Four hundred pounds cash	Five hundred pounds cash

Whilst the lists above may accurately reflect what Alex owns and what he owes we cannot easily see whether he is better or worse off at the end of the year than he was at the start. We could perhaps say with the benefit of our own knowledge of the world that he must be worse off because everything is one year older. This, however, assumes that the value of his possessions decreases with time. In most cases that is a reasonable assumption but clearly there are some cases where the value is increasing. For example, would our attitudes change if the car was a 1906 Bentley? Leaving that question aside for a minute, you will have noticed that once we started to discuss the measurement of wealth we also started talking of the more abstract concept of value.

This raises two questions, one of which relates to value which we shall discuss in some more detail later, and the other relates to the way in which we assign value. In the case of the list of possessions above the easiest item to deal with in terms of value is the cash. This is because it has already had a value assigned to it with which we are all familiar, i.e. a monetary value. On the face of it, therefore, it would seem that if we assigned a monetary value to each of the items in the list we would have solved part of our problem at least. In fact it is not as easy as that as the value of money is not stable. We only have to listen to our grandparents or even our parents talking about what money used to buy to realize that the value of money has decreased over time.

We shall leave the problem of the changing value of money aside for the present and return to it later in the book. For the present, if we use money as a measure of value, then we have no problem with the value of the cash in the bank, but what of the other items? What is the value of the car, for example? Is it worth less because it is one year older, and if so how much less? The same line of argument can be applied to the suits and shirts. We do not even know if they are the same suits and shirts. In the case of the sweatshirts at least one more has been acquired during the year as he has five at the end compared with four at the beginning. We also have yet to establish whether their age is important for the purposes of arriving at a value.

In order to be able to decide on that question we need to first look at the possibilities available to us. Although numerous alternative measures have been proposed many are combinations of those dealt with in this chapter. We shall limit our discussion at this stage to the most commonly quoted possibilities. For convenience, and in order to help understanding, we shall first deal with those that relate to cost and then discuss those that are based on some concept of value. We start with original cost and then look at historic cost and finally replacement cost.

The definitions of these terms will be explained later in this chapter. The important point to note at this stage is the relationship between wealth and profit and the way in which a change in the measurement of one affects the other. This will be explored in more detail, using the example of Alex.

Commentary

The debate about the most appropriate method of arriving at a figure for the capital or wealth of a business has been going on for many years and is still going on. In terms of the Companies Act legislation accounts can be prepared under the historic cost convention or under the current cost accounting system. Given below are the two balance sheets included in the 1991 Annual Report of British Gas Plc. As can be seen there is a vast difference between the two balance sheets, all of which relates to the tangible fixed assets which are shown at a figure of £9953 million using the historic cost as the basis, and at £21 715 million on a current cost basis. The fact that the wealth is different under the two methods means, if we take the connection between wealth and

CASE 3.1

ALTERNATIVE METHODS OF MEASUREMENT OF WEALTH

Continued over page

Continued from previous page capital explained above, that we would expect the profit figure also to differ. This is in fact the case and British Gas reported a profit of £1211 million on a historic cost basis and £918 million on a current cost basis. The majority of the difference between the two is attributable to the charge for the use of the fixed assets which of course is higher under current cost as they are represented at a higher figure.

British Gas Plc
Current Cost Balance Sheets
at 31 March 1991

		Group 1991 £m	1990 £m (as restated)	Company 1991 £m	1990 £m (as restated)
	Notes				
Fixed assets					
Intangible assets	9	686	558	–	–
Tangible assets	10	21 715	19 858	17 370	16 530
Investments	11	92	76	2 223	1 651
		22 493	20 492	19 593	18 181
Current assets					
Stocks	13	366	338	285	312
Debtors	14	3 147	2 374	5 525	3 874
Investments	15	838	623	561	449
Cash at bank and in hand		61	32	50	27
		4 412	3 367	6 421	4 662
Creditors (amounts falling due within one year)	16	(3 790)	(3 220)	(3 447)	(3 113)
Net current assets		622	147	2 974	1 549
Total assets less current liabilities		23 115	20 639	22 567	19 730
Creditors (amounts falling due after more than one year)	17	(2 763)	(1 442)	(3 173)	(1 404)
Provisions for liabilities and charges	18	(191)	(132)	(60)	(52)
		20 161	19 065	19 334	18 274
Capital and reserves					
Called up share capital	21	1 065	1 065	1 065	1 065
Share premium account	22	34	33	34	33
Current cost reserve	22	16 452	15 732	16 332	15 580
Profit and loss account	22	2 253	1 912	1 903	1 596
		18 739	17 677	18 269	17 209
British Gas shareholders' interest		19 804	18 742	19 334	18 274
Minority shareholders' interest		357	323	–	–
		20 161	19 065	19 334	18 274

II. Group Historical Cost Balance Sheet
at 31 March 1991

Continued from previous page

	Notes	1991 £m	1990 £m (as restated)
Fixed assets			
Intangible assets		**686**	558
Tangible assets	d	**9 953**	8 523
Investments		**92**	76
		10 731	9 157
Current assets			
Stocks		**366**	338
Debtors		**3 147**	2 374
Investments		**838**	623
Cash at bank and in hand		**61**	32
Creditors (amounts falling due		**4 412**	3 367
within one year)		**(3 790)**	(3 220)
Net current assets		**622**	147
Total assets less current liabilities		**11 353**	9 304
Creditors (amounts falling due after			
more than one year)		**(2 763)**	(1 442)
Provisions for liabilities and charges		**(191)**	(132)
		8 399	7 730
Capital and reserves			
Called up share capital		**1 065**	1 065
Reserves	e	**6 977**	6 342
British Gas shareholders' interest		**8 042**	7 407
Minority shareholders' interest		**357**	323
		8 399	7 730

It is worth noting here that British Gas Plc is a recently privatized company and this may have affected the choice of the current cost basis of accounting for the main accounts. The basic ideas underlying current cost are discussed in Chapter 17 whilst the issue of different definitions of wealth and income are discussed further in Chapter 15.

KEY CONCEPT 3.5

ORIGINAL COST

The cost of the item at the time of the transaction between the buyer and seller.

Cost-based measurements

Original cost

The original cost of an item is the cost of the item at the time of the transaction between the buyer and seller. It should be noted that we have made a number of implicit assumptions about there being a willing buyer and a willing seller which do not need to concern us at this point. Although, on the face of it, the original cost seems to be a fairly easy figure to arrive at, it is in fact not so easy. Consider the case of this book. Is the original cost the price you paid in the bookshop? Or is it the price the bookshop paid the publisher? Or do we go back even further to the cost to the publisher? Or further still to the cost to the author? Each of these is a possible measure of the original cost, but the question is: Which is the right cost? The answer lies in the idea that the cost is the cost to the individual or enterprise on which you are reporting. This cost is normally referred to as the historic cost.

Historic cost

Historic cost is the cost incurred by the individual or enterprise in acquiring an item measured at the time the transaction took place. It is extremely important as it underpins most current accounting practice. The historic cost of the book to you will be different from the historic cost to the bookshop as these costs represent two separate transactions taking place at different points in time. Hopefully, the cost to the bookshop is less than the cost to you as this is what keeps the bookshop in business. But let us take our example a stage further. Let us assume, for whatever reason, at the end of the year you decide you no longer need this book; you therefore decide to sell it. In this situation you will probably find that the book is no longer worth what you paid for it and therefore the historic cost is no longer a fair representation of the book's worth or of your wealth. In order to tackle this problem, when measuring your wealth at the end of the year, you could write the historic cost down to some lower figure to represent the amount of use you have had out of the book.

KEY CONCEPT 3.6

HISTORIC COST

The cost incurred by the individual or enterprise in acquiring an item measured at the time of the originating transaction.

The amount that would have to be paid at today's prices to purchase an item similar to the existing item.	**KEY CONCEPT 3.7** _____ **REPLACEMENT COST**

Accounting follows a similar process and the resulting figure is known as the written-down cost. This written-down cost can be described as the historic cost after an adjustment for usage.

This adjustment for usage is commonly referred to as depreciation, and there are a number of alternative ways of arriving at a figure for depreciation which we shall deal with in more detail in Chapter 9.

The problem with historic cost and written-down historic cost is that with the value of money and goods changing over time it is only likely to be a fair representation of value at a particular point in time, i.e. at the time of the original transaction. At any other time it will only be a fair representation of value by chance unless the world is static, i.e. with no innovation etc. Clearly this is not the case and so we should look for alternative measures. One such alternative to the historic cost of an item is its replacement cost. This is certainly more up to date and allows for the changes that will take place in a non-static world.

Replacement cost

The replacement cost of an item is the amount that would have to be paid at today's prices to purchase an item similar to the existing item. It is often very relevant as those of us who have had cars written off will know. In those cases the amount the insurance company pays you often bears no relationship to what it would cost to replace your car, because yours was better than average or had just had a new engine put in. The problem that arises in using replacement cost is, first, that you have to want to replace the item. You may not want to replace a textbook that you used at school as it would no longer be of use to you. Even if we assume that you do want to replace the item, you may find that it is difficult to find the replacement cost, as would be the case with a specialist item such as the Post Office Tower.

It may also be the case that even if you could replace an item with an exact replica you may not wish to do so. For example, you may wish to obtain a newer version or one with extra features. The most obvious example of this sort of problem is the replacement of computer equipment, which is constantly expanding in power whilst its size and its price are generally decreasing. This leads us to the same problem as we had with historic cost in that the replacement cost of a computer does not take into account the age of the machine that we actually own. The solution is the same as for historic cost, i.e. estimate the effect of usage and arrive at a written-down replacement cost.

There are clearly problems with using either historic cost or replacement cost. In a number of situations these are unlikely to be useful measures of

KEY CONCEPT 3.8	Economic value is, or would be, an ideal measure of value and wealth. It is the value of the expected earnings from using the item in question, discounted at an appropriate rate to give a present-day value.
ECONOMIC VALUE	

value or of wealth. Historic cost is unlikely to be useful when prices change, whatever the reason for that change. Replacement cost, on the other hand, whilst overcoming that problem by using up-to-date costs, is itself irrelevant if there is no intention of replacing the item with an exact or close replica.

Before reading the next section on alternative measures based on value rather than cost, it is worth spending a few minutes thinking of the situations in which historic cost and replacement cost are appropriate and those situations when they are unlikely to be appropriate. This is important because any measure is only useful if it is the appropriate measure to do the job in hand. For example, whilst the acceleration of a car may be appropriate in certain circumstances it is irrelevant when doing an emergency stop. Similarly the historic cost or replacement cost of a motor car is unlikely to be useful if we wish to sell that car as the selling price will be governed by other factors. The alternative to these cost-based measures are measures which are related to value. However, as we shall see, these value-based measures also have their own set of problems.

Value-based measurements

Economic value

The economic value of an item is the value of the expected earnings from using the item in question discounted at an appropriate rate to give a present-day value. The problem is not in defining the measure but in actually estimating the future earnings as this implies a knowledge of what is going to happen in the future. The problems of foreseeing technological change, fashion changes, changes in taste, etc., all make the estimation of future earnings problematic. Even if we assume that this can be done, we are then left with the question of finding an appropriate rate at which to discount the estimated future earnings. The problem here is that every individual may wish to use a different rate depending on his or her circumstances. For example, a millionaire may not worry overmuch if money is available in a year rather than now, but if you have no money to buy your next meal the situation is entirely different. We should not totally discount the possibility of using this measure because of these problems since with the use of mathematical techniques relating to probability it is still a useful tool in decision-making. In fact it is the basis underlying techniques such as net present value which are often used in investment appraisal decisions and which we shall discuss in more detail later.

The net realizable value is an alternative measure of value to economic value. It is the amount that is likely to be obtained by selling an item, less any costs incurred in selling.	KEY CONCEPT 3.9<hr>**NET REALIZABLE VALUE**

Net realizable value

The net realizable value is the amount that is likely to be obtained by selling an item, after taking off any costs incurred in selling. On the face of it this should be easily obtainable but in practice the amount for which an item can be sold will vary with the circumstances of the sale. The problems of arriving at the net realizable value are very apparent in the second-hand car market where there is a trade price and a range of retail prices. Another good example is the house market where independent valuers can differ as much as £40 000 on a property worth between £110 000 and £150 000. Apart from the problem of arriving at a value other factors will affect the net realizable value. For example, if you are hard up you may be prepared to accept less than the market value in order to get a quick sale. The value in the latter situation is known as the forced sale value and this is the most likely value to be obtained where circumstances are unfavourable to the seller. If, on the other hand, the market conditions are neutral as between buyer and seller then the net realizable value is likely to be the open market value.

Comparing the methods of measurement

It should be clear from the above that plenty of alternative measures are available each of which has its own problems. Remember the starting point for this discussion was that we wished to establish whether Alex was 'better off' at the end of the period than he was at the start; had he made a profit? The problem is not one of finding a concept of profit as there are plenty available within the economics literature apart from the one we have already referred to provided by Hicks (see for example, Fisher's (1930) income concept and that of Kaldor (1955)). We shall be returning to consider some of these income concepts and their applicability to enterprises in more detail in Chapter 15. However, at present, all we are concerned with is the problem of measurement as most of these concepts either rely on a measurement of future income streams or on the measurement of wealth.

We have already pointed out that to measure future income streams is extremely difficult in the real world because of the effects of uncertainty. This then leaves us with the alternative of measuring wealth and leads us to the question of finding the most appropriate measure. As we have seen all the measures discussed have inherent problems, and it may be that the solution lies in combining one or more of these measures to obtain the best measure. For the purposes of this introductory chapter it is unnecessary to probe this area in greater depth as we shall be returning to it later in the book. Before leaving this area completely, however, let us reconsider our example based on the wealth of Alex and assign some monetary values to see what effect the choice of measure will have:

Year T$_0$

Description	Replacement cost £	Historic cost £	Net realizable value £
Ford Fiesta 1.0L	6180	6180	5000
Suits	390	360	60
Shirts	75	75	10
Sweatshirts	60	60	20
Cash	400	400	400

If you study the figures carefully you will notice that the only figure common to all three columns is the cash figure. Apart from the cost of the suits the replacement cost and the historic cost are also identical. In reality this will always be the case at the time the goods are bought, but it is unlikely to be the case at any other time. In this example the fact that the replacement cost of the suits is different from the historic cost would indicate that some or all of these suits were bought when the price of suits was lower than it was at the start of the year in question. In other words the point of time at which we are measuring is different from the date of acquisition and, as we said, in these circumstances the replacement cost is likely to differ from the historic cost.

You should also have noticed that the net realizable value is lower than the historic cost and replacement cost even though some of the items were clearly bought new at the start of the year. Once again this is obviously going to be the case in most situations because personal goods being resold are effectively second-hand goods even though they may not have been used. The situation for a business enterprise is not necessarily the same as some goods are not bought for use but for resale, e.g. a retailer or wholesaler. In these cases the net realizable value of the goods bought for resale should be higher than the cost – otherwise the enterprise would not stay in business very long.

Let us now look at Alex's situation at the end of the year and assign some values to the items owned at that point in time. We shall then be in a position to measure the profit or increase in wealth and use this as a basis for discussion and illustration of some of the problems of measurement which we referred to earlier:

Year T$_1$

Description	Replacement cost £	Historic cost £	Net realizable value £
Ford Fiesta 1.0L	4475	6180	3550
Suits	450	360	50
Shirts	80	75	5
Sweatshirts	80	70	15
Cash	500	500	500

You will notice that the figures have changed in all cases except under historic cost where they are the same as at the start of the year except for the cash. This highlights one of the problems with this measure in that it only tells us what an item cost and gives no clue to what it is worth.

It is also worth looking more closely at the car. As you can see the replacement cost is lower than at the start of the year. This is because the car we are replacing at the end of the year is a one-year old model rather than a new model. You will also see that the replacement cost is higher than the net realizable value. This is because there would be costs incurred in selling the car so the amount you would get would be reduced by these costs.

Let us now look at our measures of wealth and profit, starting with historic cost:

Description	Year T_0 £	Year T_1 £
Ford Fiesta 1.0L	6180	6180
Suits	360	360
Shirts	75	75
Sweatshirts	60	70
Cash	400	500
	7075	7185

We can now measure the profit under historic cost as we have a figure for wealth at the start and end of the year. Thus using the formula

$$\text{Wealth } 1 - \text{Wealth } 0 = \text{Profit}$$

we get:

$$£7185 - £7075 = £110$$

Let us now look at replacement cost:

Description	Year T_0 £	Year T_1 £
Ford Fiesta 1.0L	6180	4475
Suits	390	450
Shirts	75	80
Sweatshirts	60	80
Cash	400	500
	7105	5585

We have a figure for wealth at the start and end of the year measured using replacement cost. Thus using the formula:

$$\text{Wealth } 1 - \text{Wealth } 0 = \text{Profit}$$

we get:

$$£5585 - £7105 = £1520 \text{ loss}$$

In other words according to the replacement cost figures we are £1520 worse off at the end of the year than we were at the start.

Finally let us see what the situation would be if we were using the net realizable value to arrive at our measures of wealth.

Description	Year T_0	Year T_1
	£	£
Ford Fiesta 1.0L	5000	3550
Suits	60	50
Shirts	10	5
Sweatshirts	20	15
Cash	400	500
	5490	4120

We can now measure the profit under net realizable value. Thus using the formula

$$Wealth\ 1 - Wealth\ 0 = Profit$$

we get:

$$£4120 - £5490 = £1370\ loss$$

Using net realizable value as the basis of measuring wealth we again find Alex is worse off at the end of year than he was at the start.

You may well be wondering at this point which is the correct answer. The answer to that question takes us back to who is to use the information and for what purpose is it to be used. Clearly this varies from case to case; however, it is more important, at the present time, that you understand that differences arise depending on the valuation method adopted. You may feel that as Alex is clearly worse off at the end of the first year than he was at the start (he no longer has a brand new car) then replacement cost or net realizable value are the better alternatives.

However, you must bear in mind that we are trying to measure the amount that can be spent whilst maintaining wealth and that there is therefore a hidden assumption that Alex would want to maintain the wealth he had at the start. This may not, in fact, be the case due to changes in circumstances – he may for example have been banned from driving which would mean that he does not want to replace his car which may lead us to the net realizable value model as he would probably want to sell his car. However, just because he has lost his driving licence it is unlikely that he will not need to go out even if only to buy food. He is going to need to wear some clothes so to value these on the assumption that they are going to be sold is not a defensible position.

Conclusion

We have seen that there are a number of alternative ways of measuring a person's wealth and each has its own problems. One of the most frequently cited problems with both replacement cost and net realizable value is that they are subjective. This is true in many cases. This subjectivity is one reason why accounts are still prepared using historic costs, even though, as we have seen with the simple example of Alex, this can lead to irrelevant information being produced which can in turn lead to wrong decisions being taken. Another reason that is often cited for retaining historic cost in the accounts is that it is a system which is based on what was actually spent and owners of enterprises need to know what their money has been spent on. But to what extent can the latter advantage of historic cost make up for its deficiencies as a measure of wealth and therefore as the basis of the profit measure? This question is, and has been, the subject of much debate and that debate will continue for many years to come.

<table>
<tr><td colspan="4">**Extracts from BP Annual Report 1984**</td><td>CASE 3.2</td></tr>
<tr><td colspan="4" align="center">Financial highlights</td><td rowspan="5">**BRITISH PETROLEUM PLC: MEASUREMENT OF PROFIT**</td></tr>
<tr><td></td><td></td><td>1984</td><td>1983</td></tr>
<tr><td>Profit after taxation before extraordinary items</td><td></td><td></td><td></td></tr>
<tr><td>Historical cost</td><td>£m</td><td>1 402</td><td>866</td></tr>
<tr><td>Replacement cost</td><td>£m</td><td>1 264</td><td>970</td></tr>
<tr><td>Earnings per share</td><td>pence</td><td>76.8</td><td>47.5</td><td></td></tr>
<tr><td>Dividends per share</td><td>pence</td><td>30.0</td><td>24.0</td><td></td></tr>
<tr><td>Return on average shareholders' interest</td><td>%</td><td>13.2</td><td>9.5</td><td></td></tr>
<tr><td>Turnover</td><td>£m</td><td>37 933</td><td>32 381</td><td></td></tr>
<tr><td>Funds generated from operations</td><td>£m</td><td>5 734</td><td>4 587</td><td></td></tr>
<tr><td>Capital expenditure and acquisitions</td><td>£m</td><td>3 815</td><td>3 301</td><td></td></tr>
<tr><td>Capital employed</td><td>£m</td><td>22 966</td><td>18 627</td><td></td></tr>
<tr><td>Government take on oil and gas production</td><td>£m</td><td>4 100</td><td>3 800</td><td></td></tr>
<tr><td>Taxation on profits</td><td>£m</td><td>1 426</td><td>1 214</td><td></td></tr>
</table>

Commentary

The financial highlights reproduced above show that profits on a historic cost basis are £1402 million whereas on a replacement cost basis they are shown as £1264 million for the same year. The confusion over the appropriate model to apply is aptly demonstrated by the following extract from the same annual report.

Accounting bases and presentation

In recent years the group has presented its financial results in three ways:

☐ Replacement cost – which identifies the profitability of continuing business activity by using the current cost of sales. It is applied in the presentation of results for individual businesses or geographical areas because we believe it improves understanding of the sources and strength of the group's profits.

☐ Historical cost – which additionally includes realized stock holding gains or losses. It is therefore a measure of the profit attributable to

Continued over page

Continued from previous page

shareholders, and the most appropriate basis for the presentation of the group's balance sheet and funds statement.

☐ Current cost – which follows the UK Accounting Standard 16. We have now concluded that current cost adjustments based on the assumptions in this Standard are not appropriate as a means of assessing profit for the industries in which we operate. However, we recognize the need and continue to support the search for an acceptable method of handling the effects of changing costs and prices. Since the UK Standard remains in force current cost figures have been provided as a matter of compliance on pages 56 to 59.

We believe that a combination of replacement and historical cost figures is necessary to provide our shareholders with financial information on the group's performance and this rationale is applied in the highlights on page 1 and in the main accounts.

Summary

We have looked at definitions of wealth and profit which are commonly used and indeed underpin current accounting practice, and we have found that there are problems in actually measuring wealth. We have looked at four alternative measures: historic cost, replacement cost, net realizable value and economic value. We have shown by way of a simple example that each of the first three produces a different answer and in the course of our discussion we have pointed to some of the problems and assumptions underlying each alternative. At the present point in time there is no generally accepted right answer, and in fact the most commonly used system is that based on historic cost (although it is worth noting that Philips, the electronics giant, has used replacement costs for a number of years). Finally it should also be pointed out that change is likely to be slow in coming as the present system, based on historic cost, is familiar to all and has, it is argued by some, worked well in the past, although it is not clear what criteria are being used to back up the latter claim.

References

Fisher, I. (1930) *The Theory of Interest*, Macmillan.
Hicks, Sir John (1946) *Value and Capital*, Clarendon Press, Oxford.
Kaldor, N. (1955) *The Concept of Income in Economic Theory: An Expenditure Tax*. Allen & Unwin, London.

Further reading

For those who wish to examine the economic value approach, a good and understandable exposition can be found in *A New Introduction to Financial Accounting* by R.G. May, G.G. Mueller and T.H. Williams (Prentice Hall, 1980).

An alternative is to read Chapter 12 in *Financial Accounting*, by J. Arnold, T. Hope and A.J. Southwood (Prentice Hall, 1985).

Review questions

1. Profit is normally seen as a flow over time whereas wealth can be described as a stock at a point in time. Explain in your own words the difference between a stock and a flow.

2. There are a number of different ways in which we can measure wealth. List the alternatives discussed in this chapter together with any drawbacks or problems that were identified with their use.

3. In certain situations we said that written-down cost could be used as an alternative. Explain in your own words the difference between cost and written-down cost and suggest when the latter would be more appropriate.

4. What effects, if any, do rapid changes in technology have on the appropriateness of the alternative ways of assigning a cost or value to an item?

Problems for discussion and analysis

1. Under certain circumstances only one of the alternative methods of valuation is the most appropriate. Giving brief reasons for your choice, suggest the most appropriate value to be placed on each item in the following example.

   Jean owns a shop which used to sell clothes but she has now decided that given the location she would make more money running a restaurant at the same premises. She has obtained planning permission for the change of use and has bought some of the equipment needed but has not yet started trading. She has made a list of the items the business owns which is reproduced below:

   (a) freehold shop;
   (b) hanging display rail for clothes;
   (c) a two-year old car which is essential for the business;
   (d) new restaurant tables and chairs;
   (e) cash till;
   (f) quantity of fashion garments that were not sold in the closing down sale.

   You may find that you need more information or have to make some assumptions. This is normal but you should state any assumptions you are making.

2. In the example of Alex in the chapter no allowance was made for the fact that an item had been in use for some time. Whilst it is intuitively obvious that the utility of most things declines over time, it is more difficult to identify the extent of that decline over a given period. In addition even if we could identify the decline in utility and the utility remaining we still have to assign some monetary amount to both parts. We said in the chapter that this was done through the medium of arriving at a written-down cost or value. For each of the following situations suggest, with reasons, the best method for arriving at the written-down cost or value:

   (a) a ticket machine which will produce 10 million tickets and then need to be replaced. Ticket production each year is matched to visitors coming through the gates and estimates are 1 million in year 1, and 1.5 million in year 2. The years after that cannot be forecast with any accuracy;

(b) a leasehold property on a five-year non-renewable lease;
(c) a company car;
(d) a microcomputer;
(e) computer software.

3. Two brothers decided to go into business as suppliers to the catering industry buying and selling ice-making machines. Details of their transactions are set out below.

They initially bought 100 machines at £200 each and a delivery van for £6000. At the end of six months they had sold 80 of the 100 machines for £300 each. Unfortunately the machine manufacturer had during that time increased the price to £250 each and this was their only source of supply. To make matters worse a competitor had come into the area and was selling the same machines at £280 each. The brothers found that on average over the six months they had incurred costs for advertising, petrol, etc., which amounted to £20 for each machine sold.

On the basis of the information above, calculate what the brothers' wealth was at the start and end of the six months and what profit had been made.

4. Having calculated the profit for the first six months discuss whether the profit figure is a useful benchmark for measuring the performance of the business, and also whether it is useful as a guide to future profitability.

Measurement of wealth and the balance sheet 4

In Chapters 1 and 2 we discussed the objectives of accounting reports, and the influence of users on financial reporting. We also discussed the limitations of accounting information. The role of accounting in business, its effect on business and some of the factors which influence accounting were discussed in Chapter 3. We then examined some possible approaches to income measurement from the point of view both of the economist and of the accountant. We will now extend that work to look more specifically at the ways in which accountants actually measure wealth and income.

We suggested in Chapter 3 that the problem facing accountants is that of finding an appropriate basis for the measurement of wealth. There is also the additional problem that with the complexity involved in the real world a system that only measures wealth and derives income from wealth will be unable to cope with the complexity of present-day enterprises. Consider the problem of a large retailing group such as Marks & Spencer having to carry out a valuation of all their premises, vehicles, stocks, etc., on one day of the year. The costs of such an operation would make it prohibitively expensive even if it were possible logistically. For companies such as Hanson Trust where operations are carried out on a world-wide basis these logistical problems would be even greater. Such a system would also lead to problems because management would not be able to make decisions on a day-to-day basis as they would only have information at hand once a year. Because of these problems we need to find separate ways of measuring wealth and income.

The measurement of income will be dealt with in detail in Chapter 5. In this chapter we concentrate on the problem of the measurement of wealth and the way in which accounting approaches that problem. We shall look in some detail at the use of the balance sheet as a proxy for a measure of wealth, at its component parts such as assets and liabilities, and finally at the format in which the balance sheet is presented and briefly review the way in which that is influenced by the type of organization, the environment, the regulatory framework and the needs of the users. We shall be considering the impact of the regulatory framework in more detail as we progress through the book.

The measurement of wealth

In the case of an individual, we have illustrated that wealth can be found by simply listing the items you own, assuming of course that you don't

KEY CONCEPT 4.1	The balance sheet is a statement, at one point in time, which shows all the items (assets) owned by the enterprise and all the claims on those
THE BALANCE SHEET	assets (liabilities and owner's equity).

owe anybody money as this will clearly reduce your wealth. To some extent the same can be said for an enterprise although the level of complexity will of course be greater. The way in which this is done for an enterprise is similar to that for an individual but the resulting statement is called a **balance sheet**. You should note that the balance sheet relates to a position at one point in time. It is because of this that the analogy to a snapshot is often found in accounting textbooks.

The definition given in Key Concept 4.1 is not intended to be comprehensive – it merely provides us with a basic idea of what we are talking about. Before looking at the balance sheet in more detail it is important to appreciate that, although an enterprise does not exist in the same way as a person, for accounting and for some legal purposes an enterprise is presumed to exist in its own right. It is therefore treated as a separate entity from the person or persons who own or operate it. In broad terms it is possible to account for any unit which has a separate and distinct focus. It may be that this is a factory, a group of shops or a more complex organization such as Forte. This idea of a separate entity is often referred to in accounting literature as the **business entity** principle. It applies equally to organizations that are not commonly referred to as businesses such as charities, clubs and societies. Whether an entity should be accounted for separately is related to the question of whether it can be seen to have a separate focus as well as the legal situation. For example, there is no legal recognition of a market trader unless it is set up as a company or partnership. However, for accounting purposes it is dealt with as a separate entity from its owner. For tax purposes the income of a company is taxed separately through corporation tax, whilst for the sole trader and partnership, the profits are taxed as one part of the owner's or individual partner's income through income tax. However, all are treated as separate entities for the purposes of accounting.

Whilst the application of this principle and the reasons for it are fairly self-evident when we are looking at large public companies such as British Airways or British Telecom, they are less clear with smaller enterprises such as the mini-cab owner, a local fish and chip shop or a small-scale bed and breakfast business. If, for example, you decided to set yourself up providing chauffeur driven cars, for accounting purposes the cars

KEY CONCEPT 4.2	The business entity principle states that transactions, assets and liabilities that relate to the enterprise are accounted for separately. It
THE BUSINESS ENTITY PRINCIPLE	applies to all types of enterprise irrespective of the fact that the enterprise may not be recognized as a separate legal or taxable entity.

purchased for hire and the money earned as a result of that activity would be treated separately from your own personal transport and money. In this case this allows the tax authority to tax you separately on the profits from your business and it also helps you to arrive at the value of your business should you wish at some stage to sell the business or take in a partner. The important point to remember is that for each business entity it is possible to account separately and therefore for each entity we can draw up a balance sheet at any point in time.

We shall now examine balance sheets in more detail.

Importance of balance sheets

The purpose of a balance sheet is to communicate information about the financial position of an enterprise at a particular point in time. It summarizes information contained in the accounting records in a clear and intelligible form. If the items contained in it are summarized and classified in an appropriate manner it can give information about the financial strength of the enterprise and indicate the relative **liquidity** of the assets.

It should also give information about the liabilities of the enterprise, i.e. what the enterprise owes, and when these amounts will fall due. The combination of this information can assist the user in evaluating the financial position of the enterprise. It should be remembered, however, that the financial statements are only one part of the information needed by users and as such the importance of the balance sheet should not be over-emphasized.

In the vast majority of cases enterprises draw up a balance sheet at least once a year. It could be done more frequently, of course, or indeed less frequently, although convention dictates that a normal accounting period is a year and tax and other legislation – for example the Companies Acts – also require annual accounts for those business entities covered by that legislation. It should also be remembered that because the balance sheet represents the position at one point in time its usefulness is limited as the situation may have changed since the last balance sheet was drawn up. For instance, you may draw up a balance sheet every December, so if you looked at the balance sheet in October it would be ten months out of date. It may be helpful to extend our earlier analogy and picture a business as a movie and a balance sheet as a still from that movie. Clearly in the case of a movie the still does not give a complete picture and the same can be said for the balance sheet.

We now need to know what balance sheets contain. We have already said that they are similar to an individual's own measurement of wealth.

Liquidity refers to the ease with which assets can be converted to cash in the normal course of business.

KEY CONCEPT 4.3

LIQUIDITY

Therefore if you think how you would measure your own wealth you will realize that you need to make a list of what you own (assets) and take away from that what you owe (liabilities). For an enterprise this listing of assets and liabilities at a particular point in time is in fact the enterprise's balance sheet.

Given this information about the contents of a balance sheet, let us look in more detail at what is meant by assets and liabilities. We shall start with assets and consider what constitutes an asset and how assets are classified.

Assets

Although we can find many definitions of assets, some of these are less useful than others. Most contain some of the vital elements of a useful description, but a clear working definition is needed. For our purposes we have taken the one provided by R.M. Lall (1968), whose definition is given in Key Concept 4.4.

This definition is not dissimilar to that adopted by the accountancy profession and included in international accounting standards. We will now examine its various components in order to make the nature of an asset somewhat clearer.

Future benefits/service potentials

The clear implication in the terms 'future benefits' and 'service potentials' is, that in order to be an asset, there must be some clear expectation that some benefit will be derived by the enterprise either now or in the future. This implies that the item must have some specific usefulness to the enterprise. An item that has no specific usefulness for the enterprise is therefore not an asset. This is particularly important in times of rapidly changing technology as it suggests that the question of what is and what is not an asset can only be decided on the basis of its usefulness to the enterprise. For example, if we consider the effect the changes in technology have had on offices we can see the move from manual typewriters, to electric, to programmable electric and finally to word processors and desk-top publishing. As a result in most large organizations a manual typewriter is no longer used and therefore is not considered an asset. This is because electric typewriters and, in most cases, word processors have replaced them. By comparison in a third world charity the same typewriter would be still in use and classified as an asset of that organization.

KEY CONCEPT 4.4	Embodiments of present or future economic benefits or service potentials measurable in terms of monetary units, accruing to the enterprise as a result of economic events, the enjoyment of which by the enterprise is secured by law.
DEFINITION OF AN ASSET	

Similarly, it is fairly obvious that a gold mine full of un-mined gold is an asset for a mining business. Eventually there will come a point where all the gold that can be removed economically has been removed and all that is left is a hole in the ground. The hole in the ground is no longer useful to the mining enterprise and as such it ceases to be an asset. However, for a different type of enterprise, e.g. a rubbish disposal business, a hole in the ground is useful. We can therefore conclude that in order to be classified as an asset an item must be useful to the enterprise itself.

Measurable in monetary units

In certain circumstances enterprises may gain future benefits from items which may be impossible or difficult to measure in monetary units. For example, a producer of jams may be able to advertise that they are jam-makers 'By Appointment'. The fact that they have a Royal Appointment may well increase their profits and as such being 'By Appointment' has a benefit to the business. The problem facing accountants is, having decided there is a future benefit, how that benefit is to be measured in monetary terms. In this particular example it would be almost impossible to isolate the effect that the Royal Appointment has in monetary terms and therefore we do not include it in the balance sheet as an asset even though the business is clearly getting a benefit from it. Other examples of items which are clearly of benefit but which are not included for accounting purposes could be a good location, a highly motivated work-force, or a reputation for excellent service. You will remember from Chapter 1 that we discussed this problem in the context of the limitations of accounting information. We will return to this discussion in more detail in Chapter 10 where we deal with intangibles.

Legal ownership

Many definitions of assets imply that in order to be an asset something must be owned. In reality most assets are owned; however, the assertion that ownership is a precondition for the recognition of an asset by an enterprise is not strictly true. For example, a rental agreement for a house entitling you to occupy the house at a rent of £20 a week obviously confers a benefit if the market rental is, say, £90 a week and thus this may be seen as an asset. On the other hand, the fact that an individual or enterprise owns an item does not necessarily mean there is any future benefit to be obtained. For example, an old motor car that has failed the MOT test may cease to be an asset, and in fact, unless it can be driven to the breakers yard, it may become a liability.

Accruing to an enterprise

Whilst it may seem patently obvious that the benefits should accrue to the enterprise, i.e. be received by the enterprise at some point in time, it is vital in many cases to be able to separate out the assets of the enterprise from those of the owner for reasons referred to earlier. For example, a factory building is likely to be an enterprise asset as the benefits from its use are likely to accrue to an enterprise. However, if the enterprise is a small restaurant with residential accommodation for the owners above, it is somewhat less clear which part of the building is an asset of the business and which is not. In practice it may well be the case that some of the food and wine stocks are actually physically stored in part of the residential accommodation. There is unfortunately no general rule which can be applied and each case must be considered on its merits. The process of distinguishing between the assets of the owner and those of the business is merely an application of the business entity principle referred to earlier. In simple terms this principle states that the business should be viewed as separate from the owner and therefore accounted for separately.

Fixed and current assets

For accounting purposes assets are normally separated, as far as possible, into sub-categories. The reasoning behind this is that accounting statements should provide information that is useful in making economic decisions. These decisions, it is suggested, will be better informed if there is some indication given regarding the nature of the assets of the enterprise. The categories most frequently used are **fixed** and **current assets**, and indeed these are the categories recognized under the Companies Acts.

Fixed assets

Although the term fixed assets is used frequently in accounting literature there is no precise definition of what constitutes a fixed asset. One possible definition of a fixed asset is:

> An asset that is retained for use in the business and is not for resale in the normal course of business.

This definition suggests that the distinction relates to the usage to which the asset is put. However, the conventional distinction between fixed and current assets requires a further element relating to time and implies some degree of permanency. For example, it is generally accepted that factory buildings are fixed assets as they are retained for use, are not resold and will last for a long period of time. It is this latter element relating to time that is missing from the above definition. If we simply used the definition above office stationery would meet the criteria of a fixed asset. It is quite clear, however, that office stationery is unlikely to be even semi-permanent and is essentially a different type of asset from the factory building previously discussed. This may lead us to a definition that includes some reference to the life of an asset. A definition that relates solely to the life of an asset, however, is not on its own sufficient. For example, a fixed asset definition could be:

> An asset that will last for a considerable period of time.

This definition is deficient because it says nothing about the use of the asset within the business. Thus, for example, a washing machine would be

An asset that is acquired for the purposes of use within the business and is likely to be used by the business for a considerable period of time.	KEY CONCEPT 4.5 **FIXED ASSETS**

classified as a fixed asset using this latter definition. However, there are clear differences between the way in which washing machines should be treated in the books of a launderette and that of an electrical retailer even though the life of the washing machine does not change merely as a result of it being owned by a different business. This leads us to the conclusion that there are two elements involved in deciding what is and what is not a fixed asset, i.e. the **use** to which the asset will be put and the **life** of the asset **within the business**. This provides us with a working definition of a fixed asset.

For companies, the definition of a fixed asset to be used is that included in the 1985 Companies Act. This broadly defines fixed assets as those intended for use on a continuing basis in the company's activities. However, the definition which we have used is more generally applicable and when used in conjunction with the definition of an asset given in Key Concept 4.4 is more than adequate for our purposes.

Current assets

As with fixed assets the definition of a current asset is not as clear as might be expected. Some accounting textbooks suggest that current assets are those known as circulating assets, i.e. those which are part of the operating cycle. This does not really help as we need to know what an operating cycle is or what circulating assets are.

The operating cycle

It is perhaps easier to understand the term operating cycle if we look at one or two examples. In the case of a shop selling clothes the operating cycle may consist of buying garments and selling them for cash. In the case of a restaurant the operating cycle may involve more processes such as buying a number of ingredients, cooking them, serving them and then collecting the cash. The operating cycle has no fixed time period as this depends on the nature of the business and it may in fact extend over a number of years as would be the case with property development, ship-building and other heavy construction industries. In the fast-food business it is unlikely to be this long as the nature of the stocks held will necessarily lead to a short operating cycle. The fact that operating cycles are of different lengths is not vital as in general those assets that are part of the operating cycle are similar and these are likely to be items such as stock, cash in the bank, etc.

The realization period

Some accounting texts suggest that what distinguishes current assets from other assets is whether or not they will be realized in the form of cash in

KEY CONCEPT 4.6	A current asset is one which is either part of the operating cycle of the enterprise or is likely to be realized in the form of cash within one year.
CURRENT ASSET	

the current accounting period. By convention accounting periods are normally one year. If we applied this test strictly we would find that in certain cases, such as the shipbuilder referred to above, something that is part of the operating cycle will in fact not be realized in the form of cash within a year.

In practice the classification is based on both these principles. For our purposes, therefore, a useful working definition is that given in Key Concept 4.6 which combines these two properties and therefore overcomes the problems inherent in using either on its own.

By looking at the definitions of fixed and current assets it should be clear that it is possible to think of some assets that a business might own that do not easily fit within either category. An example of such an asset is a trade name, such as McDonalds, and a trade mark or a patent on a product or process which has been developed by the enterprise itself, e.g. Coca Cola. A number of ways of dealing with this problem have been suggested. However, the American solution of coining the title *indeterminate assets* and including those assets not easily classified as fixed or current under that heading overcomes most of the main problems and is sufficient for our purposes at this stage.

Having looked at what constitutes an asset, and the way in which assets are divided into sub-categories on the balance sheet, we can now turn to the other part of the balance sheet – what is owed or, to use accounting terminology, the liabilities.

Liabilities

As with the general term assets a useful working definition of liabilities must contain a number of components. A suitable definition is that put forward by Bull (1984) in Key Concept 4.7.

The definition implies that the liability must exist at the present time. It also implies that the date by which that liability must be paid is known. A simpler definition which is adequate for our purposes is:

Liabilities are what the business owes.

KEY CONCEPT 4.7	The existing obligations of the business to provide money, goods or services to an agent or entity outside the business at some time in the future.
LIABILITIES	

| Those liabilities falling due to for payment within one year. | KEY CONCEPT 4.8 |
| | **CURRENT LIABILITIES** |

An alternative way of looking at them is to view them as claims on the assets of the business. Such an approach neatly avoids the question of whether owners' equity is in fact a liability in the same way as those discussed below.

Current liabilities

Given that we have used a simple definition for liabilities we can also use a simple definition of current liabilities (Key Concept 4.8).

This definition is in fact in line with the heading under which current liabilities are shown in the published accounts of companies as you shall see later in the section dealing with balance sheet formats. A common example of a current liability is a bank overdraft which, in theory at least, would have to be repaid to the bank on demand. Another example would be where goods or services were bought on credit terms and the supplier had not been paid at the balance sheet date.

Other liabilities

Clearly there are other types of liability which do not have to be repaid in full in one year; an everyday example of this type of liability is a mortgage on a house. In the case of a business, however, this type of liability may take a number of forms such as a bank loan, hire purchase, a lease, debenture or a commercial mortgage. It may be repayable over any period from one year upwards. Liabilities of this sort are longer-term liabilities and are normally put under the heading of:

Amounts falling due after more than one year

Owners' equity

The owners' equity can be viewed in a number of ways. In a sense it is a liability of the business in so far as it is a claim on the assets. However, it differs from other liabilities in that they have definite dates by which they are to be paid and they are fixed in amount. The owners' equity, on the other hand, is normally left in the business as long as it is required. Another way of viewing the owners' equity is as a residual claim on the assets of the business after all the other liabilities have been settled. In general, the owners' equity is normally shown under two headings, i.e. that which is put into the business and that which is earned by the business and left in the business. This latter category we will refer to initially as retained profits, although, in reality, these may be subdivided

KEY CONCEPT 4.9	Owners' equity is in one sense a claim on the assets of the enterprise. It is different from other liabilities in that the amount cannot necessarily be determined accurately. It can be viewed as a residual claim on the assets of the enterprise.
OWNERS' EQUITY	

into a number of other reserves. In the case of the individual the equity could be seen as analogous with wealth, whereas in the case of a business this owners' equity is often referred to as capital. As we showed in Chapter 3, the amount at which this wealth or capital is stated is dependent upon the measure used to arrive at a figure for assets, i.e. historic cost, replacement cost, net realizable value, etc. It is therefore better to view owners' equity as a residual claim rather than as capital or wealth as the latter terms could be taken to imply that an absolute measure is possible.

The balance sheet equation

As we have already indicated the balance sheet of an enterprise can be viewed as a statement of assets and liabilities at a particular point in time. Because the business is an artificial entity, by definition all its assets belong to someone else. This idea is summed up fairly simply in the balance sheet equation.

$$\text{Assets} = \text{Liabilities}$$

This equation describes the balance sheet in its simplest form and must always hold true. However, it uses a very loose definition of liabilities and can be further refined to highlight the differences between normal liabilities and owners' equity as follows:

$$\text{Assets} = \text{Liabilities} + \text{Owners' equity}$$

This latter equation can be rewritten to highlight the fact that owners' equity is a residual claim on the assets as follows:

$$\text{Assets} - \text{Liabilities} = \text{Owners' equity}$$

Simple balance sheets

To illustrate the equation above a simple balance sheet may be constructed using the information contained in Example 4.1.

Example 4.1
Harry Keel has just been made redundant and he has decided to start up a small business making safety harnesses which he calls Keelsafe Safety Harnesses. For this purpose he purchased:

One industrial sewing machine	£550
A quantity of heavy duty webbing material	£300
A quantity of sewing materials	£100
A second-hand typewriter	£ 50

A supply of office stationery and letterheads   £ 50
One cutting machine   £400

The remaining £50 of his redundancy money was put in a business bank account.

At this stage we could draw up a list of assets of the business as follows:

Assets	£
Sewing machine	550
Webbing	300
Sewing materials	100
Typewriter	50
Stationery	50
Cutting machine	400
Cash in bank	50
	1500

We could also identify the owner's equity in the business as being £1500, i.e. the amount he put in. Thus the other side of the balance sheet – and indeed the accounting equation – would be.

	£
Owner's equity	1500
	1500

Before moving on it is worth thinking about how we obtained the figure for owner's equity. All we did was to list what Harry's business owned and then as it did not owe anything to anybody but Harry, the owner, we made the balance sheet balance by recording the amount the business owed to Harry, the owner's equity.

Let us take this example a bit further.

Example 4.1 contd
As the business was just starting Harry decided that until the business got off the ground he would operate from home and use the garage to manufacture the safety harnesses and the front room of his house as an office. His house had originally cost him £20 000 in 1979.

This additional information, on the face of it, presents us with a problem as we do not know how much of the £20 000 relates to the garage or to the front room. We know that the business uses some of the house and that the house is an asset. The question is whether it is an asset of Harry himself or of the business, and if it is the latter how should we record it and at what amount? To answer this question we need to go back to our definition of an asset (see Key Concept 4.4).

Definition of an asset:

Embodiments of present or future economic benefits or service potentials measurable in terms of monetary units, accruing to the enterprise as a result of economic events, the enjoyment of which by the enterprise is secured by law.

Bearing in mind the business entity principle, we can see from the definition that the garage is not an asset of the business as the business is viewed as a separate entity from the owner. It is Harry Keel himself who owns both the house and the garage and he also retains the legal right to enjoy the benefits from their use. Thus the garage is not an asset of the business, as the business has no legal right to use the garage, it therefore does not need to be included in the balance sheet of the business. A similar argument can be applied to the front room which is being used as an office.

Example 4.1 contd

When Harry starts to make up the harnesses he realizes that he needs to buy some fasteners before he can sell them. He therefore approaches a supplier and finds that enough fasteners to fit all the harnesses he can make up with his existing materials will cost him £300. As he has used up all his redundancy money except £50 he approaches his bank who agree to make a loan of £500 to his business for a period of two years. He borrows the £500, puts it in the business bank account and then buys the fasteners with a cheque drawn on that account.

We shall look first of all at this transaction and then draw up a new balance sheet. The reason we have to draw up a new balance sheet is that we are now at a different point in time – remember that a balance sheet shows the position at one point in time only.

    The actual transaction on its own can be looked at in two stages:

Stage one

The first stage is that we borrow the money from the bank. This has two effects, i.e. we increase the business assets as the business will get a future benefit from the use of that money, and we also increase the business liabilities as the business now owes the bank £500. Thus viewed on its own this can be depicted as:

$$\text{Assets} \quad = \quad \text{Liabilities}$$
$$\text{Cash in bank} \quad +\pounds500 = \text{Loan} \quad +\pounds500$$

Stage Two

If we now look at the second stage where some of the money in the bank is used to buy the fasteners we can extend stage one and depict this as:

Assets		=	Liabilities	
Cash in bank	£500	=	Loan	£500
Cash in bank	−£300			
Fasteners	+£300			

We can see that all that has happened is that we have exchanged one asset for another and the totals on either side of the equation have remained the same.

Before going on to draw up a new balance sheet we should draw your attention to an important principle that we have just illustrated. That principle is that there are two sides to every transaction. At the first stage

| The principle of duality is the basis of the double-entry book-keeping system on which accounting is based. It states that:

Every transaction has two opposite and equal sides. | KEY CONCEPT 4.10

THE PRINCIPLE OF DUALITY |

the two sides of the transaction were an increase in assets with a corresponding increase in liabilities, whereas at the second stage there was a decrease in one asset with a corresponding increase in another asset. This principle is often referred to as the **principle of duality** which is essentially a grand sounding title for the principle that all transactions have two sides.

We can now draw up the new balance sheet of Keelsafe. Unlike the previous balance sheet this time we will classify the assets into fixed and current assets and group these together to make the balance sheet more meaningful. Another way in which we can make the balance sheet more meaningful is to order the assets in descending order of liquidity, i.e. the more difficult the item is to turn into cash the less liquid it is. Thus the sewing machine as a fixed asset is less liquid than the stocks of fasteners etc. Similarly these are shown as less liquid then the cash at the bank.

You will also note that each of the groups of assets are subtotalled and the subtotal is shown separately. The total of all the assets is then shown, the fact that it is a final total denoted by the fact that it is double underlined. (It is conventional to use single underlining for subtotals and double underlining to denote final totals.)

Having classified and listed the assets of Keelsafe we then show the amounts owed by the business classified into the amount the business owes to Harry, the owner's equity, and the amount it owes to others.

Balance sheet of Keelsafe
as at 31 December 1991

Fixed assets	£	£
One sewing machine		550
One cutting machine		400
Typewriter		50
		1000
Current assets:		
Office stationery	50	
Webbing material	300	
Sewing materials	100	
Fasteners	300	
Cash at bank	250	1000
		2000
Financed by:		
Owner's equity	1500	1500
Bank loan		500
		2000

The balance sheet shown has been rearranged to emphasize the differences between the various types of assets and Harry's residual claim on the assets after the other liabilities have been paid. It should be noted that the balance sheet is headed up with the name of the business and the date at which the balance sheet is drawn up.

It is worthwhile, before you proceed any further, to re-examine the definitions of fixed and current assets and ensure that you understand why the items above have been classified as they have.

Having done that we can now proceed to examine the determinants of

---

CASE 4.1

THE BODY SHOP INTERNATIONAL Plc

Balance sheet
28 February 1989

	Note	28 February 1989		30 September 1987	
		£000	£000	£000	£000
Fixed assets					
Tangible assets	11		12 930		3 895
Investments	12		189		183
			13 119		4 078
Current assets					
Stocks	13	13 544		3 994	
Debtors	14	15 455		5 441	
Cash at bank and in hand		–		783	
		28 999		10 218	
Creditors: amounts falling due within one year	15	17 424		7 583	
Net current assets			11 575		2 635
Total assets less current liabilities			24 694		6 713
Creditors: amounts falling due after more than one year	16		(44)		(96)
Provisions for liabilities and charges					
Deferred tax	17	(133)		–	
			24 517		6 617
Capital and reserves					
Called up share capital	18		2 131		1 013
Share premium account	19		9 671		–
Profit and loss account	20		12 715		5 604
			24 517		6 617

Continued from previous page

Commentary

As you will see the balance sheet classifies the assets between fixed assets and current assets. It then lists the amounts owing currently to arrive at a figure of net current assets. This is followed by the other liabilities leaving a balance sheet total of net assets, i.e. assets minus liabilities. This is then balanced on the other side of the balance sheet by the owners' equity. This balance sheet is therefore a variation on the equation:

$$\text{Assets} - \text{Liabilities} = \text{Owners' equity}$$

The meaning of the various subheadings and classifications will be discussed in later chapters.

the format of balance sheets and the ways in which they can be used, together with their limitations.

Determinants of the balance sheet format

We shall now examine the purpose of the balance sheet and its limitations. We shall also consider some of the influences affecting the way in which it is presented and the extent to which this is determined by the type of organization, the regulatory framework and the users of the financial statements.

Purpose and limitations

The balance sheet is in essence a listing of the assets and liabilities of the enterprise or organization at a point in time. The fact that it represents the position at one point in time is itself a limitation as it is only fully relevant at that point. At any other point in time, as we have seen in the case of Keelsafe, a new balance sheet has to be drawn up. This means that in order for the balance sheet to be useful it should be as up to date as possible, and that its utility diminishes the more out of date it becomes. This is borne out in the empirical research with bankers, referred to earlier, where this was the improvement to published accounting information most bankers – 88 per cent of those surveyed – would like (Berry *et al.*, 1987). Similarly, in order for it to be an accurate measure of the assets and liabilities the values of those assets and liabilities should be as up to date as possible, and herein lies another limitation.

As we saw in Chapter 3 there are a number of ways in which assets can be valued, some of which are more subjective than others. The choice of value is in part related to the purpose for which the balance sheet is to be used. For example, if we want to know how much each item cost then the original, or historic, cost would be appropriate. If, on the other hand, we wanted to know how much each item could be sold for then the net realizable value may be appropriate. Alternatively if we wanted to know how much the business as a whole was worth it is likely that neither of the aforementioned would be appropriate. Partly because of the difficulties involved in choosing an appropriate valuation and partly because of convention accountants have traditionally used the historic cost as a basis of valuation of assets in the balance sheet.

Clearly in certain cases this has led to assets being stated at a figure which bears little if any relation to the current value of the asset. The most obvious example of this in recent years has been the changes in prices and values of land and buildings. Because of this one often sees land and buildings shown in published accounts at a valuation rather than at cost.

An allied problem to the changes in the prices of specific assets is the fact that the unit of measurement, in our case the pound sterling, does not itself represent a constant value over time. For example you cannot buy as many goods with a pound today as you could, say, ten years ago. This once again limits the usefulness of the information contained in the balance sheet. This problem has been recognized for a number of years as we shall explain in Chapter 14, and in the 1981 Companies Act there is provision for the annual accounts to be provided using a system known as current cost accounting. If a company chooses to produce current cost accounts it is also required to provide the historic cost information. In practice there has been a great deal of resistance to any change from the historic cost system despite its acknowledged limitations.

Influences on the format of the balance sheet

There are many influences on the format and content of the balance sheet. At one level there are factors relating to the type of business and the objectives of the preparers of the balance sheet. Then there is the effect of the size and type of organization and who owns the organization. Finally and perhaps most obviously is the effect of the regulatory framework which itself varies from country to country. We will consider each of these in turn and then round off our discussion with a look at the requirements of users and their impact.

The type of business and preparers' objectives

As we have already shown in some of the examples we have used, the activity in which the organization is involved can have dramatic effects on the classification of an asset, as in the case of a car belonging to a car dealer as compared to a manufacturing business. Similarly we have illustrated in the example relating to gold mines that what might not be an asset for one business would be an asset of another business undertaking a different activity. Apart from these cases which are to some extent reasonably clear cut, the activity can have dramatic effects on the difficulty or otherwise of drawing up a balance sheet. Consider for example the problems of a football club when trying to account for star players – Paul Gascoigne is a good example – or of a high technology business in trying to decide whether the cost of the patent on a new product is going to yield any future benefit when the state of the art and the environment is changing so rapidly. Given the current concern with the ozone layer and the effect of motor vehicles was the Sinclair C5 electric car simply ahead of its time and will the patent on the design now become valuable? Similar problems can be seen in virtually every industry. For example, how do you value a brand name such as Mars Bars, a reputation such as the reputation for quality of a Rolls Royce, a world-class chef at the Savoy, a prime location? How do Disney or MacDonalds value their trade names?

Apart from the issues raised by the type of activity in which an organization is involved there are issues relating to the ways in which a business is perceived and the ways in which management would wish the business to be perceived. For example, research by Carsberg *et al.* (1985) has shown that the management of smaller organizations perceive that bankers are interested in the amount of assets available as security for a loan or overdraft. There is therefore a temptation to try to enhance the value of assets, perhaps by revaluing the land and buildings prior to applying for a loan. Similarly, in a number of cases where a business is in trouble, the assets have been revalued in order to bolster the image of the business and to promote the impression of it having 'a sound asset base'. These are some examples of where the objectives of preparers and of users could be in conflict.

The size and type of organization

One of the prime determinants of the content and format of the balance sheet is the type of organizational structure involved. For example, an incorporated business, i.e. a company, is subject to certain rules and regulations imposed by the state whereas a partnership or sole proprietorship has no such restrictions. A company has to produce annual accounts and file a copy of these at Companies House, whereas in the case of a partnership there is no such requirement. Similarly a business that is part of a larger organization may well have to comply with the rules and formats of accounts that suit that organization as a whole.

The need to comply with the organizational needs may also be affected by who owns the business. For example a company operating in the UK which is owned by an American company would have to comply with UK regulations but would also report to its owner, the US company, in a format that complies with US regulations. If we contrast this with a business that is owned by two partners, there are no restrictions or rules imposed on the latter organization and the partners can decide for themselves what format the balance sheet should take and indeed how often it should be drawn up.

Another factor affecting the format of the balance sheet will be the size of the organization. In the example used we have assumed a very small operation and as such all the assets could be individually listed. In the case of a larger, more complex organization there will be a need for assets to be summarized under broad headings as otherwise the level of detail would be such that the user of the statement would find it extremely difficult if not impossible to get an overall picture.

Finally, although they are to some extent interconnected with the type of organization, we should mention the influence of organizational goals.

Consider, for example, an organization set up for charitable purposes, which may or may not be incorporated. Of what relevance to that organization is a classification such as owners' equity? Similarly, if you looked at the accounts of your local authority, you would not expect to see a heading for owners' equity or retained profits.

The regulatory framework

Perhaps the most pervasive influence on the form and content of the balance sheet is the state through the medium of legislation. As we have already indicated the format and content of balance sheets as well as the way in which they are drawn up is different in some respects in the UK and in the USA. In recent years the EC has had a major influence, commencing with the 4th Directive which was incorporated into the 1981 Companies Act. Within the UK, as we saw in Chapter 2, there are different rules concerning the format and level of sophistication depending on whether the organization is a charity, whether it is a local authority, a company registered under the Companies Acts or a cooperative registered under the Provident and Friendly Societies Act. Even within these categories there can be different rules. For example, a small company may produce abridged accounts for filing with the registrar of companies. A quoted public company, on the other hand, also has to comply with the rules and regulations laid down by the Stock Exchange.

Apart from the Companies Acts there are other rules governing the presentation and content of the annual accounts which are laid down for companies by the professional accounting bodies. These are known as Statements of Standard Accounting Practice (SSAPs). Finally, company accounts should comply with the International Accounting Standards. In general, compliance with the SSAPs usually ensures that the requirements of the international standards are also met. We will be considering some of these detailed requirements both in terms of legislation and accounting standards in the course of this text. At present we will confine ourselves to looking at the format of accounts as prescribed by the legislation and comparing it with alternative formats available for an unincorporated business.

Users of accounts

As we discussed in Chapter 1 there are a number of different users who may have conflicting needs in terms of their information requirements. To some extent the rules and regulations laid down by the state could be said to encompass some of these needs. However, those rules only lay down a minimum requirement. For example, whilst the Companies Acts require that loans and overdrafts should be shown, research (Berry *et al.*, 1987) shows that bankers would like to see details of the repayment dates of those loans in the accounts. On the other hand, the owners of the company may not wish to have that information made public. A similar conflict arises between the needs of managers who may wish to know what it would cost to replace an asset rather than be presented with a statement which shows them what the asset cost when they bought it, whereas the owners may wish to know what management has spent their money on and how much each item cost.

Conclusion

In this chapter we have defined the nature, purpose and content of balance sheets and highlighted some of the problems in drawing up such a statement. We have also introduced you to the wider context in which accounting reports can be viewed. It is important before proceeding further that you make sure that you understand the definitions involved and can apply them to real problems. As you have seen, the balance sheet can take many forms and clearly in a book of this nature there is no necessity to cover all of them. For the sake of simplicity therefore we will use the format below initially and then move to the format required by the 1981 Companies Act. The sample format given below is followed by an explanation of what the balance sheet contains and the reasons for the choice of format. It is important that you understand the reasons for the choice of the suggested format as this will aid you in interpreting accounting information at a later stage. We then provide an illustration of the same accounts under the format required by the Companies Acts and briefly discuss the differences between the formats.

Suggested balance sheet format

Balance sheet of 'Simple'
as at 31 January 1992

Fixed assets	£	£
Land and buildings		200
Machinery		100
Motor vehicles		50
		350
Current assets		
Stocks of raw materials	200	
Stocks of finished goods	110	
Cash in hand	20	
	330	
Current liabilities		
Bank overdraft	190	
	190	
Net current assets		140
		490
Financed by		
Owners' equity	100	
Retained profits	240	340
Bank loan		150
		490

As numerous formats are available, and these to some extent at least are dependent on the type of organization, we have started with a format which we consider to be appropriate to an introductory level text. If you wish to look at other formats you will find these referred to in the additional reading at the end of this chapter. Before following a different format, you should ensure that you understand the reasons behind the alternative format and you should consider whether the information given is as clear as in the format suggested above.

Reasons for choosing this format

The balance sheet is headed with the name of the organization and the date to which the balance sheet relates. As we have already explained, a balance sheet relates to one point in time and that date needs to be clearly stated in the heading.

Within the balance sheet itself we commence with the 'Fixed assets' which are shown in descending order of permanence and liquidity – for example, the land and buildings will probably outlast the motor vehicles. They will also take longer to sell if we wished to sell them as we would first have to empty them whereas the motor vehicles could be sold almost immediately.

The 'Current assets' are also shown in descending order of liquidity. For example, in order to turn the raw materials into cash we first have to turn them into finished goods then sell them, whereas in the case of the finished goods no manufacturing or assembling process is required. Note also that all the current assets are added together and a total is given.

A similar rationale applies to the 'Current liabilities' and once again these are totalled. You will find that the current liabilities are often headed up 'Creditors: amounts falling due within a year', this latter heading being taken from the legislation on company accounts in the Companies Acts.

The next heading is 'Net current assets' and this is arrived at by subtracting the total of the current liabilities from the total of the current assets. If this figure is positive it indicates that, assuming a one-year period, then we should realize enough from selling our current assets to pay the liabilities due within one year. Obviously in reality things are not so clear cut as we may need to pay large amounts almost immediately whereas some of our current assets may take a relatively long time to turn into cash. Also there are certain types of business, for example some retailers, where the figure could in fact be negative. If it is negative then the term 'Net current liabilities' is used.

The final figure on the top half of our balance sheet is the total of all the assets less the current liabilities and this is the figure to which the other half of the balance sheet should total. You will see that this total is different from the previous totals in that it is double underlined. This is simply a device for differentiating a subtotal from the final total.

The other half of the balance sheet shows the way in which the assets are financed by long-term capital. It is again subdivided in so far as the loans are separated from the amounts due to the owners. Similarly the amounts due to the owners are separately classified between those that the owner contributed to the business and those that the business generated as a result of trading, i.e. the retained profits. As was the case with the other half of the balance sheet, the liabilities of the enterprise are in order of liquidity in that the owners' equity is the last amount to be repaid after all the loans and other liabilities are repaid.

Companies Act formats

The 1981 Companies Act laid down specific formats to be followed for both the balance sheet and profit and loss account together with other disclosure requirements. As far as the balance sheet is concerned there are two prescribed formats contained in the Act. These both require the same information to be disclosed, the difference being that one is in a vertical format as given above and the other is for a horizontal format. We will illustrate the vertical format as it aids comparison with the balance sheet format suggested above.

Balance sheet of 'Simple'
as at 31 January 1992

	£	£
Fixed assets		
Tangible assets		
Land and buildings		200
Machinery		100
Motor vehicles		50
		350
Current assets		
Stocks of raw materials	200	
Stocks of finished goods	110	
Cash in hand	20	
	330	
Creditors: amounts falling due within a year		
Bank overdraft	190	
	190	
Net current assets		140
Total assets less current liabilities		490
Creditors: amounts falling due after more than one year		
Bank loan		150
Total net assets		340
Capital and reserves		
Called up share capital	100	
Profit and loss account	240	340
		340

Differences in formats

The first difference in the formats is the subheading of tangible assets under fixed assets. The Act requires fixed assets to be shown under three subheadings: intangible assets, tangible assets and investments. As we have said in the chapter there are assets which may not be easily classified as fixed or current and we suggested that the American term indeterminate assets was appropriate. However, if the business entity on which we are reporting is a company, then we need to classify its assets as either fixed or current.

The next difference is one of wording where the phrase 'Creditors: amounts falling due within one year' is used instead of current liabilities. The figure for net current assets is given and a subtotal entitled 'Total assets less current liabilities' is arrived at. From this is deducted any liabilities and charges under the heading 'Creditors: amounts falling due after more than one year', not forming part of the equity capital. The balance sheet is then totalled to give a figure of total net assets. This figure may in theory be useful to shareholders as it appears to tell them the assets that they would own after all the liabilities are paid. That of course assumes that the figure at which the assets are shown is what they are worth. This, as we have explained in Chapter 3, is unlikely to be the case and as such it may be misleading to the unsophisticated user of accounting information.

The other side of the balance sheet shows the owners' equity. As this is a company this takes the form of share capital. There are a number of classes of share capital and these are dealt with in Chapter 12.

Summary

In this chapter we have seen that a balance sheet is an attempt to show the financial position at one point in time. We have also introduced the idea that a business is viewed for accounting purposes as a separate entity from its owner (the business entity principle). From this starting point we have gone on to define assets, liabilities and owners' equity and to look at the balance sheet equation. Before moving on to the next chapter you should ensure that you have understood what is contained in this chapter by working through the review questions and the problems given below.

References

Berry, A., Citron, D. and Jarvis, R. (1987) *The Information Needs of Bankers Dealing with Large and Small Companies*, Certified Accountants Research Report 7, Certified Accountants Publications, London.

Bull, R.J. (1984) *Accounting in Business*, 5th edn, Butterworths, p. 22.

Carsberg, B.V. *et al.* (1985) *Small Company Financial Reporting*. Prentice Hall International, London.

Companies Act 1985, Section 262(1), HMSO.

Lall, R.M. (1968) An enquiry into the nature of assets, *The New York Certified Public Accountant*, November, pp. 793–7.

Further Reading

Students who wish to examine the regulatory framework in greater depth are referred to *Form and Content of Company Accounts* Coopers & Lybrand (Financial Training Publications, 1986).

Alternatively, looking at the annual accounts of a bank, a manufacturing business and a service sector business would also provide valuable insights.

Review questions

1. What are the essential elements of a useful definition of an asset?

2. What are the deficiencies, if any, in the following definition of an asset: 'Assets are the things a business owns.'

3. What are the essential elements of a useful definition of a fixed asset?

4. Explain in your own words the difference between fixed assets and current assets and why it is important to classify assets into subgroups.

5. Explain in your own words what a liability is, and the differences between liabilities and owners' equity.

6. What is the purpose of a balance sheet and what information does it contain?

7. In the chapter we gave examples of situations such as Harry's garage where the question was raised about whether the asset was a personal asset or a business asset. Identify similar examples that are likely to occur in the following industries and state what test you would apply to them to decide whether they were a business asset:

   (a) hospitality;
   (b) retailing;
   (c) auto repairers;
   (d) computer software design.

Problems for discussion and analysis

1. In each of the following situations decide whether the item should be classified as a business asset and if so suggest how you would arrive at a figure for inclusion in the balance sheet.

   (a) You are running a restaurant and have just been included in a prestigious list of the top ten restaurants of the year.
   (b) You have as one of your employees a world-famous chef who has attracted and continues to attract a high class of clientele. He has been with you for the past ten years and is extremely loyal.
   (c) You own the Savoy hotel in the Strand and are thinking of including the name in the balance sheet as a business asset.
   (d) You have just opened your own theme park and as you have some Disney characters in it you have decided to call it Disneyland and feel that the name should be shown in your balance sheet as it will undoubtedly attract customers.
   (e) You own Compass Airlines which is the largest domestic carrier in your country and you are considering including your routes which you were granted rights to under a government tender as an asset.
   (f) You have just been made the sole agent for a major package holiday company for the next three years with options to renew the contract if both sides are satisfied with the arrangements.
   (g) You have just installed new technology in your factory and in order to get it working you have had to get new software written. Some of this was

done by an external bureau at a cost of £25 000 and some was done in-house by your own people who spent six weeks solving the problems.

2. Prepare the balance sheet of Smallstays from the following information and comment on the position of the business as shown by that balance sheet.

	£
Freehold land and building	240 000
Mortgage on land and building	168 000
Cash in tills	500
Furniture fixtures and fittings	43 600
Office furniture	2 300
Bank overdraft	20 700
Courtesy car	3 200
Bank Loan	23 000
Owners' equity	?

3. Prepare a balance sheet from the following information and comment on the position of the business as shown by that balance sheet.

	£
Stock of goods held for resale	6 500
Freehold land and building	34 000
Mortgage on land and building	29 000
Cash in tills	1 800
Fixtures and fittings	7 600
Office furniture	3 000
Bank overdraft	29 000
Delivery van	6 100
Owners' equity	?

4. In each of the following situations identify whether the item should be included in the balance sheet of Transport of Delight at 31 December 1991, and if so at what amount and under which heading. Transport of Delight is a tour operator specializing in safari holidays. In all cases reasons for your decision must be given.

(a) A freehold shop bought in July 1991 for £88 000.
(b) A mortgage of £50 000 taken out to buy the shop in July 1991.
(c) Brochures and publicity material which cost £8000 and office supplies which cost £200.
(d) Three jeeps each costing £16 000, which Transport of Delight ordered on 20 December 1991 but which were finally delivered and paid for on 2 January 1992.
(e) Shop fittings which were worth £3000 and had been bought at an auction by Transport of Delight for only £1500 prior to opening the shop in July 1991.
(f) A VW Golf costing £3500 which the owners of Transport of Delight had bought in November 1991 for their son to use.
(g) One photocopier which was rented from Office Equipment Supplies at an annual rental of £200.
(h) One fax machine which Transport of Delight had bought in November 1991 for £600.
(i) A bank overdraft which amounted to £6500 on 31 December 1991.
(j) Three large frame tents which Transport of Delight had bought for £1200 in October. One of these had unfortunately been badly damaged when there was a small fire in the storage area and is no longer usable.

5. Using the information in question 4 above and your decisions, draw up the balance sheet of Transport of Delight as at 31 December 1991 and calculate the owners' equity.

6. For each of the following, decide whether the item should be included in the balance sheet of Transom Trading at 31 March 1992, and if so at what amount and under which heading. Transom Trading is a retailer of motor spares and accessories. In all cases reasons for your decision must be given.

   (a) A freehold shop bought in August 1991 for £38 000.
   (b) A loan of £30 000 taken out to buy the shop in August 1991.
   (c) Goods on the shelves at the end of the day on 31 March 1992. These goods had a resale value of £12 000 and had been purchased by Transom Trading for £8000.
   (d) Delivery van, costing £6000, which Transom Trading ordered on 20 March 1992 and paid for on 30 March but which was not delivered until 5 April 1992.
   (e) Shop fittings which were worth £4000 and had been acquired from a customer in exchange for motor spares with a retail value of £3500 and a cost price of £2000.
   (f) A Ford Fiesta costing £5500 which the owner of Transom Trading had bought in October 1991 for his wife to use. He had found that the Ford Granada Estate which he had bought second-hand in September for £4000 was being used exclusively for collecting and delivering goods for Transom Trading and not as a family car as originally intended.
   (g) One telephone answering machine which was rented from British Telecom at an annual rental of £40.
   (h) One cash register which Transom Trading had bought in November 1991 for £600.
   (i) A bank overdraft of £3500 on 31 March 1992.
   (j) A supply of seat belts which the owner of Transom Trading had bought for £600 in September from a market trader in good faith and which were subsequently found to be defective.

7. Using the decisions in question 6 above calculate the owners' equity and draw up the balance sheet of Transom Trading as at 31 March 1992.

8. Fred owns a garage and has tried to get everything together ready for the business accounts to be drawn up. He has drawn up the list of items below. You are required to identify with reasons the balance sheet heading under which each item should be classified, and the amount at which it should be included.

   (a) A motor car bought for resale at a cost of £3500, the retail price of which was £5000.
   (b) Various loose tools for car repairs which cost £700.
   (c) Two hydraulic jacks which had each cost £120.
   (d) Freehold premises which had cost £40 000.
   (e) The cost of digging and finishing a pit for repairs £600.
   (f) Spare parts held as a general stock having originally cost £790.
   (g) Spare parts bought from the previous owner when the garage was bought. At that time the value was agreed at £600 but it was subsequently discovered that only £200 of these spares were of any use.
   (h) Breakdown truck which cost £3000 for the basic truck and £600 to have the crane fitted.
   (i) A customer's car worth £1500 which was being held because the customer had not paid an outstanding bill of £300.

(j) Fred's own car which cost £4000. This is used mainly for business but Fred also uses it in the evenings and at weekends for the family.

(k) Customer goodwill which Fred reckons he has built up. He thinks that this would be worth at least £7000 if he sold the garage tomorrow.

(l) A bank loan for £1500 repayable within three months.

(m) A twenty-year mortgage taken out on the property amounting to £24 000 has not been fully repaid. The amount still outstanding is £18 000.

9. Jane owns a free house and has provided the following information for you to draw up her balance sheet. You need to decide the balance sheet heading under which each item should be classified, and the amount at which it should be included. You should be prepared to give Jane explanations of what you have done and why you have done it.

(a) A motor car bought from a hard up customer at a cost of £3500, the retail price of which was £5000.

(b) Pub furnishing which cost £4000.

(c) Optics and bar equipment which cost £1000.

(d) Freehold premises which had cost £280 000

(e) The cost of refurbishing and redecorating the pub £2000.

(f) Stock of beers etc. which had cost £790.

(g) Toasted sandwich-maker bought from the previous owner when the pub was bought. At that time the value was agreed at £200 but it was subsequently discovered that it was faulty and Jane has had to pay out £40 to get it repaired.

(h) A new washing machine and tumble drier which cost £600. These Jane tells you are used to wash tea-towels as well as doing the family washing.

(i) A television which is sited in the public bar and is rented from Radio Rentals at an annual cost of £96.

(j) Jane's own car which cost £4000. This is used mainly for business but Jane also uses it for the family when she can get time off.

(k) Customer goodwill which Jane reckons she has built up. She thinks that this would be worth at least £20 000 if she sold the pub tomorrow.

(l) A bank loan for £3500 repayable within three months.

(m) A twenty-year mortgage taken out on the property amounting to £184 000 has not been fully repaid. The amount still outstanding is £120 000.

(n) Takings awaiting banking and cash floats of £1300.

The profit and loss account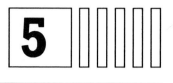

We have already seen that we can measure profit by measuring wealth at two points in time. We have also shown that the way in which wealth is measured in accounting terms can be roughly equated with balance sheets, and we have looked at some of the issues arising from the alternative choices in respect of assigning monetary values to wealth measurement.

In this chapter we will be concerned with an alternative way of measuring profit, using a profit and loss account. Our starting point and approach is very similar to that taken in the previous chapter. We look at what a profit and loss account is, why it is important, why it is produced and what it contains. We then consider some determinants of the content of a profit and loss account and some of the issues that have to be dealt with when drawing up a profit and loss account.

Importance of profit and loss accounts

Unlike a balance sheet which communicates information about a point in time, the profit and loss account relates to a period of time. It summarizes certain transactions taking place over that period. In terms of published reports the period is normally one year although most businesses of any size produce profit and loss accounts more regularly, usually quarterly and often monthly. These monthly or quarterly accounts are normally for internal consumption only except in the case of the interim reports of quoted public companies. In the case of a small and medium size business banks often request copies or make the production of such accounts a condition of lending money. The reason the banks require these accounts on a regular basis is that they need to monitor the health of the business they are lending to. They want to be confident that the managers of the business are aware of what is happening and are taking action to rectify the situation if the business is making losses. In fact banks place particular emphasis on the profit and loss account with the vast majority seeing it as very important (Berry *et al.*, 1987).

As far as owners and managers are concerned, if they want the business to flourish, there is little point in finding out at the end of the year that the price at which goods or services were sold did not cover what it cost to buy those goods or provide those services. By that stage it is too late to do anything about it. If the problem is identified at the end of the first month it can be dealt with immediately by putting up prices, reducing the level of services, buying at a lower price or whatever is appropriate to the particular business.

Clearly the profit and loss account is a very important statement as it tells you whether a business is profitable or not. We have all heard the expression 'the bottom line'. The bottom line is the amount of profit made by a project or business. By comparing that profit with how much wealth is needed to produce it, you can decide whether to invest in the business or undertake the project. Other factors which also need to be taken into account when making such a decision, are the risks involved and your own judgement of future prospects. These will help you decide whether the return as measured by the profit and loss account is adequate. Therefore, it can be argued that the profit and loss account provides some of the basic financial information for a rational decision to be made. We should remember, however, that although most of us think of business as being primarily motivated by profits, this is not always the case. Many small businesses make profits which are unsatisfactory from the point of view of a rational economic assessment, but the owners may not be profit orientated, they may simply hate working for any boss, or they may value leisure more than additional profits. This is a clear example of the dangers of looking at accounting results out of context.

Having talked about why a profit and loss account is important let us now look at what it is and what it contains. We have said that it is a statement covering a period of time, normally one year, and that its purpose is to measure profit, i.e. the increase in wealth. It does this by summarizing the revenue for that period and deducting from that the expenses incurred in earning that revenue. The process is therefore simple but to be able to do it we need to look at the definitions of revenue and expenses.

Revenue

Let us take a fairly standard definition of revenue and look at it in some detail so that we understand what it means. The definition which is reproduced as Key Concept 5.1 comes from International Accounting Standard 18 on revenue recognition.

As is usual with definitions, the one in Key Concept 5.1 seems on the face of it fairly complex. This is because it is trying to cover all eventualities. In most cases revenue is so obvious that it hits you between the eyes. For example, we would all agree that in a greengrocers the

KEY CONCEPT 5.1	Revenue is the gross inflow of cash, receivables or other consideration arising in the course of the ordinary activities of the enterprise from the sale of goods, from the rendering of services, and from the use by others of enterprise resources, yielding interest, royalties and dividends.
REVENUE	

revenue is going to be the amount that the fruit and vegetables were sold for, and in most cases that amount will all be in cash in the till. However, if we complicate it a bit more and we find our greengrocer supplies fruit and vegetables to a couple of local restaurants who settle their bill every month we find that in order to define revenue we have not only to include cash sales but also these other sales for which we have not been paid. These latter amounts are referred to as receivables by American text-books or as debtors in the UK. These debtors of course are shown in our balance sheet as assets because we will get a future benefit from them. We shall discuss the treatment of debtors in more detail in Chapter 7.

Let us develop our example of the greengrocer a bit further to illustrate other parts of the definition. Let us assume that, as well as supplying the local restaurants who pay monthly, he also supplies his accountant but instead of the accountant paying cash the arrangement is that the accountant does the accounts for nothing instead of charging the normal fee of £520 per year. These goods are effectively being sold to the accountant; all that has happened is that instead of the accountant paying the greengrocer £10 per week and then the greengrocer paying the accountant £520 at the end of the year they have simply agreed to exchange goods for services. These services are an example of what is referred to in the definition as 'other consideration'.

At this stage we should have a fair idea of what revenue is and the essence is that it relates to goods and services sold. However, we need to be careful to ensure that we only include in revenue sales that are part of our normal business activity. To illustrate let us assume that the green-grocer sells one of his two shops. Should this be seen as revenue or is it different from selling fruit and vegetables? Clearly the answer is that it is different because without a shop the business will cease to exist, whereas one cauliflower more or less does not threaten the existence of the business. Thus we need to differentiate normal sales of goods and services from the amounts arising from the sale of what is essentially the fabric of the business. These latter amounts will be dealt with separately and we will explore their treatment in more detail in Chapters 9 and 10.

Finally before leaving our greengrocer illustration let us assume that, having sold one of the shops, the greengrocer decides to invest the money in some shares or in the building society until such time as a new shop can be found. In this situation the money invested, which is effectively surplus to immediate requirements, will generate additional revenue in the form of interest or dividends. This is a form of revenue which is different from our main source of revenue. It would, in this case, be shown separately but included in the total revenue for the period. In certain cases, how-ever, the interest may be the major source of revenue – if for example, the main activity of a business is lending money, similarly dividends may be the main source of revenue for an investment trust.

So we can see that, although broadly speaking revenue is synonymous in many cases with sales, the actual revenue of a business is dependent upon the type of business and the particular activity giving rise to the revenue. In the example we have used we have seen that in its simplest form revenue was equal to cash sales. However, for some business activities the distinctions are not so clear and this leads to problems in deciding what revenue relates to a particular period. This of course would not be a problem if accounting periods were the same as the period of a business cycle. For example, if a housebuilder takes eighteen months to build and sell a house there is no problem in finding the revenue for the eighteen months. Unfortunately, the normal accounting period is twelve months and, as we have pointed out earlier, management and others need information on a more regular basis than that. What then is the revenue of our housebuilder for the first six months, or for the first year? This leads us to the question of when revenue arises and when should it be recognized. To help in answering this we use the realization principle.

The realization principle

This principle is defined in Key Concept 5.2.

You may have noticed that, unlike our definitions which tend to be fairly precise and all inclusive, this principle is carefully worded to avoid too much precision. It is meant to provide some basic criteria which can then be applied to the particular circumstances. The final decision on whether revenue is recognized is in practice often a matter of judgement rather than fact. The realization principle is part of what the Statement of Standard Accounting Practice 2 defines as the accruals concept. This is, however, broader than the principle referred to above and includes elements of the matching principle which we discuss later in this chapter. Returning to our discussion of the realization principle, before looking at an example, let us look at the wording used. First you will see that it talks of 'process', which implies a period rather than a point in time. It also talks of 'substantially complete', which leaves the question of what is substantial: is it two-thirds, or ninety per cent, or what? The principle also talks of payment being 'reasonably certain' – once again this leaves room for the exercise of judgement and raises the question of what is 'reasonable certainty' in an uncertain world.

Obviously if we sell services or goods to a reputable customer of long standing we are going to be reasonably certain that we will be paid. If, on the other hand, we sell to a shady character then we may be a lot less confident that we shall be paid. Interestingly, in a report prepared in 1989 for the Research Board of the Institute of Chartered Accountants in England and Wales, Carsberg and Noke suggested that realization should be equated with 'reliability of measurement' and not 'convertibility to cash'. However, at present the definition being used relates to convertibility to cash. Rather than looking at numerous examples of this type let us start by looking in general terms at a production and selling process

KEY CONCEPT 5.2	The realization principle states that revenue should only be recognized:
THE REALIZATION PRINCIPLE	☐ when the earning process is substantially complete; and ☐ when the receipt of payment for the goods and services is reasonably certain.

and examine the possible points at which we could recognize revenue in accordance with the realization principle:

Point 1   Inputs
           ↓
Point 2   Production
           ↓
Point 3   Finished goods
           ↓
Point 4   Sale of goods
           ↓
Point 5   Receipt of cash

Clearly it is unlikely that revenue would ever be recognized at point 1 but as we shall see all the others could be appropriate to different circumstances. We will start at the end of the process, i.e. point 5. On the face of it, this seems to be a safe place to recognize revenue as the earnings process is likely to be complete and payment is certain because the cash has been received. In many cases point 5 is the appropriate point – as, for example, in the case of our greengrocer. However, he also had some other sales which were paid for monthly in arrears so those may have to be recognized at point 4 as at that point the earning process is complete and payment is reasonably certain. On the other hand, if we take our builder and used either of these points we would get a situation where there was no revenue for the first seventeen months but a lot in the eighteenth month. Of course in practice, even in the case of our builder, if there was a contract to build the house for a third party then cash would have been paid on account. The point we are making here is that point 4 and point 5 are not necessarily appropriate in all cases.

One could argue that for a shipbuilder points 4 and 5 are inappropriate as cash is received throughout a contract and the point of sale is in fact before the production process starts. In this case, as a ship takes a number of years to build, it is also inappropriate to choose point 3 as this would lead to all the revenue arising in one year. Therefore it may in fact be that point 2 is appropriate if the earning process is 'substantially' complete and it is likely that payments on account will have been received. A similar argument applies to the cases of a property developer or building subcontractor.

From the discussion above it should be obvious that each case needs to be judged on its merits. If we consider industries that do not involve production in the sense used above, the fact that each case has to be judged on its merits is even more obvious. For example, in the case of an airline or a passenger railway service, the payment is normally received in advance of any service being provided to that particular customer. The cycle in these cases is quite different from that depicted above. Bearing in mind that not all cycles are the same you may like to think about when the appropriate time for revenue recognition would be for the following businesses:

☐ a local newsagent;
☐ a hotel with a fixed-term contract to provide rooms for aircrew from a major airline at a fixed price;

KEY CONCEPT 5.3 **THE MATCHING PRINCIPLE**	We must match the revenue earned during a period with the expenses incurred in earning that revenue.

☐ a supplier of components to Ford Motors;
☐ a gold mine where all output is bought by the government at a fixed price;
☐ an aircraft manufacturer.

If you have applied the realization principle you should have had little problem with the first example but the others are more problematic and are discussed more fully at the end of the chapter. If you feel unsure of your own solutions you may wish to refer to that discussion before proceeding any further.

The problem of when to recognize revenue is very important because the profit and loss account is based upon the revenue for a period and the expenses for that period. Before going on to discuss expenses we should first discuss how we establish which expenses to include. This is done by means of the matching principle (Key Concept 5.3).

We can therefore see that the realization principle is of prime importance as it defines the revenue with which the expenses have to be matched. If we include additional revenue then we must also include expenses incurred in earning that additional revenue. On the face of it this matching is fairly straightforward. However, there are a number of areas where problems may arise. These may be to do with timing (as we discuss later) or a combination of timing and uncertainty as we illustrate in Case 5.1.

Expenses

Whilst the definition given in Key Concept 5.4 is fairly straightforward it leads us on to having to define what a cost is. There are numerous ways of arriving at a cost as a perusal of any management accounting textbook will quickly show. Some of these are discussed in Chapter 8 which deals with stock and work in progress. However, for our present purposes we can say that a cost means a money sacrifice or the incurring of a liability in pursuit of the business objectives. Some examples of costs are:

☐ wages, which normally involve a money sacrifice;
☐ use of electricity, which normally involves incurring a liability to pay at the end of a quarter;
☐ purchase of equipment, which will normally incur a money sacrifice or a liability;
☐ purchase of goods for resale, which will normally incur a money sacrifice or a liability.

CASE 5.1

BP ANNUAL REPORT
1991

Extract from accounting policies statement

Exploration expenditure

Exploration expenditure is accounted in accordance with the successful efforts method. Exploration expenditure is initially classified as an intangible fixed asset. When proved reserves of oil and gas or commercially exploitable reserves of minerals or coal are determined the relevant expenditure is transferred to tangible production assets. All exploration expenditure determined as unsuccessful is charged against income. Exploration leasehold acquisition costs are amortized over the estimated period of exploration.

Exploration costs incurred under production sharing contracts are classified as loans within fixed asset investments. Provisions are initially made against these loans in accordance with the successful efforts method. On the determination of proved oil and gas reserves in contract areas provisions against expenditures, which are recoverable under contracts from future production, are written back to income.

Commentary

This extract from the Accounting Policies Statement illustrates the problems of matching in conditions of uncertainty. In this case BP, like many other oil companies, has to decide how it should treat the expenditure on exploring new oil fields etc. The problem is really whether an asset exists, i.e. is there a future benefit to be obtained, and is that benefit reasonably certain? Clearly we can assume that BP only spends money on exploration if there is a chance of a future benefit but, taking into account the uncertainty of that benefit, BP exercises prudence where there is some doubt of the eventual outcome. The concept of prudence is explored in more detail later in this book (Chapter 7). At this stage the reader should be aware that in reality life is not as simple as it would appear and hard and fast rules are often inappropriate. Thus some judgement needs to be exercised, as we illustrated when discussing the realization principle.

An expense is an expired cost, that is a cost from which all benefit has been extracted during an accounting period.

KEY CONCEPT 5.4

EXPENSE

Although all of these examples can clearly be seen to fit our definition of costs they are not necessarily expenses of the period. For example, the equipment is likely to last more than one period so it cannot be seen as an expired cost. Similarly the goods bought for resale may not, in the case of a furniture retailer for example, be sold during the period and they therefore cannot be seen as an expense of the period for two reasons. First the benefit has not expired as we will be able to sell those goods at some time in the future. Secondly they cannot be matched against the revenue earned during the period. There are other situations where the point at which a cost is incurred and the point at which the benefit arises do not coincide. These we will discuss in more detail shortly.

Before we do that it is worth emphasizing once again that we are dealing with a separate business entity and only costs relating to the business objectives can ever become expenses. This is very important as in many cases, especially with small businesses, the owner and the business are to all intents and purposes the same, but we are only drawing up accounts for the business. Thus if we find that a bill has been paid to buy a new double bed for a newsagent's business this cost is not an expense of the business because it relates to the owner personally not the business. Obviously if the business was a hotel then it is more likely that it would relate to the business. Personal items, such as the newsagent's purchase of a double bed, often go through a business bank account but need to be separated out and shown as withdrawals of the owner's capital rather than business expenses.

These withdrawals are often referred to in accounting literature as drawings. We could provide numerous examples of these some of which are less obvious than others. For example, is the tax and insurance of the car a business expense if the car is also used for family transportation? The guiding principle, however, in making a judgement is whether or not the cost has been incurred in pursuit of the objectives of the business.

We shall return to the discussion of drawings later, but let us now consider some possible situations in which we have to decide whether a cost which is clearly a business cost is an expense of the period. There are three possible situations that we need to discuss. These are where:

☐ costs of this year are expenses of this year;
☐ costs of earlier years are expenses of this year;
☐ costs of this year are expenses of subsequent years.

Costs of this year are expenses of this year

This is the most normal situation and is also the simplest to deal with. It occurs when an item or service is acquired during a year and consumed during that same year.

Note that no reference is made to whether the item acquired has been paid for. It may be that it has still not been paid for even though it has been acquired and used. A common example is telephone calls which are only paid for at the end of the quarter. The question of the timing of payment is not relevant to the process of matching expenses and revenues.

Costs of earlier years are expenses of this year

These can be divided into those that are wholly used up in the current period and those that are partly used up in the current period.

Wholly expenses of this year

The most obvious example of this is the stock of goods in a shop at the end of the year. The cost of buying those goods has been incurred in the year just ended but at the year end the benefit has not expired; they are therefore assets at the year end. However, in the next year they will be sold and thus will become expenses of the next year. The process that has occurred can be illustrated with an example.

Example 5.1

In this example we are asked to look at what should be included in the accounts for the year to 31 December 19X2.

Assume that we bought additional goods for our shop in November 19X1 but did not sell those goods until January 19X2. As we have a year end on 31 December 19X1 then that stock of goods is an asset at that date, i.e. 31 December 19X1, as the benefit is not used up. The cost has, however, been incurred in that year (the year to 31 December 19X1). In 19X2 the goods are sold and therefore the benefit is used up and there is an expense for the year ended 31 December 19X2 although the cost was incurred in the previous year. This is an example of a situation where the costs of an earlier year are wholly expenses of this year, in this case 19X2. It can be shown diagrammatically as follows:

$$1.1.X1 \longrightarrow 31.12.X1 \longrightarrow 31.12.X2$$

Cost incurred: Asset at   Goods sold:
goods bought   year end   expense

A similar situation arises when services are paid for in advance and are not fully used up at the end of the accounting period. For example, if the rent is payable quarterly **in advance** on 31 March, 30 June, 30 September and 31 December and the enterprise has a year end on 31 December, then the cost will be incurred in Year 1 for the quarter to 31 March, Year 2. However, the benefit will be used up in the first quarter of Year 2 and thus the expense belongs to Year 2. The rent for the first quarter of Year 1 would, of course, have been paid in the December preceding the commencement of Year 1.

These expenses are normally referred to as 'prepaid expenses' and frequently arise in respect of rent and water rates. For an individual the most obvious example of this type of expense is annual subscriptions to clubs and societies, car insurance, road fund licence, etc., although in many of these cases they are more likely to fall under the next heading where part of the benefit is used in one year and part in the following year.

Partly expenses of current year

An everyday example of this is any consumer durable, e.g. a car, washing machine, television, etc. In all these cases the costs are incurred at a point in time but the benefits are expected to accrue over a number of years. In a business enterprise the equivalent of our consumer durable is a fixed asset such as equipment, fixtures and fittings, etc. The allocation of the cost of these items to subsequent accounting periods is called depreciation and this will be dealt with in more detail in Chapter 9.

Other situations, for a business, where a cost may relate to more than one period arise frequently. For example, if we assume that the car insurance on the business cars was payable on 1 July 19X2 then half of that cost would be used up and become an expense for 19X2 and half would be used up and be an expense of 19X3. The crucial test is whether the benefit has been used up at the year end. If not there is a future benefit and we therefore have an asset.

Costs incurred this year which are expenses of later years

In the last two paragraphs we have given examples where although the cost was incurred last year, part of the expense relates to the current year. A similar situation can arise when a cost is incurred this period which partly relates to the next period.

In these cases some of the costs incurred in the current period may also be expenses of future periods. Examples which we have already mentioned are car tax, insurance, rates, etc. The due date for payment of these is unlikely to coincide with the end of the accounting period, nor would we want them to as this would lead to an uneven cash flow. Other examples are goods held in stock at the year end and fixed assets bought during the year. In the case of goods held in stock the whole of the costs are incurred this year but the expense relates to next year. In the case of a fixed asset some of the expense may relate to the current period if the asset has been used in the current period to generate revenue, and the remainder will relate to one or more future periods.

If we take as an example annual car tax we can see that if we pay for that in the current year 19X2 on 1 July then part of that cost will relate to this year, i.e. the proportion of the cost relating to the period 1 July to 31 December 19X2. The other part of the cost relates to next year, i.e. the year to 31 December 19X3, and will be accounted for as an expense of that period:

$$1.1.X2 \longrightarrow \quad 31.12.X2 \quad \longrightarrow \quad 31.12.X3$$

$$\uparrow \qquad\qquad\qquad \uparrow$$

$$\text{Tax paid} \qquad\qquad \text{Tax paid}$$

$$\longleftarrow \quad \text{Expense period} \quad \longrightarrow$$

Having looked at revenues and expenses we now need to recap on how these fit together in the profit and loss account before looking at a simple numerical example.

The profit and loss account

The purpose of this statement is to measure the profit or loss for the period. It does this by summarizing the revenues for the period, matching the expenses incurred in earning those revenues and subtracting the expenses from the revenues to arrive at the profit or loss. This could be depicted as:

$$R - E = P$$

or:

$$\text{Revenue} - \text{Expenses} = \text{Profit}$$

Before going on to examine what the profit figure could be used for let us see how this fits with the measurement of wealth described in Chapter 4.

In Chapter 4 we said that profit is the difference between wealth at the start and end of the year, i.e.

$$\text{Wealth 1} - \text{Wealth 0} = \text{Profit } P_1$$

or:

$$W_1 - W_0 = P_1$$

The alternative way of measuring profit was to take expenses from revenue. We also said in Chapter 4 that wealth in accounting terms was measured by assets minus liabilities. The resultant figure, i.e. the residual, was referred to as the owners' equity. Thus we said that at a point in time T_0 the owners' equity is

$$\text{Assets } T_0 - \text{Liabilities } T_0 = \text{Owners' equity } T_0$$

If we add to the owners' equity at T_0 the profit for the period T_0 to T_1, then the resultant figure will be our wealth at T_1 which will equal our assets minus liabilities at T_1, i.e.

$$\text{Assets at } T_1 - \text{Liabilities at } T_1 = \text{Owners' equity at } T_0 \pm \text{Profit } P_1$$

or:

$$A_1 - L_1 = O_0 \pm (R - E)_1$$

This shows us that there is a relationship between the profit and loss account and balance sheet. The nature of that relationship will become clearer in Chapter 6. However, let us now look at an example of a profit and loss account and then consider what it is used for, its format and its limitations. In Example 5.2 we use the following transactions of Blake's Enterprises, a paint shop, and see what should go into the profit and loss account for the year to 31 December 1991.

Example 5.2

Blake's Enterprises is a new retail paint outlet set up at the start of the year. Its transactions for 1991 its first year are summarized below.

Dates	Description	Amount £
1 January	Purchase of freehold shop	60 000
1 January	Rent for the year	2 000
1 April	Van purchased	8 000
1 April	Van – tax and insurance for a year	600
1 July	Purchase of washing machine	300
Various	Wages to shop assistant for year	6 000
Various	Goods bought and resold	18 000
Various	Goods bought but unsold	4 000
Various	Cash from sales	45 000
Various	Motor expenses and petrol	1 200
Various	Money withdrawn by Blake	6 000

☐ **Purchase of freehold**. The benefit arising from this cost has clearly not expired during the period although some part of the benefit may have been used up. At this stage we will not try to measure the part used up but we should bear in mind that at a later stage we will need to make such allocations.

☐ **Rent for the year**. This is clearly a cost and an expense of the year in question and should be included in the profit and loss account.

☐ **Purchase of van**. As with the freehold shop the benefit is likely to be available over many periods and we should theoretically allocate to the profit and loss account for the year the amount of the benefit used up. This allocation is done by means of a depreciation charge which we will deal with later in this book. At this stage therefore we will merely note the idea that an allocation should be made.

☐ **Van – tax and insurance**. This was paid for in advance on 1 April for a full year. At the end of our accounting period, i.e. 31 December, we shall have used nine months' insurance and tax, i.e. 9/12ths of the total. The expense for the period therefore is 9/12 of £600, i.e. £450. The remaining £150 relates to the next year and is an asset at the end of the year as the business will receive some future benefit. This and similar items are discussed in more detail in Chapter 7.

☐ **Purchase of washing machine**. We know that Blake's Enterprises is a retail shop selling paint. It is therefore highly unlikely that the washing machine was bought for use by the business although it has been paid for out of the business bank account. This is not therefore an expense of the business nor is it an asset of the business as the business will not get any future benefit. It is, in effect, a withdrawal of capital by the owner and should be treated as drawings.

☐ **Wages for year**. This is clearly a business expense as the wages are paid to the shop assistant and the benefit has been used up. From the information we have, the whole £6000 relates to the accounting period, and therefore the expense charged to the profit and loss should be £6000.

☐ **Goods bought and resold**. These goods have been sold to customers – we therefore no longer own them and are therefore not entitled to any future benefit. Thus the whole of the £18 000 is an expired benefit and as such should be charged as an expense in the current year's profit and loss account.

☐ **Goods bought but unsold**. These goods are still held by the business at the end of the year. The benefit from these goods is still to come in the form of cash when they are sold. These goods held in stock are therefore an asset rather than an expense of the period we are dealing with. Note that the test being applied is whether there is a future benefit or whether the benefit is past. If the former is the case there is an asset; if the latter then there is an expense.

☐ **Cash from sales**. This is the revenue of the business for the year and as far as we can tell it is the only revenue. The full amount of £45 000 should be shown as sales revenue in the profit and loss account.

☐ **Motor expenses and petrol**. Once again the benefit from these has expired. The whole of the £1200 should therefore be charged as an expense to the current year's profit and loss account.

☐ **Money withdrawn by Blake**. Given the present information we cannot categorically say whether this is a business expense or not. If it is in effect wages for Blake's work it could be argued that it is a genuine business expense. If, on the other hand, it has simply been withdrawn because Blake has decided to buy a new boat for personal use then it is clearly drawings. For the present we will classify it as drawings and therefore exclude it from the calculation of the enterprise's profit.

We can now draw up the profit and loss account of Blake's Enterprises for the year ended 31 December 1991:

Profit and loss account of Blake's Enterprises
for the year ended 31 December 1991

	£	£
Sales revenue		45 000
Cost of the goods sold		18 000
Gross profit		27 000
Rent	2000	
Van tax and insurance	450	
Wages	6000	
Motor expenses	1200	9 650
Net profit		17 350

You will notice that we have shown a gross profit and a net profit. Gross profit can be defined as:

Sales less cost of goods sold

and net profit can broadly be defined as:

Gross profit less operating costs, administrative costs and other charges

The reason for showing a gross profit is to enable Blake to see that the business is doing as well as it should. Most retail businesses know what percentage of the selling price is profit and what is cost; Blake's, for example, has costs of 40 per cent of the selling price and would expect a gross profit margin of 60 per cent of the selling price. If next year the gross profit margin was only 50 per cent Blake would want to know why. The answer must lie with either the sales figure, i.e. the price has been reduced or all sales have not been included, or with the cost of goods sold figure, i.e. the price from the supplier may have risen, the amount sold has been incorrectly calculated or the mix of sales, e.g. of paint to brushes, has changed. The latter case, i.e. where the sales mix has changed, can only be an explanation if the gross profit on the brushes is different from that on paint.

The net profit figure, as can be seen from the definition above, can be affected by numerous expenses. It is the figure often referred to as the bottom line. You may see sets of accounts in which the owner's drawings are deducted from this figure to arrive at a figure of profit retained in the business. The reason for not taking drawings off the net profit figure is twofold. First it does not fit the definition of an expense and cannot be matched with any revenue. The second point is similar to the argument for a gross profit in that a business will normally incur similar expenses year to year, i.e. Blake's will probably need a shop assistant next year, will have to pay rates, etc. These amounts will be reasonably constant and the net profit as a percentage of sales should therefore be reasonably constant. The owner's drawings, on the other hand, may fluctuate widely from year to year and therefore to include these in the calculation of net profit would mean that the net profit would fluctuate widely as well. This would make any analysis of the performance of the business more difficult than if the drawings are taken after the net profit has been determined.

Determinants of the format of the profit and loss account and its uses

Unlike the balance sheet which represents the position at a point in time the profit and loss account tries to represent a series of transactions over a period of time. Let us look first of all at what determines the format of the profit and loss as this also, to some extent, determines its usefulness and its limitations. For this we will follow a similar format to Chapter 4 in that we will look at the type of business and the preparers' objectives, the size and type of organization, the regulatory framework and the influence of users of accounts.

The type of business and the preparers' objectives

To a limited extent the type of business activity will determine the presentation and context of the profit and loss account. For example, in the case of a small retail business such as Blake's arriving at a gross profit figure may be useful but in a service business such as a hotel, which is highly labour intensive, the revenue earned may bear little, if any, relationship to inputs of physical goods. Thus the type of activity has an effect on what is being reported and how it should be reported. Similarly the objectives of the preparers of information often has an effect on the profit and loss account. If, for example, the accounts are being prepared for tax purposes the owner may wish to reduce profit, or defer it to the next year if at all possible. On the other hand, if the accounts are to be used to borrow money then a healthy profit may be what is required to be portrayed. Whilst we should not give the impression that the profit figure can be manipulated at will, it is clear from our discussion that there are a number of areas of judgement which allow slightly different results to be obtained from the same basic data. The extent to which mani-pulation is practised is often limited by the fact that there are a number of conflicting requirements which mean that manipulation of the profit one way for one purpose is detrimental for another purpose. It should also be borne in mind that the accuracy of the profit and loss account can only be as good as the information on which it is based. Thus if Blake's only records every second sale through the till the accounts will only record those takings that go through the till as they will be drawn up from till records and money banked. They will therefore not reflect the actual level of activity for the period.

The size and type of organization

As with the balance sheet a prime determinant of the content and format of the profit and loss account is the type of organizational structure involved. The content and format of the profit and loss account for a company is determined by the relevant Companies Acts as well as being subject to regulations imposed by the professional accounting bodies. These latter regulations are, as we have said, contained in Statements of Standard Accounting Practice (SSAPs) and the International Accounting Standards. As was the case with the balance sheet the 1981 Companies Act laid down that certain formats had to be followed. In the case of the profit and loss account four formats were given in the Act, although in reality there are two alternative formats, each of which can be presented in a vertical or horizontal format. In addition to the information included in the prescribed formats the 1981 Act also required additional disclosure of any movements on reserves and of the aggregate dividends for the period. These will be explored in more detail in Chapter 11 where the alternative formats will be illustrated.

Another important determinant is ownership in so far as a company may have to produce accounts that comply with UK and US regulations for example, or with regulations of a number of countries as is the case with multinationals such as Volkswagen etc.

For other types of organizations such as sole proprietorships and partnerships there are virtually no regulations covering format. Because the profit and loss is being prepared for owners who are also managers, it is normally the case that for these organizations the level of detail in the profit and loss account is greater than you would find in the published accounts of a public company. The reason for this is that the annual report, as well as being a report on performance, also acts as a basis for management decisions about the organization. In a large organization the accounts for external consumption are only one form of accounts as regular profit and loss accounts are normally prepared for internal use by the managers and these internal reports will generally be more detailed than the reports produced for external users.

Finally it is important to remind ourselves that the type of organization and the organizational goals may make a profit and loss account less relevant and in some cases irrelevant. Should charitable organizations make profits, from providing nursing care for example, or is the prime interest in how any surplus monies have been used to further the aims of the charity? In many cases a different statement is more appropriate to the needs and aims of the particular organization.

The regulatory framework

As we said in Chapter 4 there are a number of environmental influences on the format and content of the published accounts including the profit and loss account. In some countries a particular influence that is more relevant to the profit and loss account than the balance sheet is the taxation legislation. This is not the case in the UK but in some other European countries such as Germany, unless an amount is in the profit and loss account it is not allowable for tax purposes. This can lead to what, in effect, are not expenses in that there is still a future benefit to be obtained being charged as expenses in the current year in order to maximize the tax advantage and minimize the tax bill for the year. In the UK as in the rest of the EC there are special regulations allowing limited disclosure in the accounts sent to the registrar for filing that apply to small and medium sized companies.

Users of accounts

The users of accounts often have different requirements from each other. This was made very clear when the government in 1985 and 1986 put forward a number of consultative documents such as *Building Businesses...Not Barriers* and opened up the arena for a long and, at times, heated debate about what information should be provided in the published accounts of limited companies. In that debate even the accounting profession was divided on the issue of what needed to be provided to meet the needs of users. In terms of user needs, as we have said, owner managers would normally require more detailed information than is in the published accounts. The tax authorities often require specific information to decide whether a particular expense is allowable for tax purposes. They may, for example in the case of Blake's, require details of the mileage done on business and the private mileage done in the van. They also use a different mechanism for dealing with assets that last for a number of accounting periods than that normally used in producing the published accounts. Apart from these influences there is also the whole issue of confidentiality, whereby each business does not necessarily want its competitors, or indeed its customers, to know how much profit it is making. Obviously the limited disclosure provisions in respect of filing accounts has increased the level of confidentiality that is possible.

Summary

In this chapter we have identified what revenue is and explained two important principles, i.e. the realization principle and the matching principle. We have also looked at the question of what constitutes a business expense and seen that:

☐ expenses are **not** necessarily the same as costs;
☐ all costs **must relate** to the business before they can even be considered as expenses.

We have also pointed out that both the definition of assets and of expenses relate to benefits to the business. The important difference is that assets give future benefits whereas expenses relate to benefits used up in the accounting period. This leads us to a series of questions relating to assets and expenses which may assist in the correct classification of items. These questions may be summarized in the form of a decision tree.

Has a cost been incurred? → NO   Unlikely to be
accounting event.

YES
↓

Is there a benefit to   → NO   Relates to the
the business?   owner or someone
                                else and should be
YES   charged
↓   appropriately.

Has the benefit been   → NO   Show the future
used in this period?   benefit as an asset.

YES
↓

Charge as an expense.

Discussion of recognition of revenue for examples in the chapter

☐ **A local newsagent**. The business is likely to be mainly cash based so Point 5 is probably most appropriate although this will depend upon how many customers buy their newspapers etc. on account.

☐ **A hotel with a fixed-term contract to provide rooms for aircrew from a major airline at a fixed price**. Clearly Point 5 is too late as prior to this the earnings process is complete and payment is reasonably certain. However, in this case the sale of the services has taken place before the services are provided, i.e. when the contract was negotiated. Thus at this point the earnings process is not substantially complete. The logical point to recognize revenue is therefore immediately after the service has been provided, i.e. after the rooms have been occupied. If, however, the hotel has a fixed contract in terms of the number of rooms and the duration of the stay, irrespective of occupancy, an earlier point may be appropriate. In this case the revenue could be recognized when the rooms are due to be used irrespective of whether the service is in fact used. This is the point at which the service is provided which would not normally be appropriate for the casual guest.

☐ **Supplier of components**. Clearly Point 5 is too late as even at Point 4 the earnings process is complete and payment is reasonably certain. However, it could be argued that if the component supplier has a fixed contract with Ford an earlier point may be appropriate such as the point at which the goods are ready to be delivered. This may well become closer to the 'norm' if more large firms adopt 'just in time' principles as these lead to dedicated stocks being held by their suppliers rather than them.

☐ **A gold mine**. A similar argument to the component supplier could be applied here as the earnings process is substantially complete at the point of production and payment is certain as the government buys all output.

☐ **An aircraft manufacturer**. Your answer here will depend on the assumptions you have made. If, for example, you have assumed that the aircraft manufacturer is making to order then your judgement of certainty of payment would be different than if you assumed that it produced aircraft and then tried to sell them. Similarly if you thought of an aircraft producer as producing Boeing 747s you may have thought of the production process as spreading over a number of years in which case Point 2 may have been your judgement. If on the other hand you thought of the manufacture of light aircraft such as Piper Cubs you may have assumed a shorter production cycle in which case Point 2 would not be appropriate.

References

Berry, A., Citron, D. and Jarvis, R. (1987) *The Information Needs of Bankers Dealing with Large and Small Companies*, Certified Accountants Research Report 7, Certified Accountants Publications, London.

Carsberg, B. and Noke, C. (1989) *The reporting of profits and the concept of realisation: A report prepared for the research board of the ICAEW*, London.

Department of Employment, (1986) *Building Businesses...Not Barriers*, HMSO, Cmnd 9794.

Department of Trade and Industry (1985) *Accounting and Audit Requirements for Small Firms: A Consultative Document.*

International Accounting Standard No. 18 (1982) *Revenue Recognition*, International Accounting Standards Committee.

Statement of Standard Accounting Practice No. 2, SSAP 2, (1981) *Disclosure of Accounting Policies*. Accounting Standards Committee.

Further reading

Readers interested in pursuing the question of when revenue should be recognized may refer to an interesting discussion in J.H. Myers, 'The critical event and the recognition of net profit', *The Accounting Review*, October 1959, pp. 528–32.

See also B. Carsberg and C. Noke, *The reporting of profits and the concept of realisation: A report prepared for the research board of the ICAEW*, London 1989.

Review questions

1. In your own words define revenue.

2. At what point should revenue be recognized?

3. In your own words define an expense.

4. How does an expense differ from a cost?

5. 'Expenses are always the same as costs for a period.' Discuss the truth of the above statement using examples to illustrate your argument.

6. What is the purpose of a profit and loss account and who would use it?

7. Describe the difference between an expense and an asset.

8. In what circumstances would it be inappropriate to recognize a cost as either an expense or an asset?

Problems for discussion and analysis

1. Early in the chapter we produced a generalized five-stage model of the production process. Whilst that model clearly fits with a manufacturing business it may be less appropriate to service industries. In each of the following situations provide a possible model of the process and the points at which revenue could be recognized.

   (a) The provision of hotel rooms.
   (b) A tourist attraction charging a flat, all-inclusive, entrance fee such as a theme park.
   (c) A restaurant.
   (d) A professional accountancy firm doing a two-stage annual audit.
   (e) A package tour operator selling directly to the public.

2. There are two partners in AB & Co., an electrical retailer. They each have withdrawn £5000 from the business in cash during the year. B has also taken a washing machine which cost £200 and which had a selling price of £280 from the business for personal use. A has been paid wages of £12 000 and B has been paid £6000 in wages.

   Discuss how each of the above should be dealt with in the accounts giving reasons for your decisions.

3. Flights of Fancy is a travel agency which deals with flights, package holidays and holiday insurance. When a customer requires a flight booking, a £50 deposit is required with the balance due one month before the flight. For package holidays a deposit of £100 per person is required with the balance due when the holiday is confirmed. In both cases the tickets are issued fourteen days before the start of the holiday or flight and at that point Flights of Fancy becomes liable to pay the tour operator or airline. In the case of the travel insurance no deposit is required but the whole premium has to accompany the final payment for the flight or holiday package.

   Discuss the point at which Flights of Fancy should recognize the revenue for each of its three services.

4. In each of the following situations, discuss whether the item would be included in the profit and loss account for the year to 31 October 1990 and at what amount. The business called Hare Today is that of a fifty-roomed hotel which also runs a restaurant and bar. It was opened a year ago.

   (a) Receipts from room booking amounted to £300 000 of which all but £2000 had been received in cash by 31 October 1990 and the remainder was received in November 1990.
   (b) Money due from conference organizers for rooms provided during September and October on a block booking at a discounted price. This amounted to £22 000 and it was received in full by 31 December 1990.
   (c) Bar and restaurant takings amounting to £200 000 of which £1500 had not been banked at 31 October. This was banked the following day.
   (d) The costs of the food bought during the year amounted to £40 000 and of this there was £1000 worth of food in the deep freeze etc. at the end of 31 October. All of this had been paid for by 31 October 1990.

(e) The bar stock at the 31 October was valued at £2000 and the costs of the liquor sold during the year amounted to £65000.

(f) Wages paid in respect of the bar and restaurant amounted to £94000 for the year.

(g) As regards the hotel the wage costs relating to that were £96000 which included the reception staff, porters and housekeeping staff.

(h) The manageress's salary was £30000 and she was also entitled to a bonus of 1 per cent of the takings from any room booking over £200000 a year.

(i) The owner who worked full time in the business paid himself a salary of £20000 and also withdrew £5000 in cash from the business to pay a pressing personal debt.

(j) The motor expenses paid in the year were broken down as follows:

Annual road tax on car and minibus paid 1 January	£300
Annual insurance on above paid 1 January	£480
Repairs and petrol for vehicles	£600
Repairs and running costs of the owner's car	£800

The owner used his car virtually solely for the business and had done so from when the hotel opened.

(k) The following bills were also paid relating to the year:

Electricity	£1500
TV licences: 1 November 1989 to 31 October 1990	£500

(l) The TVs were on a rental contract which was paid monthly in arrears. Up to 31 October 1990 there had been eleven payments of £800 made.

5. Based upon your decisions, draw up a profit and loss account for 1990 using the information above.

6. In each of the following situations, discuss whether the item would be included in the profit and loss account for the year to 31 December 1990 and at what amount. The business is that of a builder and builders' merchant.

(a) Sales of general building materials by the builders' merchant to third parties amounted to £26000 of which £24000 was received in cash by 31 December 1990 and the remainder was received in January 1991.

(b) Three house conversions were started and completed during the year at a price of £24000 each. These amounts were received in full by 31 December 1990.

(c) One office conversion which had been 60 per cent complete at the end of 1989 was completed in 1990 at a price of £40000. Invoices on account amounting to £24000 had been sent out in 1989.

(d) The building materials sold to third parties during the year had cost £14000 of which all but £1000 had been paid for by December 1990.

(e) The building materials used on the three houses referred to in (b) above had cost £18000 and had all been paid for by December 1990.

(f) Wages paid in respect of the houses mentioned in (b) above amounted to £20000 for the year.

(g) As regards the office mentioned in (c) above the costs relating to that were:

Wages paid in 1989	£8000
Wages paid in 1990	£6000
Materials used in 1989	£8000
Materials used in 1990	£7000

(h) The storeman's wages in the yard amounted to £8000 for the year.

(i) The owner who worked full time in the business paid himself a salary of £9000 and also withdrew £1000 in cash from the business to pay a pressing personal debt.

(j) The motor expenses paid in the year were broken down as follows:

Annual road tax on three vans paid 1 April	£380*
Annual insurance on vans paid 1 April	£480*
Repairs and petrol for vans	£600
Annual road tax on owner's car paid 1 June	£100*
Annual road tax on owner's wife's car paid 1 June	£100*
Annual insurance on owner's car paid 1 June	£120*
Annual insurance on owner's wife's car paid 1 June	£120*
Repairs and petrol for the two cars	£800

*The charge for road tax had gone up by £20 per vehicle on the previous year and insurance premiums had risen by 20 per cent. All these charges are paid annually in advance.

(k) The following bills were also paid during the year:

Electricity	1 February	£54
(payable at end of each quarter)	1 May	£45
	1 August	£45
	1 November	£60
Rent – for 1 year to 1 April 1991	1 April 1990	£400*
TV licence 1 April 1990 to 1 April 1991		£60*

*The rent had remained the same as in 1989 but the TV licence had gone up from £50 to £60.

7. Based upon your decisions, draw up a profit and loss account for 1990 using the information above.

6 Introduction to the worksheet

In Chapter 4 we discussed the question of how we measure the wealth of a business at a particular point in time using the balance sheet, whilst in Chapter 5 we discussed the measurement of the profit for a period of time through the use of the profit and loss account. We also indicated that the profit could be measured either using the profit and loss account or by taking the increase in wealth over a period of time. Because of the complexity of most business organizations and the number of transactions involved we need to have a system from which the details for inclusion in the balance sheet and profit and loss account can be drawn. This system also needs to have some built-in checks and balances to ensure as far as possible that transactions are not omitted and to allow us to trace back to the original source any errors that are identified. To cope with these and other demands a form of recording known as double-entry book-keeping was developed. This system of double-entry book-keeping is based on a rule known as the principle of duality (see Key Concept 4.10). This was discussed in some detail in Chapter 4, and it was further exemplified in our discussion of the balance sheet equation which we defined as:

$$\text{Assets} = \text{Liabilities} + \text{Owners' equity}$$

We also showed that the owners' equity was increased by the profits made by the business and decreased by any losses. We defined profit as:

$$\text{Profit} = \text{Revenue} - \text{Expenses}$$

We can therefore see that if the balance sheet at the start of the period is stated as:

$$\text{Assets at } T_0 = \text{Liabilities at } T_0 + \text{Owners' equity at } T_0$$

then the balance sheet at the end of the period can be depicted as:

$$\text{Assets } T_1 = \text{Liabilities } T_1 + \text{Owners' equity } T_0 \pm (\text{Revenue} - \text{Expenses})$$

From these equations it should be clear that there is a relationship between assets, liabilities, owners' equity, revenue and expenses and that with every transaction recorded we must ensure that there are two sides in order that the equation remains in balance. This may seem complicated but it will become much clearer when you see how the double-entry system of recording works.

Applying the duality principle to our equation we find that, if we increase our assets, we must have:

either   increased our liabilities;
   or   made a profit;
   or   increased our owners' equity.

In other words, the principle of duality when applied to the balance sheet equation holds that both sides of the equation must always be equal.

KEY CONCEPT 6.1

APPLICATION OF THE PRINCIPLE OF DUALITY

Basic double-entry book-keeping

We shall deal with fairly simple examples to illustrate the principles, which are the same no matter how complex the business. It is normally the number of transactions that is the problem rather than the complexity, and most large businesses and indeed some fairly small businesses have to have very sophisticated recording systems to deal with the thousands of transactions that take place during a year. This is of course one of the major uses, if not the major use, of computers in business today. Computers not only provide a vehicle for recording the accounting transactions but the more sophisticated systems will also analyse the data and produce reports such as balance sheets, profit and loss accounts and other reports tailor-made to the particular needs of the users of those reports. For our purposes, however, we do not need to introduce a high level of sophistication to understand the principles involved and we can in fact set up a perfectly adequate double-entry book-keeping system using a spreadsheet approach in the same way as computer packages such as Lotus 1-2-3 use a spreadsheet. We will refer to our manually produced spreadsheet as a worksheet and we will use the worksheet to illustrate the basics of double-entry book-keeping.

The worksheet is set out in the form of the balance sheet equation with columns being headed up as appropriate to the situation. We will use the following simple data to illustrate the worksheet.

Example 6.1
Jim started a business buying and selling sailing dinghies. His first transactions were.

1. To open a business bank account and deposit £5000 of his own money.
2. To buy a car to enable him to view dinghies for £3000.
3. To buy a trailer for transporting boats for £700.
4. To get a bank loan of £1000.
5. To buy five racing dinghies for £2000.

Each of these transactions have been entered on the worksheet (version 1) and you should look at that whilst reading the description of what has been done.

Before looking at the transactions in detail let us briefly talk about the way in which the worksheet has been set up. You will notice that there is a column in which the transaction is identified and described. This identification and description in our case has been done via the item number. You could include a fuller description, however: the date, the invoice number, the name of the suppliers involved or whatever is appropriate.

After the column containing the description there are columns for each asset purchased and these are separated from the liabilities and owner's equity by a double space. Thus we have in effect across the top of our worksheet the balance sheet equation:

$$\text{Assets} = \text{Owner's equity} + \text{Liabilities}$$

Having made that very important point let us now examine each of the transactions in turn and see how they have been entered into our double-entry worksheet. To make things easier the transactions are first repeated below, are followed by the worksheet and then by descriptions of how they are entered on the worksheet.

1. To open a business bank account and deposit £5000 of his own money.
2. To buy a car to enable him to view dinghies for £3000.
3. To buy a trailer for transporting boats for £700.
4. To get a bank loan of £1000.
5. To buy five racing dinghies for £2000.

Jim's worksheet version 1

| | Assets | | | | = Equity + Liabilities | |
| | | | | | Owner's | |
	Bank	Car	Trailer	Dinghies	equity	Loan
Item 1	5000				5000	
Item 2	−3000	3000				
Item 3	−700		700			
Item 4	1000					1000
Item 5	−2000			2000		
Balances	300	3000	700	2000	5000	1000

☐ **Item 1**. In the case of this transaction Jim expects to get a future benefit, therefore we have an asset. So we have opened a column for cash and entered the amount paid into the bank account. On the other side of our worksheet we have opened a column entitled owner's equity and have entered in that column the amount the owner, Jim, has put into the business – in effect the amount the business owes the owner. Before moving on to the next item it is worth noting that if we were to total up our worksheet we would have the figures for the balance sheet at that point in time. This holds true at every stage as long as all transactions up to the balance sheet date have been recorded.

☐ **Item 2**. For this transaction we have opened another column in which we have recorded the car as an asset as it will give a future benefit, and we have also deducted the amount we paid for the car from the bank column. The worksheet if totalled now would still balance and would correctly record that the business owns a car which cost £3000 and has £2000 in the bank.

☐ **Item 3**. Next we used some of our cash to purchase a trailer to transport the dinghies. We therefore need to record that our asset bank is reduced by £700 and that we have a new asset trailer which cost us £700.

☐ **Item 4**. In this transaction we borrowed some money and put it in our bank. The amount in the bank is therefore increased by the amount of the loan £1000 and on the other side of the worksheet we open a column in which we record the fact that the business has a liability, i.e. it owes somebody money, in this case £1000. Once again if we were to total up our worksheet at this point in time we would find that it balances.

☐ **Item 5**. This transaction involves using one asset, our cash in the bank, to purchase another, the dinghies. Once again the stock of dinghies can be viewed as an asset of the business as the business is going to get some future benefit when the dinghies are sold. So all that is needed is to open a column for our new asset, the dinghies, and show that they cost £2000 and reduce the amount we have in our bank by the same amount.

From an examination of the worksheet it should be obvious that every transaction involves two entries. For example, when the owner pays in the money an entry is made in the bank column and one is made in the owner's equity column. It should also be apparent that if all the columns are totalled the worksheet will always balance. If either of these points is not clear to you it is important that you look again at what has been done so that you understand both these points before moving on.

You may have noticed that so far all the transactions are ones that only affect the balance sheet. In order to provide a clearer understanding of the way in which the worksheet is used and how profit and loss account transactions are recorded we will extend our example by a few more transactions.

Example 6.1 – further information
6. Jim hired a local boatbuilder to check the dinghies out and modify them to improve their performance. For this he paid £300.
7. Jim paid £200 for an advert in the local paper.
8. Jim sold the dinghies for £3000.

☐ **Item 6**. We can assume that when Jim paid the boatbuilder there was an expectation that there would be a future benefit because the modifications would enhance the value of the dinghies. We can there-fore record this payment either as an asset in its own right or add it to the cost of the dinghies bought and held in stock. We will take the latter course in this example. Thus the entry we need to make is to reduce the bank by £300, and record the £300 spent in the dinghies column.

☐ **Item 7**. Here we have incurred expenditure on an advert from which we may or may not get a future benefit. This time, to be safe, we will classify the £200 as an expense. We therefore reduce the cash in the bank by £200 and open a new column which we will title 'Profit and loss account' and in this we will enter the expense of £200.

☐ **Item 8**. Clearly we have some sales revenue here so we can enter sales of £3000 in the profit and loss account. We also need to enter the increase in cash of £3000 in the bank column.

If at this stage we were to draw up a balance sheet it would balance and show us that a profit of £2800 had been made. However, that would be incorrect because we have not applied the matching principle, that is we have not shown all the expenses incurred in producing the sales of £3000. We can either try to identify these expenses directly as we know they consist of the cost of the dinghies and the modifications, in other words the amount in the dinghies column. An alternative would be to look at each of our assets and ask ourselves the question: is there a future benefit to be obtained or has the benefit expired? If there is a future benefit then we have an asset; if the benefit has already passed then we have an expense. If we did this, in this case, we would have to come to the conclusion that as we had sold the dinghies represented by the figure of £2300 in the dinghies column and had received the benefit from selling them in the form of £3000 in cash then these are clearly not an asset any longer and should be charged as an expense of the period. We thus have to make a further adjustment to our worksheet which we will call item 8(a). Our new worksheet will now be as follows:

Jim's worksheet version 2

	Assets				=	Equity + Liabilities		
						Owner's		Profit
	Bank	Car	Trailer	Dinghies		equity	Loan	& loss
Item 1	5000					5000		
Item 2	−3000	3000						
Item 3	−700		700					
Item 4	1000						1000	
Item 5	−2000			2000				
Balances	300	3000	700	2000		5000	1000	
Item 6	−300			300				
Item 7	−200							−200
Item 8	3000							3000
Balances	2800	3000	700	2300		5000	1000	2800
Item 8(a)				−2300				−2300
Balance	2800	3000	700	0		5000	1000	500

Before leaving this simple example let us extract from the worksheet a balance sheet at the end of the period in question and a profit and loss account for the period.

Jim's balance sheet at the end of the period

Fixed assets	£	£
Car		3000
Trailer		700
Current assets		
Bank	2800	
	2800	2800
		6500
Financed by:		
Owner's equity		5000
Profit		500
		5500
Loan		1000
		6500

A careful study of the figures in the balance sheet and a comparison with the last line of the worksheet will make it clear that the balance sheet is in fact the bottom line of the worksheet after appropriate classifications have been made.

Jim's profit and loss account for the period

	£
Sales	3000
Cost of sales	2300
Gross profit	700
Expenses	200
Net profit	500

You will notice that the profit and loss account is simply a summary of the profit and loss column in the worksheet.

If we consider what we have done in the example we can see that the system of double-entry is merely a convenient way of recording transactions in a logical manner. The system is not complex – all it requires is an understanding of addition and subtraction together with the knowledge that the equation must always balance. It also requires the application of our definitions to classify a particular transaction correctly so if you have had problems in understanding why a transaction is dealt with in a particular way you should return to Chapters 4 and 5 and reread the definitions.

Before going on to try an example yourselves it is worth spending some time reflecting on what we have just said by reference to the last example. If we look at any of the columns we can see that there is simply addition and subtraction taking place; a good example is the cash column where we make additions as money comes into the business and make deductions as money is spent. Another feature of the system that is not so obvious is that if we make mistakes there is an automatic check because in the end the worksheet will not balance. If this turns out to be the case we have two ways of finding the error: we can either do a line by line check to ensure that each of our lines balances or we can total the columns at various stages to see where the error is likely to be. For example, if we had an error in the worksheet we have just done we could look at the totals after entering item 4 or item 5 or whatever. Quite often the error is reasonably obvious as the amount involved gives us a clue. The easy way to illustrate this is to put some deliberate errors into the context of the worksheet we have just completed.

Single-entry errors

Let us assume that we forgot the basic rule that each transaction has two sides and when we paid the boatbuilder we simply deducted the £300 from the bank column. Our worksheet would appear as follows:

Jim's worksheet version 3

	Assets				=	Equity + Liabilities		
						Owner's		Profit
	Bank	Car	Trailer	Dinghies		equity	Loan	& loss
Balances	300	3000	700	2000		5000	1000	
Item 6	−300							
Item 7	−200							−200
Item 8	3000							3000
Balances	2800	3000	700	2000		5000	1000	2800
Item 8(a)				−2000				−2000
Balance	2800	3000	700	0		5000	1000	800

You will notice that because we did not record the other side of the payment to the boatbuilder the amount charged to the profit and loss account in respect of the dinghies we sold is only £2000 and the profit is increased to £800. If we now add up the two sides of our worksheet we find that the assets side totals £6500, i.e. £2800 + £3000 + £700, whereas the other side totals £6800, i.e. £5000 + £1000 + £800. The difference beween the two is £300 which, of course, should direct us to the payment to the boatbuilder as the likely cause of the problem.

Incorrect double-entry

Another common cause of errors is incorrect double-entry. In this case two sides are recorded but they do not leave the equation in balance. Let us assume for example that we had got the entry for the boatbuilder correct but that we had incorrectly classified the £3000 Jim obtained from selling the goods as an increase in bank and an increase in dinghies rather than as sales revenue. The resultant worksheet would then be as follows:

Jim's worksheet version 4

	Assets				=	Equity + Liabilities		
						Owner's		Profit
	Bank	Car	Trailer	Dinghies		equity	Loan	& loss
Balances	300	3000	700	2000		5000	1000	
Item 6	−300			300				
Item 7	−200							−200
Item 8	3000			3000				
Balance	2800	3000	700	5300		5000	1000	−200

You will notice that we no longer have a cost of goods sold which is of course logically consistent because due to our error we no longer have any goods sold. What we have instead is a worksheet that has assets that total £11 800 while the other side totals £5800. The difference in this case is £6000 which is twice the amount involved in the error.

Addition, subtraction and transposition errors

Another common cause of errors is that we have simply failed to add or subtract correctly. The only way round this problem is to re-check all our totals and all our addition and subtraction. We can reduce the size of that task by balancing our worksheet on a regular basis so that we know where the error is likely to be.

A similar problem is a transposition error where, for example, we recorded the total of our cash column as £8200 instead of £2800 – in other words we transposed the order of the 2 and the 8. This is a common error and happens to all of us. In this case we can identify that it may be a transposition error because the difference of £5400 is divisible by 9. This will always be the case if we simply transpose two figures, for example 45 as 54, 97 as 79, etc. Notice that although the difference is divisible by 9 it does not necessarily have the number 9 in the difference.

Before moving on we suggest that you draw up your own worksheet for the following set of transactions and compare them with the answer given at the end of the chapter. If your answer varies from the one given try to identify what you have done, e.g. classified an item as the purchase of an asset. When you have done this you can then compare your explanation with our explanation of that item. Your entries do not necessarily have to be identical to ours as there are many different ways of setting up the worksheet and of arriving at the correct answer to show the position at the end of the month. We can illustrate this by reference to the example based on Mary's business which is set out below.

Example 6.2

Mary decided to start a business selling second-hand cars. She had saved up some money of her own but this was not enough to start so she had obtained an interest-free loan from her parents. The transactions of the business, which were all cash, for the first month were as follows.

Day 1   Opened a business bank account and paid in five hundred pounds of her own money.

Day 2   Paid in to the bank two thousand pounds she had borrowed from her parents for use by the business.

Day 3   Found a suitable showroom and paid a fortnight's rent of one hundred pounds.

Day 4   Went to the car auction and bought the following cars for cash:
1980 Ford Fiesta for £1000;
1977 Ford Escort for £500;
1975 Volkswagen Beetle for £300.

Day 5   Bought some office furniture for £120.

Day 6   Employed a teenager who was on the dole to clean cars for her at the rate of £10 per car and paid out £30.

Day 8   Placed adverts for all three cars in the local paper. The cost of advertising was £20 per day for each car. She decided that all three should be advertised for two days, so the total cost was £120.

Day 9   Sold the Ford Fiesta for £1500 cash.

Day 10   Sold the Ford Escort for £700 cash.

Day 11   Returned to the car auction and bought a Sunbeam Horizon for £1500.

Day 12   Employed her teenage friend to clean the Horizon for £10.

Day 15   Re-advertised the Volkswagen for three days at £20 per day, total cost £60.

Day 17   Advertised the Horizon using a special block advert which cost £75 in total.

Day 18   Paid rent of showroom for the next fortnight amounting to £100.

Day 19   Was offered £400 for the Volkswagen.

Day 20   Accepted the offer for the Volkswagen and was paid £400.

Day 22   Sold Horizon for £1800.

Day 23   Went to the car auction and bought a Vauxhall Cavalier for £2300.

Day 24   Had the Cavalier professionally valeted at a cost of £40.

Day 25   Advertised the Cavalier using the special block advert at a cost of £75.

Day 26   Decided that as things were going so well she would repay her parents £200.

Day 27   Took Cavalier on a test drive with a customer and seized the engine.

Day 29   Had Cavalier repaired at a cost of £300.

Day 30   Sold the Cavalier for £2700.

Day 31   Paid electricity bill of £40 for the month.

To illustrate the different treatments possible let us consider the transaction on day 3 where Mary paid a fortnight's rent in advance. The question arises – is this an expense or an asset? Let us consider the alternatives.

On day 3 it is reasonably clear that we have an asset in that we will get a future benefit in the form of the use of the showroom for two weeks. On the other hand, if we are recording the transaction for the first time at the end of the month we can then argue that the transaction is an expense because at that point in time the benefit has expired. Thus, we could

The prudence principle can be summed up as: Anticipate no profits and provide for all possible losses.	KEY CONCEPT 6.2 ――――――――― **PRUDENCE**

record on day 3 the payment and an asset and then re-evaluate all our assets at the end of the month as we have done on our worksheet. Conversely, we could wait till the end of the month and just record an expense. We would recommend at this stage that you adopt the former treatment for two reasons: first, it ensures that you re-evaluate all your assets at the end of the month, and secondly that short-cuts often cause more problems than they are worth if you are unfamiliar with the area.

Another transaction that is worthy of mention is the advertisements on day 8 and other days. In these cases a similar dilemma to that already identified with the rent exists. However, there is another problem in that, whereas with the rent we knew that there was going to be a future benefit, in these cases it is far from certain that there will be a future benefit. In other words we do not know when we place the advert whether anyone will reply to it, and even if they do whether they will buy the car. In these cases we apply a principle known as 'prudence' which basically argues that unless you are reasonably certain of the future benefit then you should not recognize an asset. This is similar to the rule for the recognition of revenue which we discussed in Chapter 5. Prudence, however, goes somewhat further as it encourages us to state assets at lower values rather than recognizing an uncertain increase in value, and it suggests that if we think that there is a reasonable chance of a loss we should recognize that loss immediately rather than waiting until it arises.

As you are probably beginning to recognize accounting is not just about recording, it is also about exercising judgement within a framework of broad and often very general principles. The important factor to remember as you work through the example above is that you are making judgements and applying the definitions set out in the previous two chapters, and you need to be aware of what you are doing and why you are doing it. You should now attempt to produce your own worksheet and extract a profit and loss account and balance sheet.

If your worksheet is correct the balances on the bottom line of your worksheet should be those in the balance sheet set out below. The profit and loss account follows the balance sheet and is merely a summary of the profit and loss column on the worksheet.

Even if you find your answer is correct, before proceeding to the next chapter, you should read the explanations for the treatment of the transactions on days 3, 6, 18, 19, 26, 27 and 29 as these are of particular interest and will assist you in the future. If your answer disagrees with ours it may be that you have made an error or it may be that you have arrived at a different judgement about the treatment of a transaction. The full worksheet and explanations for our decisions are given at the end of this chapter before the review questions and problems. You should check both our answer and the explanations where you differ from us.

Balance sheet of Mary's business at the end of the month

	£
Fixed assets	
Furniture	120
Current assets	
Cash	2730
	2850
Financed by	£
Owner's equity	500
Profit for the month	550
	1050
Loan	1800
	2850

Profit and loss of Mary's business for month one

	£	£
Sales revenue		7100
Cost of cars sold		5600
Gross profit		1500
Expenses		
Rent	200	
Cleaning	80	
Advertising	330	
Repairs	300	
Electricity	40	950
Net profit		550

Summary

This chapter has introduced you to the worksheet and the concept of duality which states that for accounting purposes there are two sides to every transaction. We have also shown the importance of asking ourselves some basic questions regarding what exactly is an asset, an expense, etc. Hopefully we have also illustrated that simply by referring back to the definitions contained in Chapters 4 and 5 most if not all the problems you are likely to encounter can be solved.

We have also provided, by means of the worksheet, a simple vehicle for recording, checking and extracting a balance sheet and profit and loss account. We have shown that the basis of accounting is very simple as long as you follow the basic principles and for those times when you do lapse the system used on the worksheet should provide you with a simple and effective check. Finally we have introduced you to the idea that accounting is not a science, that it involves elements of judgement, and we have provided you with the 'prudence' concept as a useful tool to assist in arriving at your judgement.

Answer to Example 6.2

Worksheet of Mary's business

	Assets				=	Equity + Liabilities		
	Cash	Cars	Rent	Furniture		Equity	Loans	Profit & loss
Day 1	500					500		
Day 2	2000						2000	
Day 3	−100		100					
Day 4	−1800	1800						
Day 5	−120			120				
Day 6	−30							−30
Day 8	−120							−120
Day 9	1500							1500
Day 9*		−1000						−1000
Day 10	700							700
Day 10*		−500						−500
Day 11	−1500	1500						
Day 12	−10							−10
Day 15	−60							−60
Day 17	−75							−75
Day 18	−100		100					
Day 20	400							400
Day 20*		−300						−300
Day 22	1800							1800
Day 22*		−1500						−1500
Day 23	−2300	2300						
Day 24	−40							−40
Day 25	−75							−75
Day 26	−200						−200	
Day 29	−300							−300
Day 30	2700							2700
Day 30*		−2300						−2300
Day 31	−40							−40
Balance	2730	0	200	120		500	1800	750
Day 31**			−200					−200
Balance	2730	0	0	120		500	1800	550

* You will notice that every time we sold a car we immediately transferred the cost of that car from our cars column to the profit and loss as an expense. This transfer was carried out because having sold the car we no longer expected a future benefit and therefore we no longer had an asset. An alternative treatment would be to do this exercise at the end of the month.

** When we complete our worksheet it is important to review our assets and ask ourselves the question: are these still assets? If, as in this case, the answer is **no** then we need to transfer their cost to the profit and loss account as an expense of the period.

Transaction summary

We have set out below the transactions that took place together with the treatment of those transactions on the worksheet and where appropriate explanations of that treatment and acceptable alternatives. If there are any items that you still do not understand you should try to examine them in terms of the basic definitions referred to in Chapters 4 and 5.

Day 1   Opened a business bank account and paid in £500 of her own money.

Here we have created a business asset in the form of cash at the bank and have also opened an account to show the owner's stake in the business under the heading of owner's equity.

Day 2   Paid in to the bank two thousand pounds she had borrowed from her parents for use by the business.

Once again the business has acquired an asset as it will get a future benefit from the cash. It has also acquired an obligation to pay somebody some money and as such has a liability for the amount borrowed.

Day 3   Found a suitable showroom and paid a fortnight's rent of one hundred pounds.

We have already discussed this transaction in the main body of the chapter. Our treatment has been to reduce our asset cash at the bank and to record an asset of the prepaid rent from which we will derive a benefit in the future.

Day 4   Went to the car auction and bought the following cars for cash:
1980 Ford Fiesta for £1000;
1977 Ford Escort for £500;
1975 Volkswagen Beetle £300.

Clearly by paying out £1800 we have reduced our cash at the bank so that is one side of the entry; the other side is to record the cars as an asset as we will get a future benefit from these.

Day 5   Bought some office furniture for £120.

This is exactly the same as the previous transaction – we have merely exchanged one asset, cash at the bank, for another, furniture.

Day 6   Employed a teenager who was on the dole to clean cars for her at the rate of £10 per car and paid out £30.

In this case one side of the transaction is clear in as much as the cash at the bank has clearly been reduced by £30. The question that then arises is whether there is an asset or an expense. We have shown the cost of the car cleaning as an expense because we are uncertain that any future benefit will arise from this particular expenditure. The fact that a car is cleaned does not add any intrinsic value and in fact it is probably necessary to clean all the cars in the showroom regularly because customers expect to buy clean cars.

Day 8   Placed adverts for all three cars in the local paper. The cost of advertising was £20 per day for each car. She decided that all three should be advertised for two days, so the total cost was £120.

You should refer back to the text for a detailed discussion of the reasons for our treatment of this item. What we have done is to apply the prudence principle and treat the item as an expense and charged the item to the profit and loss at the same time as reducing our cash at the bank by £120.

Day 9   Sold the Ford Fiesta for £1500 cash.

Clearly we have another £1500 in our bank so we increase our cash at the bank column and we also have a sale which accords with our definition of revenue so we bring that revenue in to the profit and loss column.

Day 9*

Here we have reduced our assets by the cost of the car we sold and charged that cost, i.e. the cost of the expired benefit, to the profit and loss column.

Day 10   Sold the Ford Escort for £700 cash.

See the explanations for day 9 above. If you have got these wrong make sure you understand why, then correct your worksheet for all similar items before reading on.

Day 11   Returned to the car auction and bought a Sunbeam Horizon for £1500.

This is in essence the same as the transaction on day 4 and if you have made an error you should re-read that explanation and check that your treatment of the transaction on day 23 is correct before moving on.

Day 12   Employed her teenage friend to clean the Horizon for £10.

This is the same as the transaction on day 6 and if you have made an error you should re-read that explanation and check that your treatment of the transaction on day 24 is correct before moving on.

Day 15   Re-advertised the Volkswagen for three days at £20 per day, total cost £60.

See the explanation for day 8 above.

Day 17   Advertised the Horizon using a special block advert which cost £75 in total.

See the explanation for day 8 above.

Day 18   Paid rent of showroom for the next fortnight amounting to £100.

This is the same situation as the transaction on day 3 – the entry should therefore be the same. At this stage you could also reduce the rent column by the rent for the first two weeks and charge this to the profit and loss as the benefit has now expired. We have not done this because we wished to illustrate the importance of the final review before a balance sheet and profit and loss account are finally drawn up.

Day 19   Was offered £400 for the Volkswagen.

There is no need to record this as the transaction is not substantially complete at this stage so we would not recognize revenue. If you have shown a sale at this stage re-read the discussion on the recognition of revenue in Chapter 5.

Day 20   Accepted the offer for the Volkswagen and was paid £400.

Now we have a sale and revenue can be recognized as in day 9 above.

Day 22   Sold Horizon for £1800.

Once again we have a sale and revenue can be recognized.

Day 23   Went to the car auction and bought a Vauxhall Cavalier for £2300.

See day 4 for the explanation of treatment.

Day 24   Had the Cavalier professionally valeted at a cost of £40.

This is the same as the cleaning on day 6 etc. The fact that it was done professionally does not alter the argument set out in respect of the transaction on day 6.

Day 25   Advertised the Cavalier using the special block advert at a cost of £75.

This should be treated in the same way as previous adverts for the same reasons.

Day 26   Decided that as things were going so well she would repay her parents £200.

This is a different transaction from any of the ones we have dealt with so far – those have dealt with expenditure of cash either for a past or future benefit. In this case we have reduced our cash at the bank in order to pay back an amount the business owes – in other words we have used some cash to reduce our liability. Thus we reduce the amount shown as owing in the loan column by £200, and we reduce the amount of cash at the bank by £200.

Day 27   Took Cavalier on a test drive with a customer and seized the engine.

Although an economic event has happened we cannot account for it as at this stage the effect of that event cannot be adequately expressed in monetary terms.

Day 29   Had Cavalier repaired at a cost of £300.

We are now in a position to account for the event as we know the effect in monetary terms. However, we are now left with the question of whether the expenditure is going to provide a future benefit or whether it is an expense. We need to ask ourselves the question has the expenditure added to the asset? If it has then there is no problem in recognizing the transaction as one which creates an asset. If, however, the expenditure merely restores the asset to the state it was in previously then it is doubtful that it relates to an asset, and applying the prudence principle we would be safer to charge it to the profit and loss account as an expense, which is what we have done. In essence this is a shorthand way of recording two events. The first is that the engine blew up so reducing the future benefit we could expect from the asset – if we knew the extent of this reduction we could have charged that as a past benefit. If we had done that then the repairs could legitimately be viewed as enhancing the future benefit to be obtained in respect of the reduced asset. This whole process is in fact shortened because we do not know what the loss in value of future benefits was. We therefore are in effect using the cost of repairs as a surrogate for that loss in value.

It is worth noting that in Example 6.1 when Jim paid the boatbuilder for the modifications to the dinghies we assumed that there was an enhanced future benefit whereas here in effect we are saying that the repairs merely restored the asset to its original state rather than enhanced it.

Day 30   Sold the Cavalier for £2700.

See previous transactions of this type on days 9, 10, etc.

Day 31   Paid electricity bill of £40 for the month.

Here we have a reduction of the cash at the bank in respect of the use of electricity over the past month. The benefit here has clearly expired and we therefore have an expense.

Review questions

1. Describe in your own words what is meant by the concept of duality.

2. In each of the following cases describe the two entries required on the worksheet.

    (a) The owner pays £500 into the business bank account.
    (b) A desk is bought for the business for £100 paid for from the bank account.
    (c) The business buys goods for resale for £200.
    (d) The rent of the premises for the first week of £50 is paid.
    (e) A potential customer makes an offer for the goods of £250.
    (f) The wages of the employee amounting to £60 are paid.
    (g) The firm receives another offer of £350 for the goods, accepts this offer and is paid immediately.

3. In situations where doubt exists as to whether a transaction has resulted in an asset or expense what questions should be posed?

4. If some doubt still remains how a choice should be made, explain any principles involved.

Problems for discussion and analysis

1. In each of the following situations discuss the potential effect on the business and suggest possible ways in which those effects could be reflected on the worksheet.

(a) The owner starts up a new business and pays into the business bank account £1000. In addition it is decided that the owner's car will be used exclusively for the business. The car was purchased last year at a cost of £5000 but a similar one-year old car could be bought for £4500 now.

(b) A reservation was made for a suite of rooms for two nights at an agreed price of £800. However, prior to taking up the reservation the customer changed his mind and decided that he did not want the suite after all.

(c) A batch of goods which had been bought for £400 and sold for £600 were subsequently found to be faulty. The options available are as follows:

(i) Give the customer a rebate on the purchase price of £100.

(ii) Refund the full selling price to the customer and reclaim the goods. If this course of action is followed a further £140 will need to be spent to rectify the faults.

(d) A guest staying at your hotel had booked for two weeks on your holiday special and paid the cost of £700 in advance. At the end of the first week she has to leave as her parents are seriously ill. The day after she leaves you are able to relet the room for the remaining six nights at the normal daily rate of £70 per night.

Your stated policy on cancellation is that if the room can be relet up to 80 per cent of the moneys paid in respect of the cancelled booking can be refunded.

2. Leech has recently gone into business selling office chairs. Details of her transactions for the first month are given below.

Day 1   Opened a bank account and paid in £5000 of her own money. Transferred the ownership of her car to the business at an agreed price of £2000.

Rented an office/showroom at a rental of £120 per month and paid one month's rent.

Bought a desk, typewriter, answerphone and sundry office equipment at a cost of £800.

Day 2   Bought 100 chairs at a price of £35 per chair and paid for them immediately.

Day 3   Received delivery of the chairs.

Day 5   Placed advert in trade paper offering the chairs for sale on the following terms.

Single chairs: £50 per chair including delivery.

Ten or more chairs: £45 per chair including delivery.

The advert cost £200 and was paid for immediately.

Day 8   Received separate orders for twelve chairs at £50 each together with accompanying cheques.

Day 9   Paid the cheques into the bank and despatched the chairs. The delivery costs were £72 in total and were paid straightaway.

Day 11   Received six orders for ten chairs each at a cost of £45 per chair together with six cheques for £450.

Banked the cheques and despatched the orders. The delivery charges were £50 for each order making a total of £300 which was paid immediately.

Day 14   Leech paid herself two weeks' wages from the business amounting to £150 in total.

Day 16   Bought another 20 chairs for £35 each and paid for them immediately.

Day 21   Paid £150 for car repairs.

Day 23   Received an order for twenty chairs at £45 each, banked the cheque and arranged delivery for £40 which was paid for immediately.

Day 24   Placed a further advert in the trade paper at a cost of £200 which was paid for immediately.

Day 27 Received one order for 15 chairs at a price of £45 each – this order totalled £675 – and another order for seven chairs at a price of £50 each, a total of £350. The cheques were banked and the chairs despatched at a total cost of £100 which was paid immediately.

Day 28 Drew another £150 from the bank for her own wages.

Sold the remaining six chairs to a customer who walked into the showroom, at a price of £250 for all six. The customer paid the £250 in cash and this money was banked. No delivery costs were incurred as the customer took the chairs away.

Paid the telephone bill, £30, and the electricity bill, £40.

Required:

(a) In each situation where there is more than one possible treatment discuss the arguments in favour of and against each alternative.

(b) Based upon the outcome of your discussions draw up a worksheet and enter the above transactions.

(c) Extract a balance sheet at the end of the month and a profit and loss account for the month.

(d) Discuss the performance of the business for the period as revealed by the accounts you have prepared paying particular attention to its cash position and its profitability.

3. Seal has recently gone into business running a small guest house providing bed and breakfast. Details of the first month's transactions are given below.

Day 1 Opened a bank account and paid in £50 000 of his own money.

Transferred the ownership of his car to the business at an agreed price of £2000.

Obtained a mortgage from the bank for £140 000 and paid £180 000 to the vendor, the balance of £40 000 coming from the business bank account.

Day 2 Contracted with a firm of decorators to paint and paper all the guest rooms at a price of £1000 payable in cash immediately.

Day 3 Bought furniture for all the guest bedrooms for £2400.

Day 5 Placed advert in local paper saying that the guest house would be re-opening in one week's time under new management. The advert cost £200 and was paid for immediately.

Day 8 Bought furniture for the dining room and guest lounge for £2800 and paid in cash.

Day 9 Bought tableware, linen, cutlery, etc., for £800.

Day 12 Bought in stocks of food £80 ready for opening the following week.

Day 14 Opened the guest house for business and was able to let all eight rooms for the week at £30 per night per room. All the guests paid in advance.

Day 15 Banked the £1680 received from the guests.

Day 20 Replenished the food stocks at a cost of £80.

Day 21 Paid laundry bill of £40.

Day 22 Let all the rooms for the next seven days on the same terms as previously and banked the £1680.

Day 25 Replenished the food stocks at a cost of £80.

Day 26 Received reservations for two rooms for the following week.

Day 27 Paid laundry bill of £40.

Day 28 Drew £300 from the bank for his own wages.

Day 29 Let five rooms for three nights at £30 per night and banked the money.

Only one of the guests who had made a reservation arrived and they paid for three days as they had decided that they were only going to stay until the end of the month. As they arrived in the evening the money was not banked until the following day.

Bought enough food to last until the end of the month for £60.

Day 31   Paid the telephone bill, £30, and the electricity bill, £60.

Required:

(a) In each situation where there is more than one possible treatment discuss the arguments in favour of and against each alternative.

(b) Based upon the outcome of your discussions draw up a worksheet and enter the above transactions.

(c) Extract a balance sheet at the end of the month and a profit and loss account for the month.

(d) Discuss the performance of the business for the period as revealed by the accounts you have prepared, paying particular attention to its cash position and profitability.

Accrual accounting 7

In all the examples we have dealt with so far, and indeed in all our discussions, we have always assumed that all transactions are on a cash basis. As we pointed out in Chapter 4, this is unlikely to be the case. Therefore we need to consider how we deal with the situation where a business buys goods or services from its suppliers on credit terms and supplies goods or services to customers on credit terms. We need to consider how to deal with the situation where a business has to pay for goods or services in advance, as is the case with insurance, or when it pays after receiving the goods or services, as would be the case with most raw materials and with services such as electricity, telephones, etc.

As these transactions impact directly on both the balance sheet and the profit and loss account, we need a system that deals with them in an appropriate way to ensure that expenses are matched with revenue and that the balance sheet reflects the position at the balance sheet date. In other words, the system must ensure that the balance sheet shows the assets held at the balance sheet date and the amounts owed at that date. The profit and loss account must record the actual sales for the period and the expenses related to those sales. Not to do so would contravene the matching and realization principles and the accounts would merely reflect the timing of cash receipts and payments rather than reflecting the economic substance of the transactions that the business has engaged in during the period.

A system that tries to reflect the economic substance of the business activity is known as accrual accounting. In this chapter we shall examine situations in which the economic substance of the transaction does not occur at the same time as the cash flow and the way in which accrual accounting deals with these situations. In particular we will look at how it deals with debtors, prepayments and bad debts, and at creditors and accruals. Finally we shall briefly consider other forms of liability and in particular contingent liabilities.

Debtors and prepayments

Debtors

In American accounting textbooks and financial statements, debtors are often referred to as amounts receivable. You may find initially that the American term is easier to remember as it is more descriptive than the

KEY CONCEPT 7.1	Debtors arise when a business sells goods or services to a third party on credit terms or, in other words, when goods or services are sold on the understanding that payment will be received at a later date.
DEBTORS	

term debtors. Debtors, which are defined in Key Concept 7.1, arise when a business has sold goods during the year for which payment is not received at the point of sale. In this situation we need to recognize the revenue from the sales even though the cash has not yet been received. If, however, we simply entered the sales on the worksheet the accounts would not balance as there would only be one side to the entry. This is in conflict with the principle of duality. However, we do have an asset, as we have a right to a future benefit in the form of cash, but we cannot use the cash account for the other side of the transaction as no cash has been received. The way in which accrual accounting solves the problem is to open an account, which we depict on the worksheet as a column, for this asset which is known as a debtor. In any sizeable business there would normally be a number of debtors, each of which would need a separate account in which the specific transactions relating to that debtor are recorded. These separate accounts are kept in a subsidiary set of books of account known as the sales ledger and the main accounts normally only reflect a summary of those transactions. As most trade credit terms are for one month or a similar period you will generally find debtors classified under current assets.

Prepayments

Prepayments, as the name implies, are payments in advance. They often arise in respect of such services as insurance, road tax, etc., which we discussed in Chapter 5. The payments must relate to the usage of such services by the business and not by the owner in a personal capacity, a distinction sometimes difficult to establish in the case of small businesses. The proportion of the payment that relates to benefits still unexpired at the year end will be shown as a current asset in the balance sheet of the business. Prepayments therefore differ from debtors in two ways. First they generally relate to payments made by the business for services rather than to sales, and secondly the future benefits will be in a form other than cash receipts.

KEY CONCEPT 7.2	The key question that must be considered is: has the benefit been used up or is there still some future benefit to be obtained? If there is a future benefit accruing to the business we have an asset; if there is no future benefit we have an expense which must be matched with revenue.
PREPAYMENTS	

We can now look at an example which illustrates the way in which accrual accounting deals with debtors and prepayments.

Example 7.1
Assume a business, Pitco, has the following transactions for the period from 1 January to 31 March:

Sales for cash	£6000
Sales on credit	£4000
Cash received from debtors	£3000
Rent for the quarter paid 1 January	£ 500
Insurance – year to 31 December, paid 1 January	£1200

We can see that the revenue consists of the sales for cash and the sales on credit. Of the latter we can also see that there is still £1000 which has not been received, i.e. £4000 less the £3000 cash received from debtors. The £1000 should be shown as an outstanding debtor at 31 March. As far as the payments are concerned, the rent is clearly all an expense of the quarter as all the benefit from using the premises for the quarter has expired. The insurance premiums paid are for the whole year so we have to decide what benefit has been used up and what is a future benefit. In this case we have used up three out of the twelve months' benefit so we have an expense of £300 and a prepayment of £900.

If we put the above information on to a worksheet it would appear as follows:

Pitco worksheet version 1

	Assets			= Equity +	Liabilities
				Owner's	Profit
	Cash	Debtors	Prepaids	equity	& loss
Cash sales	6000				6000
Credit sales		4000			4000
Cash from sales	3000	−3000			
Rent	−500				−500
Insurance	−1200		900		−300
Balance	7300	1000	900		9200

You will note that in our worksheet we have shown the credit sales in the profit and loss and recorded at the same time an asset, debtors, of £4000. This asset was subsequently reduced by the cash received of £3000. You may also have noticed that we charged the rent as an expense straightaway and have split the insurance premium paid between the prepaid column and the expenses.

An alternative approach would have been to enter both the rent and the insurance as prepayments when they were paid on 1 January and then to consider at 31 March whether they were still assets. This we would do by answering the question, has the benefit been used up? If we had adopted that approach our worksheet would appear as follows:

Pitco worksheet version 2

	Assets			= Equity +	Liabilities
				Owner's	Profit
	Cash	Debtors	Prepaids	equity	& loss
Cash sales	6000				6000
Credit sales		4000			4000
Cash from sales	3000	−3000			
Rent	−500		500		
Insurance	−1200		1200		
Balance	7300	1000	1700		10000
Rent expense			−500		−500
Insurance expense			−300		−300
Final balance	7300	1000	900		9200

As you can see, the end result is the same. The advantage that this presentation has is that it shows clearly what we have done which always helps in case an error is made. The choice of which presentation to use is a personal one but we would recommend that you use the latter one and that you get into the habit of reviewing all the balances, in terms of whether they are still assets or liabilities, before finally extracting a balance sheet and profit and loss account. The advantages of this approach will become more obvious as we proceed through the next few chapters.

Bad Debts

Before leaving the question of debtors and prepayments let us consider how we would deal with a situation where when we come to the end of the quarter and review the balances we find that some of the amounts owed by customers are not likely to be collectable.

Example 7.1 contd
Of the £1000 Pitco is showing as debtors it is only likely to receive £800 because a customer who owed £200 has left the country and is very unlikely to pay up. In this situation the £200 is not an asset as any future benefit expired when our customer skipped the country.

The first question that arises is, was it a genuine sale? In other words, at the time of making the sale were we reasonably certain that we would receive payment. If the answer is yes, then we have correctly recognized the revenue and the debtor. What needs to be done now is to deal with the situation that has arisen as a result of later events. This is done by reducing the amount shown as debtors by £200 and charging the £200 as an expense of the period. The worksheet would now appear as follows:

Pitco worksheet version 3

	Assets			= Equity +	Liabilities
				Owner's	Profit
	Cash	Debtors	Prepaids	equity	& loss
Cash sales	6000				6000
Credit sales		4000			4000
Cash from sales	3000	−3000			

	Assets			= Equity +	Liabilities
				Owner's	Profit
	Cash	Debtors	Prepaids	equity	& loss
Rent	−500		500		
Insurance	−1200		1200		
Balance	7300	1000	1700		10 000
Rent expense			−500		−500
Insurance expense			−300		−300
Bad Debts		−200			−200
Final balance	7300	800	900		9 000

It should be noted that the bottom line now represents assets which have a future benefit at least equal to the amount shown.

Of course we have to some extent simplified the situation as it is not always known in advance that a debt is going to become uncollectable at some point in the future. If we were able to predict this then if we acted rationally we would not sell goods to that person or company. However, in reality when Polly Peck was put into liquidation it owed a lot of other people money. The way in which accountants deal with the problem of uncertainty in this case is to make an estimate of the amount that may not be collected and make provision for this, which is of course in line with the principle of prudence. The way in which they normally arrive at a figure is based on past experience and/or an analysis of the age of the debts due to the business. The latter is based on the presumption that the longer people take to pay the less likely they are to pay. In many small businesses one of the reports that their banks require if they are experiencing cash flow problems is an aged debtor analysis.

An example of the problems caused by uncertainty over whether a debt is collectable or not is shown in Case 7.1 later. In most commercial organizations the level of detail shown in respect of what is commonly referred to as a 'provision for doubtful debts' is not so great as in the example in the case study.

Before leaving debtors and prepayments we need to look briefly at how these provisions for doubtful debts are accounted for.

Provisions for doubtful debts

Provisions for doubtful debts may be general provisions, e.g. 3 per cent of debtors at the year end, or specific as a result of an aged debtor analysis, or they may be a combination of the two. The exact method varies from business to business. We need not concern ourselves at this stage with the mechanics of how the figure is arrived at. Instead we need to understand what a provision is and how it is dealt with.

A provision is the amount charged to the profit and loss in respect of a diminution in the value of an asset, or for the use of goods or services for which the exact cost is not known at the balance sheet date. We shall deal with the latter situation more fully under our discussion of accruals. At present we shall look at provisions in respect of diminutions in the value of assets. We have said in earlier chapters, for example, that as we use our fixed assets they will gradually wear out. However, in the same way as we don't know who will fail to pay their debts we also don't know exactly how much use and over what period we will get a benefit from our fixed assets. Thus in order to deal with this uncertainty we make a provision each year for the diminution in future benefits by means of depreciation with we shall consider in Chapter 9.

For now we shall concentrate on provisions in respect of doubtful debts and their effect on the balance sheet and profit and loss account.

Example 7.1 contd

Based on past experience Pitco knows that, of the debtors outstanding at any point in time, 2 per cent are likely not to pay. Thus having already taken out the bad debt where we knew payment was extremely unlikely, we now need to make a provision for the anticipated 2 per cent, of the remainder who may not pay. By doing this we will end up with a figure for the balance sheet which will be a more reasonable reflection of the future benefit we expect to gain from our debtors.

The first thing we need to do is to calculate how much the provision needs to be. In this case it is 2 per cent of £800, i.e. £16. Note, that the provision is made after the specific bad debts are dealt with otherwise you would end up providing for more than 100 per cent of the bad debt, in this case 102 per cent of the bad debt. Having established the amount of the provision, we then need to charge the £16 to the profit and loss account and either reduce our asset debtors by this amount or set up a separate account for this provision which will need to be on the opposite side of the balance sheet to the asset. Thus our worksheet would be as follows:

Pitco worksheet version 4

	Assets			=	Equity + Liabilities		
					Owner's	Profit	Provision
	Cash	Debtors	Prepaids		equity	& loss	for debts
Cash sales	6000					6000	
Credit sales		4000				4000	
Cash from sales	3000	−3000					
Rent	−500		500				
Insurance	−1200		1200				
Balance	7300	1000	1700			10 000	
Expenses							
Rent			−500			−500	
Insurance			−300			−300	
Bad debts		−200				−200	
Balance	7300	800	900			9000	
Provision						−16	16
Final balances	7300	800	900			8984	16

In terms of the balance sheet presentation in the final accounts the normal way in which this is presented is that the debtors figure is reduced by the provision and a net figure is shown. In this case the balance sheet would show £784 for debtors, i.e. £800−£16.

The following extract from the 1991 annual report of Midland Bank Plc shows the general provision that is made against doubtful debts and the specific provision. The specific provision relates to debts that have been separately identified as potentially uncollectable and you can see that during the year debts amounting to £640 million were in fact written off as bad debts. In general the level of disclosure in respect of bad debts is not so high outside the banking sector as in many cases the amounts are not material.

CASE 7.1

BAD AND DOUBTFUL DEBTS PROVISIONS

Extract from the notes to Midland Bank Plc annual accounts for 1991

ADVANCES AND OTHER ACCOUNTS	Group		Midland Bank plc	
	1991	1990	**1991**	1990
	£m	£m	**£m**	£m
Loans to customers				
Advances	**34 246**	37 084	**28 936**	31 979
Instalment finance	**1 280**	1 368	**–**	–
	35 526	38 452	**28 936**	31 979
Lease financing	**2 431**	2 482	**–**	–
Total loans and lease financing	**37 957**	40 934	**28 936**	31 979
Less provisions	**3 026**	2 693	**2 762**	2 456
	34 931	38 241	**26 174**	29 523
Placings with banks (over 30 days)	**3 239**	2 044	**2 037**	882
Accrued interest and other customer accounts	**1 416**	1 840	**1 176**	1 497
	39 586	42 125	**29 387**	31 902
Of which				
Sterling	**27 451**	31 727	**22 352**	26 169
Currency	**12 135**	10 398	**7 035**	5 733
	39 586	42 125	**29 387**	31 902

Advances are stated after deduction of amounts refinanced with the Export Credits Guarantee Department and the Department of Trade and Industry.

Included in instalment finance above are amounts in respect of hire purchase contracts amounting to £653 m (1990 £745 m).

The cost of assets acquired in 1991 for the purpose of letting under lease financing and hire purchase contracts amounted to £682 m (1990 £745 m) and £451 m (1990 £549 m), respectively.

Continued over page

Continued from previous page

Movements on provisions for bad and doubtful debts were as follows

	1991 £m Specific	1991 £m General	1991 £m Total	1990 £m Specific	1990 £m General	1990 £m Total
Group						
Provisions at 1 January	2497	196	2693	2598	224	2822
Currency translation and other adjustments	60	–	60	(360)	(11)	(371)
Charge for the year	863	40	903	720	(17)	703
Amounts written off	(640)	–	(640)	(476)	–	(476)
Less recoveries of amounts written off in previous years	10	–	10	15	–	15
	(630)	–	(630)	(461)	–	(461)
Provisions at 31 December	2790	236	3026	2497	196	2693
Midland Bank plc						
Provisions at 1 January	2314	142	2456	2405	165	2570
Currency translation and other adjustments	64	–	64	(338)	(17)	(355)
Charge for the year	756	34	790	656	(6)	650
Amounts written off	(556)	–	(556)	(423)	–	(423)
Less recoveries of amounts written off in previous years	8	–	8	14	–	14
	(548)	–	(548)	(409)	–	(409)
Provisions at 31 December	2586	176	2762	2314	142	2456

The Group makes specific provisions against loans to and interest due from borrowers in developing countries. The level of such provisions is reviewed against exposure on a country by country basis and adjusted when the economic, political or regional circumstances of a country change, assessed by a scoring system consistent with Bank of England guidelines. In addition, interest is normally reserved when it is more than 90 days overdue.

Having looked at how debtors, prepayments and bad and doubtful debts are dealt with we can now consider how to deal with the situation where we receive goods or services before paying for them.

Creditors and Accruals

When an established business buys goods it rarely pays cash. In fact it is normally only when a business is just starting, or in exceptional cases, that trade credit is not used. The question we have to address is, how a business would deal with goods supplied on credit when it may have used them or sold them before it has to pay the supplier. However, before we deal with that question we need to explain the difference between creditors and accruals.

Creditors arise as a result of goods or services being supplied to an

KEY CONCEPT 7.3

CREDITORS AND ACCRUALS

enterprise for which an invoice is subsequently received and for which no payment has been made at the date of receipt of the goods or services. As we have already said, most established businesses will receive most of their raw materials and components on the basis of payment being due within a certain time period after delivery. At the date at which we draw up a balance sheet therefore we need to acknowledge that there are amount owing 'liabilities' in respect of these supplies. These are normally referred to as creditors in the UK or as amounts payable in the USA.

Accruals are in some ways similar to creditors in that they relate to amounts due for goods or services already supplied to the enterprise. They differ because at the time of drawing up the balance sheet, the amounts involved are not known with certainty. This is usually due to the fact that the invoice for the goods has not been received. A common example of a situation where this arises is telephone bills which are always issued in arrears. Other examples are electricity and gas bills. These are also generally received after the end of the quarter to which they relate. In these situations therefore all we can do is to estimate what we think is owed for the service the business has used during the period. This estimate may be based on the last quarter or the previous year or on some other basis which the business considers more appropriate.

An example may help to clarify the treatment of creditors and accruals and the differences between the two.

Example 7.2

For the year to 31 December 1991 Archie & Co. had the following transactions:

Item 1   Paid £6000 of Archie's own money into a business bank account together with £5000 borrowed from a friend.
Item 2   Bought 1000 items from a supplier for £9 per unit.
Item 3   Paid the electricity bills for lighting and heating for three quarters amounting to £1500.
Item 4   Paid supplier £7000 for items purchased.

If we enter the above transactions on a worksheet and explain how they are dealt with, we can then deal with the other transactions of Archie's business. Our worksheet for the first transactions will look like this:

Archie's worksheet version 1

	Assets		=	Equity		+	Liabilities	
				Owner's	*Profit*			
	Bank	*Stock*		*equity*	*& loss*		*Loan*	*Creditors*
Item 1	6000			6000				
	5000						5000	
Item 2		9000						9000
Item 3	−1500				−1500			
Item 4	−7000							−7000
Balance	2500	9000		6000	−1500		5000	2000

Let us examine each of the transactions in turn.

☐ **Item 1**. By now we are familiar with transactions of this type which create an asset and a corresponding liability either in the form of money owing to the owner or to some other party.

☐ **Item 2**. This is slightly different from the previous examples which have dealt with the purchase of stock. Up to now we have assumed that the stock was paid for when we received it. In this case, however, we are only told that during the year we bought items for £9000. We have no idea, at present, how much we have actually paid out in respect of these items or how much is still owing. Therefore we show that we are owing money for all the items, opening up a column for our creditors and showing £9000 in that column.

☐ **Item 3**. Once again, this is a familiar item as we receive a bill which is paid for in cash. However, it should be borne in mind that we have in fact only paid for three quarters whereas we have consumed a year's supply of electricity. We therefore need to make some provision for the other quarter. One estimate could be that the fourth quarter's bill would be the same as the other quarters, i.e. approximately £500. It may of course turn out to be more or less. We are not, however, attempting 100 per cent accuracy – we simply need to give a reasonable picture of the situation.

☐ **Item 4**. We now know that, of the £9000 we owe to suppliers, £7000 was paid in the year. We therefore need to reduce our cash by that amount and reduce the creditors by the same amount.

Let us now return to the question of the electricity bill. We said that we need to make an accrual which we estimated to be £500. Let us see how this affects our worksheet using the balances from the worksheet above:

Archie's worksheet version 2

	Assets		=	Equity		+	Liabilities		
				Owner's	*Profit*				
	Bank	*Stock*		*equity*	*& loss*		*Loan*	*Creditors*	*Accruals*
Item 1	6000			6000					
	5000						5000		
Item 2		9000						9000	
Item 3	−1500				−1500				
Item 4	−7000							−7000	
Balance	2500	9000		6000	−1500		5000	2000	
Accrual					−500				500
Balance	2500	9000		6000	−2000		5000	2000	500

As we can see the balance sheet still balances and it now gives a truer picture of the goods we own and the amounts we owe.

Before leaving the subject of debtors and creditors here are some more transactions for Archie & Co. which you should try to work through yourself and then compare your answer with the answer shown below.

Example 7.2 contd
Archie & Co's other transactions in the year to 31 December 1991 were as follows:

Item 5   Paid loan interest of £300 in respect of the half year to 30 June 1991.
Item 6   Sold 1000 items at £20 per item all on credit.
Item 7   Received £14 000 from customers in respect of sales.
Item 8   Paid rent £1500 for five quarters as rent of the premises is due quarterly in advance.

Note our answer shown below combines the debtors and prepayments in one column and the creditors and accruals in one column. You may prefer to keep them in separate columns which is perfectly acceptable and arguably clearer.

Archie's worksheet version 3

| | Assets | | | = Equity | + | | Liabilities |
	Bank	Stock	Debtors & prepaids	Owner's equity	Profit & loss	Loan	Creditors & accruals
Balance	2 500	9000		6000	−2 000	5000	2500
Item 5	−300				−300		
Item 6			20 000		20 000		
Item 7	14 000		−14 000				
Item 8	−1 500		1 500				
Balance	14 700	9000	7 500	6000	17 700	5000	2500

If we now review the position at the year end as shown on our worksheet we find that the asset 'prepaids' is no longer going to give us a future benefit of £1500 as four quarters' rent relates to the year just gone and therefore the benefit has been used. We also find that the interest paid is only for the first half of the year yet we have had the benefit of the loan for the full year and we therefore need to make a provision or accrual for a further £300. We should also realize that our stock figure represents 1000 items at £9 each and that all of those items were sold so our cost of sales should be £9000. Our worksheet will now be as follows:

Archie's worksheet version 4

| | Assets | | | = Equity | + | | Liabilities |
	Bank	Stock	Debtors & prepaids	Owner's equity	Profit & loss	Loan	Creditors & accruals
Balance	14 700	9000	7500	6000	17 700	5000	2500
Rent			−1200		−1 200		
Interest					−300		300
Cost of sales		−9000			−9 000		
Balance	14 700	0	6300	6000	7 200	5000	2800

We can now extract the balance sheet and the profit and loss account for the first year of Archie's business. These are shown below:

**Profit and loss account of Archie & Co.
for the year ended 31 December 1991**

	£	£
Sales		20 000
Cost of goods sold		9 000
Gross profit		11 000
Electricity	2000	
Loan interest	600	
Rent	1200	3 800
Net profit for the year		7 200

Balance sheet of Archie & Co. at 31 December 1991

	£	£
Current assets		
Debtors	6 000	
Prepayments	300	
Cash at bank	14 700	
		21 000
Current liabilities		
Creditors	2 000	
Accruals	800	
		2 800
Net current assets		18 200
		£
Financed by		
Owner's equity		6 000
Profit for year		7 200
		13 200
Loan		5 000
		18 200

You will note that on the balance sheet debtors and prepayments are shown under current assets, and creditors and accruals under current liabilities. Although we have shown the figures for debtors and prepayments separately you would normally only see a single figure in company accounts and the detail would be found in the notes to the accounts. The same situation would apply to creditors and accruals.

Having now established how to deal with debtors, creditors, accruals and prepayments and how they are disclosed on the balance sheet, let us examine what happens in the second year of Archie's business.

Example 7.2 contd
For the year to 31 December 1992 Archie & Co.'s transactions were as follows.

Item 1   Bought 1000 items on credit at £9 per item.
Item 2   Paid suppliers £10 000.
Item 3   Paid electricity of £2300, £500 for last year and £1800 for the first three quarters of 1992.
Item 4   Paid loan interest of £600.
Item 5   Sold on credit terms 1000 items at £22 per item.
Item 6   Received £18 000 from customers.
Item 7   Paid rent of £1200.

It is worth briefly discussing some of these items before we enter them on a worksheet.

Let us consider the payments to suppliers and the payment for electricity. In the former case we do not know exactly which parts of the payments relate to this year or to last year. However, for our purposes it does not really matter as we are looking at amounts owing at the balance sheet date, not at the amounts due to the individual suppliers or how long those amounts have been due for. That information would in fact be kept for each supplier in a subsidiary book of accounts known as the bought ledger. In the case of the electricity we know £500 relates to last year and £1800 to the first three quarters of this year. As with last year we have to make an estimate of the amount due in respect of the last quarter. Based on the same quarter the previous year we would estimate £500 but this is clearly too low as, based on the first three quarters of this year, electricity is now costing £600 a quarter, therefore a reasonable estimate would be £600.

In the case of the loan interest, £300 relates to the previous year and £300 to this year. Therefore, we need to make an adjustment in respect of the £300 we still owe for the current year.

The situation with debtors is the same as for creditors – we cannot identify the individual payments, but for our purposes it does not make any difference.

Finally, as regards the rent, the annual rent is £1200, payable in advance. As the first quarter was paid for last year, this payment relates to three quarters for the current year and one quarter for next year.

After entering these transactions the worksheet should look something like the one below. It is possible to take some short-cuts and get the same answer but you should bear in mind that such short-cuts can lead to errors.

Archie's worksheet 1992 version 1

	Assets			=	Equity	+	Liabilities	
			Debtors		*Owner's*	*Profit*		*Creditors*
	Bank	*Stock*	*& prepaids*		*equity*	*& loss*	*Loan*	*& accruals*
Balance	14 700		6 300		6000	7 200	5000	2 800
Item 1		9000						9 000
Item 2	−10 000							−10 000
Item 3	−2 300					−1 800		−500
Item 4	−600					−300		−300
Item 5			22 000			22 000		
Item 6	18 000		−18 000					

| | Assets | | | = Equity | + | Liabilities | |
	Bank	Stock	Debtors & prepaids	Owner's equity	Profit & loss	Loan	Creditors & accruals
Item 7	−1 200		300		−900		
Balance	18 600	9000	10 600	6000	26 200	5000	1 000
Cost of sales		−9000			−9 000		
Rent			−300		−300		
Electric					−600		600
Interest					−300		300
Balance	18 600	0	10 300	6000	16 000	5000	1 900

There are certain items in the worksheet that warrant some further explanation. These are dealt with below.

☐ **Item 3**. Here there has been a payment of £2300 in respect of electricity. We know that of this £1800 relates to this year so that amount is charged to the profit and loss account. The other £500 relates to last year and we find that we made an accrual of exactly that amount which is contained in the balance of £2800 brought forward in respect of creditors and accruals. Thus in this case all we have to do is reduce the accruals column by £500.

☐ **Item 4**. This is the same as item 3 above except in this case the accrual was in respect of loan interest.

☐ **Item 7**. Here the situation is that we have paid rent of £1200 of which only £900 relates to this year and £300 is a prepayment of next year's rent. So we charge the profit and loss with £900 and set up a prepayment for 1993.

At this stage we can balance our worksheet and then review the balances. If we do this we find that all the stock has been sold, and that we still have an amount of £300 for the rent for the first quarter of 1992 included as a prepayment. In both these cases the benefit has been used up in the period so we charge the respective amounts of £9000 and £300 to the profit and loss account. Reviewing our expenses we see that we only have three quarters' electricity and half a year's interest and so we make accruals for the rest and charge the amounts of £600 and £300 respectively to the profit and loss account.

The balance sheet at the end of 1992 and the profit and loss account for that year can now be extracted. These are shown below:

Balance sheet of Archie & Co. at 31 December 1992

| | 1992 | | 1991 |
	£	£	£
Current assets			
Debtors	10 000		6 000
Prepayments	300		300
Cash at bank	18 600		14 700
		28 900	21 000

Current liabilities

Creditors	1 000		2 000
Accruals	900		800
		1 900	2 800
Net current assets		27 000	18 200

Financed by		£	£
Owner's equity		6 000	6 000
Profit for year		8 800	7 200
Profit from 1991		7 200	
		22 000	13 200
Loan		5 000	5 000
		27 000	18 200

Profit and loss account of Archie & Co.
for the year ended 31 December 1992

	1992		1991
	£	£	£
Sales		22 000	20 000
Cost of goods sold		9 000	9 000
Gross profit		13 000	11 000
Electricity	2400		2 000
Loan interest	600		600
Rent	1200	4 200	1 200
Net profit for the year		8 800	7 200

As you can see both the balance sheet and profit and loss account have the comparative figures for the previous year. This is required for companies but is good practice in any case as it enables some comparisons to be made. For example, we can see from the profit and loss accounts that the sales and gross profit are increasing and that the cost of electricity has gone up. From the balance sheet we can see that the cash and debtors have also increased. By looking at both statements together we can see that in the case of the debtors they have increased more than would have been expected from the increase in sales, i.e. sales have increased by 10 per cent and debtors by over 60 per cent.

Returning to creditors and accruals, you will have noted that in our examples the estimates made for accruals turned out rather conveniently to be exactly right. In reality this is unlikely to happen every time and we then end up with a situation where, for example, we had accrued £500 for electricity and the bill when it arrives is for £520. The question is what to do in this situation as clearly the expense relates to last year and should not be matched with the revenue of this year.

Prior year adjustments, extraordinary and exceptional items

At first sight the obvious thing to do is to adjust the previous year's accounts by the amount, £20 in this case. Unfortunately the accounting standard on extraordinary items and prior year adjustments (SSAP 6) precludes this as it defines a prior year adjustment as either a fundamental error or a change in accounting policy, and says that prior year adjustments do not normally include recurring corrections of adjustments to accounting estimates made in prior years.

Can we then show this as either an extraordinary or exceptional item? The simple answer to the first is no. An extraordinary item has to be material, outside the normal activities and not expected to recur frequently or regularly. Our example in fact is likely to recur frequently and arises from the ordinary activities of the business. Can we therefore classify it as an exceptional item? Once again the answer is no as these are material items which, although they arise out of the normal activities, are such that they need to be disclosed separately in order for the accounts to show a 'true and fair view'. There are two points at issue here, first whether the amount is material, and secondly whether by including it in the normal expenses the accounts would no longer show a true and fair view. In this case the fact that the amount involved is only £20 on an annual electricity bill of over £2000 in a business that is making a profit of in excess of £7000 a year means that it would not be considered material. Materiality has to be judged against the total background of the business. For instance, what is material for a small business may be of little or no consequence in a multinational. A simple way to think about it is in respect to exam marks. If the pass mark is 40 per cent and you have scored 75 per cent, one mark either way is not really material to the decision to pass or fail you. If, however, you had only achieved 39 per cent that one mark becomes very material to the decision.

Other liabilities

Before leaving the subject of creditors, accruals and other forms of liability it is worth briefly mentioning some of the other types of liability that need to be dealt with. Perhaps the most common one is the bank overdraft which we have already discussed. This is a current liability as the bank has the right to call in the money when it wishes and in this way an overdraft differs from a loan or debenture which are for fixed periods and are generally, at least in theory, longer term. We will discuss long-term liabilities in more detail in Chapter 12. As far as current liabilities are concerned the other common ones in company accounts are taxation and dividends. These are specific to company accounts as sole traders and partnerships as business entities are not liable to tax. Instead the owners or the partners are themselves liable to pay tax on the profits. As far as dividends are concerned these are in fact the payments to the owners of

KEY CONCEPT 7.4	An item is material when it would affect the evaluation of a business or where it would affect decisions.
MATERIALITY	

some part of profit and once again in the case of sole traders and partnerships these amounts would be dealt with as drawings. A type of liability that is common to all businesses is a contingent liability which is neither current or long term. This is discussed briefly below.

Contingent liabilities

Contingent liabilities are often similar to accruals in that in many cases the amount is not certain and estimates may have to be made. For example, if your business is being sued for negligence at the end of the year, you can only estimate the amount of the potential liability, as the actual amount will only be decided by the court if you are proved to have been negligent. Contingent liabilities do, however, differ on one fundamental point which is that they will only become liabilities if a future event happens. Accruals and other liabilities that we have discussed to date in this book actually exist at the balance sheet date. Because of this fundamental difference contingent liabilities are not included in the balance sheet but are required to be disclosed in the notes to the annual accounts in order that the accounts comply with SSAP 18.

An example of the disclosure of contingent liabilities is given below. The first extract from the 1990–91 accounts of British Airways covers two types of contingent liability. Here, British Airways has guaranteed the borrowing of other companies. In this case the liability is contingent upon the other companies failing to meet their obligations. If this did happen, the lender would then have recourse to British Airways to pay the outstanding amounts.

CASE 7.2

CONTINGENT LIABILITIES

Extract from the notes to the accounts

CONTINGENCIES
Contingent liabilities exist for which no provision has been made in the accounts covering obligations of the Company and guarantees given by or on behalf of subsidiary and associated undertakings. For the Group they amount to £107 million (1990: £77 million) and for the Company £614 million (1990: £593 million). The figure for the Company includes £527 million (1990: £519 million) in respect of Convertible Capital Bonds and borrowings by subsidiary and associated undertakings.

There are a number of identified legal and other claims which emanate from international airline operations. Where the Board considers that a material liability may arise from such claims relevant sums have been provided. In addition, experience with litigation and regulation in the USA and elsewhere has led the Board to conclude that it is prudent to carry forward the provision of £25 million made in prior years (see Note 17).

British Airways Plc Annual Report & Accounts 1990–91.   Continued over page

Continued from previous page

In the second example, which is taken from the 1990 Annual Report and Accounts of BAT Industries, the contingent liability is in respect of court cases. These are either cases still to be heard or pending appeal, and the liability is contingent on the outcome of those cases. You will see that the directors include in the note their opinion of the likely outcomes and, where appropriate, the amounts involved. In addition, like British Airways, BAT Industries has guarantees as contingent liabilities.

Extract from the notes to the accounts

Contingent liabilities and financial commitments

There are contingent liabilities in respect of litigation, overseas taxes, guarantees and social benefits in various countries.

B.A.T Industries' subsidiary, Brown & Williamson Tobacco Corporation (B&W), and other leading US cigarette manufacturers are defendants in a number of the actions which have been brought in different states in the USA asserting that tobacco companies should be held legally responsible to individual plaintiffs for damage to their health allegedly resulting from cigarette smoking. At December 1989, the number of cases pending at the Trial Court level involving B&W was 12; this number is now 6. All such actions will be vigorously defended. While it is not possible to predict the outcome of the litigation, the Company does not believe these actions will have a materially adverse effect upon the financial condition of the Company or the Group.

Brown & Williamson Tobacco Corporation (B&W) is the defendant in an action in the USA by the Liggett Group Inc. The jury rejected four trade mark and unfair competition claims but proposed the award to Liggett of US$49.6 million in damages (which would be automatically trebled under the relevant US federal law) for violation of the Robinson Patman Act. The jury's decision on the anti-trust claims was set aside by the Trial Court which entered judgement for B&W on all claims. Liggett has filed a notice to appeal this decision to the US Court of Appeals for The Fourth Circuit. The Directors do not consider it appropriate to make any provision.

Farmers has received management fee revenues from its affiliated insurance exchanges some of which would be refunded if its rates were found 'excessive' during the period from November 1988. Under the Cal-Farm vs. Deukmejian California Supreme Court ruling, which was rendered subsequent to passage of Proposition 103, insurance companies are entitled to a 'fair and reasonable' rate of return. Farmers believes that the rates of return of insurance exchanges it manages are well within that constitutional standard, and thus there will be no material revenue reduction to the exchanges or to Farmers.

B.A.T Industries has guaranteed borrowings by subsidiaries of **£545 million** 1989 £1988 million and given guarantees to third parties of **£168 million** 1989 £92 million.

Summary

In this chapter we have dealt with the question of how accruals accounting deals with the fact that in many cases the timing of cash flows is such that if accounts were prepared on the basis of cash flows the matching principle would be contravened. We have shown how sales on credit are included as revenue and how the amounts not received at the end of the year are dealt with as debtors and shown as current assets as they will provide the business with a future benefit. We have also examined the way in which payments in advance can be dealt with in order that expenses are matched against revenue. In addition we have shown how accrual accounting allows bad debts, where the future benefit has expired, and doubtful debts, where the amount of the future benefit is uncertain, to be dealt with. From the point of view of goods supplied to the business we have seen how creditors are dealt with and how accruals arise. The principle that is common to all these items is that the accounts should comply with the matching principle and the balance sheet should record the rights to future benefits and what the business owes at a particular point in time. Finally we have introduced the idea of materiality as defined under SSAP 2, looked at the classification of items as prior year adjustments and extraordinary or exceptional items under the rules of SSAP 6, and considered the idea of contingent liabilities in terms of disclosure as required by SSAP 18.

References

Statement of Standard Accounting Practice 2 (1971) *Disclosure of Accounting Policies*, Accounting Standards Committee.

Statement of Standard Accounting Practice 6 (1986) *Extraordinary Items and Prior Year Adjustments*, Accounting Standards Committee.

Statement of Standard Accounting Practice 18 (1980) *Accounting for Contingencies*, Accounting Standards Committee.

Further reading

Further detail on the content of the accounting standards mentioned in this chapter can be found in *Accounting Standards*, 3rd edn, by John Blake (Pitman, 1991).

Detailed explanations of the mechanics of dealing with provisions for doubtful debts and bad debts can be found in *Accounting and Finance: A Firm Foundation*, 3rd edn, by Alan Pizzey, (Cassell, 1990).

Review questions

1. In your own words describe what a creditor is and when it arises.

2. Explain the difference between creditors and accruals.

3. Why are debtors and prepayments classified as current assets?

4. When do prepayments arise and how do they differ from accruals?

5. Explain the matching principle.

6. Why is it necessary to identify debtors and creditors?

7. How do debtors affect the profit and loss account?

8. Explain the difference between a contingent liability and other liabilities.

9. Explain the concept of materiality.

10. What is a prior year adjustment, an extraordinary item and an exceptional item, and how do they differ?

Problems for discussion and analysis

1. In each of the following situations describe the way the transaction would be dealt with in the accounts of the business and identify, where appropriate, the effect on the balance sheet and profit and loss account.

   (a) Purchase of stock of raw materials on credit terms.
   (b) Purchase of production machines for cash.
   (c) Receipts from customers in respect of credit sales.
   (d) Repayment of a loan.
   (e) Payment in respect of research expenditure.
   (f) Sale of goods on credit.
   (g) Payment to supplier in respect of goods already delivered.
   (h) Payment of wages to clerical workers.
   (i) Payment of wages to production workers.
   (j) Payment of loan interest.
   (k) Payment of an electricity bill from last year.
   (l) Payment of rent quarterly in advance.
   (m) Withdrawal of cash from the business by the owner.
   (n) Receipt of cash from the owner.
   (o) Withdrawal of stock for personal use by the owner.
   (p) A customer going into liquidation owing money.
   (q) A guarantee of another business's bank overdraft.

2. A business which has been trading for a number of years and whose terms are to sell goods on 30 days credit has the following balances on its sales ledger at the year end. It has annual credit sales of £140 000 and last year made a profit of £40 000.

Name	Amount £	<1 month £	2 months £	3 months £	7 months £
Barker	900	900			
Bertles	70	70			
Brains	860	860			
Cresto	680	680			
Dabbler	460		460		
Easicome	530	270	260		
Estcorp	570	90	420	60	
Failsafe	820	820			
Frinders	540	540			
Goforit	660	660			
Gorrit	60			60	
Helpless	990	50	260	680	

Name	Amount £	<1 month £	2 months £	3 months £	7 months £
Jarvis	12 000				12 000
Manson	420	420			
Nickels	540	540			
Portilas	430	430			
Restles	200		200		
Strapped	700			700	
Tolittle	270	270			
Viners	300	300			
	22 000	6900	1600	1500	12 000

The managing director has informed you that, as far as he knows, all the debts are collectable. However, your auditors have informed you that Jarvis is in voluntary liquidation and the chances of any payment are extremely dubious. Given this information you ask your assistant to look up past records and you find that in general debts that go to two months old have a 5 per cent chance of not being paid while those that go to three months have a 10 per cent chance of not being paid.

(a) Based on the information you have, suggest what should be done in terms of bad debts and doubtful debts.
(b) What additional information might you require in order to improve on the estimates upon which your answer to (a) was based?

3. On 1 May 1992 Barbara paid £3000 into a business bank account as capital for her new business which she called Barbie's Bikes. The transactions during May were as follows:

May 3 Bought van for £800 cash.
6 Bought goods on credit from Drake for £700.
8 Paid rent for the quarter of £480.
14 Bought goods on credit from Gander for £300.
16 Made cash sales of £200.
18 Made credit sales of £400 to Bill's Bikes.
21 Paid the garage account for petrol and oil of £20.
23 Sold more goods on credit for £600 to Swans.
24 Paid Drake £682 after taking advantage of a 2.5 per cent discount for prompt payment.
30 Received £360 from the liquidator of Bill's Bikes and was advised that no more would be forthcoming. Received back from Swans goods with an invoice price of £80 which they had not ordered.
31 Paid monthly salary to shop assistant of £400. Sold the remaining goods for £380 and received the payment in cash.

(a) Discuss how each transaction should be treated.
(b) Discuss what, if any, accruals and prepayments are or should be involved.
(c) Draw up a worksheet, balance sheet and profit and loss account.
(d) Comment on the results for the month.

8 Stocks and work in progress

In all the examples we have looked at so far we have made some simplifying assumptions in relation to the goods purchased which we referred to as the stock of the business. The first assumption was that no stocks were held at the end of the period. The use of this assumption meant that we had no problem in identifying what had been sold or what it cost. It also meant that the question of whether the goods held in stock at the end of the period were still worth what we had paid for them did not arise. We also only dealt with single-product businesses which had fairly straightforward processes for converting the goods purchased into saleable commodities. Finally, our examples only dealt with start-ups, i.e. businesses in their first year. This meant that the question of how to deal with the stock held at the beginning of the year did not need to be considered.

Clearly the real world is more complex than this. Businesses are also generally more complex. They may have multiple processes or multiple stock lines or both. In this chapter, we will be relaxing all these assumptions and discussing the effects on the balance sheet and profit and loss account. We will also be considering

- ☐ the nature of stocks in different types of business;
- ☐ the problems of accounting for stocks in more complex businesses and in particular those associated with work in progress and finished goods;
- ☐ the determination of the cost of stock sold during a period;
- ☐ the accounting entries needed to record stock on the worksheet;
- ☐ the issue of valuation and how a change in the basis of valuation will affect the balance sheet and profit and loss account.

Stocks and work in progress

The points made above give some indication of the importance of stock. In reality, it is very important because there is often a high level of resources invested in the stock held by a business. This has, in many businesses, led to a reappraisal of the way in which they operate and the adoption of techniques such as just-in-time management which can lead to savings in the costs associated with holding high levels of stocks. Often the reason that businesses held high levels of stocks was that these were felt to be necessary in order to meet customer demand and to ensure that the production process was not held up. The costs involved in holding these high levels of stocks were twofold. First there was the obvious one that in order to hold stock you need space and space costs money. There was also the opportunity cost associated with using money to maintain the stock levels rather than for another purpose.

The adoption of just-in-time techniques led to a reappraisal of the production process and demand cycle in order that the level of stocks was reduced to a minimum. A side-effect of this was that many of the large manufacturing firms who have adopted this technique have had to take a closer look at their suppliers to ensure that they have the capability to provide supplies regularly and on time. It has in some cases led to a situation where stocks previously held by the manufacturer are now being held by the component supplier, so shifting the cost of holding stock down to smaller businesses.

So far we have discussed stock and work in progress without really defining these terms. Rather than attempting to find one generic definition it is probably easier to look at what comprises stock and work in progress as this will lead to a better understanding of the terms. Stock can be said to comprise the following.

☐ **Goods purchased for resale**. For example, packets of cereal are purchased by a supermarket to be sold to their customers; cars are purchased by motor dealers to resell to their customers.
☐ **Raw materials**. These are purchased for incorporation into the product or products being manufactured or assembled for sale, e.g. wood purchased by a furniture manufacturer, or steel purchased by a car manufacturer.
☐ **Consumable goods**. These are goods which are not bought for resale but for use within the business. These could consist of supplies of oil for heating or machine maintenance, supplies of stationery or cleaning materials.

You may have noticed from the examples used that the stocks are related to the type of business. For example, cars owned by a furniture manufacturer will not be classified as stock because they are held for use in the business and not for resale. You may also have noticed that the last category mentioned is different from the others as this is also not held for resale. It is in fact actually another form of current asset which is called stock only because it is a stock of items which are held by the business and we have no more suitable term.

Stock comprises goods purchased for resale, goods purchased for conversion into goods for resale, or consumable stores. The distinguishing feature of stock is the intention to resell the item in some form or to use it in a short period of time.

    Having looked at some ideas to give an indication of what comprises stock let us now look at work in progress and finished goods. These are in fact both merely different types of stock – the difference lies in the fact that they have normally gone through some production or assembly process.

KEY CONCEPT 8.1

STOCK

KEY CONCEPT 8.2	Work in progress is the term applied to products and services that are at an intermediate stage of completion; for example, if you envisage an
WORK IN PROGRESS	assembly line for microcomputers, at any point in time there will be some partially assembled machines somewhere on that assembly line. An even more obvious example which we can observe merely by walking around any town centre is partially completed buildings which are work in progress for some building contractor. A less obvious but equally valid example is an architect with some half-finished plans.
FINISHED GOODS	Finished goods are goods that have been through the complete production or assembly cycle and are ready for resale to the customer. Examples are cars for Ford, computers for Apple or IBM, or video recorders for Amstrad.

In general all these forms of stock and work in progress fall within the definition of current assets which we adopted in Chapter 4. That definition was 'a current asset is one which is either part of the operating cycle of the enterprise or is likely to be used up or realized in the form of cash within one year'. You will notice if you consider the examples given that in some cases the goods will be realized within the year as in the case of the cereals for the supermarket, and in some cases the reason something is classified as stock is because it is part of the operating cycle of the business as in the case of the building contractor. You will also probably have noticed that the nature of the business is a major determinant of what is classified as stock or work in progress. We will now explore this aspect of stock and the question of stock valuation in more detail.

The nature of the business and stock valuation

It is fairly obvious that the nature of the business has an impact on the type of stock held. We would all expect the type of stock held by a greengrocer to be different from that of a company like British Petroleum. What may be less obvious is the way in which the nature of the business affects the question of stock valuation. To illustrate this let us first of all look at a retailer and a manufacturer and then compare the latter with a provider of services such as a firm of solicitors.

In the case of a retailing business the stocks held are those goods purchased for resale. Because of the nature of the business there is generally little if any change between the goods bought by the business and the goods it sells. Its operating cycle could be seen as:

$$\text{Purchases} \rightarrow \text{Stock} \rightarrow \text{Sales}$$
$$\text{(input)} \qquad\qquad \text{(output)}$$

If we can establish what the goods cost we can arrive fairly easily at a valuation of stock, because the operating cycle is very simple.

If we now examine the situation of a manufacturing company we find

Raw materials
Car components

Work in progress
Half-assembled car

Finished goods
Completed car

Figure 8.1 Stocks and work in progress.

that in order to manufacture goods we need an input of raw materials, of labour and of other items such as the nuts and bolts needed to assemble a car or paint to protect and colour it. These inputs can and often do occur at multiple points in the production process. However, for our purposes a simplified version of the manufacturing process, such as that given below, will suffice to illustrate the points being made:

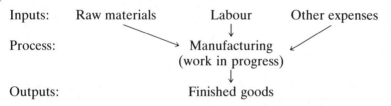

Inputs: Raw materials   Labour   Other expenses

Process: → Manufacturing ←
                                     (work in progress)

Outputs: Finished goods

A business with a process similar to that described is likely to have, at any point in time, a stock of raw materials, a stock of goods in the process of completion, its work in progress, and a stock of finished goods. This can be illustrated by a simple diagram such as Figure 8.1.

In the case of the raw materials the question of stock valuation is similar to that faced by a retailer. For the other categories, however, the question of valuation is often more complex. Do we include the cost of labour in the value of partially completed goods and, if so, which labour? One possible answer would be to include labour involved in the production process and exclude other labour. This is easy in theory but in practice it is not that clear cut. For example, are the foreman and production manager involved in the production process and, if so, what part of their labour cost is attributable to a particular product? The whole question of what should and should not be included is vital as it has a direct effect on profit. In some industries where pricing is on a 'cost plus' basis it could be the difference between survival and bankruptcy. If, for example, we quoted a selling price that did not cover all our costs we could end up entering into a contract which could lead to the downfall of the business. Indeed some commentators have suggested that the Rolls Royce collapse in 1972 was caused by being tied into an unprofitable contract.

The discussion so far has emphasized the manufacturing sector. What of the service sector? In this sector the question of stock valuation can be very straightforward as in the case of a newspaper vendor or a travel agent. On the other hand it can be more complex as in the case of solicitors, architects and accountants. If we consider the case of a firm of solicitors, the inputs will not be raw materials but will be in the form of labour and expenses such as travelling expenses to see the client, attend court, etc. Thus in some ways the problem is simplified. However, it is quite likely that some proportion of the work handled by solicitors will take a considerable amount of time between inception and completion, especially if a case goes to appeal etc. Thus for this particular service activity there will be a problem of valuing the work in progress every time the annual accounts are prepared. The same will be the case for a firm of accountants, architects or even management consultants. Thus in many ways these particular examples from the service sector face similar problems to manufacturing firms in terms of the valuation of their work in progress.

The determination of the cost of stocks sold

In previous chapters we have assumed that all goods bought in the period were sold in the period and that we could clearly identify the actual goods we sold during the period. In practice, except in fairly simple businesses, it is doubtful whether it would be possible to identify the goods actually sold and, even if it were possible, we would need to consider the question of whether to do so was cost effective. Because of the difficulties involved in recording every item sold and the question of the cost effectiveness of such an exercise some smaller businesses have little if any formal stock records. Instead they rely on keeping accurate records of purchases and the annual stock count to establish the cost of goods sold during a period. This annual stock count is carried out at the balance sheet date, so the stock figure in the balance sheet represents a snapshot of the stock level at that particular point in time. You will notice that in essence what is happening here is what we described in Chapter 3, i.e. the wealth in the form of stock is measured at two points in time to establish the change over the period. Whilst, at first sight, this may seem to be an odd way to run a business, it is in fact quite sensible if you consider the impossible job a sweet-shop would have in trying to keep track of every Mars bar, Kit-Kat, or Milky Way bought and sold. In fact if you talk to owners of small businesses you may be quite surprised at how accurately they can value their stock simply by looking at what they have in the shop and on the shelves of their storerooms.

What we have just said should not be taken to imply that all retailers have poor stock records. In fact some of the major retail chains have very sophisticated stock record systems that operate at the point of sale, such that every time the cashier enters the sale of a tin of baked beans the stock records for that store are automatically updated via a computer link from the tills to the stock recording system. Similar systems are operated by a number of well-known fast-food franchises. However, whilst such an investment may be necessary and cost effective for large multiples it is at present outside the grasp of smaller retailers and in fact is probably more sophisticated than they need.

Clearly, for a business that has accurate and detailed stock records arriving at the value of stock and the cost of goods sold is reasonably simple. Therefore let us look at the situation where detailed stock movement records are not kept and see how we can arrive at the cost of the goods sold and the cost of those still in stock at the end of the year. In these cases we need to count the stock at the start of the year and at the end of the year. From these two figures and the figure for goods purchased during the year we can derive the cost of the goods sold during the year. In other words if we add the purchases to the stock of goods we had at the start of the year that will tell us the total of the goods we have held during the year. If we then subtract what we have left at the end of the year the resultant figure must be the cost of the goods we have sold during the year, assuming of course that we have allowed for any taken by the owner for personal use etc. This relationship, which is perhaps difficult to describe, can be more easily understood if it is shown in the form of an equation:

Opening stock + Purchases − Closing stock = Cost of goods sold

The information to solve the equation can be derived as follows:

Opening stock: from the balance sheet at the start of the year;
Purchases: from the suppliers' invoices;
Closing stock: from a physical stock-count at the end of the year.

The importance of determining stock is examined in Key Concept 8.3.

Let us look at a simple example to illustrate the process referred to in the equation above and see how it is entered on the worksheet.

Example 8.1
The summarized transactions of Tento during the year were:

Sales	£20 000
Purchases	£12 000
Other expenses	£ 6 000

The stocks at the end of the period had been counted and were valued at £7000. The balance sheet of Tento at the start of the period was as follows:

	£
Fixed assets	
Premises	20 000
Current assets	
Stocks	5 000
Cash	11 000
	36 000
Financed by	£
Owner's equity	36 000
	36 000

The opening and closing stock levels are vital in determining the cost of goods sold. They therefore have a dual role in the balance sheet in determining wealth and through the cost of goods sold in determining profit.

KEY CONCEPT 8.3

THE IMPORTANCE OF THE DETERMINATION OF STOCK LEVELS

Solution 8.1

We start by entering the opening balances on to our worksheet which will now appear as follows.

Worksheet of Tento – version 1

	Assets			= Equity + Liabilities	
				Owners'	Profit
	Cash	Stock	Premises	equity	& loss
Balances	11 000	5000	20 000	36 000	

If we now enter the transactions for the year and draw up a preliminary total our worksheet will look like this:

Worksheet of Tento – version 2

	Assets			= Equity + Liabilities	
				Owners'	Profit
	Cash	Stock	Premises	equity	& loss
Balances	11 000	5 000	20 000	36 000	
Sales	20 000				20 000
Purchases	−12 000	12 000			
Expenses	−6 000				−6 000
Subtotal	13 000	17 000	20 000	36 000	14 000

The worksheet at this stage shows that we have a stock of goods of £17 000 whereas we know from our stock-count that what we actually have is £7000. In other words the asset at the end of the year, i.e. the part that will provide a future benefit, is only £7000. Using our equation we can establish that the cost of goods sold during the year was £10 000. This is of course an expense because the benefit is in the past. The figure of £10 000 was arrived at as follows:

$$\text{Opening stock} + \text{Purchases} - \text{Closing stock} = \text{Cost of goods sold}$$
$$\text{£5000} \quad + \quad \text{£12 000} \quad - \quad \text{£7000} \quad = \quad \text{£10 000}$$

Having found that the cost of goods sold is £10 000, we can now enter this on our worksheet and draw up our balance at the end of the year. This is done as follows:

Worksheet of Tento – version 3

	Assets			= Equity + Liabilities	
				Owners'	Profit
	Cash	Stock	Premises	equity	& loss
Balances	11 000	5 000	20 000	36 000	
Sales	20 000				20 000
Purchases	−12 000	12 000			
Expenses	−6 000				−6 000
Subtotal	13 000	17 000	20 000	36 000	14 000
Cost of sales		−10 000			−10 000
Balance	13 000	7 000	20 000	36 000	4 000

We would show the calculation included in the worksheet above on a profit and loss account as follows:

Profit and loss of Tento for the year

	£	£
Sales		20 000
Opening stock	5 000	
Purchases	12 000	
	17 000	
Less: Closing stock	7 000	
Cost of sales		10 000
Gross profit		10 000
Other expenses		6 000
Net profit		4 000

An alternative simplified presentation would be as follows:

Profit and loss of Tento for the year

	£
Sales	20 000
Cost of sales	10 000
Gross profit	10 000
Other expenses	6 000
Net profit	4 000

This latter format which does not show how the cost of goods sold is calculated is closer to that which you are likely to see in the published accounts of quoted companies.

Before we move on to the area of valuation it is worth pointing out that, because of the relationship between the balance sheet and profit and loss account, an error in the opening stock figure, the purchases figure or the closing stock figure will not only change the profit but it will also change our balance sheet. For example, if we had miscounted the stock at the end of the year and thought we only had £5000 our assets would be reduced by £2000 and our profit would also be reduced by £2000.

Valuation of stocks

In general if prices of goods stayed constant over time, tastes did not change and there were no changes in technology then we would have no problem with stock valuation. However, the real world fortunately is not like that – this has the advantage that civilization can progress but it creates some problems for accountants (a small price to pay you might think!). The question of how changes in prices can affect stock valuation is fairly wide ranging and is allied to the question of how the cost of stock is arrived at. We will therefore first of all consider the effects of changes in taste and technology, then we will look at the question of how cost is arrived at before finally considering the effects of price changes.

KEY CONCEPT 8.4	Net realizable value can be defined as the estimated proceeds from the sale of items less the costs likely to be incurred in selling those items.
NET REALIZABLE VALUE	

Changes in technology and tastes

We have grouped these two together because although the causes are different the effects on stock valuation are likely to be the same. Let us consider the effect of changes in technology, of which there are hundreds of everyday examples such as the use of microcomputers as compared to mainframe machines, and the advances in microcomputer technology. A fairly dramatic example of this effect was the introduction of the Sinclair QL, a microcomputer which retailed at £399. This undoubtedly made a number of other machines seem heavily overpriced. In turn when other manufacturers had caught up with the technology the QL was overpriced and Sinclair had to reduce the retail price to £199. For the purposes of our illustration let us assume that we are a retailer who has a stock of ten QLs bought (before the price reduction took effect) at a cost of £300 per machine. If we valued our closing stock on the basis of the cost our asset would be shown as £3000.

However, we said in Chapter 4 that an asset is the right to a future benefit. In the retailer's situation the future benefit that can be obtained is only £199, the new retail price. Thus in this case the cost does not reflect the future benefit the retailer is likely to get – a fairer reflection would be the amount it could be sold for. However, even the £199 is probably overstating the benefit as there will undoubtedly be some costs incurred in selling the QLs. If, for example, these costs were estimated to be £10 per machine then the amount of the future benefit would in fact be £189. This is referred to as the net realizable value of the goods.

A similar effect would have arisen if the goods could either only be sold at a reduced price or sold for scrap because of changes in people's tastes. In each of these cases the cost is not relevant to the future benefit and a better valuation would be the net realizable value. This leads us to the idea that we should compare the cost of an item with what we can get for it and if the latter figure is lower then that should be the figure used to value our stock. Or to express that in more formal terms, we have a rule which states that stocks should be valued at the lower of cost and net realizable value.

KEY CONCEPT 8.5	Stock should be valued at the lower of cost and net realizable value.
THE VALUATION RULE	

Under this concept profits are not anticipated and revenue is not recognized until its recognition is reasonable. This concept has to be used in conjunction with the realization principle which we discussed in some detail near the start of Chapter 5.	KEY CONCEPT 8.6 **THE PRUDENCE CONCEPT**

This rule will need to be applied where the stock is becoming obsolete as would happen with changes in tastes and technology. It also needs to be applied if the stock is damaged, if there is a fall in the market price, a decision to sell the stock at below cost as a loss leader and where the costs of production, for some reason, have exceeded the selling price.

You may well wonder why, if the net realizable value is higher than the cost, that higher value is not used. The reason for this is that the attainment of the higher value is uncertain as tastes etc. may change, thus we apply the prudence principle in these cases. This was simply defined in Chapter 6 as Key Concept 6.2. In Key Concept 8.6 we expand on that definition to emphasize its particular importance in stock valuation.

Having established the general rule for stock valuation and seen the reasons for the rule, the next question that we need to consider is the effect of price changes on the cost of goods sold and the closing stock.

Effects of price changes

Although we have considered the effect of downward movements in price under the heading of changes in technology we also need to consider the effect of increases in the input price of our stocks, i.e. increases in the prices we pay to our suppliers. As we have already indicated there would be no real problem if all sales could be identified with the actual goods sold. In practice, however, a builders' merchant has a pile of bricks and sells them in any order depending on the ease of access. We therefore cannot work out whether a particular brick sold was bought by the builders' merchant when the price of bricks was 30 p or whether it was bought after the price had gone up to 33 p. It is not feasible or cost effective to trace each brick through the process. We therefore have to find some system that will give a reasonable approximation of the cost of the goods we have sold and of the cost of the stock remaining. There are of course numerous possibilities at various levels of complexity. For our purposes we will concentrate on three which exemplify the problem and illustrate that solutions tend to be arbitrary.

In order to illustrate the differences between the methods let us take some fairly simple data.

Example 8.4
Brenda started the year with some goods in stock and bought additional goods as required during the year. The price of the goods she bought also rose steadily during the year. The summarized data for her transactions is:

	Units	Cost per unit
Goods in stock at the start of the year	400	£1.00
Purchases, quarter 1	500	£1.10
Purchases, quarter 2	400	£1.20
Purchases, quarter 3	400	£1.25
Purchases, quarter 4	300	£1.40

Goods sold during the year 1800 units for a total of £2400.

Using the data above we shall illustrate how the adoption of different valuation rules affect not only the stock value at the end of the year but also how it affects the cost of sales and therefore the profit. We shall start by considering a method of valuation called first in first out (FIFO).

First in first out

This method is based on the artificial assumption that the first goods bought are the first sold. This means that in effect the stock held at the end of the period is assumed to be that purchased most recently. It is probably the most common basis of stock valuation in the UK and there are many situations when it is clearly the obvious choice, as would be the case for any industry or business dealing in consumables, although it should be pointed out that generally the choice of method for arriving at the cost of stock has little if anything to do with actual stock movements.

In our example this method would mean that all the opening stock together with that purchased in the first three quarters would be assumed to have been sold together with 100 units bought in the fourth quarter. This would leave a closing stock of two hundred units which were bought in the fourth quarter.

FIFO

Opening stock	400	£1.00	£400.00	Sales	£2400.00
Quarter 1	500	£1.10	£550.00		
Quarter 2	400	£1.20	£480.00		
Quarter 3	400	£1.25	£500.00		
Quarter 4	100	£1.40	£140.00		
Cost of goods sold			£2070.00		£2070.00
				Profit	£330.00
Closing stock	200	£1.40	£280.00		

Last in first out

The last in first out (LIFO) method is based on the assumption that the last goods bought are the first sold. In therefore charges the latest price from suppliers against the revenue, and leaves the closing stock at a value based upon outdated prices. It is argued that in industries where prices are rising steadily this is more likely to give a profit figure that can be maintained in the future. It is similar in its profit and loss charge to that which would occur if we had used replacement cost.

In our example this method would mean that all the stock purchased in the year together with two hundred units of the opening stock would be assumed to have been sold. This would leave a closing stock of two hundred units which were in stock at the start of the year. These would be included at the original price and as such the balance sheet value is deliberately understated.

LIFO

Quarter 4	300	£1.40	£420.00	Sales	£2400.00
Quarter 3	400	£1.25	£500.00		
Quarter 2	400	£1.20	£480.00		
Quarter 1	500	£1.10	£550.00		
Opening stock	200	£1.00	£200.00		
Cost of goods sold			£2150.00		£2150.00
				Profit	£250.00
Closing stock	200	£1.00	£200.00		

Average cost

The average cost method is basically a compromise between the two methods we have already discussed. It makes no assumptions about the way in which goods flow through the business and is probably more neutral than either of the previous methods.

For the purposes of arriving at the profit and loss charges all that is needed is to work out the average cost per unit of stock and multiply that by the number of units sold. Similarly the closing stock is arrived at by taking the number of units left in stock times the average cost per unit. This would lead to a profit and stock figure which is between the two identified under FIFO and LIFO, and which is calculated as shown below:

Average cost

Opening stock	400	£1.00	£400.00	Sales	£2400.00
Quarter 1	500	£1.10	£550.00		
Quarter 2	400	£1.20	£480.00		
Quarter 3	400	£1.25	£500.00		
Quarter 4	300	£1.40	£420.00		
			£2350.00		
Average cost	1	£1.18			
Cost of goods sold	1800	£1.18	2115.00		£2115.00
				Profit	£285.00
Closing stock	200	£1.18	£235.00		

Having dealt with the question of rising prices and their effects on the cost we now need to consider what is included in cost, i.e. how to establish the cost that is referred to in the lower of cost and net realizable value rule. Before moving on to that however, there is one bit of good news, which is that the use of LIFO is not allowed under SSAP 9, *Accounting for Stock and Work in Progress*.

Establishing the cost of stocks

As we have already indicated, the more complex the process involved the more difficult it is to establish the cost of the stock. The problem is what should and what should not be included. The debate on this subject has been going on for some considerable period of time in the literature relating to management accounting. Fortunately, for our purposes at present we need only be aware in fairly general terms what the alternative methods are as the choice between the methods has to some extent been made for us through custom and practice and the rules laid down for companies in SSAP 9 – *Accounting for Stocks and Work in Progress*. Before looking at what the Standard says let us briefly consider some of the alternatives available. These are best considered by means of a simple example.

Example 8.2

Let us assume that a business produces spanners. Each spanner requires £0.30 of steel, and takes 15 minutes labour to produce. The business employs ten people to make spanners and they each produce 140 spanners per week and are paid £70 each per week. We also assume that supervising our workers we have a foreman who is paid £100 per week, and that at the end of the year we have one week's production, i.e. 1400 spanners, in stock. The question that we have to answer is what is the cost of the 1400 spanners we have in stock at the end of the year?

Solution 8.2

One solution might be to establish how much it would cost to produce one extra spanner.

Clearly one spanner would cost £0.30 for materials and we would need to pay a worker for 15 minutes to produce it. This would cost £0.50, i.e. £70 per week divided by the number of spanners produced which was 140. Thus the marginal cost of producing one spanner is £0.80. If we then applied this cost to our stock we would value our stock at 1400 × £0.80 = £1120. This would be the cost using a marginal cost basis.

On the other hand, it could legitimately be argued that the cost of producing 1400 spanners, i.e. a week's production, is made up as follows:

	£
Steel 1400 × £0.30	420
Direct labour 10 staff at £70	700
Foreman's wages	100
Total cost	1220

This latter method of arriving at the cost is known as absorption costing. You will note that the difference between the two is £100, i.e. the cost on a marginal cost basis is £1120 and on an absorption cost basis it is £1220. This is because the foreman's wages are not included on a marginal cost basis.

To some extent the choice between the two has been made for us by the requirements of SSAP 9 which states that cost is:

... that expenditure which has been incurred in the normal course of business in bringing the product or service to its present location or condition.

(para. 19)

Later on in the same paragraph it says:

... this expenditure should include, in addition to cost of purchase, such costs of conversion as are appropriate to that location and condition.

(para. 19)

The costs of conversion referred to include direct costs, similar to our labour and materials in the example above, production overheads, such as our foreman's wages, and any other overheads that are attributable to bringing the stock to its present location and condition. An example of these would be the cost to Ford of transporting engines from its production plant to the assembly line factory. It should be noted that these overhead costs have to be allocated based on a normal level of activity. If, in example 8.2, we only produced 700 spanners during the week because the workers were on strike we should not allocate the overheads, in this case the foreman's wages, to those 700 spanners. Instead, based on a normal level of activity of 1400 spanners we would allocate £50 of the foreman's wages, i.e. $700/1400 \times £100$, to the stock. The other £50 would be charged to the profit and loss account as an expense of the period as there is no future benefit that will arise from it.

In all the examples we will deal with from here on we will adopt a method of arriving at cost which will include all the costs which are obviously attributable to the stock, work in progress or finished goods. This can be done on the worksheet as illustrated in the following example.

Example 8.3

Bertie had his own business which assembled bicycles from a number of components. This involved the following processes.

Process 1 Assembling of frames, saddles and handlebars.
Process 2 Adding wheels to the partially completed frames.

The first process takes one hour and costs £5 in wages, whilst the second process takes less time and costs £3 in wages. Thus to assemble a complete bicycle costs £8 for labour. The frames, saddles and handlebars are bought from one supplier for £40 per set, and the wheels come from a different supplier at a cost of £20 per set.

We shall assume for the sake of simplicity that it is the first year of the business. During the year Bertie bought 500 frame sets at a total cost of £20 000 and 600 pairs of wheels at a total cost of £12 000. He paid wages of £3200 and sold 350 bicycles for £140 each making a total of £49 000 in revenue. His only other expenses were the rent of a showroom which cost him £5000 for the year.

At the end of the year he had in stock 50 completed cycles, 100 untouched frame sets and 200 pairs of wheels.

If we summarize the information we have been given in total and enter it on our worksheet we can then deal with the closing stock and the cost of goods sold.

Summary of the information:

Frame sets bought	£20 000
Wheels bought	£12 000
Wages paid	£ 3 200
Other expenses	£ 5 000
Sales revenue	£49 000

The relevant extracts from our worksheet would now appear as follows:

Bertie's worksheet – version 1

	Assets				= Equity + Liabilities
					Profit
	Cash	*Frames*	*Wheels*	*Wages*	*& loss*
Frames	−20 000	20 000			
Wheels	−12 000		12 000		
Wages	−3 200			3200	
Rent	−5 000				−5 000
Sales	49 000				49 000
Subtotal	8 800	20 000	12 000	3200	44 000

You will notice that the rent of the showroom has been included as an expense as it is a selling expense and by no stretch of the imagination could it be classified as an overhead attributable to bringing the goods to their present state and condition.

Turning now to the wages, we were told that each bicycle cost £8 for labour and that he has sold 350 bicycles. The labour in respect of the bikes sold is therefore 350 × £8 = £2800. The completed bicycles in stock cost 50 × £8 = £400 for labour. If we do similar calculations for the frames and the wheels we find that the cost of goods sold should be as follows:

Frames 350 × £40 = £14 000
Wheels 350 × £20 = £ 7 000
Wages 350 × £ 8 = £ 2 800

The amounts to be included in our stock of finished goods are:

Frames 50 × £40 = £2 000
Wheels 50 × £20 = £1 000
Wages 50 × £ 8 = £ 400

If we now wish to put this on the worksheet we will first need to open a column for our finished goods and then enter the above information. The relevant extracts from our worksheet will now be as follows:

Bertie's worksheet – version 2

		Assets				= Equity
					Finished	*Profit*
	Cash	*Frames*	*Wheels*	*Wages*	*goods*	*& loss*
1 Frames	−20 000	20 000				
2 Wheels	−12 000		12 000			
3 Wages	−3 200			3200		

		Assets				= Equity
					Finished	*Profit*
	Cash	*Frames*	*Wheels*	*Wages*	*goods*	*& loss*
4 Rent	−5 000					−5 000
5 Sales	49 000					49 000
6	8 800	20 000	12 000	3200		44 000
7 Frames		−14 000				−14 000
8 Wheels			−7 000			−7 000
9 Wages				−2800		−2 800
10 Frames		−2 000			2000	
11 Wheels			−1 000		1000	
12 Wages				−400	400	
13	8 800	4 000	4 000	0	3400	20 200

We shall briefly examine what we have just entered on our worksheet. On lines 1 to 5 we have simply included the items on the worksheet under various asset headings assuming that the frames, wheels and wages will give us a future benefit and are therefore assets. On lines 7, 8 and 9 we have dealt with the cost of the goods sold and have transferred the costs of the raw materials, frames and wheels, together with the labour costs associated with the assembly process, to the profit and loss as an expense of the period. You will note that here we have employed the matching principle and matched the costs of assembling 350 bicycles with the revenue earned from selling 350 bicycles. We have then opened an account for the finished goods we have assembled but not sold and on lines 10, 11 and 12 we have transferred the costs associated with those bicycles to a finished goods column. Now if we look at our final balances we find that what is left in stock is 100 frames at £40, 200 pairs of wheels at £20 and finished goods which have cost £3400 to get to their present state and condition.

Another way of looking at what is happening in Bertie's business is to see it as a flow through a factory which is represented by the accounting system. Thus the inputs are the frames, wheels and labour. These together form the work in progress, which then becomes finished goods ready for resale. The worksheet would therefore look something like that illustrated below:

Bertie's worksheet – version 3
Raw materials → WIP → Finished goods → Sales

	Cash	*Frames*	*Wheels*	*Wages*	*Work in progress*	*Finished goods*	*Profit & loss*
1 Frames	−20 000	20 000					
2 Wheels	−12 000		12 000				
3 Wages	−3 200			3200			
4 Rent	−5 000						−5 000
5 Sales	49 000						49 000
6	8 800	20 000	12 000	3200			44 000
7 Frames		−16 000			16 000		
8 Wheels			−8 000		8 000		
9 Wages				−3200	3 200		

Raw materials → WIP → Finished goods → Sales

	Cash	Frames	Wheels	Wages	Work in progress	Finished goods	Profit & loss
10 Finished					−27 200	27 200	
Cost of							
11 Goods Sold						−23 800	−23 800
12	8 800	4 000	4 000	0	0	3 400	20 200

Worksheet version 3 follows the production process through. The entries for lines 1 to 5 are the same. On lines 7, 8 and 9 the costs are transferred into work in progress, thus if at the end of the day we had some half finished goods the costs would be in this account. In this particular example all the bicycles were completed and therefore on line 10 we transfer the cost of all the completed bicycles to our finished goods account. However, not all those goods were sold, so on line 11 we transfer the costs that relate to the goods sold to the profit and loss account. This leaves a balance of £3400 in the finished goods account which is the same as in worksheet version 2. What version 3 shows is the way in which the flow of materials can be traced in the accounts from raw materials through work in progress and finished goods into sales.

Before moving on you might like to try to identify what would have happened had the 50 bicycles been partially completed, in other words only process 1 had been completed. You may assume that there were no other changes in costs. A worksheet headed 'Example 8.3 (part 2)' showing that situation is included at the end of the chapter for you to compare your answer with.

Having discussed the methods of arriving at the cost of stock it should be clear that applying the rule of the lower of cost and net realizable value is not in fact as straightforward as it seems at first sight. This is due to the problems in establishing the net realizable value and the cost. These problems are of course exacerbated in the case of long-term contracts which we shall consider next.

Long-term contracts

As we have pointed out stock valuation is even more difficult when we are concerned with long-term contracts and in these cases the importance of keeping good stock records cannot be over-emphasized. As far as the accounting standard is concerned the emphasis is on what can be recognized as revenue rather than on the stock figure. However, as we have shown in this chapter, these two are inextricably linked. The accounting standard's requirements are broadly that attributable profit to date on a long-term contract can be taken to the profit and loss account when the earnings process is sufficiently far advanced and there is reasonable certainty of a profit. All foreseeable losses, on the other hand, should be recognized immediately irrespective of how complete the project is. This is of course what one would expect given the realization principle and the prudence concept.

The situation with long-term contracts is normally fairly complex as firms tend to invoice on account during the progress of the contract. This would be reasonably straightforward if the invoices related precisely to the work completed. In reality this tends not to be the case and the reasons for this are to do with cash flows and time lags in the payment system. For example, a building subcontractor will know that when they invoice the contractor, they in turn will send somebody to the site to assess the progress on site. They may then invoice their client who may also check on the completion before passing an invoice for payment. Even then the subcontractor is likely to have to wait thirty days before getting paid. Therefore what happens is that invoices are sent out in advance of the work having reached the stage of completion to which the invoice relates. These invoices are sometimes paid before the work is done, which raises the problem of how to deal with this cash which in effect is a prepayment. SSAP 9 answers this question by allowing the prepayments to be used to reduce the stock and work in progress for that contract as long as it does not make the stock figure negative. The actual stock and work in progress in these cases is normally related to the next phase of the project where, for example, a central heating contractor has bought the boiler for the next phase, has invoiced for installation of the radiators and been paid but has not yet installed all the radiators. If the advance payments exceed the work in progress for that contract then the amount of the prepayment is included in the creditors.

As you can surmise from the above this is a complex area where the accounting standard has reflected practice rather than an application of principles. This argument is fortunately outside the remit of an introductory text. However, there are certain points that are worthy of note. These are the use of the principles of realization and prudence in terms of recognizing revenue. It should also be clear that the analysis of a set of accounts of a contracting business has to be approached in a different way from a straight manufacturing business as the treatment of stock and the receipt of payments in advance make even year-on-year comparisons fraught with problems.

Disclosure requirements for stock and work in progress

SSAP 9 on stocks and work in progress lays down the following requirements regarding disclosure in respect of stock. These are that the accounting policies that have been used in calculating cost, net realizable value attributable profit and foreseeable losses should be stated. The standard also requires that stock and work in progress should be classified in the balance sheet or the notes to the accounts in a manner which is appropriate to the business so as to indicate the amounts in the main categories. The categories which the standard has in mind are raw materials, work in progress and finished goods.

CASE 8.1

ACCOUNTING FOR STOCKS AND WORK IN PROGRESS

The extract from the 1991 annual report of GKN Plc in respect of stock is reproduced below. It provides a good example of the three main categories of stock, i.e. raw materials, work in progress and finished goods held for resale. The heading 'Payments on account' relates to work in progress and need not concern us here. The accounting policy note, while being reasonably clear, does not tell us what basis is used for arriving at cost, i.e. FIFO, average cost or whatever. However, the fact that the cost is not materially different from the replacement cost does tell the user that the figure is not heavily understated.

Stocks – extract from GKN Plc notes to the accounts

	1991	1990
STOCKS	**£m**	£m
Raw materials and consumables	**89.1**	96.9
Work in progress	**78.0**	99.0
Finished goods and goods for resale	**124.9**	137.8
Payments on account	**(1.2)**	(5.4)
	290.8	328.3

Stocks are valued at the lower of cost and estimated net realisable value, due allowance being made for obsolete or slow-moving items. Cost includes the relevant proportion of works overheads assuming normal levels of activity. The replacement cost of stocks is not materially different from the historical cost value.

By Contrast, in the case of Bentalls Plc, a retailer, there is only one category of stock. However, the accounting policies note in respect of stock, which is reproduced below, is worthy of mention. Here we see that the cost of the stock is an estimate based upon the selling price less the normal gross profit margin for that type of stock. Here also there is no specific mention made of obsolete and slow moving stock and how those are dealt with.

Stocks – extract from Bentalls Plc accounting policies
Stocks have been valued at the lower of cost and net realisable value. Cost is arrived at by valuing stocks at normal selling prices less the appropriate departmental gross profit margin.

The example of Bentalls is an industry-specific problem in respect of arriving at the cost of stock. Another industry-specific problem of a different kind is revealed in the accounting policy of Guinness Plc below:

Stocks – extract from Guinness Plc accounting policies
Stocks are stated at the lower of cost and net realisable value. Cost includes raw materials, duties where applicable, direct labour and expenses and the appropriate proportion of production and other overheads, including financing costs in respect of whisky stocks during their normal maturation period.

In this case the interest charges attributable to the costs of holding the whisky in stock while it matures are included in the cost of stocks held as are some excise duties. Once again the basis of arriving at cost is not stated.

Continued from previous page

An example of where the information on the way in which cost is arrived at is given in the extract from the accounting policies of British Petroleum Plc reproduced below. Here we see that a different basis is used for different types of stock. It is also worth noting the lack of precision in respect of the stores which are either at or below cost and the costs are mainly calculated using the average method.

Stocks – extract from British Petroleum Plc accounting policies
Stocks are valued at cost to the group using the first in first out method or at net realisable value, whichever is the lower. Stores are stated at or below cost calculated mainly using the average method.

Summary

In this chapter we have relaxed some of our assumptions about the business being a start-up and have shown how we establish the cost of goods sold during a period and the closing stock. We have also looked at what constitutes cost when dealing with stock and have introduced the ideas of marginal and absorption costing. In the latter part of the chapter we have looked at the effects of changes in technology which can lead to stock being sold at less than cost and at the effect of changes in prices both on the balance sheet and profit and loss account. We have considered three possible methods for arriving at the cost of goods sold during a period and at the closing stock figure. It can be seen that some of the issues faced in accounting for stock are often a direct result of the management strategies adopted such as 'just in time' which will affect the amount of stock held. Other factors at the organizational level that will have an impact are the size of the organization. For example Tesco are likely to hold a wider range of goods than the corner shop. Similarly the problems associated with arriving at a figure for stock and work in progress are different in different sectors, e.g. retailing, manufacturing and long-term contracting.

Answer to Example 8.3 (part 2)

Bertie's worksheet – version 4

	Cash	Frames	Wheels	Wages	Work in progress	Profit & loss
Frames	−20 000	20 000				
Wheels	−12 000		12 000			
Wages	−3 200			3200		
Rent	−5 000					−5 000
Sales	49 000					49 000
	8 800	20 000	12 000	3200		44 000

	Cash	Frames	Wheels	Wages	Work in progress	Profit & loss
Frames		−14 000				−14 000
Wheels			−7 000			−7 000
Wages				−2800		−2 800
Frames		−2 000			2000	
Wheels			−1 000		1000	
Wages				−250	250	
Balance	8 800	4 000	4 000	150	3250	20 200
Wages				−150		−150
	8 800	4 000	4 000	0	3250	20 050

You will notice in this case that the wages column ends with a balance of £150 still in it. Given our assumptions this cannot be attributed either to the cost of the bicycles or to the work in progress, nor is it an asset at the end of the year as there is no identifiable future benefit. It is therefore treated in the same way as the showroom rent, i.e. as a period expense and charged to the profit and loss account. This treatment is in line with the requirements of SSAP 9.

References

Statement of Standard Accounting Practice No. 9 (1989) *Accounting for Stocks and Work in Progress*, Accounting Standards Committee.
Statement of Standard Accounting Practice No. 2 (1971) *Disclosure of Accounting Policies*, Accounting Standards Committee.

Further reading

An interesting article on just-in-time is by Robert A. McIllhattan, 1987, 'The JIT philosophy', *Management Accounting*, 7 September pp. 20–6.

A more detailed illustration of the business as a series of inputs and outputs can be found in Chapters 1 and 6 of D. Needle, *Business in Context* (Chapman & Hall, 1989).

Review questions

1. What main categories of stock are likely to be held by a manufacturing business?

2. In arriving at a figure for stock in a business manufacturing and assembling furniture what questions would need to be considered?

3. What would be the effect on the profit if goods costing £6000 were excluded from the opening stock figure?

4. What are the effects of omitting goods costing £500 from the year end stock figure?

5. Why is it necessary to value stock at the lower of cost and net realizable value?

6. Explain in your own words the difference between absorption costing and marginal costing.

7. Which of the following costs would be appropriate to include in a marginal costing system.

   (a) director's salary?
   (b) foreman's wages?
   (c) machine operators' wages?
   (d) cost of raw materials?

8. Of the costs above which would be appropriate to include in arriving at cost under a marginal costing system?

9. Name three methods of stock valuation and describe the differences between them and the effects of those differences.

10. Think of examples of types of business where one method would be more appropriate than the others.

Problems for discussion and analysis

1. In the situation described in the following example discuss which costs, if any, should be included in the stock valuation, and at what point in time they should be included.

   Hasp is in business manufacturing sails. The sail material is purchased in one hundred metre lengths and these are delivered to the storeman who sorts the materials according to quality and width. The material is then issued to the cutting room where five people are employed, one of whom is the cutting room supervisor. After cutting the material is passed through to the machining room where the sails are sewn up and the hasps etc. are put on. The machining room has seven staff employed full time including a supervisor. From the machining room the sails go through to the packaging department where they are folded, inserted in sail bags and sent either to the despatch department or put into stock. The packaging department and the despatch department each employ one member of staff working on a part-time basis. The whole operation is under the control of a production manager who also has responsibility for quality control.

2. Discuss the ways in which your answer to question 1 above would be affected by the use of a marginal cost basis of stock valuation.

3. Gilco had been in business for a year buying and selling home water purifiers. During the year 400 units had been sold and installed; of these 220 were Model 2 and the remainder were the upgraded model, Model 3. Model 2 is still selling but at a reduced price which is of course less than the price of Model 3 as it has less features. Since Model 3 was introduced in August the sales of Model 2 have fallen but have now stabilized at 10 a month. The stock count at the year end shows that Gilco has 60 Model 3 purifiers and 20 Model 2 purifiers in stock. The price of Model 2 is now £70 and Model 3 is selling at £110. The pattern of purchases for the year are provided below. Gilco estimates that the costs incurred in selling either of the purifiers are £20 per unit.

	Model 2		Model 3	
	Units	Price	Units	Price
Quarter 1	80	£50		
Quarter 2	100	£50 55		

	Model 2		*Model 3*	
	Units	Price	Units	Price
Quarter 3	60	£50	80	£60
Quarter 4			160	£65

(a) Calculate the cost of the goods sold on a FIFO basis.

(b) Calculate the cost of the goods sold using average cost.

(c) Calculate the balance sheet figure for stock on a FIFO basis, having regard to the lower of cost or net realizable value rule.

4. Simon has recently gone into business making meat pies. Details of his transactions for the first month are given below:

Day 1   Opened a bank account and paid in £20 000 of his own money.
Purchased an oven to make pies at a cost of £10 000.
Paid rent for production space for the first month of £200.

Day 2   Bought the following supplies and paid cash:
1100 lb of flour at 60 p per lb;
1100 lb of meat at £1 per lb.

Day 3   Withdrew £1000 to pay a pressing personal debt.

Day 3 to 31:
Made 4000 pies and sold 3900 pies.
Each pie takes 4 oz of flour and 4 oz of meat and was sold for £1.
At the end of the month he still had in stock the expected 100 lb of flour, 100 lb of meat and 100 finished meat pies.

Day 31   Paid himself £1600 wages for the month. He estimates that half his time is spent on production and the rest on selling and administration.
Paid production overheads of £120 for the month.
Paid administration expenses of £50 for the month.

(a) Draw up a worksheet, balance sheet and profit and loss account for Simon's business.

(b) Comment on the performance of the business.

4. Using the information in the example below, discuss the accounting treatment of each transaction and the possible value of the stock at the end of the month.

Stern has recently gone into business assembling hang gliders. Details of the transactions for the first month are given below:

Day 1   Opened a bank account for the business and paid in £50 000 of his own money.
Purchased for cash assembly machinery for £40 000.
Rented factory space at a rental of £200 per month and paid one month's rent in advance.

Day 2   Bought 1000 metres of tubing for the hang glider frames at price of £250 per hundred metres and paid the £2500 in cash

Day 3   Purchased one hundred and fifty sets of material for sails for £20 per set and paid the £3000 immediately. Each hang glider takes one set of sails.

Day 8   Received an order for twenty hang gliders at £400 each together with a cheque for £8000.

Day 9   Banked the cheque and commenced manufacture of the hang gliders.

Day 14   Completed manufacture of the twenty hang gliders and despatched the completed order to the customer, paying the delivery charges of £200 immediately.

At this stage it was possible to do some preliminary calculations relating to the manufacture of each hang glider. These calculations showed that each hang glider required the following:

> Labour: Sail machining – 30 minutes per unit
>   Frame assembly – 2 hours per unit
>   Final assembly – 30 minutes per unit
> Materials: Metal tubing   – four metres per unit
>   Sails   – one set per unit

Day 15 Received an order for another 200 hang gliders at a price of £250 each. Payment is to be made on a cash on delivery basis.

Day 16 Commenced work on the new order.

Day 26 Puchased another hundred sets of sails, and paid for them in cash. The price had gone up to £22.00 per set making a total of £2200.

Day 30 Paid wages of £320 for the month based on 4 40-hour weeks at £2 per hour.

Day 31 Established the position at the end of the month as follows:

> Completed hang gliders ready for delivery – 20
> Manufactured frames   – 10

> Stocks of materials were as follows:

> Steel tubing in stock – 800 metres
> Sets of sails in stock – 210 sets

5. Draw up a worksheet and enter the transactions outlined in the example above.

6. Draw up a balance sheet and profit and loss account for Stern.

7. Comment on the situation as revealed by the balance sheet and profit and loss account of Stern.

8. Spain has recently gone into business manufacturing office chairs. Details of the transactions for the first month are given below:

Day 1   Opened a bank account and paid in £10 000 of her own money. Purchased machinery to make the chairs at a cost of £4000 paid for immediately. Rented factory space at a rental of £200 per month and paid one month's rent in advance. Bought office equipment at a cost of £400.

Day 2   Bought 1000 metres of steel tubing at a price of £50 per hundred metres and paid for this immediately.

Day 3   Purchased 250 packs of end fittings for £125, together with a quantity of screws costing £40. Both of these purchases were paid for immediately.

Day 4   Purchased 150 sets of ready-cut seat bases and backrests at a price of £5 per set, and paid for them.

Day 5   Bought upholstery materials and cloth for seat covers for £400.

Day 8   Received an order for 20 chairs at £50 each together with accompanying cheque.

Day 9   Paid the cheques into the bank and commenced manufacture of the chairs.

Day 14 Completed manufacture of chairs for order and despatched these to the customer, paying £40 total delivery charges.

At this stage it was possible to do some preliminary calculations relating to the manufacture of the chairs. These showed that each chair required the following:

Labour: Manufacturing 2 hours per frame.
                       Upholstering seats and backrests $\frac{1}{2}$ hour per set.
                       Assembling chairs $\frac{1}{2}$ hour per chair.
Materials per chair: Four metres of metal tubing.
                       One pack of end fittings.
                       One set of seat/backrest.
                       Quantity of upholstery materials etc.

Day 15   Received an order for another 200 chairs at a price of £50 each. Payment was to be on the basis of cash on delivery.
Day 15   Commenced work on the new order.
Day 26   Purchased and paid for another 100 sets of seats and backrests. The price per set had, however, gone up to £6.
Day 30   Paid himself wages for the month of £320 calculated on the basis of £80 per week for a 40-hour week.

The position at the end of the month was established as follows.

Completed chairs ready for delivery   20
Manufactured frames   10

In addition there was in stock:

800 metres of steel tubing.
210 packs of end fittings.
210 seat and backrest sets.
Half the screws and upholstery materials.

(a) Draw up a worksheet for Spain and enter the above transactions.
(b) Draw up a balance sheet at the end of the month and a profit and loss account for the month for Spain.
(c) Discuss the performance of Spain's business for the period.

Fixed assets and depreciation 9 ||||||

Review of fixed and current assets

In Chapter 4 we discussed the definitions of assets and of fixed and current assets. We defined an asset in accordance with the definition suggested by R.M. Lall reproduced from Key Concept 4.4 below:

Embodiments of present or future economic benefits or service potentials measurable in monetary units, accruing to an enterprise as a result of economic events, the enjoyment of which by the enterprise is secured by law.

The distinction that we made in earlier chapters between assets and expenses is that an asset relates to present or future benefits whereas an expense relates to past or expired benefits. Thus we have stocks of goods held at the year end shown as an asset and the cost of the stocks sold during the year charged as an expense. Similarly some of the assets we hold change form during a period or from one period to the next. For example, debtors become cash, or they become expenses as is the case when a debt becomes uncollectable. This applies to all assets in the long run but in the case of fixed assets it takes longer to use up the future benefits than it does with current assets. We defined fixed assets in Chapter 4 and that definition is reproduced from Key Concept 4.5 below:

An asset that is acquired for the purposes of use within the business and is likely to be used by the business for a considerable period of time

The fact that these assets neither change form or get used up in a short period poses some problems for accountants. These problems are in some ways similar to those we identified when discussing stock valuation. In that case we found that there was a problem in allocating costs such as the wages of the foreman and deciding which part of that cost should be allocated to the costs of the goods sold during the period, i.e. the expired benefit. There was also the question of how much should be allocated to the stock held at the end of the period which is an asset as there is a future benefit to be derived.

The problem can be looked at on a more general level. From the point of view of the balance sheet, which tells us what we own at a particular point in time, we have to try to identify the amount of the future benefit left at the end of each year. On the other hand, from the perspective of

KEY CONCEPT 9.1	Income is that amount which an individual can consume and still be as well off at the end of the period as he or she was at the start of the period.
INCOME – HICKS' DEFINITION	

the profit and loss account, we need to measure the amount of the future benefit used up during the year in order that we can match this expense with the revenue earned during the year. Whichever way we choose to look at the problem, we are still left with the issue of how to measure the future benefit to be derived from the use of the asset. This is because the balance sheet and profit and loss are linked and in fact it was argued in Chapter 3 that accounting largely adopted a definition of profit based on Sir John Hicks' definition of income reproduced in Key Concept 9.1.

This we said could be illustrated diagrammatically as:

Wealth T_0 Wealth T_1 Wealth T_2
T_0 T_1 T^2
$\longleftarrow$ —— Profit —— $\longrightarrow$ $\longleftarrow$ —— Profit —— $\longrightarrow$

We can see from this that wealth at T_0 plus the profit for the period will give us wealth at T_1. Thus we can either measure the wealth in the form of future benefits at the end of each period, which brings with it the problems of valuation discussed in Chapter 3, or we can try to measure the profit by matching the revenue with the benefits used up during the period. This brings its own problems as we found with stock and cost allocation in Chapter 8.

Theoretically it may be possible to measure the future benefits from the use of our fixed assets. We could, for example, measure the benefits to be derived from selling the products which our fixed assets help us to produce. In a world in which there is uncertainty, however, this process is far from straightforward. For example, what effects do technological advances have on the market for our products? How does that affect the future benefits to be derived from the use of our asset? What is the effect of competition on our market share? What is the effect of a change in production technology? It may be that the change allows competitors with newer equipment to produce the same product at a cheaper price thereby reducing our competitiveness.

In fact, it is extremely difficult to measure the future benefit in the long term as we do not know what changes the future will bring, therefore we cannot estimate their effects. This leaves us with the alternative approach, i.e. measuring expired benefits and matching those with revenues. The problem with this approach is that if you were able to tell how much benefit had expired you would then be able to work out what the unexpired or future benefit was. This, we have just argued, is extremely difficult to do in reality because of the problems of uncertainty.

Traditionally accounting has solved this conundrum by the simple expedient of valuing assets at cost unless there is reasonable certainty that this value is incorrect, either because it is lower, as would be the case if changes in technology made the fixed assets obsolete, or because it is clearly considerably higher, as has happened in recent years with land and buildings. In general, however, the problem of identifying future benefits is avoided by simply recording fixed assets at cost. Accounting does, however, try to take some cognizance of the fall in value of the fixed assets and the need to match revenue with expenses. This is done by means of a depreciation charge which is a way of spreading the original cost of a fixed asset over its useful life and thereby charging the profit and loss account with some amount relating to the use of the asset.

This approach, although avoiding the problem of how to deal with uncertain future benefits, does not, in itself, solve the problem of how to deal with uncertainty as the useful life of a fixed asset is itself uncertain. There are also other issues arising out of the approach. For example, how does a fixed asset differ from a current asset and how do we deal with what we referred to earlier as indeterminate assets? What is the cost of a fixed asset? How should we spread the cost over the useful life? We need to examine each of these issues if we are to understand what the profit and loss and balance sheet figures mean.

Difference between fixed and current assets

We have already defined fixed and current assets in Chapter 4 and if you look at the definitions you will see that the difference is in the main related to the intention regarding the use of the asset, and to the nature of the business. In simple terms a car is not a fixed asset in the case of a motor dealer because it is not the intention of the dealer to use it within the business for a considerable period of time. The problem with a definition that relies on the intentions of the business is that these change from time to time as the nature of the business changes or the product changes. This may mean that an asset that was classified as a fixed asset may be re-classified with corresponding effects on whether the asset is subject to depreciation. These problems rarely arise, thus for our purposes we can safely ignore them. However, the question of how to deal with indeterminate assets such as patents, research and development, etc., do arise regularly and we shall be discussing these in more detail in Chapter 10.

The cost of a fixed asset

On the face of it the question of what an asset cost should present few if any difficulties. This is true in some cases, but in a great many cases the answer is less clear. To illustrate the point let us look at the situation where an individual buys a house. If we were to read the legal contract between the seller and the buyer we would find within that contract an agreed price. We could therefore argue that the cost is that agreed price, but were you to talk to someone who has recently purchased a house you would find that there were other costs associated with buying that house such as solicitors' fees, surveyors' fees, etc. The question is whether these should be treated as part of the cost of the asset or whether they are expenses. In this particular situation the way in which accounting might answer the question is to argue that the amounts involved would not be material when compared to the cost of the house. This is not really a very satisfactory solution as it merely avoids the question rather than answering it.

Accounting does not, in fact, provide an answer to this problem. There are some broad guidelines, however, which accountants use which we will illustrate by examining some possible examples and identifying the basis of the decision.

Example 9.1
Purchase of a delivery van by a retailer of office stationery for £7600. The price includes number plates and one year's road fund licence.

Discussion
It is clear that in this example we have a fixed asset. The question is only how much did the fixed asset cost? Included in the £7600 is the cost of number plates and one year's road fund licence. The road fund licence could hardly be described as a fixed asset as it only lasts for one year, whereas the number plates are clearly part of the cost of the fixed asset in that they will remain with the van over its useful life.

Example 9.2
Let us now assume that, as the retailer did not have the cash to buy the van outright, it was purchased on hire-purchase. The hire-purchase contract allowed the retailer to put down a deposit of £3400 and then make 24 monthly payments of £200. Thus the total cost of buying the same van would be £8200 compared to the cash price of £7600.

Discussion
The fact that the retailer has decided to finance the purchase in a different way has, on the face of it, added to the cost of purchasing the van. However, this is somewhat misleading as the cost of the van is in fact the same. What has happened in this case is that the retailer has incurred an additional cost which does not relate to the van itself. This additional cost relates to the cost of borrowing money, which is effectively what hire-purchase is. If the retailer had borrowed money through a bank loan and then paid cash for the van the cost of the van would have been the cash price and the interest on the loan would be dealt with separately. Thus in the case of hire-purchase all that needs to be done is to identify the part of the payments that are interest charges and deal with those in the same way as we would interest on loans. In this particular example the interest is £600, i.e. the full HP price of £8200 less the cash price of £7600. The £600 interest would of course be charged to the profit and loss account as an expense over the 24 months it takes to pay the hire-purchase company.

Example 9.3
A business decides that as it does not have the money available to buy a new piece of highly specialized machinery it will lease it from a specialist leasing company as this is virtually the same as buying the machine, the difference being that ownership remains with the leasing company. The

lease is for ten years and the annual lease payments are £11 000 whilst the cash price of the machine is £98 000.

Discussion

This is similar to the situation with hire-purchase. The business has the right to use the machinery for the next ten years, although it does not own the machinery. The machinery therefore fits our definition of an asset and of a fixed asset. The cost is £98 000, the other £12 000 is interest charges and these should be charged to the profit and loss account over the period. It is worth noting that there is an accounting standard dealing with leasing and hire-purchase, SSAP 21 *Accounting for Leases and Hire Purchase*. The standard distinguishes between an operating lease where a business rents some equipment, e.g. a photocopier, and a finance lease where the intention is that the business has the use of the asset and all the risks and rewards that go with it. In the latter case what is happening is really the same as hire-purchase, i.e. the asset is being purchased by an alternative form of finance. In the case of an operating lease there is no intention that the lessee, the business renting the photocopier, will ever purchase it from the lessor, the business that owns the photocopier.

Example 9.4

A manufacturer bought a second-hand machine for £8000 which had cost £15 000 new. The cost of transporting the machine to the factory was £500 and the costs of installation were £400. When it was installed it was found that it was not working properly and had to be repaired which cost £300. At the same time a modification was carried out at a cost of £500 to improve the output of the machine. After two months' production the machine broke down again and was repaired at a cost of £200.

Discussion

The starting point is the basic cost of the machine which was £8000. The fact that it had cost £15 000 when it was new is not relevant. What we need to bring into the accounts of our manufacturer is the cost to that business, not the original cost to the seller. With the other costs though, the decisions are less clear cut – For example, should the cost of transport be included? One answer would be to argue that in order to obtain the future benefits from the asset we needed to incur this cost so this is in fact a payment for those future benefits. If we followed that line of argument we could then include the costs of installation, the initial repairs and the modifications. This would seem a reasonable line of argument as long as we are happy that the future benefits are likely to exceed the costs incurred to date. This is clearly a question of judgement because of the uncertainty surrounding the estimation of future benefits.

You will have noticed that we referred specifically to the initial repairs rather than all the repairs. The reason for this is that, in the first case, it could be argued that the reason the business was able to buy the machine cheaply was because it was not working properly. In the second instance, however, the argument is less clear cut, as the repairs might simply be due to normal wear and tear and should therefore be judged as part of the cost of running the machine in much the same way as we would view the cost of car repairs as a part of the costs of running a car.

We can see from these examples that there is no nice easy solution to the problem of what should and should not be included in the cost of fixed assets. Each case is judged upon its merits and a decision is made about whether the cost should be included in the expenses for the year or added to the cost of the asset. The broad rule of thumb that can be used to assist in these decisions is, has there been an enhancement of the potential future benefits? If there has, then the cost should be added to the asset. If, on the other hand, the effect is simply to restore the status quo, as is the case with car repairs, then it is more reasonable to treat those costs as expenses of the period in which they arise. This approach conforms to the prudence concept which we have referred to earlier.

The useful life of fixed assets

In our introduction we mentioned the useful life of the asset and how we spread the cost over the useful life. This raises a number of issues: How do we judge the useful life? What cost do we spread over the useful life? How do we spread it? The latter point will be dealt with below in our discussion of depreciation, but it is worth examining the other two before we move on to that discussion. The first point is how do we judge the useful life. The answer is that all we can hope for is a reasonable approximation of the useful life. The reason we can only approximate comes back to the question of uncertainty in respect of the future. Similarly if we try to arrive at the cost that we wish to spread over the useful life we could argue that we should take into account anything that we will be able to sell our asset for when it is no longer viable to use it in our business. This amount, the residual value, is only a guess because of the uncertainty involved. In reality it is quite likely that such issues are sidestepped and that assets are classified into broad groups which are then assumed to have a useful life based upon either past practice or the norm for the industry. All too often one can visit factories where a vital machine in the production process has no book value in the accounts because the estimate of the useful life was incorrect.

It should be clear from our discussion that there is no magic formula for arriving at either the cost or the useful life. Bearing this in mind we can now examine the way in which we spread the cost over the useful life. This as we have already mentioned is done by means of depreciation.

Depreciation

We have suggested some reasons for charging depreciation which we will discuss more fully shortly. What we have not done is to define depreciation precisely – instead we have tried to give a flavour of what depreciation is. However, no discussion of depreciation would be complete without at least looking at the definition provided in SSAP 12 *Accounting for Depreciation* (see Key Concept 9.2).

> . . . the measure of the wearing out, consumption or other loss of value of a fixed asset whether arising from use, effluxion of time or obsolescence through technology or market changes.

This definition is, in fact, difficult to comply with because, as we have already pointed out, the fixed asset is normally included at cost not at value, therefore to measure the loss in value would be inconsistent. It also assumes that we will be able to take into account changes in technology and the market. This might be possible in the short term but it is much more difficult in the long term. As fixed assets are essentially long-term assets the requirement to take into account these changes in technology and the market is, in practice, difficult to comply with. Whilst we could spend considerable time analysing the definition it is more important that we consider the question of why we depreciate assets and what depreciation can and cannot be expected to achieve.

Why depreciate?

One reason already mentioned is that of matching the revenue earned in a period with the expense connected with earning that revenue. In essence the argument for matching the cost of goods sold with sales or of matching expenses with sales is the one being applied here. The major difference is that some of these other items are ascertainable with a reasonable degree of accuracy, whereas depreciation as we have pointed out is only an estimate and subject to all sorts of inaccuracies.

A second and more contentious reason for providing for depreciation is in order to maintain the capacity of a business to continue its production or whatever, i.e. to maintain operating capacity. Clearly if a machine comes to the end of its useful life the business will need another machine if it is to carry on producing the goods that the worn out machine produced. This of course assumes that it would wish to replace the machine which in itself has underlying assumptions about the product still being produced, the technology in terms of production processes being the same, etc. This question is directly related to our original problem in Chapter 3 of measuring one's wealth or how well-off one is. Such a measure depends on how you define wealth and whether that changes over time. For example, a car may be seen as an asset until such time as the world runs out of petrol reserves. At that stage we probably will not want to include a car in our measurement of wealth. Therefore to have retained profits in order to ensure we always had a car would not have been appropriate.

Maintenance of operating capacity is also contentious because in fact all accounting depreciation does is to spread the original cost and maintain the original money capital. This means that in fact operating capacity is not maintained through depreciation as no account is taken of changes whether they be in prices, in technology or in consumer demand. Neither is any account taken of changes in the size of the business. These may have implications in terms of economies of scale. All of this means that we cannot guarantee that we will have enough money left in the business as a result of our depreciation charges to replace an existing machine with one of equal capacity should we so wish. Having made the point that there is no guarantee that the depreciation charges will equal the requirements for replacement because of changes in those requirements and in the environment, let us look at how depreciation would maintain capital if the requirements and the environment did not change.

We will start by looking at an example to see what happens if we ignore depreciation and then how it is dealt with in terms of the accounts.

Example 9.5

Toni buys a van for £4000 and sets up as an ice-cream seller. In addition to the van £1000 cash is put into the business which is subsequently used to buy stocks of ice-cream.

At the end of the first year the sales have been £6000 and the total expenses including the cost of ice-creams, van repairs and running costs were £3000. All the stock has been sold so all the money is in cash. Thus the business has £4000 in cash – the original £1000 plus the money from sale of £6000 less the expenses paid of £3000.

Toni therefore withdraws £3000 on the assumption that the business is still as well off as it was at the start. That is the business had at the start of the year a van plus £1000 in cash; it still has the van so there only needs to be £1000 left in for the status quo to be maintained. Let us assume for convenience that the situation is repeated for the next three years.

Under these assumptions the profit and loss accounts and balance sheets of the business would be as follows:

**Profit and loss accounts
of Toni's business**

	Year 1	Year 2	Year 3	Year 4
Sales revenue	6000	6000	6000	6000
Cost of sales	3000	3000	3000	3000
Profit	3000	3000	3000	3000
Withdrawal	3000	3000	3000	3000
Retained profit	0	0	0	0

**Balance sheets
of Toni's business**

	Year 1	Year 2	Year 3	Year 4
Fixed assets				
Van	4000	4000	4000	4000
Current assets				
Cash	1000	1000	1000	1000
	5000	5000	5000	5000
Financed by				
Owner's equity	5000	5000	5000	5000
	5000	5000	5000	5000

If we assume the van would last four years we can see that in fact the balance sheet at the end of year 4 is wrong as the van has come to the end of its useful life and there is no future benefit to be derived from keeping it. If we want the balance sheet to include as assets only items that reflect future benefits the balance sheet at the end of year 4 should be:

Fixed assets	
Van	Nil
Current assets	
Cash	1000
	1000
Financed by	
Owner's equity	1000
	1000

We can see from this balance sheet there is not enough money left in the business to replace the van and in this situation the business cannot continue. If we compare our results with our definition of profit in Chapter 3 it is clear that our profit measure must have been wrong as Toni is not as well off at the end of year 4 as at the beginning of year 1.

The problem has been that the profit has been overstated because no allowance has been made for the fact that the van has a finite useful life which is being eroded each year. If we assume that the cost should be spread evenly over the four years and call this expense depreciation then our profit and loss accounts would appear as follows.

Revised profit and loss accounts of Toni's business

	Year 1	Year 2	Year 3	Year 4
Sales revenue	6000	6000	6000	6000
Cost of sales	3000	3000	3000	3000
Gross profit	3000	3000	3000	3000
Depreciation	1000	1000	1000	1000
Net profit	2000	2000	2000	2000
Withdrawal	2000	2000	2000	2000
Retained profit	0	0	0	0

As can be seen the net profit has been reduced by £1000 for the depreciation each year and Toni has withdrawn only £2000 each year. The balance sheets would now be:

Revised balance sheets of Toni's business

Fixed assets	Year 1	Year 2	Year 3	Year 4
Van	4000	4000	4000	4000
Depreciation	1000	2000	3000	4000
Net book value	3000	2000	1000	0
Current assets				
Cash	2000	3000	4000	5000
	5000	5000	5000	5000
Financed by				
Owner's equity	5000	5000	5000	5000
	5000	5000	5000	5000

As we have seen, the effect of charging depreciation in the profit and loss account was to reduce the net profit which in turn led to a reduction in the amount withdrawn each year. The reduced withdrawal has led to the cash balance increasing each year by £1000 until at the end of year 4 there is £5000 in the bank and Toni is in a position to replace the van, assuming of course that the price of vans has not changed. If you compare the two sets of balance sheets there is another change – this is that the fixed asset reduces each year by the amount of the depreciation charge. These two effects should not be mixed up – the increase in cash is as a result of withdrawing less and **not** as a result of providing for depreciation. The latter does not in itself affect the cash balance as is obvious if we work through year 1 of this example on a worksheet:

Worksheet showing year 1 of Toni's business

	Cash	Van	Owner's equity	Profit & loss	Depreciation
Start	1000	4000	5000		
Sales	6000			6000	
Expenses	−3000			−3000	
Depreciation				−1000	1000
Withdrawal	−2000			−2000	
Balance	2000	4000	5000	0	1000

As you can see the depreciation charge does not affect the cash column in any way. You will also have noticed that the way in which we have dealt with the accounting for the other side of the charge to the profit and loss account is the same as when we created a provision for doubtful debts.

An alternative way of dealing with depreciation on a worksheet is to reduce the asset column by the depreciation. If we did this our worksheet would appear as shown below. We would, however, recommend that wherever possible the worksheet should include a separate column for depreciation as this adds to the clarity and allows one to identify roughly how far through its useful life the asset is at the end of the year. In our example we can see that it cost £4000 and £1000 depreciation has been charged so we know we are a quarter of the way through its estimated useful life. This of course assumes that we know either the useful life or the rate of depreciation being used. In fact we will know one of these – probably the rate of depreciation – from the notes to the accounts where the method and rates of depreciation are required to be disclosed by SSAP 12.

Alternative worksheet of Toni's business for year 1

	Cash	Van	Owner's equity	Profit & loss
Start	1000	4000	5000	
Sales	6000			6000
Expenses	−3000			−3000
Depreciation		−1000		−1000
Withdrawal	−2000			−2000
Balance	2000	3000	5000	0

This is the cost of the fixed asset less the total depreciation to date. In certain cases, such as buildings, where the asset has been revalued, the written down value is the valuation less the total depreciation to date.

In the example of Toni's business we have assumed that the cost should be spread evenly over the life of the asset. This is known as straight line depreciation and is one of a number of alternative methods that can be used as the basis for providing depreciation. Each of these alternatives will give a different figure for the depreciation charge for the year and as a result the 'written down value', often also referred to as the 'net book value', will change. This is illustrated in more detail in Example 9.6 after our discussion of methods of depreciation. Before going on to that discussion it is worth refreshing your memories on what 'written down value' is through Key Concept 9.3.

Methods of depreciation

There are a number of alternative methods of depreciation. The choice of the appropriate method, at least theoretically, would depend upon the nature of the asset being depreciated. In practice, however, the only methods in common usage are the straight line method and the reducing balance method, and the former is used by the vast majority of businesses. The reason for this is probably to do with simplicity of calculation. In this regard it would be useful for you to look at the accounting policies statements in published accounts to try to ascertain the reasons underlying the choice of depreciation method. As we shall see a case can be made for using different methods for different assets or classes of assets. It may be the fact that assets are put into broad categories that account for the predominance of straight line depreciation in practice.

Straight line method

We have already seen, in Example 9.5, that this is a very simple method which may also explain why so many companies use it. The assumption, with regard to asset life, that underlies the choice of this method is that the asset usage is equal for all periods of its useful life. The way in which the depreciation charge is calculated is to take the cost of the asset less the estimate of any residual value at the end of the asset life and divide it by the useful life of the asset. Thus an asset which cost £130 and which has an estimated life of four years and an estimated scrap value of £10 would be depreciated by £30 per year. This was arrived at by using the formula:

$$\frac{\text{Cost} - \text{Residual value}}{\text{Useful life}}$$

In our case this works out as follows:

$$\frac{£130 - £10}{4} = £30 \text{ per annum}$$

Reducing balance method

This method assumes that the asset declines more in the earlier years of the asset life than in the later years. In fact it is likely that in most cases the cost of repairs would rise as the asset gets older so this method when combined with the cost of repairs is more likely to produce a more even cost of using an asset over its full life. It is less frequently used than the straight line method probably because it is slightly more difficult to calculate, although with the increasing use of computers this should not really cause any problems. The method applies a pre-calculated percentage to the written down value, or net book value, to ascertain the charge for the year. In order to arrive at the percentage we use the following formula:

$$\text{Rate of depreciation} = 1 - \sqrt[\text{Useful life}]{\frac{\text{Scrap value}}{\text{Cost of asset}}}$$

Comparison of the two methods

This is best illustrated through an example.

Example 9.6
Let us assume a situation where a business has an asset which has an estimated useful life of three years, cost £20 000 and has an estimated scrap, or residual, value of £4000.

For the straight line method we need to depreciate at £5333 a year, i.e.

$$\frac{20\,000 - 4000}{3} = £5333 \text{ per annum}$$

For the reducing balance method we first need to find the rate of depreciation to apply. In this case it will be 41.5 per cent which we arrive at by using the formula above.

$$\text{Rate of depreciation} = 1 - \sqrt[3]{\frac{£4000}{£20\,000}}$$
$$= 0.415 \text{ or } 41.5\%$$

This rate is then applied to the net book value, i.e. the cost less depreciation to date.

The results of using both methods are set out below and should be read with the commentary that follows.

Year	Straight line method		Profit & loss	Reducing balance method		Profit & loss
	Balance sheet			Balance sheet		
	Cost	20 000		Cost	20 000	
1	Depreciation	5 333	5333	Depreciation	8 300	8300
	Net book value	14 667		Net book value	11 700	
	Cost	20 000		Cost	20 000	
2	Depreciation	10 666	5333	Depreciation	13 160	4860
	Net book value	9 334		Net book value	6 840	
	Cost	20 000		Cost	20 000	
3	Depreciation	16 000	5334	Depreciation	16 000	2840
	Net book value	4 000		Net book value	4 000	

As can be seen from the example the charge to the profit and loss account in each year and the accumulated depreciation in the balance sheet is quite different under the two methods, although both methods charge, in total, the same amount and come to the same residual value.

Under the straight line method the charge to the profit and loss is £5333 each year so the accumulated depreciation rises at £5333 a year.

Under the reducing balance method the charge to the profit and loss is based on 41.5 per cent of the balance at the end of the previous year. Thus in year one it is 41.5 per cent of £20 000, in year two it is 41.5 per cent of £11 700 and in year three 41.5 per cent of £6840.

As we have said both methods achieve the same result in the end as under both methods the asset is written down to its residual value at the end of year 3. It is the incidence of the charge to the profit and loss account which varies, not the total charged. Whilst in theory the choice of depreciation should be governed by the nature of the asset and the way in which the benefit is used up, in practice little, if any, attention is paid to this. However, it is worth spending some time discussing when each method would be appropriate.

We have said that the straight line method implies that the benefit is used up in an even pattern over the asset's useful life. This suggests that it is time that is the governing factor rather than use. Only in a situation where there is no growth in output would a machine be used evenly throughout its useful life. In the case of a machine therefore it would seem that the straight line method would not be appropriate. On the other hand, if we think of a building, the fabric of the building is likely to erode as a result of the passage of time rather than use and for this asset the straight line method would seem more appropriate.

For assets where the reduction in the useful life relates to usage, the question that arises is: what method should we use? There is, in fact, no generally accepted method that relates depreciation directly to use. However, it could be argued that the reducing balance method is more appropriate in these situations as it charges more in the earlier years when the machine or vehicle is likely to give the most benefit in terms of trouble-free use. In most cases the cost of establishing precisely how long a machine will run or a car will last is likely to be greater than the benefit to be gained from having a more accurate depreciation charge. However,

CASE 9.1

DEPRECIATION

In many cases the accounting policies notes with respect to depreciation do not provide much information beyond the method of depreciation used and the fact that the assets are depreciated over their useful lives. However, the examples below from British Gas Plc and Bentalls Plc do provide more than the minimum information. You may notice however that whilst Bentalls Plc judges the useful life of its building to be 100 years, British Gas Plc uses a maximum of 50 years as the useful life of its buildings.

Extract from the 1992 accounts of Bentalls Plc
Tangible Fixed Assets
The policy of the directors is to review the depreciation of all assets and continue to write down the cost to the estimated residual value by equal annual instalments over the estimated useful life of each asset as follows:

Freehold land	– No depreciation
Freehold buildings	– 100 years
Long leaseholds	– 100 years or the remaining period of the lease whichever is the shorter
Short leaseholds	– remaining period of lease
Fixtures, plant, machinery and vehicles	– 5 to 25 years

Completion of the development at Kingston later in 1992 will result in the receipt of rental income and depreciation charges on the freehold buildings on the Kingston site occupied by the company.

Extract from the 1991 accounts of British Gas Plc
Depreciation. Freehold land is not depreciated. Other tangible fixed assets, except exploration and production assets, are depreciated on a straight-line basis at rates sufficient to write off the current replacement cost of individual assets over their estimated useful lives.

The depreciation periods for the principal categories of UK assets are as follows:

Distribution mains	55 years	Gas storage	40 years
Freehold and leasehold buildings	up to 50 years	Services	35 years
		Meters	20 years
Transmission pipelines	48 years	Plant and machinery	5 to 20 years
National transmission system	43 years	Motor vehicles and office equipment	5 years

Exploration and production assets are depreciated from the commencement of production in the fields concerned, using the unit

Continued from previous page

of production method based on the proved developed reserves of those fields excepting that a basis of total proved reserves is used for acquired interests. Changes in these estimates are dealt with prospectively.

The depreciation lives of the assets of Consumers' vary from 9 to 56 years for utility plant and 4 to 38 years for other equipment.

methods based on establishing the potential of an asset have been used as is evident from the extract from the British Gas Plc annual report reproduced in Case 9.1.

Revaluation of fixed assets

Over the last thirty or more years the price of land and buildings have risen virtually every year. Given the fact that these assets have a long life, their inclusion in the balance sheet at historic cost is likely to seriously understate their value. Thus, in recent years, there have been more and more cases where these assets are shown at valuation rather than cost and this is now the norm rather than the exception. The reluctance to show land and buildings in the balance sheet at a figure that seriously under-states their value is understandable given the profits made in the 1960s by asset strippers who bought up businesses at a cheap price solely to realize the value of the property through selling the land and buildings. In general there is no problem with the use of valuation. However, the recent exposure draft on the recognition of fixed assets states that where a fixed asset is carried at a valuation that value should be measured 'with reliability'.

For our purposes we need to understand the way in which these revaluations are dealt with in the accounts and the reasons for that treatment.

In all cases of revaluation the asset account is increased by the amount of the revaluation. However, in order for the balance sheet to balance there needs to be another entry. We cannot use the profit and loss account because to recognize this gain which is at present unrealized would be in contravention of the prudence and realization principles. We therefore create another reserve, known as the revaluation reserve, in which we can record the difference between the valuation and the historic cost, written down value or the last valuation as appropriate. Once again a simple example will serve to illustrate the point.

Example 9.7
A business decided to have its land and buildings valued and the land was found to be worth £50 000 and the buildings £60 000. The owners decided that this should be reflected in the accounts. The balance sheet before the revaluation was:

Balance sheet before revaluation

Fixed assets	Cost £	Depreciation £	Net book value £
Land	20 000		20 000
Buildings	40 000	10 000	30 000
	60 000	10 000	50 000
Current assets			
Bank		7 000	
		7 000	
Net current assets			7 000
			57 000
Financed by			£
Owners' equity			30 000
Retained profits			27 000
			57 000

Before we show how to deal with the revaluations on a worksheet, it is worth reflecting on the difference between the land and buildings as shown on the balance sheet above. You will notice that, whereas the land has no depreciation, the buildings have been depreciated by £10 000. This is in fact in line with the requirements of SSAP 12 and was the subject of some controversy when the standard was introduced as many leading business people were unconvinced that buildings should be depreciated at all. They argued strongly that the value was in fact increasing in the same way as the value of the land was increasing. The thinking behind the standard's requirements is that buildings do wear out over time. If you think about the rent you would pay for an office in a brand new office block as compared to an office in an older block you will realize that you have to pay more for the new block. This is a reflection of the fact that the older building has lost some of its value, or used up some of its useful life.

For our purposes, if we accept the arguments underlying the SSAP's requirements, we then need to know how the buildings in our example are being depreciated. We will assume that the buildings are depreciated over 40 years using straight line depreciation. This means that they have 30 years' life left which is important for calculating future years' depreciation charges. We shall first consider what the situation would be if the land alone was revalued and then move on to deal with the revaluation of the building.

Worksheet – land revaluation only

	Bank	Land	Buildings	Owners' equity	Profit & loss	Depreciation	Revaluation reserve
Balances	7000	20 000	40 000	40 000	21 000	10 000	
Revaluation		30 000					30 000
Balances	7000	50 000	40 000	40 000	21 000	10 000	30 000

As you can see all that we have done is to put £30 000 in a new account called a revaluation reserve and increase our asset – land – by £30 000. If we now look at the building which is valued at £60000 and which is carried in the books at £30000, i.e. £40000 less the depreciation to date (known as accumulated depreciation) of £10000, the new worksheet will be as follows:

Worksheet – land and building revaluation

	Bank	Land	Buildings	Owners' equity	Profit & loss	Depreciation	Revaluation reserve
Balances	7000	20000	40000	40000	21000	10000	
Revaluation		30000					30000
Balances	7000	50000	40000	40000	21000	10000	30000
Revaluation –						−10000	10000
building			20000				20000
Balances	7000	50000	60000	40000	21000	0	60000

You can see that what we have done is to transfer the accumulated depreciation to the revaluation reserve and then to revalue the building from its original cost to its new value. The depreciation charge for next year will be based on that new value of £60000 and the remaining useful life of 30 years. The balance sheet after the revaluation will be:

Balance sheet after revaluations

Fixed assets	Depreciation	Net book value
£	£	£
Land	50000		50000
Buildings	60000	0	60000
	110000	0	110000
Current assets			
Bank		7000	
		7000	
Net current assets			7000
			117000
Financed by			£
Owners' equity			30000
Retained profits			27000
Revaluation reserve			60000
			117000

You will notice that the revaluation reserve is kept separate from the profit and loss account as the latter is realized gains whereas the former is unrealized gains. Another change which is not so obvious is the removal of the heading cost over the fixed assets as they are no longer at cost. This fact must be reflected in the notes to the accounts.

Sale of fixed assets

Before leaving the discussion of fixed assets and depreciation we should examine the situation that arises when we sell a fixed asset. It should be obvious from our discussion above that the net book value of the asset, i.e. the cost less depreciation to date, is unlikely to bear any resemblance to the market price of that asset. This means that when an asset is sold the selling price will either be less than or exceed the net book value and a paper loss or profit will arise. If, for example, we sold the asset in Example 9.6 at the end of year 2 for £8000, then under the straight line method there would be a paper loss of £1334, i.e. the net book value of £9334 compared with the proceeds of £8000. On the other hand, if we had been using the reducing balance method we would show a paper profit of £1160, i.e. the net book value of £6840 compared to the sale proceeds of £8000. We have referred to these as paper profits and losses because what they really are is the difference between our estimate of the future benefit being used up and the actual benefit used up. In other words they are a measure of the error in our estimates which of course cannot be treated as a prior year adjustment even though that is what they relate to as they do not meet the criteria laid down in SSAP 6 *Extraordinary Items and Prior Year Adjustments*. We shall now look at the way in which the disposal of an fixed asset is treated using the worksheet to illustrate the effect on the profit and loss account and the balance sheet.

Example 9.8
A business bought an asset for £15 000. It estimated the useful life as three years and the scrap, or residual, value as £3000.

The business uses straight line depreciation. For the purposes of illustration we shall assume that its sales are £14 000 a year and the total expenses are £9000 each year for years 1 and 2. We shall also assume that at the end of year 2 it sold the fixed asset for £6000.

Solution
The depreciation charge calculated using the formula given earlier is £4000 a year.

Worksheet

Year 1	Cash	Asset	Disposal	Owners' equity	Profit & loss	Depreciation
Asset	−15 000	15 000				
Sales	14 000				14 000	
Expenses	−9 000				−9 000	
Depreciation					−4 000	4 000
Balance	−10 000	15 000		0	1 000	4 000
Year 2						
Sales	14 000				14 000	
Expenses	−9 000				−9 000	
Depreciation					−4 000	4 000
Balance	−5 000	15 000		0	2 000	8 000
Asset		−15 000	15 000			
Depreciation			−8 000			−8 000
Sale proceeds	6 000		−6 000			
	1 000	0	1 000	0	2 000	0
Loss on sale			−1 000		−1 000	
Final balance	1 000	0	0	0	1 000	0

You will notice when you look at the worksheet that the full depreciation is charged both in year 1 and in year 2. The reason for this is that the asset was used for the full year in both years. If it had been used for less than a full year then to be correct we would have needed to time apportion the charge. In practice, because businesses own many assets which are constantly changing they often adopt a policy of depreciating fully in the year of purchase or of sale irrespective of when the asset was bought or sold. However, in our example this is not a problem as it is at the end of year 2, having used the asset for the full year, that we decide to sell the asset. As you can see this involves a number of entries on our worksheet which we will examine in turn.

For clarity we have opened a separate account in our worksheet which we have called a 'Disposal' account. An alternative way would have been to deal with all the entries in the fixed asset column but that is more difficult to follow. First, as we have sold the asset we need to transfer the cost and any associated depreciation to a disposal column. We receive some cash in exchange for the asset so we show the cash in our cash column and in our disposal column. This leaves us with a balance on our disposal column of £1000 which is the amount of the paper loss we have made. This paper loss is transferred to the profit and loss account.

Our worksheet once again shows the correct position as we have no asset or depreciation associated with an asset. The profit to date is reduced by £1000 because of the underestimate or paper loss in respect of the use of the asset for the two years.

The alternative way of dealing with the disposal on a worksheet is as follows.

Note: The worksheet given below starts from the balances at the end of year 2 after the depreciation for the year has been charged but before the disposal of the asset has been dealt with. The major difference is that instead of opening a new account to deal with the disposal all the entries are put through the existing accounts.

Worksheet – alternative presentation

	Cash	Asset	Owners' equity	Profit & loss	Depreciation
Balance	−5000	15 000	0	2000	8000
Depreciation		−8 000			−8 000
Sale proceeds	6000	−6 000			
	1000	1 000	0	2000	0
Loss on sale		−1 000		−1000	
Final balance	1000	0	0	1000	0

Some find this latter format easier to follow and work with. The choice of which way the entries are put on the worksheet is in fact irrelevant – it is the principle involved that is important.

Before leaving the topic we should briefly consider how the profit or loss could be disclosed. In Chapter 7 we introduced the idea of exceptional and extraordinary items as defined by SSAP 6 *Extraordinary Items and Prior Year Adjustments*. It may be that because of the size of the gain or loss on the sale of fixed assets or the nature of the disposal it

CASE 9.2

FIXED ASSETS

The extract from the notes to the accounts of Guinness Plc provides a useful illustration of the content of a note to the accounts in respect of fixed assets. You will note that it includes acquisitions of fixed assets, disposals and revaluations.

14. Tangible fixed assets

	Land and buildings £m	Plant and machinery £m	Casks, containers and road vehicles £m	Total £m
Cost or valuation				
At 1 January 1989	486	543	131	1160
Capital expenditure	25	66	26	117
Revaluation	165	–	–	165
Acquisitions	–	3	6	9
Disposals	(9)	(26)	(16)	(51)
Distillers fair value accounting review (Note 11)	27	24	–	51
Exchange adjustments	18	43	12	73
At 31 December 1989	712	653	159	1524
Depreciation				
At 1 January 1989	32	175	33	240
Charge for year	12	46	16	74
Revaluation	(37)	–	–	(37)
Disposals	(1)	(19)	(12)	(32)
Exchange adjustments	1	17	9	27
At 31 December 1989	7	219	46	272
Net book amount				
At 31 December 1989	705	434	113	1252
At 31 December 1988	454	368	98	920

will fall under one of these headings. If not, then it would be put through the current year's profit and loss account and, if material, disclosed in the notes to the accounts. In any case the acquisitions and sales of fixed assets during the year will be disclosed in the note to the balance sheet in respect of fixed assets as Case 9.2 illustrates.

Summary

In this chapter we have re-introduced the definitions of assets and of fixed assets, and examined some of the problems associated with arriving at the cost of a fixed asset and estimating the useful life and the residual value. We have also considered the nature of depreciation and why it is charged to the profit and loss account together with the way in which it is treated in the balance sheet. We have seen that there are two methods of depreciation in common usage and examined the differences between these and the effects on the profit and loss account and the balance sheet. Finally we have discussed and illustrated the way in which a revaluation and a sale of a fixed asset is dealt with via the worksheet and how a revaluation is reflected in the balance sheet.

References

Statement of Standard Accounting Practice 6 (1986) *Extraordinary Items and Prior Year Adjustments*, Accounting Standards Committee.
Statement of Standard Accounting Practice 12 (1987) *Accounting for Depreciation*, Accounting Standards Committee.
Statement of Standard Accounting Practice 21 (1984) *Accounting for Leases and Hire Purchase*, Accounting Standards Committee.

Further reading

A fuller treatment of alternative methods of depreciation can be found in *Accounting and Finance: A firm foundation*, by Alan Pizzey (Cassell, 1990) or in *Modern Financial Accounting* by G.A. Lee (Van Nostrand Reinhold, 1986).

A full discussion on depreciation can be found in *Depreciating Assets: An Introduction* by W.T. Baxter (Gee & Co., 1980).

Review questions

1. What is the purpose of depreciation?

2. Why is it unlikely that depreciation will provide for replacement of the fixed asset?

3. What factors need to be taken into account in determining the useful life of an asset?

4. On what basis do we decide what should and should not be included in the cost of a fixed asset?

5. Describe what is meant by the net book value and the written down value of an asset.

6. What are the assumptions underlying the two main methods of depreciation?

7. An expense has been defined as a past or expired benefit. In what way does depreciation differ from other expenses?

8. In the chapter we described the profit or loss arising on the disposal of a fixed asset as a paper profit or loss. Explain how this profit differs from that arising on the sale of stock.

Problems for discussion and analysis

1. In each of the following situations discuss the most appropriate method of depreciation giving reasons for your choice.

   Land and buildings. The land was purchased for £300 000 and £400 000 was spent on the erection of the factory and office accommodation.

   Motor vehicles. The business owns a fleet of cars and delivery vans all of which were bought from new. The owners have decided to trade in the vehicles for new models after four years or 60 000 miles, whichever is sooner. The anticipated mileage figures are 12 000 miles per annum for the cars and 20 000 miles per annum for the vans.

   Plant and machinery. The plant and machinery owned by the business can be broadly classified into three types as follows:

   Type 1. Highly specialist machinery used for supplying roller bearings to Manicmotors Ltd. The contract for supply is for five years, after which it may be renewed at the option of Manicmotors; the renewal would be on an annual basis. The machinery is so specialist that it cannot be used for any other purpose. It has an expected useful life of ten years and the residual value is likely to be negligible.

   Type 2. Semi-specialist machinery which is expected to be productive for ten years and have a residual value of 10 per cent of its original cost. However, other firms operating similar machines have found that after the first three years it becomes increasingly more costly in terms of repairs and maintenance to keep machinery of this type productive.

   Type 3. General purpose machinery which has an estimated useful life of 80 000 running hours. Based on present levels of production the usage is 8000 hours a year but as from next year this is expected to rise to 12 000 hours a year if the sales forecasts are correct.

2. Notafewl's draft balance sheet at 31 March 1992 is given below. During the year to 31 March 1992 the business made a profit of £20 000 before depreciation had been charged and before dealing with items 1 to 3 below.

   Item 1   On 30 September 1991 a new car had been acquired at a cost of £6000. The amount has been included under the fixed asset total but no depreciation has been charged.

   Item 2   The freehold property was revalued on 1 April 1991 and the values are still to be reflected in the accounts. The valuations were Land £50 000 and Buildings £60 000.

   Item 3   On 31 March 1992 some of the machinery was sold for £7000. The cheque from the purchaser was banked on that day but is not reflected in the bank balance as no accounting entries have been made in respect of this sale. At 31 March 1991 the machinery sold was recorded at cost of £20 000 and had accumulated depreciation of £12 000.

   Notafewl follows the following accounting policies in respect of depreciation:

   Land   – not depreciated.
   Buildings   – 4% per annum straight line.
   Machinery   – 20% per annum straight line.
   Cars   – 25% per annum straight line.

In the year of acquisition or disposal assets are depreciated on a time apportionment basis.

Draft balance sheet of Notafewl at 31 March 1992

Fixed assets	Cost	Depreciation	Net book value
	£	£	£
Land	20 000		20 000
Buildings	50 000	20 000	30 000
Machinery	40 000	24 000	16 000
Cars	30 000	12 000	18 000
	140 000	56 000	84 000
Current assets			
Bank		18 000	
		18 000	
Net current assets			18 000
			102 000
Financed by			£
Owners' equity			30 000
Retained profits			52 000
Profit for year			20 000
			102 000

(a) Discuss, with reference to appropriate accounting principles and standards, the way in which each of the items above should be treated.

(b) Make appropriate accounting entries on a worksheet, calculate the revised profit for the year ended 31 March 1992 and extract a revised balance sheet at that date.

3. Using a worksheet draw up the balance sheet and profit and loss account for the business whose transactions are set out below:

Month 1   Bert put in £9000 of his own money and transferred his own car into the name of the business. At the time of the transfer it would have cost £6000 to buy a new model of the same car but as the car was one year old its second-hand value was only £4000.

The business then bought a machine for £4000, paying for this in cash, and at the same time bought a second machine on credit terms. The credit terms were a deposit of £1000 which was paid in cash and two equal instalments of £900 payable at the start of month four and seven respectively. The cash price of the machine was £2500.

Month 2   Bought raw materials for £3000 and paid cash and also made cash sales of £3000.

Month 3   Paid rent in arrears for the three months amounting to £600 in cash. Paid wages of £1500 for the three months to date.

Made cash sales of £4000 and purchased more raw materials again for cash amounting to £2000.

Month 4   Paid instalment on machine of £900 in cash and made cash sales of £4000.

Months 5 to 7

Bought raw materials for cash for £2000 and made cash sales of £5000; paid wages for three months of £1500, the rent for three months of £600 and the second and final instalment on the machine of £900.

Months 8 to 12

Made cash sales of £14 000, bought raw materials for cash for £6000, paid wages for six months of £3000 and paid rent for three months of £600.

At the end of the year he has raw materials in stock which cost £2000. He calculates the car will last two more years after which he thinks he will be able to sell it for £400. The machines have useful lives estimated at three years and will then be sold for £100 each. Bert not being that clever with figures opts for straight line depreciation on all the fixed assets.

Investments and intangible assets | 10 |||||

In Chapter 4, we defined fixed and current assets and, at that stage, used the American term indeterminate assets to describe all other assets. In the UK, the Companies Act allows for only two classes of assets, i.e. current assets and fixed assets. In most enterprises the main fixed assets will be land and buildings, fixtures, vehicles, etc. However, enterprises also have some assets, such as investments in other businesses, that are essentially permanent in nature and could be classed as fixed assets. In addition, enterprises may have assets, such as a patent or trade mark, that are also permanent in nature, but are sufficiently different from other fixed assets such as vehicles to warrant separate discussion. These assets are referred to as intangible assets. In this chapter, we shall deal with investments, which may be classified as current assets or fixed assets, and with intangible assets.

Investments

There are two types of investment that we shall consider. These are investments in debt and investments in equity. An investment in debt is an investment in an interest-bearing security. These securities could be government bonds, corporate bonds, loan stock or the debentures of another enterprise. We shall use loan stock as a general term when discussing this type of investment. The other type of investment is an equity investment. This is where an enterprise buys part of the owners' equity of another enterprise.

Investments are purchased for a number of reasons. As we shall see, in order to assist in their classification as either fixed or current assets, it is important to ascertain the reason for an investment. If, for example, an investment is made to utilize surplus funds in the short term then it will fall under our definition of a current asset, which is reproduced as Key Concept 10.1.

A current asset is one which is either part of the operating cycle of the enterprise or is likely to be realized in the form of cash within one year.

KEY CONCEPT 10.1

CURRENT ASSET

KEY CONCEPT 10.2	An asset that is acquired for the purposes of use within the business and is likely to be used by the business for a considerable period of time.
FIXED ASSET	

However, not all investments are short-term investments. Many businesses have long-term investments, particularly equity investments, in other enterprises. These are normally held for strategic reasons. For example, if you hold a substantial part of the equity of one of your suppliers you may be able to exert pressure to obtain better terms or preferential deliveries of supplies. On the other hand, you may have invested in that supplier's equity because you wish to influence the future policy and direction of that business, or even to control that business.

If the investment is for any of those reasons, it is unlikely to meet the definition of a current asset. Assuming that we adopt a broad interpretation of the wording of the definition of a fixed asset, it would fall under our definition of a fixed asset, which is reproduced as Key Concept 10.2.

Therefore, the first thing that we have to establish with investments is the reasons for the investment and the type of investment, i.e. debt or equity, that we are dealing with. This will enable us to decide whether they fall under the definition of a current asset or a fixed asset. We shall now consider both types of investment and examine some of the accounting problems encountered in dealing with investments.

Fixed-interest investments

We shall consider the treatment of interest-bearing investments first. As we have said, from the point of view of the balance sheet, we need to be able to classify the investment as either a current asset or as a fixed asset. We then need to establish the amount at which the investment is to be included. This is not as straightforward as it appears because of the nature of interest-bearing securities and their earnings pattern. The return to the investor on interest-bearing securities is in the form of interest and this is normally paid either half yearly or yearly.

Earning the interest is a function of time. For example, if interest is payable annually in December and you buy the fixed interest investment on 1 August, it will already have earned seven months' interest, i.e. January to July. The previous owner will not get that interest as it is only paid out in December. Therefore, the price at which the investment is sold will include an amount for the seven months' interest. You will receive that interest in December as part of the twelve months' interest due to be paid at that time. Assuming that the accounting year end is December, the interest for the full twelve months cannot all be shown as revenue, as to do so would contravene the matching principle. This is because you have only held that revenue producing asset for five months, i.e. August to December. You should therefore only recognize five months' interest, i.e. the interest from the date the investment was purchased to the end of your accounting year, in your profit and loss account.

This may appear to be somewhat complex, but in fact it is reasonably straightforward as the following example will illustrate.

Example 10.1

Pringle started in business in January 1991 with £40 000 which she put in her business bank account. Her transactions, in relation to investments, for the first year to 31 December 1991 were as follows.

☐ **1 January**. Purchased £10 000, 12 per cent fixed interest loan stock in B, at a price of £10 000. Interest is payable annually on 31 December.
☐ **1 April**. Purchased another £6000, 12 per cent fixed interest loan stock in T, at a price of £6180. Interest is payable annually on 31 December.
☐ **1 May**. Purchased £4000, 9 per cent fixed interest, irredeemable loan stock in P, at a price of £3120. Interest is payable on 31 December.
☐ **On 31 December 1991** she received interest from B of £1200, interest from T of £720 and interest from P of £360.

Discussion

In the case of the first transaction, we have no problem with time apportioning the interest as we have held the investment for the full year. The investment in B cost £10 000 and the interest earned for the year is £1200. The full interest should be included in the profit and loss account as revenue for the year because the investment has been held for the whole year. We therefore include interest from B of £1200 in the profit and loss account and an asset of £10 000 in our balance sheet.

The second transaction, involving the purchase of loan stock in T, is slightly more complex. Here, the purchase price includes three months' interest. The interest on this investment is 12 per cent per annum on an investment of £6000. Therefore, three months' interest amounts to £180:

$$\text{i.e. } £6000 \times 12\% \times \frac{3}{12} \text{ months} = £180$$

Thus, the cost, excluding the interest, is £6000, i.e. £6180 − £180. The amount of interest earned by Pringle is nine months' interest, i.e. from the date of purchase to the end of the accounting year. This amounts to £540:

$$\text{i.e. } £6000 \times 12\% \times \frac{9}{12} \text{ months} = £540$$

The sum of £720 received on 31 December includes the interest for the first three months of £180, and the £540 for the remaining nine months. The £180 is, in effect, a repayment of part of the cost of the investment. It should therefore reduce the carrying value of that investment. The other £540 is interest earned for the period since acquisition, and should be included as revenue in the profit and loss account for the year.

In the case of the investment in P, the price paid on 1 May includes a payment for four months' interest at 9 per cent per annum. This amounts to £120:

$$\text{i.e. } \pounds4000 \times 9\% \times \frac{4}{12} \text{ months} = \pounds120$$

Thus the cost, excluding the interest, is £3000, i.e. £3120 − £120. The amount of interest earned by Pringle since purchasing the investment in P is eight months' interest which amounts to £240:

$$\text{i.e. } \pounds4000 \times 9\% \times \frac{8}{12} \text{ months} = \pounds240$$

The interest for the first four months of £120 and the £240 for the remaining eight months is all included in the sum of £360 received on 31 December. Therefore, the £360 has to be split between the £120 which reduces the carrying value of the investment, and the £240 interest earned since acquisition. The £240 should be included in the profit and loss account.

You should note that, in this case, Pringle only paid £3000 for £4000 of loan stock in P. The reason for the price being less is that the rate of interest offered is only 9 per cent and alternative investments yield 12 per cent. Investors would therefore only pay a price that would give them a return of 12 per cent per annum. Thus, if the annual interest payable is £360, i.e. £4000 × 9 per cent, then the amount that would be paid is £3000, i.e. the amount that would need to be invested at 12 per cent to produce interest amounting to £360 per annum. Because the loan stock in P is irredeemable the calculation of the market price is easy, as it is only affected by the rate of interest. In the case of redeemable debt the price will be affected by the time period up to redemption and the rate of interest currently ruling in the market, and, as such, the calculation is more complex.

To consolidate your understanding of the discussion above, consider the way in which the transactions have been dealt with on the worksheet below:

Worksheet of Pringle for 1991

Date	Bank	B stock	T stock	P stock	Accrued interest	Owner's equity	Profit & loss
1 Jan	20 000					20 000	
1 Jan	−10 000	10 000					
1 Apr	−6 180		6000		180		
1 May	−3 120			3000	120		
31 Dec	1 200						1200
31 Dec	720				−180		540
31 Dec	360				−120		240
Balance	2 980	10 000	6000	3000	0	20 000	1980

As you can see, when the investments are made, the amount paid is split between the cost and the accrued interest. When the interest is received it is split between that part earned by Pringle as a result of owning the loan stock, and the part that represents the accrued interest purchased with the asset. The investments are carried forward at their real cost.

You would need to make the same sort of differentiation if the loan stock was subsequently sold with accrued interest attaching to it. This would ensure that the proceeds of sale were divided between investment income in the form of interest, and any capital gain or loss that may arise on the sale of the investments. These capital gains and losses arise as a result of changes in the market rate of interest which in turn affects the value of the loan stock. For example, if the market rate of interest rose to 18 per cent then the £4000 irredeemable loan stock in P would have a market value of approximately £2000. This is arrived at by looking at how much you would have to invest at 18 per cent to earn the £360 interest that is paid each year on the loan stock in P. If Pringle sold the loan stock in P at a price of £2000 she would make a capital loss of £1000, i.e. £3000 − £2000.

Equity investments

Where a business invests in the equity of another business, the accounting treatment is essentially dependent upon the substance of the transaction and the purpose of the transaction. If, for example, you buy a controlling interest in another company, i.e. more than 50 per cent of the equity, then the company in which you have invested is treated as a subsidiary company in accordance with SSAP 14 which covers group accounts (often referred to as consolidated accounts). If your investment is not sufficient to control the other company, but is sufficient to allow you to exercise a significant influence over the policies of the company, the investment must be accounted for as an associate company in accordance with SSAP 1 *Accounting for the Results of Associated Companies*. In both these cases the detailed accounting treatment is outside the scope of this book. We shall, however, return briefly to the subject of consolidation under our discussion of goodwill later in this chapter.

We will now consider the situation where the investment is a relatively small proportion of the total equity and, as such, you have no influence over the policies of the company in which you have invested. In this case, you will receive income in the form of dividends. Dividends are paid once or twice a year depending on the decisions of the directors of the company paying the dividend. In terms of accounting for the investment and the dividends, the same issues arise as those we have discussed with fixed interest securities. The accounting treatment and the problems that may arise depend largely upon the timing of the purchase of the shares. They can be purchased before a dividend is declared and this creates no accounting problems. If they are purchased after a dividend has been declared but before it has been paid they can either be purchased cum div, i.e. with dividend, or ex div, i.e. without the dividend. If they are purchased cum div, the price paid has to be split between the cost of the shares and the payment for the dividend. This is done in the same way as we dealt with the loan stock and accrued interest. If, however, they are bought ex div no such problems arise as the dividend is paid to the previous owner and the price at which the share is traded reflects this fact.

This completes our discussion of investments and their accounting treatment. It has provided an introduction to a wide and, at times, complex area which you will undoubtedly come across again as you continue your studies. We shall now move on to consider intangible assets, what they are, and how they should be treated in the financial accounts. We shall commence with a discussion of intangible assets in general and then look in more detail at some specific intangible assets.

Intangible assets

In terms of the Companies Acts, intangible assets are seen as a class of fixed asset and should be shown separately under that heading. Intangible assets that may produce future profits could be knowledge, skill, reputation, location or other factors. As we pointed out earlier, the historic cost accounting model would exclude many of these, from the definition of an asset on the grounds that the future benefits are uncertain, i.e. applying the prudence concept, or on the grounds that no cost can be separately identified. This rather pragmatic approach relying, in the main, on prudence has been strengthened through the issue of an Exposure Draft by the Accounting Standards Committee. The exposure draft, which is a document for discussion that precedes the issue of a full accounting standard, codifies some of the existing practices. The exposure draft in question, ED 52 *Accounting for Intangible Fixed Assets*, provides a definition of an intangible asset and sets out conditions under which intangible assets should be recognized. The definition of an intangible asset given in that exposure draft is given in Key Concept 10.3.

These assets can include such thing as patents, trade marks, copyright, exploration and development costs, research and development costs, and goodwill. The latter two are the subject of separate accounting standards and we shall deal with them in more detail later in this chapter. In recent years, the question of intangible assets has been the subject of much debate. This debate largely arose because a number of major companies decided to include a value for their brand names in their balance sheets. The issue of whether brand names, such as Coca Cola, have a value and should be included as an asset caused such controversy that the accounting profession was prompted to issue some guidance on the subject of intangible assets.

The exposure draft referred to above has, to some extent, clarified the issue by suggesting some rules that should be adopted. These are that an intangible asset should only be recognized on the balance sheet if the following conditions are met:

KEY CONCEPT 10.3	'A fixed asset that is non-monetary in nature and without physical substance'.
INTANGIBLE ASSET – **A DEFINITION**	*Source*: ED 52, para. 37.

☐ either the historic costs incurred in creating the asset are known or it can be clearly demonstrated that they are readily ascertainable;

☐ its characteristics can be clearly distinguished from those of goodwill and other assets;

☐ its cost can be measured independently of goodwill, of other assets and of the earnings of the relevant business or business segment.

It should be borne in mind that an exposure draft is a document issued for discussion and its contents may change before a full accounting standard is issued. However, the contents of the exposure draft do give an indication of the way in which the profession is thinking.

Brands

Returning to the issue of accounting for brand names, the exposure draft makes it clear that the view of the Accounting Standards Committee, or Accounting Standards Board as it is currently called, is that brands cannot be separately identified as an intangible asset and that they should be treated as part of the value of the goodwill of the business. This, in effect, means that the practice of including brands on balance sheets will effectively be stopped if the exposure draft in its present form becomes a standard.

The reason for this is that, as we shall see, the accounting standard on goodwill only allows goodwill to be recognized when it is purchased, in other words when one business takes over another business. In any case, if we look at the conditions set out above, we would need to be able to identify the historic cost of creating and maintaining a brand name. This, of course, means that we have to put a figure on effective and ineffective advertising and marketing expenditure. In actual fact, those companies that have included brands in their balance sheets have generally arrived at a value for brands rather than attempting to find the historic cost, although as can be seen from Case 10.1 this is not always the case.

The exposure draft only allows an asset to be included at its fair value if the historic cost of the asset is the same as the fair value. If this is the case, it states that 'there will normally need to be an active market in intangible assets of the same kind independently of the purchase and sale of a business or business segments'. This, in effect, means that, in most circumstances, value is not acceptable and intangible assets have to be included at their historic cost.

Other intangible assets and their treatment

These may include, patents, trade marks, copyright, software, and exploration and development costs. As long as they fall within the definition and conditions set out above, they can be recognized in the balance sheet of the enterprise as intangible fixed assets. Once they are recognized as fixed assets they should be written off over their useful economic life in the same way as other fixed assets. The exposure draft suggests that the useful life should normally not exceed twenty years although, in exceptional circumstances, a life of up to forty years may be used. The

CASE 10.1

**ACCOUNTING FOR
BRAND NAMES**

The effects of the decision to include a figure for brands in the balance sheet is perhaps best illustrated by the following extract from the 1988 annual report of Rank Hovis McDougall Plc. As you can see, a comparison of the balance sheet for 1988 with that for 1987 reveals that the intangible assets have risen from £0 in 1987 to £678 million in 1988. The owners' equity had also risen in line with the rise in the intangibles from £251.6 million in 1987 to £928.2 million in 1988. Thus in effect the owners' equity had more than trebled in the year.

Note 12 to the accounts, which is shown after the balance sheets, reveals that the whole of the £678 million increase in the intangibles figure relates to brands.

Balance sheets of the Rank Hovis McDougall Plc group

	Note	1988 £m	1987 £m
Fixed assets			
Intangible assets	12	**678.0**	–
Tangible assets	13	**463.7**	422.3
Shares in subsidiary companies	14	**–**	–
Investments	15	**0.7**	3.4
		1142.4	425.7
Current assets			
Stocks	16	**184.6**	168.6
Debtors	17	**234.3**	215.6
Cash at bank and in hand	18	**65.2**	46.2
Creditors due within one year			
Borrowings	19	**(45.1)**	(53.0)
Other	19	**(347.3)**	(286.7)
Net current assets		**91.7**	90.7
Total assets less current liabilities		**1234.1**	516.4
Creditors due after more than one year			
Borrowings	20	**(139.8)**	(133.7)
Other	20	**(96.6)**	(78.6)
Provisions for liabilities and charges	21	**(19.0)**	(38.9)
		978.7	265.2
Capital and reserves			
Called up share capital	23	**93.2**	91.4
Share premium account	24	**27.5**	28.0
Revaluation reserve	25	**622.6**	24.9
Other reserves	26	**184.9**	107.3
		928.2	251.6
Minority interests		**50.5**	13.6
		978.7	265.2

Extract from Rank Hovis McDougall Plc notes to the accounts   Continued from previous page

12 INTANGIBLE ASSETS

	The Group 1988 £m	The Company 1988 £m
Brands		
At 5 September 1987	–	–
Valuation at 3 September 1988	678.0	–
At 3 September 1988	678.0	–

The Group has valued its brands at their 'current use value to the Group' at 3 September 1988 in conjunction with Interbrand Group plc. branding consultants.

This basis of valuation ignores any possible alternative use of a brand, any possible extension to the range of products currently marketed under a brand, any element of hope value and any possible increase of value of a brand due to either a special investment or a financial transaction (e.g. licensing) which would leave the Group with a different interest from the one being valued.

Note 12 above also reveals that in the case of Rank Hovis McDougall Plc the figure of £678 million is a valuation based on a 'current use value to the group', and that Interbrand Group Plc had been involved in the valuation.

By contrast, Guinness Plc in the notes to the 1991 annual accounts, extracts of which are reproduced below, reveals that the basis that it has used to arrive at a figure for brands is the historic cost. This would be more in line with the view of the Accounting Standards Board discussed in the chapter.

Interestingly, although, in both cases, no attempt is made to amortize the brands over their useful lives, there is provision for an annual review of the figure and a write down if the figure is thought to be too high.

Extract from Guinness Plc accounting policies

BRANDS

The fair value of business acquired and of interests taken in related companies includes brands, which are recognised where the brand has a value which is substantial and long term. Acquired brands are only recognised where title is clear, brand earnings are separately identifiable, the brand could be sold separately from the rest of the business and where the brand achieves earnings in excess of those achieved by unbranded products.

No amortisation will be provided except where the end of the useful economic life of the acquired brand can be foreseen. The useful economic lives of brands and their carrying value are subject to annual review and any amortisation or provision for permanent impairment would be charged against the profit for the period in which they arose.   Continued over page

Continued from previous page

Extract from Guinness Plc notes to the accounts

13. ACQUIRED BRANDS AT COST

Acquired brands represent the historical cost of brands acquired on the purchase of businesses. The Directors have reviewed the amounts at which brands are stated and are of the opinion that there has been no impairment in the value of the brands recognised and that the end of the useful economic lives of the brands cannot be foreseen.

Another view on the subject of amortization of brands can be found in the following extract from the 1991 annual accounts of Cadbury Schweppes where the brands represent approximately one-third of the balance sheet total. As can be seen from the extract, the fact that the brands are not amortized is defended on the basis of the money spent during the year to support the brands, i.e. the advertising and marketing expenditure, and on the basis that the figure is reviewed annually. As we shall see later in the chapter, this treatment would contravene the accounting standard if it were applied to goodwill and indeed the arguments being used by Cadbury Schweppes are reminiscent of the debate that occurred at the time of the introduction of that accounting standard.

Extract from Cadbury Schweppes accounting policies

Intangibles Intangibles represent significant owned brands acquired since 1985 valued at historical cost. No amortisation is charged as the annual results reflect significant expenditure in support of these brands and the values are reviewed annually with a view to write down if a permanent diminution arises.

figures of twenty years and forty years are purely arbitrary and pragmatic responses to a problem and have no theoretical basis.

In order to be consistent with other fixed assets, the question of revaluation needed to be addressed. On this subject, the exposure draft suggests that a revaluation should only be permitted if:

☐ it is based on depreciated replacement cost and this can be measured with some certainty;
☐ depreciated replacement cost equals current cost.

We shall be looking at replacement cost and current cost in more detail in Chapter 17. However, it is worth noting here that the concern is once again with certainty and reliability rather than relevance. As we pointed out in Chapter 1, there will always be a certain amount of trade-off between these two qualitative characteristics. In terms of intangibles, the trade-off, generally, is towards reliability rather than relevance and the accounting standards on research and development and goodwill – which we shall now consider – are no exceptions.

Research and development expenditure

Research and development expenditure, exploration and development expenditure and software development costs all have some similarities. However, the accounting treatment of these items in the UK does not necessarily reflect those similarities. Of the three types of expenditure, the treatment of research and development is the most clear cut, mainly because it is laid down in SSAP 13 *Accounting for Research and Development*. The basis of the treatment is to distinguish between expenditure on pure research, on applied research and on development.

Pure research is defined as experimental or theoretical work undertaken primarily to acquire new knowledge for its own sake rather than directed towards any particular aim or application. Applied research is distinguishable by the fact that it is directed towards a specific practical aim or objective. SSAP 13, having distinguished between these two types of research, then goes on to treat them in exactly the same way, by writing off any costs related to them in the year in which the costs were incurred. This, of course, is in line with the prudence principle.

Development expenditure is defined as the use of knowledge in order to produce substantially new or substantially improved materials, products, processes or systems for commercial application. The standard, in effect, distinguishes this type of knowledge from other knowledge and says that under certain circumstances development expenditure can be classified as an asset. The circumstances laid down are very stringent and are as follows.

☐ There must be a clearly defined project.
☐ Related expenditure must be separately identifiable.
☐ The outcome must be assessed with reasonable certainty as to its technical feasibility and commercial viability.
☐ Future revenues must be reasonably expected to cover all costs including the development costs, administration costs, production and selling costs.
☐ Adequate resources must be available, or reasonably expected to be available, to complete the project.

If all the above criteria are met, the development expenditure can then be capitalized as an intangible fixed asset and depreciated over its useful life, like any other fixed asset. If the conditions are not met then the expenditure should be written off to the profit and loss account as it is incurred. The problem for many companies, especially smaller companies, is how to prove that the conditions are met. For the auditors the application of this standard has the potential to be a nightmare. How are they to judge whether a new product being developed is technically feasible or commercially viable?

SSAP 13 also contains a requirement that a company having chosen to capitalize development expenditure must apply that policy consistently to all development projects. The alternative is to choose a policy of writing off all development expenditure as it is incurred. This requirement is, of course, necessary if we are to stick to a rigid interpretation of SSAP 2 *Disclosure of Accounting Policies*, and the need for consistency.

If a company decides to capitalize all its development expenditure, it can still write off expenditure in the year that it is incurred simply by claiming that the development no longer meets the criteria. Thus a company choosing a policy of capitalization can, in effect, either capitalize or write off immediately according to the particular circumstances of each project and still be consistent in its accounting policy. On the other hand, it would appear that a company, which chooses a policy of immediate write off in the year the expenditure is incurred would have to do that on all projects irrespective of the particular circumstances, or change its accounting policy.

Thus, to sum up, the accounting treatment of development expenditure as suggested by the standard is either to write it off immediately or to capitalize it if it meets certain conditions. Once a policy is chosen it should be applied consistently. In the case of those companies choosing an immediate write off policy, based upon a project currently being undertaken, they must apply that policy consistently, irrespective of the underlying economic substance. The alternative policy allows more flexibility. However, in order to capitalize development expenditure, conditions of near certainty have to be met. This is perhaps an extreme example of the prudence principle being applied.

We commented at the start of this section that there are many similarities between research and development expenditure and the exploration and development cost incurred by oil companies. There are also similarities with the development costs incurred in designing and developing new computer software. However, as there is no accounting standard covering either of these other areas the accounting treatment is largely at the whim of the company involved.

CASE 10.2	It is interesting to compare the accounting policies adopted in respect of research and development expenditure and in respect of exploration and development expenditure as it would appear that these two types of expenditure are very similar in nature. In the case of British Gas Plc the accounting policies adopted are shown in the following extract from the 1991 Annual Report. It is worth noting that the research and development expenditure for 1991 was £86 million and is therefore a material amount in relation to the profit of British Gas Plc.

RESEARCH AND DEVELOPMENT

Extracts from the accounting policies of British Gas Plc

Research and development expenditure
Research and development expenditure is written off when incurred.

Exploration expenditure
Exploration expenditure is accounted for in accordance with the successful efforts method. Under this method exploration and development expenditure is capitalised as an intangible fixed asset when incurred and certain expenditure, such as geological and geophysical exploration costs, is expensed. A review is carried out, at

Continued from previous page

least annually, on a field by field basis to ascertain whether proved reserves have been discovered. When proved reserves are determined the relevant expenditure is transferred to tangible fixed assets. Expenditure deemed to be unsuccessful is written off to the profit and loss account.

Prior to 1 April 1990 exploration and development expenditure was capitalised as a tangible fixed asset. Comparative figures have been restated.

Another example of the different treatment is provided by the following extract from the accounting policies of British Petroleum Plc.

Extracts from the accounting policies of British Petroleum Plc

Exploration expenditure

Exploration expenditure is accounted for in accordance with the successful efforts method. Exploration expenditure is initially classified as an intangible fixed asset. When proved reserves of oil and gas or commercially exploitable reserves of minerals are determined and development is sanctioned, the relevant expenditure is transferred to tangible production assets. All exploration expenditure determined as unsuccessful is charged against income. Exploration leasehold acquisition costs are amortised over the estimated period of exploration.

Exploration costs incurred under production-sharing contracts are classified as loans within fixed asset investments. Provisions are initially made against these loans in accordance with the successful efforts method. On the determination of proved oil and gas reserves in contract areas provisions against expenditures, which are recoverable under contracts from future production, are written back to income.

Depreciation

Oil and minerals production assets are depreciated using a unit-of-production method based upon estimated proved reserves. Other tangible and intangible assets are depreciated on the straight line method over their estimated useful lives.

Research

Expenditure on research is written off in the year in which it is incurred.

It is interesting to speculate whether the accounting policies in respect of exploration and development would change if a standard such as SSAP 13, which as we have pointed out relies heavily on prudence, was brought in.

Goodwill is the difference between the value of a business as a whole
and the aggregate of the fair value of its separable net assets.

Having looked at research and development, the other major area of
intangibles that we shall examine is the accounting treatment of goodwill.
Not only is goodwill potentially important in its own right, it also has
implications for other intangible assets. This is because, as we have seen,
one of the conditions that had to be met for these other intangible assets
to be shown as fixed assets is that the cost could be measured independently of goodwill.

Goodwill

Goodwill is basically the difference between what a business as a whole is
worth and the sum of its individual net assets. Once again, this is a fairly
contentious area in accounting and it is covered by an accounting standard issued in 1984 and revised in 1989. In addition, there is currently an
exposure draft on the subject which proposes some fairly radical changes
to the present accounting standard. The definition of goodwill given in
SSAP 22 *Accounting for Goodwill* is shown in Key Concept 10.4. Note
that separable assets are those that can be identified and sold separately
without disposing of the business as a whole. They may, in fact, include
other intangible assets.

The accounting standard separates goodwill into two categories, i.e.
purchased goodwill and non-purchased goodwill. Purchased goodwill, as
the name implies, arises when one business purchases another. Non-
purchased goodwill is all other goodwill. This is also sometimes referred
to as inherent goodwill. The accounting treatment for non-purchased
goodwill is that it should not be included in the accounts at all. This is, of
course, in line with the prudence principle. Purchased goodwill, on the
other hand, can be written off immediately or it can be capitalized.
A company chooses between the two alternatives for each acquisition.
Having made the choice, that becomes its accounting policy which must
be consistently applied in respect of that particular acquisition.

The alternatives are, as we have pointed out, to write off goodwill
immediately or to capitalize it. In terms of the first alternative of an
immediate write off, this write off is direct to reserves. This means that
no transactions go through the profit and loss account and, as such,
the bottom line is unaffected. However, the adoption of this treatment
amounts to saying that the price paid for an acquisition was in fact more
than the business was worth. The goodwill is, in effect, being treated as
having no value. In other words no future benefit will be derived from it.

The alternative treatment is to capitalize the goodwill, show it as an
intangible fixed asset in the balance sheet, and write it off over its useful

economic life. This treatment recognizes that there is a future benefit to be derived from the goodwill and that this benefit has a finite economic life. Some commentators have argued that, in fact, goodwill does not necessarily have a finite life as the purchased goodwill is constantly being replaced and replenished through expenditure on advertising etc. The supporters of this view would argue that the asset should be capitalized but not amortized. However, this view was explicitly rejected when the accounting standard was issued.

SSAP 22 is slightly unusual as an accounting standard because although it identifies two alternative treatments, it actually recommends that one should 'normally' be followed. Most accounting standards are not so prescriptive – for example the standard on stock allows three different alternatives. The treatment that is recommended for goodwill is that the policy of immediate write off should 'normally' be followed. This is interesting, as it represents a view that goodwill is not an asset but some sort of anomaly that is best got rid of as quickly and quietly as possible. If we look at the definition of an asset we have been working with, reproduced as Key Concept 10.5, we can see that there is no reason, assuming that the purchasing company acts rationally, why goodwill should not accord with that definition.

It would appear that the two accounting treatments proposed in the standard arise as a result of different views of the nature of goodwill. The Accounting Standards Committee, in the original SSAP 22 and its subsequent revision, come down firmly on the side of immediate write off, which is in line with the prudence principle. This would imply that the ASC does not view goodwill as an asset. However, in its latest exposure draft on the subject of goodwill, ED 47 issued in 1990, the use of the immediate write off policy is ruled out and it is recommended that goodwill should be capitalized and written off over its useful life. This represents a complete reversal of the previous recommendation. Whether that will be the view adopted in a revised standard only time will tell.

Goodwill and consolidated accounts

As we indicated earlier, we shall briefly examine consolidated accounts and the treatment of goodwill in consolidated accounts. Consolidated accounts are in fact a massive area of study on which whole books have been written. However, we shall keep our discussion to a very elementary level. For our purposes we can assume that when one company owns more than 50 per cent of the equity of another company it will produce

| Embodiments of present or future economic benefits or service potentials measurable in terms of monetary units, accruing to the enterprise as a result of economic events, the enjoyment of which by the enterprise is secured by law. | KEY CONCEPT 10.5

 DEFINITION OF AN ASSET |

CASE 10.3

GOODWILL

In general goodwill is written off to reserves as the extract from the 1989 annual accounts of Cadbury Schweppes, reproduced below, illustrates. However, in this case, it is interesting to contrast the wording of the accounting policies statement in respect of goodwill with that in respect of brands which we included in Case 10.1. Clearly Cadbury Schweppes views these two intangibles in quite different ways. However, it would appear from the wording of the note in respect of goodwill that given that all assets, tangible and intangible, are included in the accounts at their fair value, the goodwill is in effect an excess price paid in order to gain control. Arguably therefore, it should not be written off to reserves but should go through the profit and loss account as it would seem to have no value and this fact would be more adequately disclosed that way.

Extract from the accounting policies of Cadbury Schweppes

d) Acquisition of subsidiaries   Results of subsidiary undertakings acquired during the financial year are included in group profit from the effective date of acquisition and those of undertakings disposed of up to the effective date of disposal. For this purpose the net assets, both tangible and intangible, of newly acquired subsidiaries are incorporated into the accounts on the basis of the fair value to the group as at the effective date of acquisition.

Goodwill, being any excess of the consideration over that fair value, is written off against reserves on consolidation.

Extract from the notes to the accounts of Cadbury Schweppes

19 Capital and Reserves (continued)   **(e) Movements on reserves – Group**

	Revaluation reserve £m	Retained profits £m	Share premium £m
At beginning of year	95.8	115.8	381.6
Exchange rate adjustments	0.3	(0.3)	–
Premium on shares issued in year	–	–	12.2
Retained profit for year	–	106.2	–
Goodwill on acquisitions	9.9	(15.1)	–
Revaluation adjustments	(1.3)	–	–
Realised on disposals	(3.8)	–	–
Transfers	(1.0)	1.0	–
Other	–	(0.5)	–
At end of year	99.9	207.1	393.8

The total goodwill written off on business continuing within the Group amounts to £762.3 m, of which £633.3 m has been written off since 3 January 1988.

group accounts and that these will be in the form of consolidated accounts. To illustrate how consolidated accounts work we shall look at a very simple example and we shall then look at a slightly more complex example to illustrate some points regarding goodwill.

Example 10.2
Assume Company A buys all the shares in Company B for £120 and that Company A and Company B have the following balance sheets. As Company A owns all the equity in Company B, which is referred to as its subsidiary, it is required to produce consolidated accounts.

Balance sheets of Company A and Company B

	Company A	Company B
Investment in B	120	
Sundry net assets	80	100
	200	100
Ordinary shares	200	100
	200	100

In order to produce the consolidated balance sheet of Company A and its subsidiary, we need to add the sundry net assets together and set off the cost of the investment against the shares we purchased. However, we find that the cost of the investment is more than the assets purchased, which are represented by the ordinary shares. The difference is the goodwill we purchased. In this case it amounts to £20, i.e. £120 − £100. This goodwill is included on the consolidated balance sheet in the same way as any other asset. The consolidated balance sheet would appear as follows:

Consolidated balance sheet of Company A and its subsidiary

Goodwill	20
Sundry net assets	180
	200
Ordinary shares	200
	200

As you can see the goodwill is included as an asset at £20. The sundry net assets figure of £180 is arrived at simply by adding the sundry net assets in Company B to the sundry net assets in Company A. The other side of the balance sheet shows the equity of Company A only.

This simple example illustrates how the goodwill figure is arrived at and how it would be shown in the accounts if it were capitalized. The treatment of the goodwill in this case causes no problems. However, as we shall see this is not always the case.

Example 10.3
In this case, we shall assume that instead of buying all of Company B, Company A buys 75 per cent of the equity of Company B for £90. The

balance sheets of Company A and Company B are given below and consolidated accounts are required.

Balance sheets of Company A and Company B

	Company A	Company B
Investment in A	90	
Sundry net assets	110	100
	200	100
Ordinary shares	200	100
	200	100

As you can see the assets of Company A are the same, in total, as in Example 10.2. Similarly the total assets of Company B are the same. The difference is that in this example Company A only acquires 75 per cent of Company B for which it pays £90.

The proprietary approach

In terms of the consolidated accounts there are a number of different approaches that we could take. The first one that we shall consider is known as the proprietary method of consolidation. Under this approach Company A would only include the proportion of Company B it owns. Thus it would include only 75 per cent of the sundry net assets of Company B, i.e. £75, with its own sundry net assets of £110, making £185 in total. The goodwill that would be included would be £15, i.e. £90 − £75. The consolidated balance sheet would be as shown below:

Consolidated balance sheet of Company A and its subsidiary using the proprietary approach to consolidation

Goodwill	15
Sundry net assets	185
	200
Ordinary shares	200
	200

As you can see, this approach shows only the amount of goodwill that was purchased as an asset. The treatment of the goodwill is consistent with the treatment of the other assets, i.e. the amount included is the amount actually owned by Company A.

The entity approach

The entity approach looks at the underlying economic entity and shows the assets of the total entity that Company A controls. This, in effect, means that it includes all the assets of Company B and also includes an amount that shows that some other party or parties owns part of Company B. This is referred to as the minority interest in Company B. Under this approach, the whole of the sundry net assets of Company B would be included. In addition the whole of the goodwill of Company B would be included. This is worked out on the basis that if Company A paid £15 for 75 per cent of the goodwill, 100 per cent of the goodwill must have a value of £20:

$$\text{i.e. } £15 \times \frac{100\%}{75\%} = £20$$

Under this approach to consolidation the consolidated balance sheet of Company A and its subsidiary would be as follows:

Consolidated balance sheet of Company A and its subsidiary using the entity approach to consolidation

Goodwill	20
Sundry net assets	210
	230
Ordinary shares	200
Minority interest	30
	230

Here we see that the minority's share of Company A is represented as £30, i.e. 25 per cent of the goodwill amounting to £5, and 25 per cent of the other sundry net assets, amounting to £25. The treatment of goodwill under this approach is once again consistent with that applied to the other assets.

Parent company method

The third approach we shall look at is the parent company method. This is the method that is normally used in the UK. Under this method 100 per cent of the sundry net assets are included in the consolidated accounts and the minority interest in those assets is also shown. However, the goodwill is included at the difference between the price paid by Company A and the assets acquired. In other words goodwill of £15 is included and the minority interest does not include an interest in the goodwill. Under this approach the consolidated balance sheet of Company A and its subsidiary would appear as follows.

Consolidated balance sheet of Company A and its subsidiary using the parent company approach to consolidation

Goodwill	15
Sundry net assets	210
	225
Ordinary shares	200
Minority interest	25
	225

As you can see the goodwill is, in fact, included on the basis of the percentage owned while the sundry net assets are included on the basis of the amount controlled. The method is effectively a combination of the proprietary and entity approaches, with the former being applied to the goodwill and the latter to the other assets. The method is therefore inconsistent in its treatment of assets. The treatment accorded to the sundry net assets is to show the future benefit to be derived from the use of those assets and divide it amongst those to whom that benefit will accrue, i.e. Company A and the minority interest. On the other hand, the treatment of the goodwill would suggest that the goodwill is not an asset as, if it is, then the future benefits would also accrue to the minority in the same way as those from the sundry net assets. It would seem that either the treatment is wrong or the goodwill should not be shown on the balance sheet as it is not an asset.

The discussion and examples above illustrate two important points. The first is that there is a lack of clarity in terms of what goodwill is and whether it is an asset. This is particularly apparent when the logic of the parent company approach is examined. The other point is that there is some confusion regarding what the consolidated balance sheet should show and what its purpose is. Thus the fact that the two logical approaches have been amalgamated to form an illogical hybrid is hardly surprising. The debate over whether an entity or proprietary approach should be adopted underlies many accounting controversies, in particular in the area of price level accounting, as we shall see in Chapters 16 and 17.

Summary

As can be seen from the discussion above, the area of intangible assets is a difficult one for accountants. In the past, the treatment recommended by the accounting profession has been heavily reliant on the prudence principle. Accountants have been very reluctant to allow an asset to be shown where there was any doubt either about its value, or about whether it should be classified as an asset. This is a good example of the tension that exists between relevance and reliability which we discussed in Chapter 1. The fact that the accounting standard on goodwill is currently being revised, and the fact that the proposed revision amounts to a complete reversal of previous practice, is illustrative of the problems with this area and with the historic cost model itself. Contributing to the problems is the fact that the purpose of a balance sheet and a profit and loss account has not been clearly defined or understood. If the balance sheet is not a statement of the assets of the enterprise at a point in time that must be made clear. If it is not made clear, it can hardly come as a surprise that companies, who feel vulnerable to takeovers by predators, wish to include items that they consider to be assets such as brand names etc. On the other hand, if it is not a statement of the assets, the question that arises is what is the balance sheet and what should it contain?

References

Statement of Standard Accounting Practice No. 1 (1982) *Accounting for the Results of Associated Companies*, Accounting Standards Committee.

Statement of Standard Accounting Practice No. 2 (1971) *Disclosure of Accounting Policies*, Accounting Standards Committee.

Statement of Standard Accounting Practice No. 13 (1987) *Accounting for Research and Development*, Accounting Standards Committee.

Statement of Standard Accounting Practice No. 14 (1978) *Group Accounts*, Accounting Standards Committee.

Statement of Standard Accounting Practice No. 22 (1989) *Accounting for Goodwill*, Accounting Standards Committee.

Exposure Draft 47 (1990) *Accounting for Goodwill*, Accounting Standards Committee.

Exposure Draft 52 (1990) *Accounting for Intangible Fixed Assets*, Accounting Standards Committee.

Further reading

Further discussion of research and development can be found in R.H. Gray, *Accounting for R & D: A review of experiences with SSAP 13* (ICAEW, London, 1984), T.A. Lee, 'Goodwill: an example of will-o'-the-wisp accounting', *Accounting and Business Research* (Autumn, 1971), and R.S. Gynther, 'Some conceptualizing on goodwill', *The Accounting Review* (April 1969).

Review questions

1. Why is it important to know the reason for an investment?

2. Why is it necessary, in certain circumstances, to split the interest received on a fixed interest investment into two parts?

3. What is an intangible asset and how does it differ from a tangible asset?

4. Give some examples of intangible assets that are unlikely to be included in accounts and the reasons for their exclusion.

5. What is the difference between research expenditure and development expenditure?

6. What conditions have to be met before development expenditure can be capitalized and shown as an asset?

7. What is goodwill and how does it arise?

8. What is the philosophy underlying the proprietary approach?

9. What is the philosophy underlying the entity approach?

Problems for discussion and analysis

1. The directors of Reefknot, which installs central heating, have recently acquired another company, Slipknot, which produces central heating radiators.

Reefknot paid £1 500 000 for the whole of the equity in Slipknot. The balance sheet of Slipknot is given below:

Balance sheet of Slipknot

Fixed assets	Cost	Accumulated depreciation	
	£	£	£
Land	100 000		100 000
Buildings	80 000	20 000	60 000
Machinery	300 000	140 000	160 000
Vehicles	60 000	30 000	30 000
	540 000	190 000	350 000
Investments			84 000
Patents			6 000
Current assets			
Stock		340 000	
Debtors		100 000	
Cash at bank		60 000	
		500 000	
Creditors: falling due in one year			
Trade creditors		50 000	
Accruals		5 000	
		55 000	
Net current assets			445 000
			885 000
Financed by:			£
Owners' equity			600 000
Retained profits			285 000
			885 000

In addition you ascertain the following information.
(a) The current value of the land is £200 000 and the current value of the buildings is £100 000.
(b) The investment consists of £80 000 of 10 per cent loan stock which was bought halfway through the year. The interest is paid annually on 31 December and the amount due of £8000 has been received and taken to the profit and loss account.
(c) The directors of Reefknot believe that the patent is worth at least £60 000.
(d) During the last year, Slipknot had spent £300 000 on research and development the details of this are given below:

Expenditure on research into the feasibility of the application of new louvre design for car radiators to central heating radiators, £80 000.
Expenditure of £220 000 in relation to the development of a new process for sealing radiator joints, which has been successful and will be introduced to the production line next year. The costs of introducing the new process are minimal and it is expected to reduce costs by £70 000 a year.

(e) When Reefknot acquired Slipknot, they got the research staff, who they believe are the best in the industry, to sign new contracts of employment which should keep them with Slipknot. The directors of Reefknot believe this expertise is worth at least £100 000 and would like to see it reflected in the accounts.

Comment on each of the items above indicating what potential accounting treatments are possible and recommend, with reasons, the ones that should be adopted.

2. Calculate the value of the goodwill that Reefknot acquired and identify what the alternative accounting treatments of that goodwill are, and their effect on the profit and loss account.

11 Financing and business structures

So far, we have largely been concerned with the assets of the organization. Although we have introduced you to some of the various forms of finance as we have worked through the book, we have not looked at the way an organization finances it assets and its operations in any detail. In this chapter, we shall be considering the different forms of finance a business uses and the effects of the organizational structure upon the sources of finance available. We shall also consider the financing structure of an organization and its effect on financial risk. For our purposes, we differentiate between business risk, which applies equally to all firms in an industry, and financial risk. Financial risk is related to the capital structure of a business, i.e. the way in which it finances its assets, and by adjusting the type of finance or the mix of equity finance to debt finance the financial risk can be altered.

In terms of the types of finance available, any attempt to classify different types of finance is problematic. However, for our purposes it is useful to look at sources of finance in some broad categories. The ones we have chosen to use relate to the period for which the finance is intended. Thus we shall consider different sources of finance under the headings of short-term finance, medium-term finance and long-term finance. Before commencing our discussion of the different types of finance it is important to appreciate that the choice of appropriate finance can be vital to the long-term success of a business. The finance should match the purpose for which it is to be used. For example, using what is essentially short-term finance for the purchase of a building merely creates problems when the financier has to be repaid. The building is still needed and therefore replacement finance has to be found. Similarly, taking out a loan repayable over twenty years to buy an asset that is only going to be needed for a few years would leave the business in the position of having to pay interest on money it does not need. These are, of course, extreme examples but they do serve to illustrate the point that the finance must be matched with the purpose for which it is to be used. In this regard, when choosing between various sources of finance, a business needs to bear in mind the use of the finance, the limitations of that source of finance, the costs, the repayment terms and timing, and the availability of alternatives. In considering the various forms of finance we shall endeavour to follow a pattern of providing a general description of the source of finance, discussing its uses, limitations, costs and availability.

Short-term finance

Although there is no generally accepted definition for short-term finance, we can think of it as being for a period less than a year. Short-term finance, in general, should be used to finance short-term capital requirements such as working capital requirements, i.e. financing stock and debtors. There are a number of sources of finance that are available. The most common are trade credit, factoring and the bank overdraft, which we shall consider below.

Trade credit

We have already come across trade credit in Chapter 7 which dealt with accrual accounting, including debtors and creditors. As we pointed out there, it is normal for a supplier to allow its business customers a period of time after the goods have been delivered before payment is required. The period of time and the amount of credit a business gets from its suppliers is dependent upon a number of factors. These include the 'normal' terms of trade of that industry, the supplier's view of the business's creditworthiness and how much it values the custom of that business customer. Thus, for example, a new clothes retailing business is likely to get less favourable terms than British Home Stores or C&A.

Trade credit is very widely used as a source of finance by all businesses. It provides short-term finance that can be used to finance, or partially finance, debtors and stock. Many small businesses rely extensively on trade credit. This is perfectly reasonable and acceptable as long as the credit is managed effectively. The objective is to take as much time to pay as is reasonable without affecting the supplier's judgement of your creditworthiness. If too long a period is taken, the supplier is likely to be reluctant to allow the same favourable terms next time. In many small businesses that are experiencing problems, the temptation to extend the repayment date has often led to withdrawal of any period of credit. This leaves the business in the position that all supplies have either to be paid for in advance or on a cash-on-delivery basis. This situation is often seen in the licensed trade where tenant publicans, because of poor financial management, end up not being able to obtain further credit from the brewery. Although, there are undoubtedly some exceptions, many publicans who have got themselves into this position by too heavy a reliance on trade credit are now ex-publicans. Although publicans provide a very visible example of the dangers of relying too heavily on trade credit, all businesses that rely too much on trade credit run the risk of losing their line of credit and ultimately of bankruptcy or liquidation. Although suppliers are generally reluctant to take such steps, if they believe that they are more likely to recover their money by such a course of action that is what they will do.

Trade credit is often thought of as cost-free credit. However, this is not strictly true as quite often suppliers allow a small discount for early payment. Therefore taking the full period to pay has an opportunity cost in the form of the discount foregone. This opportunity cost has to be weighed against the availability of funds within the business or the cost of raising additional funds.

Factoring

If a business makes sales on credit, it will have to collect payment from its debtors at some stage. Up until that point, it will have to finance those debtors, either through trade credit, an overdraft, or its own capital. The costs of this finance can be very high and many small businesses will be hard up against their limits in terms of their overdraft and the amount and period of trade credit taken. In order to release the money tied up in debtors the business can approach a factoring company, which is a finance company which specializes in providing a service for the collection of payments from debtors. Often these companies are subsidiaries of, or are associated with, banks. As such bank managers are now advising clients to use this form of finance as an alternative to, or as supplementary to, other forms of short-term finance such as overdrafts.

Essentially, the way the system works is that the factoring organization assesses the firm's debtors in terms of risk and collectability. It then agrees to collect the money due on behalf of the business concerned. Once an agreement is reached the factoring company pays the business in respect of the invoices for the month virtually straightaway. It is then the factoring organization's responsibility to collect from the debtors as soon as possible. The factoring company charges for this in the form of a fee, or by 'buying' the debtors at a discount. This form of finance is therefore more expensive than trade credit but can be useful as it allows the business to concentrate on production and sales and improves the cash flow. This improvement in cash flow may mean that the business is not as heavily reliant on other forms of short-term finance and, as such, there may be some cost savings involved.

Clearly for growing firms, which tend to experience problems with finance, factoring could be very useful. However, the factoring organizations are fairly careful about which debts they will take on. They assess the 'quality' of the firm's customers in terms of their creditworthiness before agreeing to take them on. In addition, they may take no responsibility for bad debts. For small businesses, unless their customers are judged to be 'quality' customers, the factoring organizations are reluctant to take on the business. Thus, although in theory this is an alternative form of finance, it is not available to all.

A point that needs to be borne in mind when discussing the use of factoring is that, in the past, factoring has had a bad name and been associated with the fact that the firm using a factoring organization is in trouble. Whether this was in fact correct or merely a common misconception is open to debate. However, it seems that this view of factoring is gradually changing, and the factoring industry is clearly trying to 'clean up' its image. It may well be the case that factoring will become an increasingly important source of short-term finance in the future, especially as a number of factoring organizations are now willing to factor debts in Europe.

Bank overdrafts

Banks provide business with short-term finance for working capital, either in the form of short-term loans or, more commonly, in the form of an overdraft. The difference is that a loan is for a fixed period of time and interest is charged on the full amount of the loan, less any agreed repayments, for the period. An overdraft by contrast is a facility that can be used as and when required and interest is only charged when it is used. Thus, if a business knows that it needs money for a fixed period of time then a bank loan may be appropriate; on the other hand, if the finance is only required to meet occasional short-term cash flow needs then an overdraft would be more suitable. We shall discuss loans in more detail under the heading of medium-term finance.

Although many businesses use overdrafts as a semi-permanent source of finance this is not how the banks would like to see this form of finance used. Bank managers like to see a business bank account, on which an overdraft facility has been provided, swinging between having money in the bank account and using the overdraft. They do not see an overdraft as a form of permanent working capital as the following comments from bank managers involved in a recent research project (Berry *et al.*, 1993), illustrate:

'They needed more capital . . . they didn't need trading finance from me.'

'What I didn't want was to take on a business where I could tell within three months he'd be banging on the door for more.'

In both these cases, the small business concerned had been financing their growth and the higher stock and debtor levels associated with that growth through bank overdrafts. The bank managers were not happy as they viewed the overdraft as a temporary source of finance and in both these cases the bank account had been more or less permanently overdrawn. Thus, although this is a common and a useful source of finance it is often misused and this can lead to problems as it can be withdrawn with very little notice.

A bank overdraft carries with it a charge in the form of interest and often a fee for setting up the facility. The latter, which is a one-off charge, has become more common in recent years. As far as the interest is concerned, the rate of interest charged is related to the risk involved and the market rates of interest for that size of business. In general, the more risk involved the higher the rate of interest. Due to the fact that they operate in a volatile market small firms tend to be charged higher rates of interest than large firms.

In addition, banks will normally require security, which can take various forms, for any overdraft. In the case of a small business, whether it is a company or not, the normal security would be a charge on the owner's home or homes if more than one person is involved. Alternatively, or in addition, the bank may require personal guarantees from the owner, or in the case of a limited company, the directors. For larger companies, the security may be a fixed charge on certain assets, or a floating charge on all the assets. In the case of very large companies the risk involved is lower and the competition between the providers of finance is greater, therefore overdrafts are not only cheaper but they are also more easily accessible and security is less of a factor.

Medium-term finance

There are a number of sources of medium-term finance that can be used by a business. We shall limit our discussion to medium-term loans, leases and hire-purchase.

Loans

As we pointed out, an alternative to overdraft finance for short-term finance requirements is a bank loan. In general loans should only be used when finance is required for a known period of time. Ideally that period should relate to the life of the asset or the purpose for which the finance is to be used. Loans can be obtained for short-term, medium-term or long-term finance. Compared to an overdraft facility which can be used as and when needed, a loan is more permanent. Repayment of the loan is negotiated at the time the loan is taken out and is generally at fixed intervals. They are often secured in the same way as overdrafts and if the repayment conditions are not met then the lender will take action to recover the outstanding amount.

Bank loans are often granted for a specified purpose and limitations may be imposed regarding the use of the loan and the raising of other finance while the loan is outstanding. Unlike an overdraft, the cost of this form of finance is known in advance as interest accrues from the time the business borrows the money irrespective of the fact that it may not use it straightaway. In common with other forms of finance discussed so far, the rate of interest charged and the availability of this source of finance is dependent upon the size of the business and the lender's assessment of the risk involved. Thus, in general, the larger and more diversified a business is, the easier will be their access to this form of finance.

Hire-purchase

An alternative way of financing the acquisition of an asset is through the use of hire-purchase. Under a hire-purchase agreement a finance company buys the asset and hires it to the business. Thus a business can acquire the asset and use it even though it has not yet paid for it in full. During the period of the hire-purchase agreement the finance company owns the asset. The hirer has the right to use the asset and carries all the risks associated with using that asset. Thus, for example, if a car is purchased on hire-purchase, the hirer would be responsible for all the repairs and costs associated with the use of that car in the same way as if they had bought the car directly. At the end of the period of the hire-purchase agreement the ownership of the asset is transferred to the hirer. A normal hire-purchase agreement consists of a deposit and a set number of payments over a number of years.

This type of finance can only be used when a specific asset is purchased, i.e. the finance is for a specified asset purchase. It cannot be used for financing working capital requirements or any other purpose. The hire-purchase company actually pays the supplier of the asset directly and the asset belongs to the hire-purchase company. If repayments are not made in accordance with the hire-purchase agreement the hire-purchase company has the right to repossess its property.

The monthly repayments consist of an amount which includes both a repayment of the capital borrowed and a charge for interest. The rate of interest charged will be dependent upon the market rate of interest but is likely to be slightly higher than the interest on bank loans. The interest charge needs to be separated out and charged to the profit and loss account. The hirer will record an asset in its accounts as there is a legal right to the enjoyment of the benefit from that asset in exchange for the regular payments. In addition the hirer needs to record a liability in respect of the amount of capital due to the hire-purchase finance company. The treatment of hire-purchase in accounts is covered by SSAP 21 *Accounting for Leases and Hire Purchase Agreements* which we shall discuss in more detail below.

Hire-purchase is available to all businesses and individuals subject, of course, to the hire-purchase company being satisfied with the credit-worthiness of the person or business using the hire-purchase. The amount of money that can be raised via hire purchase is limited to the price of the asset.

Leasing

A lease is an agreement between a lessor, the person who owns the asset, and a lessee, the person who uses the asset. It conveys the right to use that asset for a stated period of time in exchange for payment but does not necessarily transfer ownership at the end of the lease period. The period can vary from a very short period to ten or more years. In common with hire-purchase, this form of finance is tied to a specific asset. Thus its use as a source of finance is limited to the purchase of capital items such as machinery, vehicles, etc.

In general the cost of leasing is similar to that of hire-purchase. The major difference between the two sorts of finance is that, in general, leases tend to be for a longer period of time and are frequently used as a source of finance for specialized assets. In essence there are two distinct types of leases and the accounting treatment of leases recognizes this fact and treats them differently. The accounting treatment is covered by SSAP 21 *Accounting for Leases and Hire Purchase Agreements*. This standard requires that leases, and hire-purchase agreements, are split between operating leases and finance leases. The standard does not define an operating lease; instead it defines a finance lease and any lease that is not a finance lease is to be treated as an operating lease.

Alternative definitions that may be useful are given in Key Concepts 11.2 and 11.3. For operating leases, the accounting treatment is very straightforward as no asset has to be recorded because, in effect, all that is happening is that the lessee is, for example, renting a photocopier in

| KEY CONCEPT 11.1 | SSAP 21 defines a finance lease as: |
| **A FINANCE LEASE** | 'A lease that transfers substantially all the risks and rewards of ownership of an asset to the lessee.' |

| KEY CONCEPT 11.2 | A lease where the underlying substance of the transaction is a rental arrangement. |
| **AN OPERATING LEASE** | |

| KEY CONCEPT 11.3 | A lease where the underlying substance of the transaction is a financing arrangement. |
| **A FINANCE LEASE** | |

the same way as they might rent premises. These operating leases are therefore dealt with in the same way. The rental is charged to the profit and loss account for the period in question and no asset is recorded in the books of the business leasing the asset. The standard requires disclosure in the accounts of the total rentals for the year, split between hire of plant and machinery and other items. There are also requirements in terms of disclosure of future commitments. These must be analysed in terms of those ending in the coming year, those ending in years two to five, and those ending after five years.

The underlying economic substance of a finance lease, on the other hand, is equivalent to borrowing money from a finance company and then using that money to buy an asset. The accounting treatment set out in SSAP 21 is that the lessee records an asset, as they have a legal right to the use of the asset, and also records a liability. The payments to the lessor are then split between the part that relates to capital repayment, which reduces the liability, and the interest charge, which is charged to the profit and loss account.

As far as disclosure in respect of finance leases is concerned, the asset should be treated in the same way as any other fixed asset, i.e. the cost, the accumulated depreciation and the net book value must be shown. They can either be shown as a separate class of assets from the other fixed assets or they can be included with the other fixed assets. In the latter case the net amount of fixed assets on lease included in the total assets must be disclosed. In addition, the depreciation charged for the year relating to assets on finance leases must be separately disclosed. As regards the liability, this needs to be analysed into three categories, i.e. amounts due within a year, amounts due in the second to fifth years and amounts due after five years. In addition, the total amount of the finance charges, in respect of finance leases, for the year must be disclosed.

Finally, in terms of disclosure, the accounting policies in respect of both finance and operating leases must be disclosed. An example of some of the disclosure requirements in respect of leases is provided in Case 11.1.

From a financing point of view, there are also a number of variations on hire-purchase and leases such as contract-hire, lease-purchase and sale and leaseback. The fact that such products and packages have been put together indicates that the leasing companies are keen to provide finance. It does not mean, however, that this is a source of finance that is available to all. The leasing companies are also interested in assessing the risk and creditworthiness of businesses before entering into any agreements.

Long-term finance

The number of alternative sources of long-term finance available are, to some extent, dependent upon the type of organization involved. We shall start our discussion with debt finance, such as long-term loans, which are more generally available, and then move on to discuss separately equity finance. The latter discussion will be subdivided in terms of organization types, i.e. sole proprietorships, partnerships and limited companies, as these affect the type of equity finance available. In respect of limited companies, we shall limit our discussion to private limited companies.

Debt finance

This is the term given to any source of long-term finance that is not equity finance. Often debt finance is seen exclusively as long-term interest-bearing finance. This is, in fact, a misconception as all the finance we have discussed so far has been debt finance. We shall look at two broad categories of long-term debt finance, i.e. long-term loans, which are available to all organizations, and debentures and loan stock, which tend to be used by incorporated businesses.

Long-term loans

As we have said, a loan can be used for short-term, medium-term or long-term finance. Long-term loans have the same characteristics as short- and medium-term loans as regards the purpose of the loan and the repayment of the loan. Interest rates are likely to be different as these will need to be adjusted to take into account the higher risk associated with lending money for a longer period of time. Long-term loans are often for a specific purpose, e.g. the purchase of property, and the time period is affected by the life of the asset, the repayments required and the willingness of the lender to lend money. For many small businesses these loans often take the form of a commercial mortgage on property.

Apart from loans related to property, which are effectively commercial mortgages, the period of these loans is less in the UK than in Germany and Japan where long loan periods are more common. This may reflect a reluctance on the part of banks and other financial institutions to lend money for long periods of time. This was starting to change in the late

CASE 11.1

LEASING AND HIRE-PURCHASE – DISCLOSURE REQUIREMENTS

An example of the disclosure of accounting policies in respect of leasing and hire-purchased assets from the 1990–91 Annual Report of British Airways Plc is given below together with relevant extracts from the notes to the accounts.

Extract from accounting policies statement

LEASED AND HIRE PURCHASED ASSETS

Where assets are financed through finance leases and hire purchase arrangements under which substantially all the risks and rewards of ownership are transferred to the Group, the assets are treated as if they had been purchased outright. The amount included in tangible fixed assets represents the aggregate of the capital elements of payments made during the lease and hire purchase term. The corresponding obligation, reduced by the appropriate proportion of lease and hire purchase payments made, is included in creditors. The amount included in tangible fixed assets is depreciated on the basis described in the preceding paragraphs, and the interest element of lease and hire purchase payments made is included in interest payable in the profit and loss account. Annual payments under all other lease arrangements, known as operating leases, are charged to the profit and loss account as they arise.

British Airways Plc Annual Report & Accounts 1990–91

In the same report under the note to the accounts relating to tangible fixed assets the following information is given:

Extract from note 10 to the accounts

10 TANGIBLE ASSETS *(continued)*

g LEASING COMMITMENTS		*Group*		*Company*
£ million	1991	*1990*	1991	*1990*
The aggregate payments, for which there are commitments under operating leases as at the end of the year, fall due as follows:				
(i) FLEET				
Within one year	220	*239*	220	*239*
Between one and five years	517	*551*	517	*551*
Over five years, ranging up to the				
year 1996	2	*9*	2	*9*
	739	*799*	739	*799*
Amounts payable within one year relate to commitments expiring as follows:				
Within one year	35	*56*	35	*56*
Between one and five years	180	*173*	180	*173*
Over five years	5	*10*	5	*10*
	220	*239*	220	*239*

Continued from previous page

(ii) PROPERTY AND EQUIPMENT

Within one year	46	*46*	44	*40*
Between one and five years	96	*86*	93	*71*
Over five years, ranging up to the year 2075	231	*215*	226	*182*
	373	*347*	363	*293*

Amounts payable within one year relate to commitments expiring as follows:

Within one year	13	*12*	12	*11*
Between one and five years	26	*25*	25	*23*
Over five years	7	*9*	7	*6*
	46	*46*	44	*40*

The fleet leasing commitments include the balance of rental obligations under operating leases in respect of 13 Boeing 747-400, five Boeing 747-200, seven Boeing 767, seven Boeing 757, 20 Boeing 737 and eight BAe ATP aircraft, but exclude nine Boeing 737 and three Boeing 757 aircraft which were converted from operating leases to finance leases with effect from 31 March 1991. In the case of most of these obligations, the Company may be required to meet a small share of any loss on resale if options to renew the leases or convert them into finance leases are not exercised.

In addition to the information about the assets that are leased, the notes to the accounts give information about the total liabilities in the form of loans, finance leases and hire-purchase arrangements. They also give a breakdown of when these are due for repayment. The latter information is reproduced below:

Extract from note 16 to the accounts

16 LOANS, FINANCE LEASES AND HIRE PURCHASE ARRANGEMENTS *(continued)*
b INCIDENCE OF REPAYMENTS

£ million	Bank loans	Other loans	Finance leases	Hire purchase arrangements	1991	*Group total 1990*
INSTALMENTS FALLING DUE:						
Within one year *(Note 14)*	59	5	28	13	105	*58*
After more than one year *(Note 15)*						
Between one and two years	1	5	32	14	52	*21*
Between two and five years	3	17	100	52	172	*70*
In five years or more	48	638	136	258	1080	*616*
	52	660	268	324	1304	*707*
Total 1991	111	665	296	337	1409	
Total 1990	*29*	*582*	*154*			*765*
Analysis of total 1991						
British Airways Plc	103	520	289	337	1249	*601*
Subsidiary undertakings	8	145	7		160	*164*
	111	665	296	337	1409	*765*

1980s and early 1990s when building societies were beginning to take advantage of the deregulation of financial services to enter this market. Unfortunately, but perhaps understandably, a number of them got their fingers badly burned. This was probably due to a number of factors, including a lack of expertise; theirs was in residential lending to individuals against income rather than to companies against a set of accounting numbers. In addition the recession was starting and interest rates were still rising. This meant that a number of organizations which had been operating on tight margins went out of business with consequential effects on the demand for, and price of, commercial property. Therefore, there are still limitations on the availability of long-term loans, especially for the purchase of assets other than property. As is the case with all the other types of finance we have discussed, the availability of this source of finance is also heavily dependent upon the lender's assessment of the creditworthiness of the prospective borrower.

Debentures and loan stock

These are terms used for particular types of long-term loans to limited companies. They basically mean the same thing and are essentially long-term loan finance. The main difference between these and the long-term loans which are also available to other types of organization is that debentures may be redeemable or irredeemable. The former type, i.e. redeemable, are the most common. The date or dates for repayment are fixed at the time of the initial agreement. In virtually all debenture deeds there is a right to repayment or appointment of a receiver if interest is not paid when due. Debentures and loan stock generally have a fixed rate of interest which may be above or below the current market rate. They are rarely restricted to a particular purpose for which the finance can be used.

In the case of irredeemable debentures, the company may choose to repay when it wishes. In addition to this type of finance there are numerous variants such as convertible debentures which are sometimes found in company accounts but which we need not concern ourselves with at this stage. The cost of this type of finance is similar to that for long-term loans and is affected by the market rate of interest when the debenture loan stock is issued, the security available, and the risk involved. For this reason, they are more commonly seen in the accounts of larger companies.

Equity finance

The other major source of long-term finance is equity finance, and here we need to look at organizational types as this can have a major effect on the type of equity finance available, and the amount of finance available.

Sole proprietorships

In the case of a sole proprietorship, as we have seen, the only sources of equity finance are those supplied by the owner, and the retained profits.

In many small businesses, the amount of funds that the owner has available to put into the business are often limited. This means that the only source of equity finance is retained profits. In a fast growing business it is unlikely that there will be sufficient retained profits to finance expansion. As such, sole proprietorships, in common with many small businesses, become very reliant on debt finance and, as we shall see, this exposes them to more risk as a downturn in the market or an increase in interest rates could have a dramatic impact on their ability to service the debt. Unlike debt finance equity finance has no limitations in terms of the use to which it is put.

Partnerships

Partnerships, as the name implies, are organizations that are owned, and often managed, by a number of individuals. They are most common among professionals, thus we see doctors, dentists, lawyers, architects and, of course, accountants working in partnerships. In essence, the sources of equity finance for partnerships are the same as for sole proprietorships, i.e. money contributed by the owners and retained profits. There are, of course, more people involved so more equity can be raised through contributions by the owners. Partnerships are governed by the legislation contained in the 1890 Partnership Act and by case law. In general the main difference between partnerships and sole proprietorships is that, whereas the sole proprietor is the only person responsible for the debts, in a partnership the partners are 'jointly and severally' liable. This means that if one partner cannot pay his or her share of the debts the other partners must pay. The other important difference is related to the division of profits, which must be divided amongst the partners in accordance with the partnership agreement.

We shall be looking at the subject of partnerships in more detail in Chapter 12 where the accounting problems of partnerships will be discussed. For our purposes here, we can look at partnerships as having the same sources of equity finance as sole proprietorships. The only difference is that they are likely to have access to a greater supply of funds. In addition there may be differences in relation to the availability of retained profits as some partners may leave more profits in the business than others. This will of course depend upon the individual partners' requirements for funds.

Limited companies

Limited companies have the advantage, from an investor's point of view, that the liability of the owners is limited to the amount they have invested in the company. As with partnerships and sole proprietorships, the major source of equity comes from the owners through the issue of ordinary shares.

Ordinary shares and retained profits
In the case of companies, the equity is divided into ordinary shares, which are the equity shares. Each share has a nominal or par value, e.g. 10p or

£1. This value has little significance, as it does not necessarily relate to the price the share can be bought or sold for. In the case of an existing company any new shares issued after the company has been trading are likely to be issued at a price in excess of the nominal value. The difference between the nominal value and the price at which the share is issued is put to a special account known as the share premium account. This is often referred to as a 'capital reserve account'. Essentially it is non-distributable except under specific circumstances laid down in the Companies Acts.

As with any other form of organization, the other main source of equity capital is retained profits. Unlike a sole proprietorship or partnership, a company distributes its profits by way of dividends. The directors decide on the amount of dividend to be paid and the timing of the dividend, and until a dividend is declared by the directors the shareholders have no prima facie right to a dividend. Dividends can be paid during the year and/or at the end of the year. If they are paid during the year they are referred to as interim dividends and the dividend at the end of the year is referred to as the final dividend. Dividends are treated differently from drawings which, as we have seen, are normally deducted from the owner's equity. They are not deducted from capital and are shown as an appropriation of profit, i.e. they are deducted from the profit after tax. There are also differences relating to tax which we shall not concern ourselves with here.

A company has the advantage over a sole proprietorship or a partnership in that it can issue shares to whoever it wishes in whatever proportions it wishes. The shareholders do not have to take part in the management of the company, and in most large companies, the vast majority of shareholders play virtually no part in the management of the company. They merely invest their money and take the risk that they will get better returns, in the form of their share of the profits, than they would by investing in safer fixed interest investments. Ultimately, all the profits belong to the shareholders, so if they do not get their share of the profits in the form of dividends, i.e. the profits are retained in the company, their share of the profits and the future profits is reflected in the price at which they could sell their shares.

Issue of shares

Companies when they are formed are set up with a specified authorized share capital. This is the maximum amount of share capital that can be raised through the issue of shares. It can be increased subsequently by the members of the company but until that happens it forms an effective ceiling on the amount of equity finance that can be raised from shareholders directly. Ordinary shares can be issued either as a full price issue, as a rights issue or as a bonus issue.

Full price issues

In the case of a full price issue, as the name suggests, the share is issued at the market price. In the case of a company quoted on the stock exchange or the unlisted securities market this price is already known. In the case of a private company a value would have to be put on the company and then divided by the total number of shares to arrive at a market price. As we have said, it is likely that this price will exceed the nominal or par value, and the excess over the par value will be shown in the share premium account. This is illustrated in Example 11.1.

Example 11.1
Brill Ltd has 10000 shares of 25 pence nominal value in issue. The directors decide to issue another 5000 shares and the value arrived at is 40 p per share.

In this case, the ordinary share capital will be increased by £1250, i.e. 5000 shares at 25 p nominal value. The share premium will be increased by £750, i.e. 5000 × 15 p (40 p, the issue price, less 25 p, the par value). The bank account would, of course, increase by £2000 less any costs related to the issue.

Rights issues

An alternative to a full price issue is to offer the additional shares to the existing shareholders only, on the basis that they have a right to buy shares in proportion to their existing holding. This type of share issue has the advantage of retaining the existing spread of shareholdings and the existing status quo in terms of relative voting power. Rights issues are normally offered at a price slightly below market price. The reasons for this are that this form of share issue is cheaper to administer than an open-to-all full price issue, and a lower price also encourages share-holders to exercise their rights and buy the shares. As can be seen in Example 11.2, the principles involved in accounting for a rights issue are no different from a full price issue.

Example 11.2
Brill Ltd has decided to raise additional equity finance by way of a rights issue. It has an existing share capital of 10000 shares of 25 p each, and wishes to make an issue of one share for every two held at a price of 38 p. All the rights are taken up.

In this case the share capital will be increased by 5000 shares at 25 p par value, i.e. £1250. The remaining 13 p per share, i.e. 38 p − 25 p, will go to the share premium account which will be increased by £650. The bank account, in this case, will increase by £1900, i.e. 5000 × 38 p.

Bonus issues

The other alternative we mentioned was a bonus issue. These are also referred to as capitalization issues and sometimes scrip issues. In this case no money is raised. The purpose of the bonus issue is to increase the number of shares in issue. This has the effect of reducing the price per share and making the shares more marketable. A bonus issue may have as its objective a reduction in the share price or it may be used for other reasons such as boosting shareholder confidence. In effect, what happens is that a transfer is made from one of the reserves to the share capital account. The accounting treatment of bonus issues differs from those already considered as no money is involved. It is illustrated in Example 11.3 below.

Example 11.3

Brill Ltd which had 10 000 ordinary shares of 25 p each in issue decided to make a bonus issue of one share at par value for every two held. The transfer was to be made from the retained profits which stood at £8000 before the issue.

Here the share capital would be increased by £1250 to £3750, and the retained profits would be reduced by £1250 to £6750. There would, of course, be no effect on the bank account as no money transaction is involved.

Preference shares

Apart from ordinary shares, a company can also issue preference shares. Unlike ordinary shares a preference share normally has a fixed dividend and even if more profits are made the preference dividend remains the same. In addition they normally carry a right to preference in the order of payment in the event of the company going into liquidation. They are therefore less risky than ordinary shares and appeal to a different sort of investor. Whether these shares should be classified as equity or debt would depend on the particular type of preference shares in question and the rights attaching to them. Preference shares may be redeemable or non-redeemable. They may carry a right to dividends on a cumulative basis, i.e. if the directors do not pay any dividends in a year the preference shareholders will have a right to be paid that year's dividend and any others that have not been paid before the ordinary shareholders can be paid any dividend. Some preference shares are participating preference shares, whereby they get a share of profits if the profit is over a certain figure.

From an accounting point of view they are shown as a separate class of shares. Any premiums on the issue of preference shares go to the share premium account in the same way as premiums on ordinary shares and are not separated in any way. If the preference shares are redeemed the company is obliged by the Companies Act to transfer an amount equivalent to the par value of the shares redeemed into a non-distributable reserve known as the Capital Redemption Reserve. This in effect means that in a legal sense preference shares are seen as more akin to equity than debt as no such legal requirement exists for redemption of loans or debentures.

Financing structures and financial risk

The mix of debt finance and equity finance is known as gearing and it affects the financial risk of an enterprise. Basically the more reliant a business is on debt finance, i.e. the more highly geared, the greater the risk. The risk we are referring to here is that if interest rates go up or the profit margin comes down the enterprise would not be able to pay the interest or repayments due on its debt finance. There are, of course, advantages of being highly geared as well as disadvantages as Example 11.4 illustrates.

Example 11.4
Highrisk has equity capital consisting of 20 000 ordinary shares of £1 each. It has retained profits of £10 000 and has £40 000 in loans on which interest at 3 per cent above the base rate, which currently stands at 12 per cent, is due.

Lowrisk has equity capital consisting of 40 000 ordinary shares of £1 each. It has retained profits of £10 000 and has £20 000 in loans on which interest at 3 per cent above the base rate, i.e. 15 per cent is due.

Situation 1
Both companies make sales of £100 000 and their net profit before interest is 10 per cent on sales.

The profit and loss accounts for the two companies would be as shown below:

	Highrisk	Lowrisk
Sales	100 000	100 000
Costs	90 000	90 000
Net profit	10 000	10 000
Interest	6 000	3 000
Available for equity shares	4 000	7 000
Profit per share	0.20	0.17

As you can see, the ordinary shareholders of Highrisk are getting a better return than the shareholders of Lowrisk. They are getting 20 p per share return as compared to 17 p per share in Lowrisk, even though both companies have the same sales, costs and net profit before interest charges.

Situation 2 – increased costs
In this situation, instead of making a net profit before interest of 10 per cent of sales, the companies find that they can only make 8 per cent.

In this case the profit and loss accounts of the two companies would be as follows:

	Highrisk	Lowrisk
Sales	100 000	100 000
Costs	92 000	92 000
Net profit	8 000	8 000
Interest	6 000	3 000
Available for equity shares	2 000	5 000
Profit per share	0.10	0.13

Here we have a situation where the net profit on sales has dropped below the interest rate. As a result, as we would expect, the profit after interest to be reduced in both cases. However, the effect on the returns to Lowrisk's equity shareholders are not as severe as the effects on the returns to the equity shareholders in Highrisk.

Situation 3 – increased interest rates
In this situation the facts are the same as in Situation 2 above, i.e. the net profit before interest is 8 per cent on the sales. However, in addition, the base rate of interest moves to 13 per cent and therefore the interest on the loans moves up to 16 per cent.

In this case the profit and loss accounts of the two companies would be as follows:

	Highrisk	Lowrisk
Sales	100 000	100 000
Costs	92 000	92 000
Net profit	8 000	8 000
Interest	6 400	3 200
Available for equity shares	1 600	4 800
Profit per share	0.08	0.12

As you can see from the profit and loss accounts the effects of the increase in interest rates on the return to the shareholders of Highrisk is that the return is reduced by 2 p, from 10 p to 8 p, or 20 per cent. The shareholders of Lowrisk, by comparison, only suffer a reduction of 1 p, from 13 p to 12 p, or 8 per cent.

These examples illustrate the effects of high gearing which are to increase the returns to shareholders but at the same time make them more vulnerable to decreases in profit. These decreases can be caused by a reduction of sales or an increase in costs. In addition, their returns are also affected more by increases in interest rates than those of a low geared company.

It is worth mentioning that the lower the share of the business that is financed by equity, the more difficult it is to raise debt finance. Banks in the UK like to see a ratio of one to one, i.e. they will lend money, all other things being equal, so that the debt finance is equal to the equity share. There is often a clause to that effect included in the loan agreement. If the clause limits the amount of borrowing to the equity total then decisions on how much profit to retain, whether to revalue land and buildings, brands etc., can have a dramatic effect on the company's ability to raise finance. A very good example of the effects of the inclusion of brands on the gearing of a business is shown in Case 11.2.

A stark example of the ways in which the gearing of a business can be altered by changes in accounting policies is provided by the balance sheets of Rank Hovis McDougall for 1988. This, you will remember from the discussion of brands, was the year in which they decided to include the brands on their balance sheet. As a result of that decision the equity was more than trebled from £269.2 million in 1987 to £978.7 million in 1988. This reduced the gearing very dramatically.

CASE 11.2

GEARING

Balance Sheets
at 3 September 1988

	Note	The Group 1988 £m	The Group 1987 £m	The Company 1988 £m	The Company 1987 £m
Fixed assets					
Intangible assets	12	678.0	–	–	–
Tangible assets	13	463.7	422.3	–	–
Shares in subsidiary companies	14	–	–	318.3	274.3
Investments	15	0.7	3.4	0.1	0.1
		1142.4	425.7	318.4	274.4
Current assets					
Stocks	16	184.6	168.6	–	–
Debtors	17	234.3	215.6	284.4	225.8
Cash at bank and in hand	18	65.2	46.2	7.7	3.9
Creditors due within one year					
Borrowings	19	(45.1)	(53.0)	(36.5)	(21.0)
Other	19	(347.3)	(286.7)	(202.0)	(190.0)
Net current assets		91.7	90.7	53.6	18.7
Total assets less current liabilities		1234.1	516.4	372.0	293.1
Creditors due after more than one year					
Borrowings	20	(139.8)	(133.7)	(102.7)	(70.9)
Other	20	(96.6)	(78.6)	–	–
Provisions for liabilities and charges	21	(19.0)	(38.9)	(0.1)	(0.7)
		978.7	265.2	269.2	221.5
Capital and reserves					
Called up share capital	23	93.2	91.4	93.2	91.4
Share premium account	24	27.5	28.0	27.5	28.0
Revaluation reserve	25	622.6	24.9	–	–
Other reserves	26	184.9	107.3	148.5	102.1
		928.2	251.6	269.2	221.5
Minority interests		50.5	13.6	–	–
		978.7	265.2	269.2	221.5

Summary

In this chapter we have considered the main types of short-term, medium-term, and long-term finance that are available to all organizations. We have also looked at equity finance in the form of contributed capital and retained profits. The effects of different organizational forms on the sources of equity finance have been discussed and the effects of the mix of debt to equity finance on the returns to equity shareholders have been discussed and illustrated. It is important to remember that one vital point raised in this chapter was that the type of finance used should relate to the purpose for which that finance will be used.

References

Berry, A.J., Faulkner, S., Hughes, M. and Jarvis, R. (1993) *Bank Lending: Beyond the theory*, Chapman & Hall, London.
Statement of Standard Accounting Practice No. 21 (1984) *Accounting for Leases and Hire Purchase Agreements*, Accounting Standards Committee

Further reading

Arnold, J., Hope T. and Southwood, A.J. (1985) *Financial Accounting*, Chapter 11, Prentice Hall.
Pizzey, A. (1990) *Accounting and Finance: A Firm Foundation*, 3rd edn, Chapter 21, Cassell.

Review questions

1. Why is it important to match the type of finance with the purpose of raising that finance?

2. What are the forms of short-term finance discussed in the chapter?

3. What are the main differences between equity finance and debt finance?

4. What are the differences between drawings and dividends?

5. What does the term highly geared refer to?

6. What are the advantages and disadvantages of being highly geared?

7. What do the following terms mean and what are their basic characteristics:

    (a) nominal or par value?
    (b) share premium?
    (c) capital redemption reserve?
    (d) rights issue?
    (e) bonus issue?
    (f) preference shares?

Problems for discussion and analysis

1. A friend who has her own company has been to see the bank manager about borrowing some money to finance the acquisition of a new van and a new

machine. The bank manager has said that, in view of the current financial structure of the company, the bank would not be prepared to provide funds unsecured. The latest balance sheet of the company is given below:

Balance sheet

Fixed assets	Cost	Depreciation	
	£	£	£
Machinery	20 000	15 000	5 000
Vehicles	12 000	4 000	8 000
	32 000	19 000	13 000

Current assets		
Stock	12 000	
Debtors	22 000	
Cash	500	
	34 500	

Creditors: falling due within one year		
Trade creditors	19 000	
Taxation	3 600	
Bank overdraft	11 300	
	33 900	

Net current assets		600
Creditors: falling due after one year		5 000
		8 600

	£
Financed by	
Ordinary shares	5 000
Retained profits	3 600
	8 600

(a) Advise your friend what alternative sources of finance are available and which would be appropriate for the purpose of buying a van and buying a new machine.

(b) Explain why, in your opinion, the bank manager was not prepared to lend unsecured.

2. Bill was planning to go into business as a hairdresser. He has produced the following projections for the first year based on his experience of the industry and some careful research:

	£
Sales	25 000
Cost of ten year lease	30 000
Repairs and refurbishment	1 000
Shampoos, laundry, etc.	1 900
Stock of shampoos, towels, etc.	500
Equipment	3 000
Rent	2 000
Electricity	900
Wages	8 000
Personal drawings	5 000

He says that the equipment will last for four years and has no residual value. He has £30 000 in savings but is reluctant to invest the whole of that. He has been offered a loan of £20 000 to help buy the lease, at an interest rate of 10 per cent per annum for the first year with no repayments required during that year. After the first year the rate will be 4 per cent above base rate. Base rate currently stands at 12 per cent.

Alternatively he can borrow money for a one year period at 17 per cent per annum.

(a) Calculate what Bill's profit would be if he put in all his own money and borrowed anything else he needs. *Hint:* The receipts and payments have to be looked at in terms of their regularity and their timing.
(b) Calculate what Bill's profit would be in the first year assuming he takes the loan.
(c) Calculate what Bill's profit would be in the second year assuming he does not take the loan and sales and costs are the same as the first year.
(d) Calculate what Bill's profit would be in the second year assuming he takes the loan.
(e) Bill has asked you to advise him on the choice between the two alternatives. How would you advise him and what reasons would you give?
(f) What, if any, alternatives could you suggest for Bill?

Final accounts and organizational structures $\boxed{\mathbf{12}} \parallel\parallel\parallel\parallel$

The first section of this chapter has been included to assist readers who wish to continue with their accounting studies. Other textbooks are more likely to use a more traditional approach for explaining accounting and the mechanics of accounting. It will also be helpful to readers who have had some exposure to that traditional approach as an aid to understanding how the two approaches relate to one another. In the next part of the chapter we will look at the trial balance and the final adjustments required before final accounts are extracted from the worksheet. The remainder of this chapter will consider how the final accounts are extracted from the worksheet, the alternative formats of final accounts, and how these relate to different forms of organization. This will involve some basic consideration of the advantages and disadvantages of the different organizational forms available. It will also require an examination of the ways in which the presentation of accounting information may differ and the impacts of the regulatory framework on the presentation of annual accounts. Before these new areas are discussed, however, we will examine the traditional approach to accounting and compare it to the worksheet approach.

The traditional approach

Under this approach, instead of using columns to portray the individual accounts such as an asset account in an organization's accounting system, these accounts are represented by 'T' accounts. In many basic book-keeping courses these 'T' accounts form a major part of the course and students are required to spend a lot of time practising entries to these accounts. Quite often this is done on the basis of rote learning and it is further complicated by the terminology used which is normally expressed in terms of 'debits' and 'credits'.

For those studying accounting for the first time the worksheet approach has been shown to be superior. Moreover, it is more in line with the increasing use of electronic spreadsheets in accounting courses and in industry. However, in terms of learning accounting, experience has shown that those who have already had some exposure to accounting often experience initial problems in converting from one representation of an accounting system, i.e. 'T' accounts, to another, the worksheet. We shall work through a simple example to illustrate that the difference between the two methods is superficial and does not in any way change the principles involved.

Example 12.1
Brian started a business and during the first year the following transactions took place.

1. Opened a business bank account and paid in £10000 of his own money.
2. Bought a van for £5000 and paid for it in cash.
3. Bought goods for £35000 on credit and had paid for £33000 at the end of the year.
4. Sold goods for £45000 all for cash.
5. Had goods in stock at the end of the year which cost £4000.
6. Paid expenses on the van of £1000.
7. Paid rent on his premises of £1500.

Let us first see what the worksheet would look like for Brian's business and we will then see how the same transactions would be represented under the traditional method.

Brian's worksheet – version 1

| | Assets | | | = | Equity + Liabilities | | |
| | | | | | Owner's | Profit | |
	Cash	Van	Stock		equity	& loss	Creditors
Item 1	10000				10000		
Item 2	−5000	5000					
Item 3			35000				35000
	−33000						−33000
Item 4	45000					45000	
Item 5			−31000			−31000	
Item 6	−1000					−1000	
Item 7	−1500					−1500	
Balance	14500	5000	4000		10000	11500	2000

You should make sure that you understand the entries on the worksheet above before moving on. If you do have problems refer back to the appropriate chapters.

Now we record the same transactions using the traditional approach of 'T' accounts:

		Cash					Owner's equity	
Item 1	10000	Item 2	5000				Item 1	10000
Item 4	45000	Item 3	33000					
		Item 6	1000				Creditors	
		Item 7	1500					
		Bal. c/d	14500		Item 3	33000	Item 3	35000
	55000		55000		Bal. c/d	2000		
Bal. b/d	14500					35000		35000
							Bal. b/d	2000

Van	
Item 2 5 000	

Stock			
Item 3 35 000	Item 5 31 000		
	Bal. c/d 4 000		
35 000	35 000		
Bal. b/d 4 000			

Profit & loss			
Item 5 31 000	Item 4 45 000		
Item 6 1 000			
Item 7 1 500			
Bal. c/d 11 500			
45 000	45 000		

A careful examination of both systems will show that they have recorded the same transactions. All that has changed is the way in which the recording has been represented. This will be made clearer if we explain some of the items and the ways in which they have been treated.

For example, with the worksheet approach, to deal with Item 1 where Brian puts some money into the business, we opened up a column entitled Cash and one entitled Owner's equity on the other side of the worksheet. We then entered the amount involved, £10 000, in each of these columns. By contrast, under the traditional approach, we opened two 'T' accounts. One of these was for Cash and the other for Owner's equity. We then entered the amount involved, £10 000, in these two accounts. All that is happening is that in contrast to the use of columns to represent accounts the traditional approach uses 'T' accounts.

Using 'T' accounts it is perhaps less clear which side of the account the entry should go on. In the case of assets the entry is put on the debit side, i.e. the left-hand side, and in the case of liabilities it is put on the credit side, i.e. the right-hand side.

We now consider the way in which Item 2, the purchase of the fixed asset, is dealt with. We find that using the worksheet approach a new column is opened for the asset and the cash column is reduced by the amount paid for the new asset, i.e. £5000. The traditional approach also starts in the same way by opening a new account for the new asset, and puts the cost of £5000 on the left-hand side because it is an asset. So far, the methods are essentially similar. The other half of the transaction is, perhaps, slightly more difficult to follow as we have to reduce the cash balance. This is done by putting the £5000 on the right-hand side of the cash account. This is called crediting an account – in this case we are crediting an asset account.

Even at this stage it may be becoming obvious that the worksheet approach is easier to follow as it relies less on jargon and rote learning

---

Under the traditional approach assets are shown as debit balances and liabilities are shown as credit balances.

KEY CONCEPT 12.1

DEBITS AND CREDITS

than the more traditional approach. Another advantage of the worksheet approach is that we know at the end of the exercise that we have balanced our accounts and if they do not balance the error can be found by working back through the worksheet as described in Chapter 6. In the case of the more traditional approach, we are as yet unsure that our accounts balance so we would now extract what is commonly known as a trial balance. If having extracted this trial balance we found that it did not balance we would have to check through most if not all of the entries in our accounts to find the error. Hopefully that will not be the case with the trial balance for Brian's business which would be as follows:

Trial balance of Brian's business

	Debit	Credit
Cash	14 500	
Equity		10 000
Creditors		2 000
Van	5 000	
Stock	4 000	
Profit & loss		11 500
	23 500	23 500

We can now see that the accounts do balance. You may have noticed that the columns are headed up debit and credit and that all the accounts from the left-hand side of our worksheet, the asset accounts, are in the debit column and all the accounts from the right-hand side of the worksheet, those that relate to claims on the business, are in the credit column. In this case we have not made an error in our double-entry as the trial balance balances, so we can move on to the next stage where final adjustments are made for accruals, depreciation, etc. These adjustments are often referred to in the literature as end-of-period or end-of-year adjustments.

End-of-period adjustments

As we have said end-of-period adjustments refer to adjustments such as those required to provide for depreciation, bad debts, accruals and prepayments, etc. These have all been covered in Chapters 7–11 and you should be familiar with the way in which they are dealt with via the worksheet. However, for the purposes of comparison we will initially show how they are dealt with through the worksheet and then look at how they are dealt with through the traditional approach.

Example 12.1 contd
At the end of the year Brian decides that the van will have no scrap value and should be depreciated at £1000 a year for five years. He also tells you that the rent is payable quarterly in advance so that only £1200 relates to this year.

Entering these adjustments on the worksheet would result in the worksheet shown below. You will notice that we have had to open two new accounts or columns to deal with the changes and then arrive at a new balance.

Brian's worksheet – version 2

	Assets				=	Equity + Liabilities		
					Owner's	Profit		
	Cash	Van	Stock	Prepaids	equity	& loss	Creditors	Depreciation
Item 1	10 000				10 000			
Item 2	−5 000	5000						
Item 3			35 000				35 000	
	−33 000						−33 000	
Item 4	45 000					45 000		
Item 5			−31 000			−31 000		
Item 6	−1 000					−1 000		
Item 7	−1 500					−1 500		
Balance	14 500	5000	4 000		10 000	11 500	2 000	
Adjustment						−1 000		1000
Adjustment				300		300		
Balance	14 500	5000	4 000	300	10 000	10 800	2 000	1000

In the traditional approach we would also have to create these new accounts and then extract another trial balance. However, there is also a short-cut which is often shown in textbooks and this involves making adjustments on what is effectively a type of worksheet. The difference between that worksheet and the one we use is that the rows and columns are transposed. This type of worksheet is also shown below and as you can see it merely extends the trial balance on the page previous to a new trial balance. This type of worksheet is often referred to as the extended trial balance.

The main differences between the two approaches in this respect is that when using the worksheet approach the final adjustments are automatically part of the double-entry system. Under the traditional approach they can be and often are outside the double-entry system. This can of course lead to errors and omissions which may be more difficult to trace. Let us look at the extended trial balance of Brian's business:

Brian's extended trial balance

	Debit	Credit	Adjustments Debit	Adjustments Credit	Debit	Credit
Cash	14 500				14 500	
Equity		10 000				10 000
Creditors		2 000				2 000
Van	5 000				5 000	
Stock	4 000				4 000	
Profit & loss		11 500	1000	300		10 800
Depreciation				1000		1 000
Prepaids			300		300	
	23 500	23 500	1300	1300	23 800	23 800

As can be seen the extended trial balance has also resulted in the need to open two new accounts and to make some adjustments to our existing profit and loss account. If these adjustments were done through double-entry in the 'T' accounts they would be shown as follows:

Prepaids		Profit & loss			
Adjustment 300		Item 5	31 000	Item 4	45 000
		Item 6	1 000		
Depreciation		Item 7	1 500		
		Bal c/d	11 500		
Adjustment 1 000			45 000		45 000
		Adjustment	1 000	Bal b/d	11 500
				Adjustment	300

We have seen that the differences between the two approaches are not differences of principle. Rather, they are alternative ways of depicting the same entries in the books of account of a firm. In the author's opinion, the advantages of the worksheet-based approach outweigh the advantages of the alternative approach and make it easier for those coming to the subject for the first time to assimilate the main principle involved in a double-entry book-keeping system. We shall now consider the way in which final accounts are produced and the rules and regulations governing their format.

Final accounts

Before we look at the regulations and the effects of different organizational form we should remind ourselves of the way in which the final accounts, i.e. the balance sheet and the profit and loss account, are derived from the worksheet. This may be more readily understood if we consider the example of Brian's business. We shall therefore extract the final accounts from the worksheet above.

**Profit and loss account of Brian's business
for the year ended on 30 June 1999**

	£	£
Sales		45 000
Cost of goods sold		31 000
Gross profit		14 000
Rent	1200	
Van expenses	1000	
Van depreciation	1000	3 200
Net profit		10 800

You will remember that the profit and loss account merely summarizes what is contained in that column of the worksheet and that it is titled the profit and loss account for the period ended on a certain date. This emphasizes that the profit and loss account is a period statement and here we can contrast it with the heading of the balance sheet below. This you will remember is a snapshot at a particular point in time.

**Balance sheet of Brian's business
as at 30 June 1999**

Fixed assets	£	£
Van at cost	5 000	
Depreciation	1 000	4 000
Current assets		
Stock	4 000	
Prepaids	300	
Cash	14 500	
	18 800	
Current liabilities		
Creditors	2 000	
	2 000	
Net current assets		16 800
		20 800
Financed by		£
Owner's equity		10 000
Profit and loss		10 800
		20 800

You will have noticed that the balance sheet merely takes the final line of the worksheet and classifies it under appropriate headings to enable the reader to interpret the information more readily. We will be dealing with the subject of interpretation in more detail in Chapter 14. Prior to that, however, we need to consider the effect of different forms of organizational structure on accounting reports.

Forms of organization

As we said in Chapter 2 there are many forms of organization possible, from a sole proprietorship, through partnerships, companies and groups of companies, to multinational conglomerates. In addition there are other less common forms such as cooperatives, friendly societies, provident societies, etc. Each of these organizational forms requires slightly different accounts. This may be due to the needs of the users being slightly different or to other factors such as the impact of legislation or other regulations, e.g. those imposed by the stock exchange. Rather than attempting to deal with all the different forms of organizations we will concentrate our discussion on the more common forms of organization, the sole proprietorship, the partnership and the limited company.

There are distinct differences in the presentation of final accounts which are related to legal requirements such as the Companies Act, the Partnership Act, the SSAPs and, to a lesser extent, case law. We shall commence our discussion with the smallest and perhaps the most common form of business organization, the sole proprietorship.

The sole proprietorship

The balance sheet and profit and loss account, in this case, are fairly straightforward as the business is set up as a simple form of organization in accounting terms. As the term sole proprietorship implies this is a business with a single owner who is also normally the manager and in many cases the only person involved in the business. As a form of business organization it is very simple to set up as all that is really required is a business bank account. Because it is so simple and has little recognition in law there are no formal guidelines for the format of the accounts. However, the fact that the business and the owner are not seen as separate legal entities could be a problem if the business gets into difficulties as the owner is liable for all the debts of the business and may have to sell personal possessions such as the family home to meet the debts of the business. In addition this form of organization relies heavily on the owner for finance and this can lead to problems if and when the business expands. This is due to the fact that small business owners often have fairly limited funds at their disposal as they have already invested their surplus funds in the business when it was started. These problems can be alleviated, if not solved, by, for example, introducing a partner to the business. The partner may bring additional funds, skills, contacts or whatever. Alternatively the owner may set up a company. This limits the liability of the owners but unless additional investors are found it does not solve any of the problems of a lack of finance, skills, etc.

Partnerships

A partnership exists where two or more people enter into an agreement to run a business together. As we have indicated above this can have a number of advantages in that the additional person may bring new finance to the business, or they may bring new skills or contacts etc. In essence partnerships are fairly simple organizations and are similar to a sole proprietorship in that the partners are jointly and severally liable for the debts of the partnership. The total risk is the same, all that happens is that the risk is spread among a greater number of people. Partnerships are also similar to proprietorships in that there are no rules governing the format of accounts so these can be tailored to meet the needs of the users of those accounts. However, as you can imagine, there is more potential for conflict when there is more than one owner and as such there is considerable case law surrounding partnerships as an organizational form.

For our purposes, we only need to consider some of the more common issues arising in accounting for partnerships. We shall start by considering the most basic situation where two people enter into an equal partnership, each putting in the same amount to the business and sharing profits equally. For accounting purposes all we need to do is to open a separate owner's equity account for each owner; these are generally referred to as 'partners' capital' accounts. We also need to open another account for each owner, or partner, to record other less permanent transactions; these are commonly referred to as 'partners' current' accounts. They record such things as the individual partner's entitlement to profit, their drawings, etc. It is important in law that the capital transactions and other transactions are separated as different legal treatments may be applied to each of these amounts if the partnership were to cease to exist. For our purposes we can work on the basis that the capital account relates only to deposits and withdrawals of permanent capital from the business and all other items are recorded via the current accounts. Let us use a simple example to illustrate how straightforward partnership accounting should be.

Example 12.2   Jane and John – part 1
Jane and John go into business together, sharing profits equally. Jane put in £1000 to the business whilst John put in £9000. They buy some fixed assets for £6000, some stock for £2000 and put the rest into a business bank account.

Before going on to the transactions of the period let us first examine how we would record the information to date on our worksheet:

Worksheet of Jane and John in partnership – version 1

	Assets		=	Equity + Liabilities	
	Cash	*Fixed assets*	*Stock*	*Jane's equity*	*John's equity*
Item 1	10 000			1000	9000
Item 2	−6 000	6000			
Item 3	−2 000		2000		

As you can see all that we have had to do is to open a separate account for each partner which we have called Jane's equity and John's equity. More correctly these should be referred to as capital rather than equity so from now on we will adopt that title.

Example 12.2   Jane and John – part 2
During the first year they sold goods for cash amounting to £30 000 and bought additional stock for £13 000; other expenses amounted to £4000 and they had goods in stock at the end of the year amounting to £3000. The fixed assets are to be depreciated over five years, straight line with no residual value.

Recording the above on the worksheet we find that at the end of the year there is a profit of £12 800 to be divided between the two partners. You will see that on the worksheet reproduced below we have opened partners' current accounts and have put their shares of the profits in their current accounts.

Worksheet of Jane and John in partnership – version 2

	Cash	*Fixed assets*	*Stock*	*= Jane's capital*	*John's capital*	*Profit & loss*	*Jane's current*	*John's current*
Cash in	10 000			1000	9000			
Fixed assets	−6 000	6000						
Stock	−2 000		2 000					
Sales	30 000					30 000		
Stock	−13 000		13 000					
Expenses	−4 000					−4 000		
Depreciation		−1200				−1 200		
Cost of sales			−12 000			−12 000		
Balance	15 000	4800	3 000	1000	9000	12 800		
Distribution						−12 800	6400	6400
	15 000	4800	3 000	1000	9000	0	6400	6400

You should also have noticed that, because the profit has been distributed to the partners via their current accounts, the final balance on the profit and loss column is nil.

As you can see, the principles involved are very simple. It is really only a question of separating the various transactions. What often makes it more complex is that the partnership agreement itself may be complicated. For example, a partnership agreement may require that interest is paid on the balances on the partners' accounts, or on just the balances on the capital accounts. It might require that certain partners get paid salaries or a bonus, and each of these may happen before or after profits are split. Finally a partnership agreement may require that profits are split according to some other formula than equal shares. Each of these situations can be easily handled if the partnership agreement is well drafted as all one does is follow the instructions contained within it.

Before we look at an example to illustrate how this is done let us examine some of the reasons why these requirements are included in partnership agreements.

Interest on capital

This is usually included in a situation where the partners contribute uneven amounts of money to the partnership. For instance, as Jane had put in £1000 to John's £9000 they may decide to compensate him for the fact he has more money at risk by giving interest on the capital before dividing the profit. This is illustrated in part 3 of our example.

Example 12.2   Jane and John – part 3
Jane and John decided that, as their capital invested was not equal, interest at 10 per cent would be paid on the balances on their capital accounts before the profit was divided. The new version of the worksheet would be as shown below.

Worksheet of Jane and John in partnership – version 3
after charging interest at 10%

	Cash	Fixed assets	Stock	= Jane's capital	John's capital	Profit & loss	Jane's current	John's current
Cash in	10 000			1000	9000			
Fixed assets	−6 000	6000						
Stock	−2 000		2 000					
Sales	30 000					30 000		
Stock	−13 000		13 000					
Expenses	−4 000					−4 000		
Depreciation		−1200				−1 200		
Cost of sales			−12 000			−12 000		
Balance	15 000	4800	3 000	1000	9000	12 800		
Interest						−1 000	100	900
Distribution						−11 800	5900	5900
	15 000	4800	3 000	1000	9000	0	6000	6800

By comparing this with the previous worksheet, you can see that the only effects are on the amounts in each partner's current account. This is because the interest is charged to the profit and loss first and this affects the resultant distribution.

Payment of salaries or bonus

A payment of a salary or a bonus is often done to reward particular partners for getting new business or for putting in more work in the business than the other partners. If, for example, Jane worked in the business every day of the week whereas John was rarely involved in the day-to-day running of the business, they may decide that Jane should receive a salary.

Example 12.2 Jane and John – part 4

Jane and John decided that Jane should receive a salary of £5000 a year before interest was paid and before the profit was divided up. The resultant worksheet would be as shown below. Once again it is important to notice that the amount of the profit has not changed but that the partners' shares of the profit have been altered to reflect their various inputs to the business. As before the final balance on the profit and loss account after the distributions is nil.

Worksheet of Jane and John in partnership – version 4
after charging salary and interest at 10%

	Cash	Fixed assets	Stock	= Jane's capital	John's capital	Profit & loss	Jane's current	John's current
Cash in	10 000			1000	9000			
Fixed assets	−6 000	6000						
Stock	−2 000		2 000					
Sales	30 000					30 000		
Stock	−13 000		13 000					
Expenses	−4 000					−4 000		
Depreciation		−1200				−1 200		
Cost of sales			−12 000			−12 000		
Balance	15 000	4800	3 000	1000	9000	12 800		
Salary						−5 000	5000	
Interest						−1 000	100	900
Distribution						−6 800	3400	3400
	15 000	4800	3 000	1000	9000	0	8500	4300

Uneven shares of profit

Because partners bring different skills, expertise and connections to a business venture it is not uncommon for the partners to decide to share profits in some other ratio than equally.

Example 12.2 Jane and John – part 4

Jane and John decided that because John had a number of contracts which were the backbone of the business that he should take 60 per cent of the profit and Jane would have the other 40 per cent. The worksheet would now be as follows:

Worksheet of Jane and John in partnership – version 5
after charging salary and interest at 10%
profits split 40:60

	Cash	Fixed assets	Stock	= Jane's capital	John's capital	Profit & loss	Jane's current	John's current
Cash in	10 000			1000	9000			
Fixed assets	−6 000	6000						
Stock	−2 000		2 000					
Sales	30 000					30 000		
Stock	−13 000		13 000					
Expenses	−4 000					−4 000		
Depreciation		−1200				−1 200		
Cost of sales			−12 000			−12 000		
Balance	15 000	4800	3 000	1000	9000	12 800		
Salary						−5 000	5000	
Interest						−1 000	100	900
Distribution						−6 800	2720	4080
	15 000	4800	3 000	1000	9000	0	7820	4980

As before the only alteration is to the distribution of the profit – the calculation of the profit itself is unaffected. This change in profit sharing arrangements, like the previous ones, affects the balance on the individual partners' current accounts. It is worth noting whilst we are on the subject of current accounts that these accounts are used not only to record distributions of profits etc. at the end of the year, but they are also used to record withdrawals from the business as these occur through the year.

Partnership final accounts

Before leaving this introduction to the subject of accounting for partnerships we shall look at the format of the partnership final accounts and compare it with those of a sole proprietorship. The important aspects of partnership accounts which are reflected in the final accounts are:

☐ each partner's equity should be separately identified;
☐ a split should be made between capital and other amounts due to the partners.

The majority of the non-capital transactions will be reflected in the balances on the current accounts. It may be that a partner makes a loan to the partnership, in which case this would be dealt with separately in the same way as any other loan rather than being included in the partner's current account.

Profit and loss account of Jane and John's partnership
for the year ended on 30 June 1994

	£	£
Sales		30 000
Cost of sales		12 000
Gross profit		18 000

		£	£
Expenses		4000	
Depreciation		1200	5 200
Net profit			12 800
Distributions			
Salary:	Jane		5 000
			7 800
Interest:	Jane	100	
	John	900	1 000
			6 800
Profit share: Jane		2720	
	John	4080	6 800
			Nil

If you compare the format of this profit and loss account with the one for Brian's sole proprietorship which we completed earlier in this chapter you will see that the only difference is that the partnership profit and loss account has a 'distribution statement' added on. Although this is often shown as part of the profit and loss account there are no hard and fast rules and it would be equally acceptable for it to be a separate report. The way in which the accounts are presented is largely up to the partners involved. This is also true for the balance sheet of the partnership. For our example the balance sheet is as follows:

Balance sheet of Jane and John's partnership
as at 30 June 1994

	£	£
Fixed assets		
Fixed assets	6 000	
Depreciation	1 200	4 800
Current assets		
Stock	3 000	
Cash	15 000	
	18 000	
Current liabilities		
Creditors	Nil	
	Nil	
Net current assets		18 000
		22 800
Financed by	£	£
Partners' capital accounts		
Jane	1 000	
John	9 000	10 000
Partners' current accounts		
Jane	7 820	
John	4 980	12 800
		22 800

We can see that the major difference in terms of the balance sheet is in the section relating to how the business is financed, where the owners' equity is divided between the owners and subdivided according to its permanency. The more permanent investment is in the capital accounts, and the less permanent in the partners' current accounts.

As we have seen, the fact that a business is set up as a partnership provides us with more accounting problems than if it were a sole proprietorship but also potentially can provide the business with greater access to skills and finance. However, the owners are still liable for the whole of the debts of the business should it go bankrupt. It is mainly for this reason that many small businesses are set up as limited companies, and it is this popular form of business organization which we shall now consider.

Limited companies

Unlike the partnership and the sole proprietorship, a limited company is recognized as a separate legal entity which is quite distinct from its owners. As such the debts incurred in the normal course of business are those of the company. In the case of a default in payment it is the company which has to be sued rather than the owners. The fact that the owners may also be the managers and the only employees is irrelevant as in the eyes of the law all these roles are different.

Generally, companies are set up in a particular form to meet the requirements of the business concerned. For non-commercial organizations requiring the legal status of a company, it is likely that the company to be set up will be a company limited by guarantee. In this type of company, the members promise to contribute a guaranteed amount should the company fail. The amount of such a guarantee is normally limited to £1 per member but may be any other amount.

For commercial organizations, the more common form of company is used. This is one where shares are issued to the owners. In this case their liability is limited to the nominal value of the shares. The owners are referred to as shareholders. These companies can be either private companies or public companies, and the latter category can be listed or unlisted. 'Listed' is a term referring to the fact that the company's shares are traded on a recognized stock exchange. We need not dwell on the detailed differences between the various types of company as this is outside the scope of this book. However, we can broadly say that private companies are generally easier to form but their shares cannot be freely traded on a stock exchange, whereas public companies (Plcs) have shares which are freely transferable and must have a share capital in excess of £50 000. Public companies are also subject to more restrictions and regulation than private companies and may well be subject to other forms of regulation such as the stock exchange requirements which would not apply to private companies. In addition some of the accounting standards apply only to listed companies and certain other large companies.

We shall limit our discussion to private companies and discuss the advantages of this type of organization over those already dealt with. The main advantage has already been mentioned – the limitation on the liability of the owners of the business in the event of the business being insolvent. Other advantages come from the ability to arrange distribution of profits and indeed of control by means of the share ownership of the various parties concerned. For example, in the case of Jane and John, although they put unequal amounts into the business, under partnership law they both would have an equal say in any decisions being made as would any new partner they took on in the future. If, however, they set up their organization as a company they could arrange the voting rights as they wished as each share issued normally carries the right to one vote but non-voting shares can also be issued. Therefore, through the issue of different types of shares they could adjust the amount of power and control each shareholder could exercise.

There are disadvantages to the limited company as an organizational form mainly to do with the fact that they are subject to various regulatory legislation. For example, they are required to produce accounts annually and to have these audited by a recognized firm of auditors. This can be expensive. A copy of the audited accounts have to be lodged at Companies House where they are available for inspection. The form of these accounts is also subject to the requirements of company law which requires that a company's accounts should comprise:

☐ the company's balance sheet;
☐ the company's profit and loss account;
☐ the directors' report;
☐ the auditors' report.

In addition to these general requirements there are detailed requirements covering the format and content of the actual accounts. Many of these requirements have already been discussed in the earlier chapters and some will be discussed in Chapter 14. To discuss the detailed requirements in depth is outside the scope of an introductory text so instead we have included below an illustrative set of accounts for a private company, and you should look at these in the light of the accompanying text which highlights areas of difference between the accounts of the limited company and the other forms of organization dealt with in this chapter. We shall commence our discussion with a look at the profit and loss account:

**Profit and loss account of Broll Ltd
for the year to 31 July 1993**

	Notes	£	1993 £	1992 £
Sales	1		60 000	45 000
Cost of sales			40 000	30 000
Gross profit			20 000	15 000
Distribution costs		4 000		(2 500)

	Notes	£	1993 £	1992 £
Administration costs		11 000	15 000	(9 000)
Profit on ordinary activities	2		5 000	3 500
Taxation	3		2 600	1 400
Profit after taxation			2 400	2 100
Extraordinary item	4		1 000	–
Profit after extraordinary items			3 400	2 100
Dividends – interim	5	1 000		–
– final	5	1 600	2 600	1 100
Transfer to reserves			800	1 000

The first difference is contained in the title of the profit and loss account where the fact that Broll is a limited company is stated. In addition the profit and loss contains comparative figures for the previous year, as well as references to a number of notes. These notes normally contain greater detail than can be shown on the face of the accounts and as such are an integral part of the analysis of the accounts of a company. The detailed disclosure contained in these notes is laid down in the Companies Act legislation and the accounting standards. The use of the notes to the accounts will be discussed in more detail in Chapter 14. We can see that apart from the notes the format as far as the gross profit is familiar. However, we then find expenses being classified into broad categories. These categories are laid down in the legislation. This is one of the two alternative formats allowed in that legislation. Those who wish to read about the alternative format and the detailed legislation will find more information in the books included in the further reading at the end of this chapter. It is worth noting that compliance with the Companies Acts means that the level of detail disclosed is generally less than one would expect for an equivalent small business.

As far as the notes to the accounts are concerned, there are detailed requirements regarding disclosure of turnover contained in the Companies Act and SSAP 25 *Segmental Reporting*, but the latter generally only applies to larger and more complex organizations than we are discussing here. In respect of the profit on the ordinary activities the note would, in most cases, include details of depreciation, and amortization charges, directors' emoluments, auditors' remuneration, and hire of plant and equipment. Other items may also be disclosed here depending on the circumstances of the company concerned.

You will remember that we said earlier that companies are recognized as separate entities for taxation purposes and are subject to corporation tax. In contrast the sole proprietorship and partnership are not separate legal or taxable entities and the profit is only taxable as income of the owners rather than in its own right. The detailed breakdown of the taxation charge is normally provided by way of note, and the disclosure must meet the requirements of SSAP 8 *The Treatment of Taxation Under the Imputation System*, and of SSAP 15 *Accounting for Deferred Taxation*.

Moving on through the profit and loss account we find that note 4 relates to the extraordinary item and this would provide details of the nature of the extraordinary item or items, and the tax charge thereon, thus meeting the requirements of SSAP 6 *Extraordinary Items and Prior Year Adjustments*. The final part of the profit and loss account relates to the distribution of the available profit. This part of the profit and loss account can be seen as analogous with the distribution statement in the partnership accounts which we have just considered. We have a note relating to the amount of profit which is distributed by way of dividend which gives details of the dividends per share. The dividends themselves are in fact a form of distribution to the owners (the shareholders) and are pro rata to the number of shares held. The fact that there is an interim and final dividend in one year and not in the other is not unusual as the declaration of any dividend depends upon the needs of the business and the availability of both profits and liquid funds to pay them. An interim dividend is in fact essentially a payment made part way through the year and is also dependent on both profitability and the availability of liquid funds. The final line of the profit and loss relates to the transfer to reserves which is the residual balance being transferred to the profit and loss or other reserves. The breakdown of the transfers to each reserve would be given as part of the requirements for disclosure in relation to the balance sheet which we will now consider:

**Balance sheet of Broll Ltd
as at 31 July 1993**

	Notes	£	1993 £	1992 £
Fixed assets				
Intangible assets	6		10 000	11 000
Tangible assets	7		50 000	56 000
			60 000	67 000
Current assets				
Stocks	8	10 000		7 000
Debtors		10 000		4 000
Cash at bank and in hand		3 500		2 000
		23 500		13 000
Creditors: amounts falling due in less than one year				
Creditors		4 000		3 000
Taxation	3	2 600		1 400
Dividends	5	1 600		1 100
		8 200		5 500
Net current assets			15 300	7 500
Creditors: amounts falling due after more than one year	9		10 000	10 000
Total net assets			65 300	64 500
Capital and reserves			£	£
Share capital	10		60 000	60 000
Retained profits	11		5 300	4 500
			65 300	64 500

As you can see the top half of the balance sheet is very similar to those we have encountered before, apart from the inclusion of dividends and taxation and the fact that a lot of the detail is left to the notes to the accounts. For example, notes 6 and 7 would contain details of the various classes of the fixed assets, the fixed assets bought and sold during the year, as well as the depreciation or amortization to date and the charges for the year. The detailed disclosure requirements in respect of the intangible fixed assets are contained in the Companies Acts and the various accounting standards we have referred to, e.g. SSAP 13 *Accounting for Research and Development* and SSAP 22 *Accounting for Goodwill*. Similarly the note on stock would provide the detail necessary to comply with the legislation and SSAP 9 *Stocks and Long-Term Contracts*, and the note on 'Creditors: amounts falling due after more than one year' would give the details of loans and debentures, repayment dates and interest rates in accordance with the requirements of the legislation.

You will note that the long-term liabilities are not portrayed in this balance sheet format as a source of long-term finance. Instead the balance sheet shows the 'Total net assets'. This reflects a proprietary view of the business whereby the accounts are being prepared for the owners rather than being a report from an entity viewpoint where the distinction between the various forms of long-term finance may be less relevant. As a result of taking this proprietary view the other half of the balance sheet is somewhat different. It consists of the owners' equity split between the share capital and the reserves. The share capital may consist of different types of share capital, details of which need to be provided in the notes. Similarly there may be a number of different types of reserves such as revaluation reserves, and once again details of the reserves and the movements on these need to be given in the notes. In our illustration the only reserve is the retained profits which is similar to the account for that purpose in the case of a sole proprietorship.

Summary

In this chapter we have introduced the idea that different organizational forms require accounts in different formats and that there are reasons for the different organizational forms which impact upon the accounting formats. For example, in the case of a partnership there is a need to differentiate between the amounts belonging to each partner and to distinguish between those amounts that are more permanent in nature and those that are temporary. It should be apparent that the requirements are in the main logically derived and that the differences that do exist are relatively minor in accounting terms. This is as it should be: the most appropriate form of organization should be governed by sound business considerations rather than by accounting requirements or burdens imposed by legislation.

The balance sheet and profit and loss account from Bentalls Plc 1992 accounts are reproduced below. They provide a good example of what can be found in a company's annual report. They contain figures that are, in the main, summary figures and without looking in the notes to the accounts they may not be that useful. For example, as you can see, although there is an operating profit of £1816, the retained profit in both years is negative. This is due to the fact that the directors have decided to recommend a dividend despite the fact that there are not enough profits to cover this. The explanation for this could be to do with having a large number of preference shares or because the directors have decided to maintain dividends regardless. We can only find out which of these two alternatives is in fact the case by looking at the notes to the accounts. These in fact reveal that the vast majority of this dividend is paid to ordinary shareholders which indicates that the directors have adopted a policy of dividend maintenance through the recession.

CASE 12.1

COMPANY FINAL ACCOUNTS

Profit and Loss Account
for the year ending 1 February 1992

	Note	1992 £'000	1992 £'000	1991 (53 weeks) £'000	1991 £'000
Turnover	2		70 997		70 727
Cost of sales			44 763		43 851
Gross profit			26 234		26 876
Selling and distribution		21 523		20 445	
Administrative expenses		2 895		3 107	
			24 418		23 552
Operating profit	3		1 816		3 324
Interest receivable		34		107	
Interest payable	6	(2 874)		(1 952)	
Interest capitalised	11	2 453		1 844	
			(387)		(1)
Profit on ordinary activities before taxation			1 429		3 323
Tax on profit on ordinary activities	7		499		1 289
Profit on ordinary activities after taxation			930		2 034
Extraordinary items	8		–		(1 419)
Profit available for appropriation			930		615
Dividends	9		1 617		1 617
(Loss) retained			(687)		(1 002)

Continued over page

Continued from previous page

Balance Sheet
1 February 1992

	Note	1992 £'000	1992 £'000	1991 £'000	1991 £'000
Fixed assets					
Investment in property	11	**35 108**			33 500
Other tangible fixed assets	12	**52 382**			51 603
			87 490		85 103
Current assets					
Stocks		**11 160**		9 290	
Debtors	14	**11 843**		10 613	
Cash at bank and in hand	15	**923**		3 911	
		23 926		23 814	
Creditors – amounts falling due within one year					
Bank overdraft	18	**1 564**		–	
Unsecured loan stock	17	**30**		30	
Trade creditors		**7 019**		8 437	
Sundry creditors	16	**7 639**		8 189	
		16 252		16 656	
Net current assets			**7 674**		7 158
Total assets less current liabilities			**95 164**		92 261
Creditors – amounts falling due after more than one year					
Creditors	17	**1 339**		1 930	
Bank loan	18	**22 000**		18 000	
		23 339		19 930	
Provisions for liabilities and charges	19	**2 169**		1 867	
			25 508		21 797
			69 656		70 464
Capital and reserves called up share capital	20		**4 294**		4 273
Reserves	21				
Share premium account		**188**		130	
Revaluation reserve		**49 531**		49 531	
Profit and loss account		**15 643**		16 530	
Total reserves			**65 362**		66 191
Shareholders' funds			**69 656**		70 464

The Financial Statements were approved by the Board of Directors on 22 April 1992

L. Edward Bentall
J.B. Ryan

The notes on pages 18 to 27 form an integral part of these accounts.

References

Statement of Standard Accounting Practice No. 3 (1972) *Earnings per Share*, Accounting Standards Committee.

Statement of Standard Accounting Practice No. 6 (1986) *Extraordinary Items and Prior Year Adjustments*, Accounting Standards Committee.

Statement of Standard Accounting Practice No. 8 (1977) *Treatment of Taxation under the Imputation System*, Accounting Standards Committee.

Statement of Standard Accounting Practice No. 9 (1975) *Stocks and Long-term Contracts*, Accounting Standards Committee.

Statement of Standard Accounting Practice No. 12 (1986) *Accounting for Depreciation*, Accounting Standards Committee.

Statement of Standard Accounting Practice No. 13 (1987) *Accounting for Research and Development*, Accounting Standards Committee.

Statement of Standard Accounting Practice No. 15 (1985) *Accounting for Deferred Taxation*, Accounting Standards Committee.

Statement of Standard Accounting Practice No. 22 (1984) *Accounting for Goodwill*, Accounting Standards Committee.

Statement of Standard Accounting Practice No. 25 (1990) *Segmental Reporting*, Accounting Standards Committee.

Further reading

Blake, J. (1991) *Accounting Standards*, 3rd edn, Pitman.

Coopers & Lybrand (1986) *Form and Content of Company Accounts*, Financial Training Publications.

Lee, G.A. (1986) *Modern Financial Accounting*, Van Nostrand Reinhold.

Limmack, R.J. (1985) *Financial Accounting and Reporting – An Introduction*, Macmillan.

Review questions

1. Explain in your own words the meaning of the terms trial balance and extended trial balance.

2. Explain the meaning of the term 'final adjustments'.

3. Explain the difference between a sole proprietorship and a partnership.

4. Explain the reasons why partnership agreements often contain clauses relating to interest, bonuses, salaries and division of profits.

5. Why is it advantageous to set a business up as a limited company?

6. What are the differences between a sole proprietorship and a limited liability company?

7. Describe how the choice of organizational form determines the format of the final accounts.

Problems for discussion and analysis

The information below forms the basis for the questions which follow.

Susan sets up a business on her own as a sole proprietorship and has the following balance sheet at the end of year 1:

Balance sheet of Susan's business at the end of year 1

Fixed assets	Cost	Depreciation	Net book value
Equipment	12 000	2 400	9 600
Vehicle	6 000	1 500	4 500
	18 000	3 900	14 100
Current assets			
Stock		7 000	
Debtors		6 500	
		13 500	
Current liabilities			
Creditors		6 000	
Bank overdraft		4 500	
		10 500	
Net current assets			3 000
			17 100
Financed by			
Owner's equity			10 000
Profit for year		12 000	
Less: Drawings		4 900	7 100
			17 100

At the end of the first year Susan realized that although the business was profitable she could hardly take out enough money to live on because she was heavily reliant on her bank and creditors already. She also found that a lot of her time which could have been used to produce more goods was being taken up selling goods, collecting debts and generally doing administrative work.

She therefore decided at the start of the second year to take in a partner who would put an additional £5000 into the business and would be able to do some of the selling and other tasks after Susan had trained him. The agreement was a verbal agreement only on the first day of the new year and the two of them agreed to share profits equally.

In the second year the summarized transactions of the business were as follows:

Sales, all on credit £70 000; Moneys received from debtors £62 000; Purchases, all on credit £40 000; Moneys paid to creditors £38 000; Moneys introduced by new partner, Bob, £5000; Other expenses incurred and paid £7000; Drawings by Susan £7000 and by Bob £5000; Goods in stock at the end of the year £9000.

1. The current partnership agreement between Susan and Bob has the advantage of being simple. If you were advising Susan would you suggest any alternatives to the present agreement and, if so, why?

2. What, if any, additional accounts need to be opened in the second year to cope with the fact that the business is now a partnership and for what reason are they needed?

3. How do you propose to deal with the following:
   (a) The balance of £7100, i.e. the profit after drawings.
   (b) The drawings from the business by Susan and Bob in year two.
   (c) The money introduced by Bob in year two.

4. Produce the final accounts of the partnership for year two in a form suitable for a partnership.

5. Discuss what changes would need to be made if Susan and Bob decided to form a company to take over the business to protect both partners' interests as they stand under the current partnership agreement.

13 Alternative financial statements

In this chapter we shall consider some of the other forms of financial reporting that have been suggested, or are currently being used, to supplement the information provided by the profit and loss account and balance sheet. The particular statements we shall be discussing are the cash flow statement, the statement of source and application of funds and the value added statement. In general these statements are perceived as supplementary although staunch supporters of the cash flow approach to accounting would argue that it should replace accrual accounting.

We shall consider the statement of source and application of funds and the cash flow statement together as these are so closely related that dealing with them separately would serve little purpose.

Funds flow and cash flow statements

The Corporate Report (1975) identified as one of the needs of users the need for information regarding liquidity. In the same year the report of the Committee on Inflation Accounting, commonly referred to as the Sandilands Report, also identified the need for information on liquidity. Also in that year the Accounting Standards Committee issued SSAP 10 which required all companies with a turnover in excess of £25 000 to produce as part of their annual accounts a statement of source and application of funds. However, from 1992 the statement of source and application of funds will be replaced by a cash flow statement.

We shall deal mainly with the latter statement in this chapter, but first we need to know what both statements show and what the differences are.

What do these statements show?

These statements tell us where we got money from, the sources, and how we have used that money, the applications. Typical sources of funds would be monies generated from trading, commonly referred to as operations, monies from new share issues or other forms of long-term finance, and any monies received from the sale of fixed assets. Typical applications for a limited company would be to buy new fixed assets, to pay tax and dividends, and to repay debenture holders or other providers of long-term capital. For reasons that will become apparent, this in-

formation could be very useful to the user of accounts, hence the degree
of interest in these statements.

What are the differences?

The easy answer to the question is that each statement has a different
definition of funds. This leads to the more difficult question of what is a
fund. This is more difficult to answer because a fund can be defined in a
number of ways. However, as Laughlin and Gray point out, there are
three main definitions of funds. The first is a cash definition of funds
which sees cash balances as the only amounts which represent an organization's purchasing power. The second is slightly broader and includes,
in addition to cash and bank balances, near cash items. (It should be
noted that these are not what the Financial Reporting Standard 1 (FRS 1)
– see below – refers to as cash equivalents.) They include debtors,
creditors, overdrafts and other short-term near cash items, whereas the
FRS 1 definition would exclude debtors and creditors and would in fact
be closer to the first definition of funds. The third definition is a working
capital definition. This includes cash, bank balances, debtors, creditors,
overdrafts and other short-term near cash items, plus stock and work in
progress.

The third definition was the one adopted, albeit implicitly, by SSAP 10.
The source and application of funds statement, illustrated in the appendix
to SSAP 10, showed the funds from operations, plus the funds from other
sources, less the applications. This produced a figure representing the
movement in working capital. SSAP 10 was in fact not very clear on the
question of how the source and application of funds statement should
be constructed and what definition of funds it had adopted. This led to
different companies using different definitions. For example, the 1986/7
Survey of Published Accounts showed 33 per cent of the companies in the
sample used net liquid funds in their source and application statement, 29
per cent used working capital and 25 per cent used net borrowing.

Not surprisingly, the source and application of funds statement was not
well understood and was not used as much as might have been expected.
For example, research by Berry *et al.* (1987) showed that only 67 per cent
of bankers rated it as very important compared with 91 per cent rating the
balance sheet and profit and loss account as very important. In terms
of the bankers' detailed analysis of the information in the source and
application of funds statement this was used by less than 50 per cent of
the respondents. This was surprising as the banking and accounting
literature – and indeed Egginton's earlier work (1975) – would lead one
to believe that bankers would be very interested in any statement relating
to liquidity. However, comments from the bankers indicated that they
redrafted the source and application of funds statement into a format
which they could understand and which they felt was more appropriate to
their needs.

As the requirement for a source and application of funds statement
no longer exists we shall not spend time explaining the mechanics of
producing that statement. Instead we shall concentrate on the cash flow
statement. We shall, however, illustrate the differences between the cash

flow statement and a source and application statement prepared using the same information.

The cash flow statement

In September 1991 the Accounting Standards Board (ASB) issued Financial Reporting Standard No. 1 (FRS 1). This standard deals with cash flow statements and requires all companies falling within the 1985 Companies Act definition of medium- and large-size companies to produce a cash flow statement as part of the annual accounts. In discussing the advantages of cash flow statements the ASB pointed out that, had such a statement been produced for Polly Peck which went into receivership in 1991, it would have shown that despite a trading profit of £139 million Polly Peck had a net cash outflow from operations of £129 million. In order to survive a company needs to be profitable and solvent, and clearly in the case of Polly Peck the company was not solvent even in the short term. The ASB, in FRS 1, claimed the cash flow statement had four advantages over its predecessor the source and application of funds statement, namely:

☐ **Funds flow data can obscure movements in liquidity**. Under SSAP 10, the source and application of funds statement showed the increase or decrease in working capital and then an analysis of that increase or decrease. What could easily happen is that an increase in working capital consists of increased stock which is not selling and an increase in debtors who may be poor payers. This disguises the fact that there is a large increase in short-term borrowing and in trade creditors. This did in fact happen in most of the companies in the toy industry that became insolvent in the early 1980s.

☐ **Cash flow is more easily understood than changes in working capital**. For anyone who has not studied accounting the concept of cash flow is part of their everyday life, therefore they are already familiar with the idea. Working capital, on the other hand, requires a lot more knowledge of the workings of business.

☐ **Cash flows can be directly input into the business valuation models used by financial analysts**. As we explained in Chapter 1, financial analysts are a user group in their own right. They also act as advisers to individual shareholders. Therefore if the information is more useful to them then it is meeting the needs of users better.

☐ **Cash flows may in certain circumstances give more information than was provided by funds flows**. These special circumstances are outside the scope of this book so we shall simply accept the statement at face value rather than go into a lengthy explanation of the circumstances to which the ASB are referring.

FRS 1 requires that the cash flow statement shows cash flows under five headings. The first of these relates to cash flow from operating activities, broadly trading activities, and the second to money earned from investments and to money paid to providers of finance in the form of interest. The third heading relates to taxation, specifically money paid out and recovered in respect of corporation tax. The fourth heading relates to investing activities, that is to purchases and sales of fixed assets etc. The final heading is the cash flows relating to the financing of the business. This would include amounts received from share issues, new loans or debentures, less any amounts paid out in terms of redemption of shares, loans or debentures.

The easiest way of understanding how cash flow statements would be constructed is to work through an example. Prior to that it is worth considering what it is we are trying to construct. For this we shall look at one of the examples of the cash flow statement illustrated in the appendix to FRS 1. We shall explain its components and the information that can be obtained from it.

Sample cash flow statement

Net cash inflow from operating activities		6889
Returns on investments and servicing of finance		
Interest received	3011	
Interest paid	(12)	
Dividends paid	(2417)	
Net cash flow from returns on investment and servicing activities		582
Taxation		
Corporation tax paid (including ACT)	(2922)	
Net cash outflow from taxation		(2922)
Investing activities		
Payment to acquire intangible fixed assets	(71)	
Payment to acquire tangible fixed assets	(1496)	
Receipts from sales of tangible fixed assets	42	
Net cash outflow from investing activity		(1525)
Net cash inflow before financing		3024
Financing		
Issue of ordinary share capital	211	
Repurchase of debenture loan	(149)	
Expenses paid in connection with share issues	(5)	
Net cash inflow from financing		57
Increase in cash or cash equivalents		3081

As you can see from the statement the first figure is the net cash inflow from operating activities. This figure is derived from the profit after allowing for movements that do not involve any cash flows, e.g. depreciation and profits or losses on sales of fixed assets. To this are added movements in stock, debtors and creditors. The detail of this would be provided in a note to the cash flow statement. An example based on the statement above is shown below:

Notes to the cash flow statement

Reconciliation of operating profit to net cash flow from operating activities	
Operating profit	6029
Depreciation charges	893

Loss on sale of tangible fixed assets	6
Profit on repurchase of debentures	(7)
Increase in stocks	(194)
Increase in debtors	(72)
Increase in creditors	234
	6889

As you can see the note provides a reconciliation between the operating profit shown in the profit and loss account and the cash flow from operating activities. If you think about it, the greater the amount of money the company has invested in depreciating fixed assets, the greater will be the depreciation charge added back, and therefore the difference between operating profit and cash flow from operations will be greater than for a company with very few depreciating fixed assets.

The next heading is self-explanatory as are its contents. As far as taxation is concerned, we have said already that companies are liable to corporation tax on their profits. Corporation tax is not due until, at least, nine months after the period to which it relates. However, if a company pays a dividend to its shareholders then it has to make a payment of corporation tax in advance of the final liability being agreed and paid. This payment on account is known as advance corporation tax (ACT). At this stage of your studies all you need to know is that it exists – later on you can look at the detailed treatment of taxation and the requirements of SSAP 8 and SSAP 15, both of which relate to taxation.

The rest of the contents of the cash flow statement are familiar and we shall not discuss them in any detail except to look at the additional notes that the standard requires. There is one relating to financing. This shows the changes in long-term finance arising from the issue or redemption of shares, debentures and long-term loans. An example based on the information in the cash flow statement above is reproduced below and, as you can see, it simply reconciles the opening and closing balances with the movements during the year:

Notes to the cash flow statement

Analysis of changes in financing during the year	Share capital	Debenture loan
Balance at 1 April 1991	27 411	156
Cash inflow (outflow) from financing	206	(149)
Profit on repurchase of debenture for less than book value		(7)
Balance at 31 March 1992	27 617	0

The other notes illustrated in the standard relate to the movements in, and analysis of, the cash and cash equivalents. The first of these would appear as follows:

Notes to the cash flow statement

Analysis of changes in cash and cash equivalents during the year

Balance at 1 April 1991	21 373
Net cash inflow for the year	3 081
Balance at 31 March 1992	24 454

This note reconciles the movement shown in the cash flow statement with the opening and closing figures. However, from the point of view of the user it does not provide enough information as there is no corresponding figure of cash and cash equivalents elsewhere in the accounts. There is therefore a need to provide an analysis of the figures which the user can then relate to the balance sheet or notes. An example based on the cash flow statement above is given below:

Notes to the cash flow statement

Analysis of the balances of cash and cash equivalents as shown in the balance sheet	1992	1991	Change
Cash at bank and in hand	529	682	(153)
Short-term investments	23 936	20 700	3236
Bank overdrafts	(11)	(9)	(2)
	24 454	21 373	3081

With the information in this note the user can reconcile the figures in the cash flow with the rest of the accounts. You will have noticed that FRS 1 and the cash flow statement are using 'cash and cash equivalent' as the funds definition. The FRS 1 definition of cash equivalents is given in Key Concept 13.1

Having examined the end product in some detail we shall now work through a simple example and use that as a vehicle for explaining the ideas involved. We shall start with a new business and see how the cash flow statement is prepared from the basic transaction information.

Example 13.1
On 1 April 1991 Downsend Ltd started business, buying and selling electrical goods. They arranged an overdraft facility of £10 000 if they needed it. The transactions for the first twelve months are summarized below:

April
The owners bought 10 000 ordinary shares of £1 nominal value at par value.
They purchased electrical goods for £8000 on one month's credit.
They purchased a van for £6000 and paid cash.
They purchased shop fittings for £4000 and paid cash.
They sold goods for £4000 of which £3000 was cash and the rest was credit sales.
They paid the van insurance and tax for the year of £300 in cash.
They paid the year's rent, in advance, of £6000 in cash.

May–March

The cash sales were £30 000 and credit sales were £25 000.

Cash amounting to £8000 was received from debtors.

They purchased another £40 000 of goods on credit and paid their creditors £34 000.

Paid wages to the assistant of £6500.

At the end of March 1992, the goods in stock had a cost price of £16 000. They decided to depreciate the van over five years and the fittings over four years using the straight line method. Neither of the fixed assets was thought to have any residual value. Their accountant calculated that they would owe corporation tax of £3000 and the directors decided to declare a dividend of £5000 for the year, none of which was paid in the year.

NB: Ignore the impact of ACT in this example.

Stage 1

The first stage is to record the transactions on a worksheet. This would appear as shown below:

Worksheet of Downsend Ltd for the year ended 31 March 1992

Description	Bank	Fixtures	Van	Stock	Debtors	Shares	Profit & loss	Creditors	Dep'n: Fixtures	Dep'n: Van	Tax	Dividend
Capital	10 000					10 000						
Goods				8 000				8 000				
Van	−6 000		6000									
Fittings	−4 000	4000										
Sales	3 000				1 000		4 000					
Tax etc.	−300						−300					
Rent	−6 000						−6 000					
Sales	30 000				25 000		55 000					
Debtors	8 000				−8 000							
Purchases				40 000				40 000				
Creditors	−34 000							−34 000				
Wages	−6 500						−6 500					
Cost of sales				−32 000			−32 000					
Depreciation							−2 200		1000	1200		
Balance	−5 800	4000	6000	16 000	18 000	10 000	12 000	14 000	1000	1200		
Tax							−3 000				3000	
Dividends							−5 000					5000
Final balance	−5 800	4000	6000	16 000	18 000	10 000	4 000	14 000	1000	1200	3000	5000

From the worksheet we can now produce the cash flow statement. The first figure we need to arrive at is the net cash inflow from operating activities. There are two ways of arriving at this figure. We can either work directly from the worksheet or we can work from the final accounts. We shall initially concentrate on using the information from the worksheet. However, in order to facilitate your understanding of the other method which will be illustrated later, we need to produce the final accounts for Downsend Ltd:

**Profit and loss account of Downsend Ltd
for the year ended 31 March 1992**

	£	£
Sales		59 000
Cost of sales		32 000
Gross profit		27 000
Administrative expenses	13 500	
Distribution expenses	1 500	15 000
Operating profit		12 000
Taxation		3 000
Profit after tax		9 000
Dividends		5 000
Retained profit		4 000

Notes

Depreciation on the fittings amounting to £1000 is included in the Administrative expenses, and £1200 depreciation relating to the van is included in Distribution expenses.

Balance sheet of Downsend Ltd as at 31 March 1992

Fixed assets	Cost £	Depreciation £	£
Fittings	4 000	1 000	3 000
Van	6 000	1 200	4 800
	10 000	2 200	7 800
Current assets			
Stock		16 000	
Debtors		18 000	
		34 000	
Creditors: falling due within one year			
Creditors		14 000	
Tax		3 000	
Dividend		5 000	
Bank overdraft		5 800	
		27 800	
Net current assets			6 200
			14 000
Financed by			£
Ordinary shares			10 000
Retained profit			4 000
			14 000

Stage 2

We can, using the information contained in the worksheet, calculate the net cash flow from operating activities. We shall do this using the information contained in the profit and loss column and the cash column. We shall start by identifying the cash coming in to the business (the cash inflows). From there we shall identify the amounts of cash being paid out of the business (cash outflows). In terms of the cash inflows we can see from the cash column that the moneys received in respect of sales amounted to £41 000, i.e. Cash sales of £33 000 plus £8000 received from the debtors in respect of credit sales. In terms of the cash outflows relating to operations, we find that £34 000 was paid to creditors in respect of stock purchased during the year. In addition, Downsend paid £300 for the insurance on the van, £6000 for rent and £6500 for wages. If you look at all the other figures in the profit and loss column you will see that they do not affect the bank column and there is therefore no cash inflow or outflow. From this therefore we can calculate our 'Net cash inflow from operating activities' as follows:

	£	£
Cash from cash sales and debtors		41 000
Less:		
Cash paid for purchases	34 000	
Tax and insurance	300	
Rent	6 000	
Wages	6 500	46 800
Net cash outflow from operating activities		(5 800)

Alternatively, we can arrive at this figure from the balance sheet, profit and loss account and notes by doing a reconciliation similar to that shown earlier:

	£
Operating profit	12 000
Depreciation – fittings	1 000
– van	1 200
Increase in stock	(16 000)
Increase in debtors	(18 000)
Increase in creditors	14 000
Net cash outflow from operating activities	(5 800)

We now need to look for the other cash flows. These are easily identified on the worksheet by looking at the bank column. There is a cash inflow of £10 000 when the shares were issued, and cash outflows in respect of the purchase of the fittings and van amounting to £4000 and £6000 respectively. Thus our cash flow statement prepared from our worksheet would appear as follows:

Cash flow statement of Downsend Ltd
for the year ended 31 March 1992

	£	£
Net cash outflow from operating activities		(5 800)
Returns on investments and servicing finance		
Dividends paid	–	
Net cash flow from returns on investment and		
servicing activities		–
Taxation		

	£	£
Corporation tax paid (including ACT)	–	
Net cash outflow from taxation		–
Investing activities		
Payment to acquire tangible fixed assets	(10 000)	
Net cash outflow from investing activity		(10 000)
Net cash inflow before financing		(15 800)
Financing		
Issue of ordinary share capital	10 000	
Net cash inflow from financing		10 000
Decrease in cash or cash equivalents		(5 800)

In this case we do not really need to add any notes as we have them in our workings above. However, for the sake of completeness and to facilitate our consideration of the contents of the full set of accounts we shall reproduce the notes that are appropriate. Before moving to these you will notice that we have included in the cash flow statement the headings under which dividends paid and tax paid would have gone had any been paid. This is deliberate as we wish to emphasize the point that it is only when there is a cash flow that an amount appears on the cash flow statement. If this is not clear go back to the worksheet and see if there is any cash flow associated with either of these items.

Notes to the cash flow statement

1. *Reconciliation of operating profit to net cash flow from operating activities*

	£
Operating profit	12 000
Depreciation charges	2 200
Increase in stocks	(16 000)
Increase in debtors	(18 000)
Increase in creditors	14 000
	(5 800)

2. *Analysis of changes in cash and cash equivalents during the year*

	£
Bank balance at 1 April 1991	0
Net cash outflow for the year	(5 800)
Bank balance at 31 March 1992	(5 800)

3. *Analysis of changes in financing during the year*

	Share capital £
Balance at 1 April 1991	0
Cash inflow from financing	10 000
Balance at 31 March 1992	10 000

Having produced a cash flow statement the next question to consider is, what does it tell us? In this case it is clear from the cash flow statement that the business has had a net cash outflow in total and that this was caused by the operating activities. In fact from note 1 we can see that what Downsend Ltd has done is used short-term finance in the form of trade creditors and an overdraft to finance the stock and debtors. This is because the business is under-capitalized – its equity capital is only sufficient to cover its fixed assets so it is having to rely on borrowing to finance its working capital requirements.

Let us now move on to compare the result obtained from producing the cash flow statement with that which we would have obtained had we produced a source and application of funds statement. We shall not go in to detail on how the statement is produced as you already have sufficient information to reconcile the figures to the accounts if you so wish.

Source and application of funds statement of Downsend Ltd
for the year ended 31 March 1992

	£	£
Net profit		12 000
Items not involving a flow of funds		
Depreciation – fittings	1 000	
– van	1 200	2 200
Funds from operations		14 200
Other sources of funds		
Issue of ordinary share capital	10 000	10 000
Total source of funds		24 200
Applications		
Purchase of tangible fixed assets	10 000	
Taxation paid	0	
Dividends paid	0	10 000
Change in working capital		14 200
Movements in working capital	£	£
Increase in stock	18 000	
Increase in debtors	16 000	
Increase in creditors	(14 000)	
Increase in overdraft	(5 800)	14 200

As you can see the impact in terms of the fact that Downsend is financing its trading through short-term borrowing is not so apparent. It would appear from the source and application of funds statement that if Downsend Ltd did the same next year as this year there would be no problems. However, the cash flow statement shows that Downsend Ltd would be in trouble if that happened. In fact if we project forward the same increases in stock, debtors and creditors the overdraft would be increased by a further £5800, added to which would be an increase of £8000 resulting from the payment of the tax due and the dividend. This would be well above the overdraft limit that has been negotiated. From the point of view of the user of accounts what the cash flow statement does is alert them to the fact that, although Downsend Ltd is making a profit, it is likely that it will have problems with its cash flow in the future. The user can then take whatever action is appropriate. The source and application statement does not alert the user in the same way and in fact the cash flow problem is being obscured by the increase in working capital caused by the stock increases and the increase in debtors. This is a good illustration of the first of the points in favour of cash flow statements put forward by the ASB.

At the start of example 13.1 we said that there were two ways of arriving at a cash flow statement. The easiest is working from a worksheet or the prime records, which is what we have done. The alternative is to work from the information in the final accounts which, although applying the same principles, uses some different techniques. We have effectively applied those techniques in discussing Downsend Ltd but it is worth looking at another example to consolidate our understanding. In this case all we have is the information from the published accounts so we have to work from there.

Preparing a cash flow statement from final accounts

Example 13.2
From the information given below, which consists of the profit and loss account of Clifton Ltd for the year ended 31 March 1990, the balance sheets for 1990 and 1989 and relevant extracts from the notes to the accounts, prepare a cash flow statement in accordance with FRS 1.

Profit and loss of Clifton Ltd
for the year ended 31 March 1990

	Notes	£
Sales	1	14 441
Cost of sales	2	12 595
Operating profit		1 846
Interest charges		768
Profit before tax		1 078
Taxation	3	579
After-tax profit		499
Dividends	4	337
Retained profit		162

Balance sheet of Clifton Ltd
as at 31 March 1990

	Notes	1990 £	1989 £
Fixed assets			
Land and buildings	5	1070	682
Plant and equipment	5	863	959
Other fixed assets	5	663	486
		2596	2127
Intangibles	6	451	470
Current assets			
Stocks	7	5289	3583

	Notes	1990	1989
		£	£
Debtors		3776	3012
Cash		15	183
		9080	6778
Creditors: falling due within one year			
Creditors		4711	4042
Taxation	3	644	996
Dividends	4	225	224
Bank overdraft		1427	86
		7007	5348
Net current assets		2073	1430
Creditors: falling due after one year			
Loans	8	427	0
Total net assets		4693	4027
Financed by			
Share capital	9	1476	1292
Share premium	9	157	157
Reserves	9	3060	2578
Total equity		4693	4027

Extracts from the notes to the accounts

2. Included in the cost of sales are the following charges:

	£
Depreciation	201
Auditors' remuneration	300
Directors' remuneration	500
Hire of plant	70
Loss on sale of plant	10
Goodwill amortization	19

4. Dividends:

	£
Interim	112
Final	225
	337

5. Fixed assets:

	Land	Buildings	Plant & equipment	Loose tools
Balance at 1 April 1989	400	350	1200	600
Additions			200	200
Revaluations	320			
	720	350	1400	800
Disposals			100	
Balance at 31 March 1990	720	350	1300	800

	Land	Buildings	Plant & equipment	Loose tools
Depreciation				
Balance at 1 April 1989		68	241	114
Charge for year			246	23
		68	487	137
Disposals and revaluations		68	50	
Balance at 31 March 1990		0	437	137
Net book value 1990	720	350	863	663
Net book value 1989	400	282	959	486

9. Share capital and reserves:

	Shares	Share premium	Retained profit	Revaluation reserve
Balance at 1 April 1989	1292	157	2578	
Share issue	184			
Movements in year			162	320
Balance at 31 March 1990	1476	157	2740	320

Stage 1

The first figure that we need for a cash flow statement is the 'net cash inflow from operating activities'. We have already seen in the previous example how this is obtained. It consists of the operating profit, adjustments for movements that do not involve cash flows such as depreciation, amortization, book profits or losses on the sale of fixed assets, and movements in stock, debtors and creditors.

From the profit and loss account of Clifton Ltd we see that the operating profit before interest charges (which are dealt with under another heading) is £1846. To this we have to add the non-fund movements. Details of these can be found in note 2. This tells us that depreciation for the year was £201, that amortization was £19 and that there was a loss on the sale of fixed assets of £10. Note 5 confirms the depreciation charge. It consists of a charge for the year of £246 and £23 less the write back on revaluation of £68. Note 5 also tells us that the asset we disposed of had a net book value of £50, so if we made a loss on the sale of £10 we must have sold it for £40. We shall use this latter information later.

For the other movements we need to return to our balance sheet and look at the changes from year to year. To make that exercise easier to follow we have reproduced the balance sheets with an extra column showing the changes below:

Balance sheets of Clifton Ltd with changes

	Notes	1990 £	1989 £	Changes £
Fixed assets				
Land and buildings	5	1070	682	388
Plant and equipment	5	863	959	(96)
Other fixed assets	5	663	486	177
		2596	2127	469

	Notes	1990 £	1989 £	Changes £
Intangibles	6	451	470	(19)
Current assets				
Stocks	7	5289	3583	1706
Debtors		3776	3012	764
Cash		15	183	(168)
		9080	6778	2302
Creditors: Falling due within one year				
Creditors		4711	4042	669
Taxation	3	644	996	(352)
Dividends	4	225	224	1
Bank overdraft		1427	86	1341
		7007	5348	1659
Net current assets		2073	1430	643
Creditors: Falling due after one year				
Loans	8	427	0	427
Total net assets		4693	4027	666
		£	£	£
Financed by				
Share capital	9	1476	1292	184
Share premium	9	157	157	0
Reserves	9	3060	2578	482
Total equity		4693	4027	666

From the balance sheet we can see the changes in stock, debtors and creditors. In addition we can see that the intangibles have reduced by £19, the amortization charge for the year. In the case of fixed assets things are more complex as there are new additions, disposals and revaluations as well as the depreciation charge to deal with.

Returning to the calculation of the 'net cash inflow from operating activities', we can now do this using the information from the balance sheet and from notes 2 and 5. As we produce the cash flow statement we shall also produce the notes to accompany it.

Net cash flow from operating activities

In this case as we do not have information on the actual cash flows through the bank account we can calculate the figure from the operating profit adjusted for depreciation etc. This we can do as shown below and at the same time produce the note to the cash flow statement:

Note to the cash flow statement

1. *Reconciliation of operating profit to net cash flow from operating activities*	£
Operating profit	1846
Depreciation charges	201
Loss on sale of tangible fixed assets	10
Amortization of goodwill	19
Increase in stocks	(1706)
Increase in debtors	(764)
Increase in creditors	669
	275

Extract from the cash flow statement

Net cash inflow from operating activities	275

Before moving on to the next heading on our cash flow statement you should ensure that you understand where the figures came from.

Returns on investments and servicing

The next figures we need to look at are interest and dividends, received or paid. In this example we find, by reference to the profit and loss account, that the interest charge was £768, but we do not know if that amount was paid. To ascertain that we need to look at the balance sheet and see if there is any creditor for interest. In this case there is no creditor either at the start or end of the year. Therefore, we can reasonably assume that the £768 was the amount actually paid.

The other item we need to consider, under this heading, is dividends. In this case we do have a creditor at the start and end of the year and we know from note 4 that there was an interim and final dividend. We can see from note 4 that the final dividend is the amount showing as a creditor at the end of 1990. Therefore the amounts paid must have been the £224 outstanding at the start of the year and the interim dividend of £112, i.e. £336. This information would appear in the cash flow statement as follows:

Extract from the cash flow statement

Returns on investments and servicing of finance		
Interest paid	(768)	
Dividends paid	(336)	
Net cash flow from returns on investment and servicing activities		(1104)

Taxation

The next item we have to deal with in terms of our cash flow statement is the taxation. Once again we need to look carefully at what has been paid and what is still outstanding. In this case we owed tax amounting to £996 at the start of the year, and we calculated that the tax due for the year, as shown in the profit and loss account, was £579. Therefore if we had not paid anything we would have owed £1575 at the end of the year.

However, from the 1990 balance sheet we can see that we only owe £644. Therefore we must have paid £931.

Extract from the cash flow statement

Taxation		
Corporation tax paid (including ACT)	(931)	
Net cash outflow from taxation		(931)

Investing activities

This heading covers all the investment and divestment activities of the business during the year in both tangible and intangible fixed assets. In terms of the tangible fixed assets we can see from note 5 that we bought new plant and equipment for £200 and sold some plant and equipment with a net book value of £50. We have already identified that, as we made a loss on the sale, the plant must have been sold for £40. The other item included in the fixed assets note is the revaluations. These, you will remember from Chapter 10, do not involve any cash flows. If you are unsure of this point return to the relevant section of Chapter 10 before proceeding. As far as the intangible assets are concerned, the change appears to be explained by the amount of the amortization which does not involve any cash flows.

Extract from the cash flow statement

Investing activities		
Payment to acquire tangible fixed assets	(400)	
Receipts from sales of tangible fixed assets	40	
Net cash outflow from investing activity		(360)

Financing activities

If we look at our balance sheet changes column we can see that we have dealt with all the fixed assets, the intangible assets and current assets and liabilities with the exception of the cash and overdraft. The only items we have not dealt with is the increase in long-term loans of £427. On the other half of the balance sheet we see that the share capital has increased by £184. This could be a new issue or a bonus issue. In the latter case, as we explained in Chapter 11, there is no cash flow but a transfer from another reserve. We therefore need to look at the reserves to see if a bonus issue has been made. This could be made from the share premium account or another reserve. In this case there is no movement on the share premium account. We can also see from note 9 to the balance sheet that the movements on reserves are accounted for by the revaluation and the retained profits. Therefore we can conclude that the increase is as a result of shares being issued for cash. Before looking at the extract from the cash flow statement it is worth noting that we have now dealt with all the changes in the balance sheet with the exception of the cash and overdraft which we shall deal with next.

Extract from the cash flow statement

Financing
Issue of ordinary share capital	184
Debenture loan	427

Net cash inflow from financing   611

We are now in a position to put together the note on financing to accompany the cash flow statement. This would be:

2. *Analysis of changes in financing during the year*	*Shares*	*Loans*
Balance at 1 April 1991	1292	0
Cash inflow from financing	184	427
Balance at 31 March 1992	1476	427

We have still to reconcile the movements on the cash which we can now do from the changes column of the balance sheets. At the same time we can produce the notes for the cash flow statement which are given below. These are followed by the completed cash flow statement.

3. *Analysis of the balances of cash and cash equivalents as shown in the balance sheet*	*1990*	*1989*	*Change*
Cash at bank and in hand	15	183	(168)
Bank overdrafts	(1427)	(86)	(1341)
	(1412)	97	(1509)

4. *Analysis of changes in cash and cash equivalents during the year*	
Balance at 1 April 1989	97
Net cash inflow	(1509)
Balance at 31 March 1990	(1412)

Cash flow statement of Clifton Limited
for the year ended 31 March 1990

	£	£
Net cash inflow from operating activities		275
Returns on investments and servicing of finance		
Interest paid	(768)	
Dividends paid	(336)	
Net cash flow from returns on investment and servicing activities		(1104)
Taxation		
Corporation tax paid (including ACT)	(931)	
Net cash outflow from taxation		(931)
Investing activities		
Payment to acquire tangible fixed assets	(400)	
Receipts from sales of tangible fixed assets	40	
Net cash outflow from investing activity		(360)
Net cash outflow before financing		(2120)

	£	£
Financing		
Issue of ordinary share capital	184	
Debenture loan	427	
Net cash inflow from financing		611
Increase in cash or cash equivalents		(1509)

Before leaving the subject of the cash flow statement, it is worth noting that, unlike the source and application of funds statement, the cash flow statement attempts to provide informative headings and subheadings for the various cash inflows and outflows. It also takes a slightly different viewpoint from the profit and loss account in that it is more entity based than proprietary based. The profit and loss statement is clearly aimed at shareholders, e.g. it shows interest on long-term finance as an expense but dividends as a distribution of profit. The cash flow statement, on the other hand, treats both of these in the same way as a cost associated with financing the enterprise. Another example of a statement that is entity based is the statement of value added which we shall now consider.

CASE 13.1

CASH FLOW STATEMENT

The cash flow statement from Bentalls Plc 1992 accounts is reproduced below. As you can see the operating profit is over six times higher than the cash inflow from operations. This is largely as a result of the increases in stocks and the reduction in creditors. Overall, we can see that there is a decrease in cash and cash equivalents in 1992 just as there was in 1991. Interestingly, as you saw when you looked at the profit and loss account in Case 12.1, the company has continued to pay a dividend despite the fact that the profits do not cover the amount of the dividend.

Cash Flow Statement
for the year ending 1 February 1992

	1992 £'000	1992 £'000	1991 (53 weeks) £'000	1991 (53 weeks) £'000
Operating activities				
Operating profit	1816		3324	
Depreciation charged	1619		1245	
Loss (profit) on sale of fixed assets	3		(114)	
Pension credit	(14)		(113)	
(Increase) in stocks	(1870)		(2113)	
Decrease in debtors	157		816	
(Decrease) increase in creditors	(1174)		2231	
Effect of other deferrals and accruals on operating activity cash flows	(249)		471	
Net cash inflow from operating activities		288		5747

Returns on investments and servicing of finance			Continued from previous page
Interest received	34	107	
Interest paid	(2737)	(1 865)	
Interest elements of finance lease payments	(137)	(87)	
Dividends paid	(1617)	(1 608)	
Net cash outflow from returns on investments and servicing of finance		(4457)	(3 453)
Taxation			
Corporation tax paid		(540)	(2 736)
Investing activities			
Expenditure on move of store	–	(1 256)	
Purchase of goodwill	(200)	–	
Purchase of fixed assets	(4055)	(19 314)	
Sale of fixed assets	9	248	
Net cash outflow from investing activities		(4246)	(20 322)
Financing activities			
Increase in borrowings	3970	17 970	
Proceeds from shares issued	79	18	
Capital element of finance lease rentals	354	753	
Net cash inflow from financing activities		4403	18 741
Decrease in cash and cash equivalents		(4552)	(2 023)
Net decrease in cash and cash equivalents			
Cash and cash equivalents at 1 February 1992			
Cash at bank and in hand		923	3 911
Bank overdraft		(1564)	–
		(641)	3 911

The statement of value added

The Corporate Report issued in 1975 suggested that:

> The simplest way of putting profit into proper perspective *vis-à-vis* the whole enterprise as a collective effort by capital, management and employees is by presentation of value added (that is, sales income less materials and services purchased). Value added is the wealth the reporting entity has been able to create by its own and its employees' efforts. This statement would show how the value added has been used to pay those contributing to its creation.

The simplest way to show what the statement contains is to consider the statement below which is based upon the accounts of Downsend Ltd. These we produced at the start of this chapter as part of the solution to Example 13.1.

Value added statement of Downsend Ltd
for the year ended 31 March 1992

	£
Sales	59 000
Cost of materials and purchased services	38 300
Value added for the year	20 700

Distribution of value added:

	£	£
To employees:		
Wages	6500	
To government:		
Corporation tax	3000	
To providers of capital:		
Shareholders	5000	
Retained in the business:		
To replace fixed assets	2200	
For expansion	4000	
Total distributions		20 700

As you will have noticed, all the value added statement does is to rearrange the information used to produce the profit and loss account and balance sheet. We shall briefly explain how the figures were arrived at and then go on to discuss the ideas behind the value added statement and its uses in more detail.

The sales figure is self-explanatory, in this case, as it comes straight from the profit and loss account. The figure for materials and services purchased consists of the cost of sales of £32 000 plus the rent of £6000 and the tax and insurance for the van of £300. By taking this from the sales we obtain the value added for the year. The statement then looks at how that value added was distributed. The first amount is the distribution to employees in the form of wages; then there is the distribution to the government in the form of the corporation tax and to financiers in the form of dividends. The final heading relates to amounts retained in the business for replacing fixed assets. This consists of the depreciation charge for the year. It also includes any amounts retained for expansion which consist, in this case, of the retained profits for the year.

Advantages of value added statements

There have been many advantages claimed for the value added statement, some of which are debatable. However, there is no dispute about the fact that the value added statement represented a radical change in the approach to financial statements which had generally been proprietary based, i.e. their purpose was to report to the shareholders on their investment. This view is, to some extent, entrenched in law. In addition FASB 1 *Objectives of Financial Reporting* limited its consideration of users' needs to investors and creditors. The value added statement approach was that it reported to all those contributing to the enterprise performance. This emphasis on collective effort was a major shift from capitalism's predominant emphasis on return on capital. Some of the other advantages claimed were that the statement focused attention on the total wealth creating ability of the enterprise, that it was clearer and more understandable than the conventional profit and loss account, and that it was potentially more neutral and less susceptible to accounting manipulation.

Apart from the question of the change in focus the other claimed advantages were never substantiated. However, it did create a lot of interest and a number of studies were undertaken for the professional accounting bodies into the potential uses and usefulness of the value added statement. These are referred to in the further reading at the end of the chapter. Perhaps most importantly, by taking an entity-based approach, the value added statement highlighted the question of what is the income we are trying to measure. This question, as we shall see in Chapters 15 to 17, is at the root of a lot of the disagreement on alternative accounting models.

Apart from the claimed advantages there were a number of criticisms of the value added statement. These ranged from questions of legal ownership of the funds reinvested in the business, to issues around classification. These classification issues included questions such as: Where should employees' tax be shown? Should the directors' remuneration be included with the employees'? Should depreciation be seen as a distribution or an expense? etc. Perhaps the biggest problem for the value added statement was finding some actual use for the information. On this subject various claims were made regarding its potential usefulness. Gray and Maunders (1980) argued that if it was shown to be useful in collective bargaining then it would be of interest to employees and management. They also posited that if it was used in collective bargaining then all the other users would be interested as the outcome of the collective bargaining process would affect the amount available for distribution to them. In reality in most companies the level of aggregation and the problems of classification on their own would have made the use of the value added statement in collective bargaining problematic. In addition the fact that the statement is based around sales, rather than production, limits its usefulness in negotiations centred around increases in productivity.

The value added statement, whilst being a very interesting and some would say radical statement, had a relatively short lifespan and is now rarely seen in published accounts, although an example of a value added statement from a 1991 annual report is given in Case 13.2. It may be that, like the statement of source and application of funds which as you have seen was radically rethought after 16 years, the value added statement will be rethought and emerge again as a useful addition to financial statements.

CASE 13.2

**VALUE ADDED
STATEMENT**

The statement of value added from Bentalls Plc 1992 accounts is reproduced below. As you can see the statement shows the total value added and its distribution to employees, the providers of capital and the government. The remainder is retained for use in the business.

**Statement of Value Added
1 February 1992**

	1992		1991 (53 weeks)	
	£'000	£'000	£'000	£'000
Turnover		**70 997**		70 727
Less goods and services bought in		**53 131**		52 290
Value added		**17 866**		18 437
Distribution of value added				
Paid and due to or on behalf of employees				
Salaries, staff restaurant subsidies and other benefits	**13 486**		12 996	
National insurance and pension scheme contributions	**945**		872	
		14 431		13 868
Paid and due to providers of capital				
Dividends to shareholders	**1 617**		1 617	
Interest on loans (net)	**387**		1	
		2 004		1 618
Paid and due to the Government				
Corporation tax		**499**		1 289
Retained by the company for the maintenance and expansion of the business				
Unappropriated (loss) profit before extraordinary item	**(687)**		417	
Depreciation and amortisation	**1 619**		1 245	
		932		1 662
Value added		**17 866**		18 437

Other statements and reports

A number of companies produce employee reports. However, there is no legislation or accounting standards making this compulsory or defining the contents of these reports. They therefore contain the information which management wishes to include and can be anything from very simplified accounts to very detailed documents. Another report that has been suggested is the 'Corporate Social Report'. Once again some of the information that would be provided in such a report is provided by some companies on a voluntary basis. Examples of these reports and further discussion can be found in the readings given at the end of this chapter.

References

Accounting Standards Steering Committee (1975) *The Corporate Report*, ASC, London

Berry, A., Citron, D. and Jarvis, R. (1987) *The Information Needs of Bankers Dealing with Large and Small Companies*, Certified Accountants Research Report 7, Certified Accountants Publications, London.

Companies Act 1985, sections 246–249, HMSO.

Egginton, D. (1975) The changes that Britain's bankers would like to see. *Accountants Magazine*, 27 July 1975, pp. 14–15.

Financial Reporting Standard No. 1 (1991) *Cash Flow Statements*, Accounting Standards Board.

Gray, S.J. and Maunders, K.T. (1980) *Value Added Reporting: Uses and Measurement*, ACA, London.

Inflation Accounting: Report of the inflation Accounting Steering Committee (1975), Cmnd 6225, London, HMSO.

Laughlin, R. and Gray, R. (1988) *Financial Accounting: Method and Meaning*, Van Nostrand Reinhold (International), London.

Statement of Financial Accounting Concepts No. 1 (1978) *Objectives of Financial Reporting by Business Enterprises*, Financial Accounting Standards Board.

Statement of Standard Accounting Practice No. 8 (1977) *Treatment of Taxation under the Imputation System*, Accounting Standards Committee.

Statement of Standard Accounting Practice No. 10 (1975) *Statements of Source and Application of Funds*, Accounting Standards Committee.

Statement of Standard Accounting Practice No. 15 (1985) *Accounting for Deferred Taxation*, Accounting Standards Committee.

Further reading

Gray, S.J. and Maunders, K.T. (1980) *Value Added Reporting: Uses and Measurement*, ACA, London.

Lee, T.A. (1984) *Cash Flow Accounting*, Van Nostrand Reinhold.

Meyer, P.E. (1973) The accounting entity. *Abacus*, December 1973, pp. 116–26, also reprinted in T. Burns and H.S. Hendrickson (1986) *The Accounting Sampler*, McGraw Hill.

Morley, M.F. (1978) *The value added statement. A review of its uses in corporate reports*, ICAS.

For further information on employee and other reports see R. Laughlin and R. Gray, *Financial Accounting: Method and Meaning* (Van Nostrand Reinhold, 1988).

For a full discussion on the subject of corporate social reporting see R.H. Gray, D.J. Owen and K.T. Maunders, *Corporate Social Reporting* (Prentice Hall, 1991).

Review questions

1. What is the main aim of a cash flow statement?

2. What are the three main definitions of funds used in the chapter and how do they differ?

3. What are the claimed advantages of the cash flow statement?

4. How does 'net cash flow from operating activities' differ from operating profit?

5. How does 'net cash flow from operating activities' differ from 'funds from operations'?

6. How does an increase in the depreciation charge affect the operating profit and the 'net cash flow from operating activities'?

7. What is meant by cash and cash equivalents?

8. What is meant by a proprietary-based statement?

9. Why is the value added statement said to give an entity view?

Problems for discussion and analysis

1. Discuss the impact of each of the items below on the balance sheet, profit and loss account and cash flow statement, giving reasons for your answer where appropriate.

   (a) During the year the company sold a fixed asset with a net book value of £5000 for £3000.
   (b) The company also revalued its land from its original cost of £130 000 to £200 000.
   (c) The building which had cost £90 000 and on which depreciation of £30 000 had been provided was revalued to £100 000.
   (d) The company had issued bonus shares to its existing shareholders amounting to £40 000 using the share premium account for that purpose.
   (e) The company had also made an issue of 100 000 8 per cent £1 preference shares at a price of £1.20 per share.
   (f) In line with a number of other companies the directors had decided to include their brands at a valuation of £190 000.
   (g) The company had paid back a long-term loan to the bank of £80 000.

2. The information on the transactions of Newspurt Ltd in its first year of trading are given below.

   May 1992
   Issued 50 000 £1 ordinary shares in exchange for £50 000 in cash.
   Purchased a machine for £30 000 and paid immediately.
   Bought a delivery van for £10 000 and paid immediately.
   Paid tax and insurance on the van of £400
   Paid a quarter's rent in advance of £2000.
   Purchased raw materials costing £10 000 on one month's credit.

   June 1992–April 1993
   Made sales of £90 000, all on credit.
   Purchased raw materials costing £40 000, all on credit.
   Paid four quarters' rent in advance amounting to £8000.
   Paid creditors £38 000.
   Received £70 000 from debtors.
   Paid wages of £25 000.

   At the end of the year Newspurt Ltd had raw materials in stock which cost £3000.
   The directors decided to depreciate the van over five years and the machine

over four years using straight line depreciation and assuming no residual value.

The accountant had calculated that no corporation tax liability would arise and the directors had decided not to pay any dividends.

(a) Produce a worksheet for Newspurt Ltd.
(b) Produce a cash flow statement for Newspurt Ltd.
(c) Identify any additional information about Newspurt Ltd that the user can get from the cash flow statement that would not have been apparent in the profit and loss account and balance sheet.

3. The information below relates to Metaltin Ltd:

**Profit and loss account of Metaltin Ltd
for the year ended 30 April 1992**

	Notes	1992	1991
Sales		4814	5614
Cost of sales	1	4299	5039
Operating profit		515	575
Interest charges		156	53
Profit before tax		359	522
Taxation	2	193	292
Retained profit		166	230

**Balance sheet of Metaltin Ltd
as at 30 April 1992**

	Notes	1992	1991
Fixed assets			
Land & buildings	3	360	227
Fixtures	3	285	320
Motor vehicles	3	221	162
		866	709
Current assets			
Stocks	4	1763	1194
Debtors		1259	1004
Cash		5	61
		3027	2259
Creditors: falling due within one year			
Creditors		1370	1147
Taxation	2	215	332
Bank overdraft		676	255
		2261	1734
Net current assets		766	525
Creditors: falling due after one year			
Loans	5	200	130
Total net assets		1432	1104
Financed by			
Share capital	6	545	483
Retained profit	6	787	621
Revaluation reserve	6	100	0
Total equity		1432	1104

Extracts from the notes to the accounts

1. Included in the cost of sales are the following charges:

	£
Depreciation	123
Auditors' remuneration	55
Directors' remuneration	240
Hire of plant	30
Profit on sale of fittings	20

3. Fixed assets:

	Land	Buildings	Fittings	Motor vehicles
Balance at 1 May 1991	120	140	600	440
Additions			100	140
Revaluations	60	40		
	180	180	700	580
Disposals			90	
Balance at 30 April 1992	180	180	610	580
Depreciation				
Balance at 1 May 1991		33	280	278
Charge for year		(33)	75	81
		0	355	359
Disposals			30	
Balance at 30 April 1992		0	325	359
Net book value 1992	180	180	285	221
Net book value 1991	120	107	320	162

5. A long-term loan amounting to £70 was repaid during the year. This was replaced with a new loan of £140 repayable in ten years.

6. Share capital and reserves:

	Share capital	Retained profit	Other reserves
Balance at 1 May 1991	483	621	
Share issue	62		
Movements in year		166	100
Balance at 30 April 1992	545	787	100

(a) Produce a cash flow statement and notes for Metaltin Ltd in accordance with FRS 1.

(b) Comment on the performance of Metaltin Ltd as reflected in the cash flow statement and the accounts.

4. Using the information in Example 13.2 together with the additional information provided below, produce a value added statement for Clifton Ltd.

(a) The full cost of the employees' wages for the year was £1575, of which £475 related to income tax etc.

(b) The income tax etc. on the employees' wages and the directors' remuneration amounted to £675.

Financial statement analysis 14

In the previous chapters we have considered the way in which accounting information is produced and what the components of financial statements mean. In this chapter we shall consider the statements themselves and more specifically the ways in which they can be analysed. This chapter is not intended to be comprehensive in its approach to the subject of financial analysis. Instead it offers some guidelines on an initial approach to the subject and provides the reader with some basic tools of analysis. The approach adopted considers the needs of the person for whom the analysis is being undertaken, in other words the 'user group'. Using this approach it is possible to establish the form of analysis most appropriate to these needs. The 'user groups' which we shall deal with are those discussed at the start of this book.

User groups

Investor group

The investor group was previously discussed as a homogeneous group with similar needs, but there are in fact different types of investor. For sole traders and partnerships the investor is normally the owner or partner. The equivalent of this type of investor in a company is the ordinary shareholder. These investors will be referred to from now on as equity investors. We need to establish what this group have in common, and what distinguishes the equity investor in a large company from the equivalent in a sole proprietorship.

In general, equity investors take on all the risks associated with ownership and are entitled to any rewards after other prior claims have been met. In the case of a sole trader the equity investor, i.e. the owner, is also likely to be heavily involved in the management and day-to-day running of the business. Where there is this direct involvement the needs of the owners will be the same as those of managers (discussed below). Generally, the smaller the organization and the greater the direct involvement of the owners in the day-to-day running of the business, the more detail will be required. In the case of larger organizations, such as large private companies and all public companies, it is likely that there will be a separation of ownership and management. For large businesses this leads to greater emphasis being placed on the final accounts as a means of meeting the information needs of the equity investors who are, in the main, properly characterized by the term absentee owners. However, the information required to meet the needs of equity investors in their role as owners of the business is broadly the same irrespective of the type of ownership involved. We therefore suggest that the basic needs of equity investors can be met with information about:

☐ profitability and growth, especially future profitability;
☐ management efficiency (for example, are assets being utilized efficiently?);
☐ return on their investment:
  – within the firm;
  – compared with alternatives;
☐ risk being taken:
  – financial risk;
  – business risk;
☐ returns to owners:
  – dividends;
  – drawings etc.;
  – capital growth.

Preference shareholders

As we discussed in Chapter 12 for investment in companies it is also possible to purchase a share known as a preference share. These shares are generally seen as less risky than ordinary shares and as such do not normally earn as great a reward. It is difficult to generalize on the differences between these shares and ordinary shares as this varies from one preference share to another. However, preference shares will normally be entitled to a fixed rate of dividend and to repayment of capital prior to the ordinary shareholders in the event of the business being 'wound up'. Because of the nature of the shares these users are in theory likely to be interested in:

☐ profitability, mainly future profitability;
☐ the net realizable value of the assets;
☐ the extent to which their dividends are covered by profit.

If we compare the need of this and the previous group of investors we can see that this group is more likely to be interested in the extent to which income is at risk rather than the growth of the business. This is because in most cases it is only ordinary shareholders who will benefit from such growth – the preference shareholders' return is in the form of a dividend at a fixed rate irrespective of the profits made.

This type of investment is similar, in some ways, to long-term loans which we shall deal with in more detail shortly. The similarity is at a fairly superficial level in that the return on the investment is at a fixed rate. There are, however, important differences beyond this superficial similarity. The main difference is that in the case of a loan the interest has to be paid whether or not profits are made. By contrast preference dividends are not due to be paid until they are declared by the directors of the company. This is one of the reasons why the interest on loans is treated as an expense in arriving at the profit before taxation whereas the preference dividend is shown as an appropriation of profit after tax. The difference in the way in which they are dealt with in the accounts also reflects the different treatments in tax legislation. Interest on a loan is allowed for tax purposes as an expense in arriving at the taxable profit whereas preference dividends are not. A further difference between loans and preference share is that loans are repayable at some specified point in time, whereas, unless specifically stated as in the case of redeemable preference shares, preference shares are permanent capital and are normally only repaid in the event of the company being wound up. In this way they are more similar to ordinary shares. Thus on balance the preference share can be seen as a hybrid between ordinary shares and loans and the information requirements of preference shareholders reflect this.

The information needs of other providers of capital, i.e. lenders, is what we shall now consider.

Lenders

This group can be conveniently subdivided into three subgroups: short-term creditors, medium-term lenders and long-term lenders.

Short-term creditors are normally trade creditors, i.e. those who supply the business with goods on credit. Their areas of interest would be:

☐ liquidity/solvency – short term;
☐ net realizable value of the assets;
☐ profitability and future growth;
☐ risk, financial and business.

Medium-term lenders may well be bankers and other financial institutions. Their areas of interest would be:

☐ profitability – future profits provide cash for repayment of loans;
☐ security and the nature of the security;
☐ financial stability.

Long-term lenders will have the same needs as medium-term lenders unless they are secured lenders. In the case of secured lenders their areas of interest are likely to be:

☐ profitability;
☐ risk, especially financial risk;
☐ security – net realizable value of specific assets;
☐ interest cover – how well their interest is covered by the profits being made.

As can be seen these different types of lender have broadly the same needs in terms of their total information requirements. It is the emphasis that changes depending on whether one is looking from a short, medium or long-term perspective.

Employees

Employees are interested in judging job security and in assessing their wages in terms of relative fairness. Their areas of interest are likely to be

☐ profitability – average profits per employee for the purposes of productivity bargaining;
☐ future trends in profits;
☐ liquidity.

There has been considerable debate over the extent to which these needs are met by conventional accounts and whether an alternative statement such as the statement of value added, which we discussed in Chapter 13, would meet their needs better.

Auditors

Auditors are not normally seen as users of accounting information. However, in order to perform an audit efficiently an analysis of accounts is frequently carried out. For the purposes of planning and carrying out their audit the auditors are likely to be interested in:

☐ trends in sales, profits, cost, etc.;
☐ variations from norms;
☐ accounting policies.

Management

It is very difficult to describe the needs of managers as they will vary greatly from situation to situation. They will, however, be interested in all the information referred to above as they are likely to be judged on their performance by outside investors or lenders. In addition, they require information to help them with planning, e.g. cash forecasts and profit forecasts. They will also require detailed information on the performance of the business and its parts to enable them to manage the business on a day-to-day basis. This information could include such things as profitability by major product, costs per product, impact of changes in sales or component mix, etc.

The list of users dealt with above is not intended to be comprehensive. We have tried to give the reader a flavour of the differing needs of the various groups discussed and to indicate that some of these will not be provided from the annual accounts. At this stage we need to establish what, if any, needs are common and what other factors need to be taken into account.

Some common needs which can be readily identified are profitability, liquidity and risk. The problem is how these are measured and how to judge good or bad performance. Before going on to discuss those issues in detail, let us first examine these common needs in more detail and look at the context in which financial analysis should be carried out.

Good financial analysis requires that the **person** for whom the analysis is being done is clearly identified together with the **purpose** of the analysis. It is unlikely to be useful if it does not take into account as many **relevant factors** as possible.

KEY CONCEPT 14.1

FINANCIAL ANALYSIS

Common Needs

The most obvious need that virtually all these groups have in common is the need for information about the profitability of the business. This can be divided up into two components, one relating to past profitability and the other to future profitability. Another factor that is common to a number of groups is the requirement for information about financial risk and about liquidity, or 'solvency' as it is often called. Another theme that emerges concerns the return on the investment in the business. This relates the income to the investment and has associated with it measures such as the riskiness of that return in the form of dividend cover or interest cover. There are also a number of needs that are more specific to particular user groups. A good example of these is the information related to security used by lenders. We shall examine how the common needs can be analysed in some detail after we have established the context in which the analysis should take place.

Context for financial statement analysis

Before doing any analysis it is important to remember that it must be seen in a wider context rather than merely being viewed as a mechanical exercise using various techniques. Some of the factors that are directly relevant to any analysis of business performance are discussed below.

The size of the business

The fact that a business is the size of, say, ICI makes it less vulnerable to the decisions of others outside the organization. A banker is likely to ask for security from the small business whereas with ICI the name itself is enough security. Similarly, to compensate for the higher risk, a banker might only lend money to a small business at a rate of 3 or 4 per cent above base rate whereas for ICI or BP the rate would be much lower. Another area of difference, apart from those relating to security and risk, is in the analysis of performance. In a small business there is little point in expecting too much consistency when doing trend analysis as, because these businesses tend to operate at the margin and have few products, there are often odd years. For a larger, more diversified business these odd years in one area of the business are often balanced by performance in other areas.

The riskiness of the business

Apart from size, the nature of the business needs to be taken into account. For example, a gold prospecting business will have a different level of risk and return than a building society. Other factors which affect the risk, known as business risk, are the reliance on a small number of products, the degree of technological innovation, and of course vulnerability to competition.

The economic, social and political environment

Examples of the way in which the economic, social and political environment affects industry can be found in virtually any daily paper. If the pound goes down relative to the dollar this will affect imports and exports and firms will gain or suffer accordingly. Similarly, changes in interest rates often have fairly dramatic effects on firms if they are financed by a large amount of borrowing in the form of loans or overdrafts. The effects of the social environment tend to be more subtle, but a study of recent history would show a movement towards acceptance of profit as the prime motivation for business, whereas in some other countries this is balanced with regard for the environment or for ensuring full employment. These social changes frequently coincide with political changes although the environmental issue is a good example of a social effect which is likely to transcend political changes. This was very apparent in the debate in 1989 on the privatisation of the water industry.

The industry trends, effects of changes in technology

In order to make any judgements about performance, and more especially about the future, it is vital to understand the pressures affecting the industry. For example, in the late 1970s and early 1980s most of the major British toy manufacturers were wound up. This was in part due to changes in the nature of the industry and the product. The industry was being affected by cheap imports, the impact of large buyers, and the high rates of inflation and interest. The product required in the market-place was also changing to more electronic toys rather than the traditional die-cast model cars such as those produced by Dinky etc.

Effect of price changes

We have just mentioned high rates of inflation, but the effects of price changes may also be more specific. For example, the price of property in recent years has been rising faster than the general increase in prices. Over the last 20 or more years, a number of proposals for taking account of price changes in corporate reports have been put forward, some of which will be discussed in the following chapters. None of these have gained general acceptance to date. However, the fact that the perfect solution has not been found does not mean that the problem can be ignored as even low rates of inflation of 5 per cent can mean that what appears to be gentle growth is in fact a decline. It should be pointed out that although we normally think of price changes in terms of price rises there are many examples where the effect of new technology, competition and economies of scale have led to reductions in price. The most obvious examples are in the electronics industries and the computer industry. For example, a calculator cost approximately £15 for the most basic model at the start of the 1970s; an equivalent today would be less than £5.

Projections and predictions of the future

While we can all take a guess at the future, clearly there is a case for taking into account the opinion of those more closely involved with the business and also those who have expertise in the industry or in analysing likely economic trends. Financial analysis must, after all, provide some clue to the future as the user needs to make a decision relating to the future. An evaluation of what has happened may provide a starting point for predicting what is going to happen. However, given the limitations of historic cost accounting how useful the past is as a guide to the future is open to question.

Sources of information

Having looked at some of the factors which need to be taken into account it should be clear that although a set of accounts may contain some of the information a lot of other information will have to be obtained from other sources. These other sources of information can be conveniently sub-divided into information from sources external to the business and those internal to the business. Some examples of these other sources are discussed below.

Sources external to the business

☐ **Government statistics**. These include the monthly *Digest of Statistics*, Department of Trade and Industry statistics and HMSO publications.
☐ **Trade journals**. These may be specific to the trade or more general professional or business journals such as *Management Today* or *Marketing Weekly*.
☐ **Financial press**. A lot of information can be gleaned from the financial pages of quality newspapers, from *The Financial Times* and from specialist publications such as the *Investors' Chronicle*.
☐ **Databases**. There are now a number of on-line databases, such as Datastream, Excel, etc., which can be accessed for information. These contain information about other companies, industry statistics and economic indicators.
☐ **Specialist agencies**. These agencies will provide an industry-wide analysis, a specific analysis of a firm, general financial reports, credit scoring services and many other services.

The first three of these sources are likely to be fairly readily accessible in good libraries. The others are more specialist and access is likely to be more limited and much more expensive.

Sources internal to the business

Chairman's statement

In the case of public companies a chairman's statement is normally included with the annual accounts. It contains summarized information on the year as well as some predictions for the future. The information contained should not be taken at face value as it is likely to reflect one point of view which itself may be biased. It may be that the statement highlights only the positive side rather than giving the whole picture. As a senior lending banker commented: 'It is as important to ascertain what is left out as it is to ascertain what has been included.'

Directors' report

This is a statutory requirement for all companies and the information contained therein is laid down in the Companies Acts. The statutes, however, lay down a minimum and that is therefore normally all the information that is given. Small companies can take advantage of provisions in the Companies Acts and produce a shortened version of the accounts for filing at Companies House. This shortened version excludes the directors' report although this still has to be produced as the shareholders are entitled to a full set of accounts as defined in the legislation.

The balance sheet

As we explained in Chapter 4 this gives information about the position at a point in time. The information is therefore really only valid at that point in time. Given that the median time for publication by large companies is over three months after the balance sheet date and for small companies it is thought to be at least ten months, the information may have very little bearing on the current position. This question of how timely the information is has a major bearing on what can be achieved from an analysis of the accounting information contained in the balance sheet in particular and the published accounts in general.

The profit and loss account

In common with the balance sheet the information contained is probably fairly old by the time it is published. Another problem is that the information tends to be summarized which may mean that the performance of the weaker parts of a business are not necessarily readily apparent as they are offset by the performance of the stronger parts.

The accounting policies statement

As we have seen there are a number of different ways of dealing with such items as stock – is FIFO or average cost being used? – and depreciation – is it the reducing balance or straight line method? This applies to many other items contained in a set of accounts. It is therefore vital to understand the basis which has been adopted and this should be given in the statement of accounting policies. Unfortunately, all too often, in reality these statements are of such generality that they are fairly meaningless. For example, it is not uncommon to find a statement on depreciation which says 'depreciation is charged on the straight line

The consistency concept states that once an accounting policy is adopted it should not be changed from year to year. This is applied fairly rigorously to limited companies as their financial reports are covered by legislation and are subject to an audit report. For unincorporated businesses such as partnerships and sole proprietorships it is likely to be less rigorously applied.

KEY CONCEPT 14.2

CONSISTENCY

method over the useful life of the assets'. The problem with such a statement is that different assets have different lives and different residual values – in fact it is quite likely that different businesses will come to different estimates of both of these for the same asset. This leads to problems of comparability between different companies as the basis adopted will affect the profits, balance sheet values, etc. Within the same business the problems are to some extent alleviated by the requirement to follow the basic accounting concept of consistency.

Notes to the accounts

These are vital to any financial analysis as they contain the detailed information. Without that information the level of analysis available is likely to be very superficial especially in complex business organizations. The problem that users often find with the notes is that the level of detail and the complexity and technical language used are not helpful to their general understanding of the treatment of various items in the accounts.

Cash flow statement

This is a statement contained in the accounts of medium and large-size limited companies. The purpose of the statement is to provide some information about the origin of the cash coming into the business and how that cash was spent. It broadly distinguishes between the cash flows arising out of the normal operations of the business and other cash flows. The latter group are then further subdivided into those relating to returns on investments and servicing of debt, those to do with taxation, those arising from the purchase or sale of fixed assets and those from changes in the long-term financing of the business. Finally the statement reconciles the above with the movements in cash and cash equivalents. The cash flow statement should not be confused with the statement of source and application of funds which it replaces. As we explained in Chapter 13, the two statements use different definitions of funds and therefore have to be interpreted differently.

Auditors' report

Every company is subject to an annual audit of its accounts and included in the accounts is a report from the auditors stating whether in the opinion of the auditors the accounts show a 'true and fair' view. As far as financial analysis is concerned this report is best treated as an exception report – in other words unless it is qualified in some way no account needs to be taken of it. Having said that it is worth mentioning that for most bankers it adds credibility to the figures. It does not, however, mean that the accounts are correct in all their details and quite often the report contains a number of disclaimers in respect of certain figures.

The common needs explained

We have identified common needs such as profitability, liquidity, financial risk, etc., but before we can carry out any analysis we need to know what is meant by these terms. We shall therefore discuss what each term means and identify what we are trying to highlight with our analysis. For this purpose we shall use the example of Broll Ltd to illustrate the issues being discussed. This example, which we introduced in Chapter 12 as an illustration and with which you are already familiar, is reproduced below:

Example 14.1

Profit and loss account of Broll Ltd
for the year to XX XXX 199X

	Notes	£	*This year* £	*Last year* £
Sales	1		60 000	45 000
Cost of sales			40 000	30 000
Gross profit			20 000	15 000
Distribution costs	2	3 000		(2 500)
Administration costs	2	11 000	14 000	(9 000)
Profit before taxation			6 000	3 500
Taxation	3		2 600	1 400
Profit after taxation			3 400	2 100
Dividends – interim	4	1 000		–
– final	4	1 600	2 600	1 100
Transfer to reserves			800	1 000

Profitability

Looking at the first of our needs relating to profitability it is intuitively obvious that the starting point for this information should be the profit and loss account. Before looking at the information contained in the profit and loss we need to establish what information is needed.

To say that we need information about the profitability of the business is not the same as simply identifying whether it is making a profit or not. It implies some sort of relative comparison. Is it more profitable than it was last year? Is it more profitable than a similar business, or even a dissimilar business? Each of these require us to measure the profit relative to something else. The last question cannot be answered by simply looking at one set of accounts. We need to compare a number of different businesses and to do this we have to make sure that the accounts are comparable. For example, are they depreciating the assets over the same time period? Remember the shorter the time period the greater the charge therefore the smaller the final profit figure. It is for these comparisons that the accounting policies statement is vital.

Leaving aside the problems of comparisons with other businesses for the present, let us look at comparisons over time within our own business. If we look at Broll Ltd we find that the business made more profits this year, when it earned £6000 profit before taxation, than last year when the figure was only £3500. The question that now arises is whether it is more profitable because it is selling more, i.e. £60 000 this year as compared to £45 000 last year, or whether it is more efficient, or is it a combination of the two?

We can go some way to answering that by simply working out what the increase in sales was and what the increase in profit was. In this case sales increase by 33 per cent, i.e.

$$£60\,000 - £45\,000 = \frac{£15\,000}{£45\,000} \times 100 = 33\%$$

The profit, however, increased by over 70 per cent, i.e.

$$£6000 - £3500 = \frac{£2500}{£3500} \times 100 = 71\%$$

Thus we have discovered that not only is Broll making more profit by selling more but it is also making a greater profit on each sale. However, we do not know whether this seemingly favourable change is because this year was a good year or whether last year was a bad year, nor do we know whether we have had to invest a lot of money in order to increase the profitability. The former question can only really be satisfactorily answered by comparisons over a longer period of time than two years and by then comparing Broll Ltd with a similar business in the same industry. The second question can perhaps be answered in the case of a small company by looking at what return the profit represents relative to the amount invested. This then begs the question: what is the amount invested? Often in the case of a small business the major investment made by the owner is the time spent in the business and this is not reflected in the balance sheet. In the case of a public company, on the other hand, there is normally very little relationship between the amount shown in the accounts and the amount you would have to pay to buy the company.

Whilst not ignoring those problems, for the present we can look at the balance sheet, reproduced below, as a rough guide in the absence of anything better. We can see that in this case the investment in the form of capital and reserves has hardly changed, £74 500 last year to £75 300 this year, therefore we can be reasonably certain that there is a real increase in profitability from last year.

Example 14.1 contd

**Balance sheet of Broll Ltd
as at XX XXX 199X**

	Notes	£	This year £	Last year £
Fixed assets				
Intangible assets	5		10 000	11 000
Tangible assets	6		50 000	56 000
			60 000	67 000
Current assets				
Stocks	7	10 000		7 000
Debtors		10 000		4 000
Cash at bank and in hand		3 500		2 000
		23 500		13 000
Creditors: amounts falling due within one year				
Creditors		4 000		3 000
Taxation	3	2 600		1 400
Dividends	4	1 600		1 100
		8 200		5 500
Net current assets			15 300	7 500
			75 300	74 500
Capital and reserves			£	£
Share capital	8		70 000	70 000
Retained profits	9		5 300	4 500
			75 300	74 500

Before leaving the question of profitability we need to discuss the question of the future profitability of the business as this was identified as a common need for many users. The fact that a company has been profitable is comforting but if you want to make a decision about whether to buy into a business or sell up you need information about the future not the past. This information is not contained in the profit and loss account although it could be argued that information on the past is the best guide to the future. In practical terms the only way you can form an opinion about the future is using a combination of information including past profits, knowledge of the industry, predictions about the economy and many other factors.

Profitability – summary

☐ Profitability requires comparisons:
  – over time;
  – with other businesses.
☐ Profitability relates to:
  – the past for evaluation;
  – the future for prediction.

Financial risk and liquidity

We shall deal with these two together as they are both related to the financing of the business. The area of financial risk or long-term solvency is of vital importance as there are many cases where a business has gone under because of cash flow problems even though it was profitable. The introduction of the cash flow statement should go some way to alerting users to this problem. There are also cases where two companies in the same line of business produce dramatically different results purely because of the way they are financed. For example, if you make a return of 15 per cent on every pound invested and can borrow money at 10 per cent it is worth borrowing money because the excess return goes to the owners. However, there is some risk involved in such a course of action as you will lose if the interest rate rises to, say, 17 per cent and you are still only making 15 per cent. A way of measuring the financial risk, often referred to as gearing, is to look at the balance sheet of a business and identify the amount of debt finance, i.e. loans, debentures, bank over-drafts and other borrowing, and compare this to the amount of equity finance, i.e. owners' capital plus reserves.

In the UK, in general, debt finance does not normally exceed the equity finance, although the extent to which this generalization holds true is to some extent dependent upon the size of the business. In large businesses the debt finance is probably likely to be around 30 per cent of the total financing. On the other hand, because of a shortage of equity finance, many small businesses rely very heavily on debt as the major source of finance. The fact that in general the debt does not exceed equity is largely a result of the banks' policies of lending on a pound for pound basis, i.e. for each pound of your money you put in the business the bank will lend a pound. Whilst this is not a hard and fast rule it is effectively used as the benchmark by bank managers in the clearing banks in the UK. It is interesting that different countries seem to adopt different benchmarks. For example, banks in Germany and Japan tend to lend well above the one for one norm.

In the case of Broll Ltd there is no long-term borrowing, nor is there even a bank overdraft. This may be a good thing as the company is only making £6000 on the capital invested of over £75 000. This is less than 10 per cent and at the time of writing is well below the rate at which money could be borrowed.

Looking now at the area of liquidity, what is generally understood by this is whether you can meet your commitments as they fall due. In general the major area for concern is the short term, which is often taken to be a year. This fits with the definition used for current assets and current liabilities, so we have a convenient measure simply by looking at the balance sheet. For example, Broll has current assets of £23 500 and current liabilities of only £8200. This means that it should get enough money in during the next year to pay what it is currently due to pay out in that year.

One of the problems that arises with this apparently simple measure is that current can mean due tomorrow or in twelve months or even more. In the case of some current assets, for example stock, it may have to be processed, then it has to be sold, then the money has to be collected. Another problem is the question of what is the correct liquidity level for the business – if, for example, there is a lot of cash sitting around in the bank that is hardly an efficient use of resources. In the case of Broll the fact that there is £3500 in the bank may be far in excess of its true needs. There is also the question of whether £10 000 tied up in debtors is excessive on sales of £60 000, especially if we compare it to last year where the debtors were £4000 on sales of £45 000.

Other problems with interpreting the information may arise if we try to compare different businesses – for example an aircraft manufacturer will have different needs from a food wholesaler. Even within the same industrial sector the needs will differ. For example, a whisky distiller will have different needs from a brewery as the former has a product that has to be matured over years whereas the latter has a product that has a fairly limited maturing cycle.

Financial risk – summary

☐ Financial risk involves long-term and short-term solvency.
☐ Requirements and norms differ widely from industry to industry.

Once again the general conclusion to be drawn is that on its own the analysis of the financial statements is only a small part of the story and that analysis needs to be put into a wider context of knowledge of the industry and the environment. The maxim that a little knowledge is a dangerous thing applies equally to business analysis as it does elsewhere. With that firmly in mind we can now move on to look at some of the techniques that can be used to analyse the financial information.

Techniques of analysis

There are many techniques used in financial analysis varying from simple techniques such as studying the financial statements (in a manner similar to the exercise we have just done) and forming a rough opinion of what is happening to sophisticated statistical techniques. It should be pointed out that this rough analysis based on 'eyeballing' the accounts is vital as it forms the base on which the more sophisticated techniques can be built. If, for example, we fail to notice that a business has made a loss for the past few years the application of the most sophisticated techniques will not help as we have failed to grasp an essential point.

We shall limit ourselves to an examination of some of the simpler techniques. The choice of technique is once again a function of what you are trying to do and the purpose of your analysis. For example, managers and auditors may be interested in establishing any variations from past norms and explaining these and, where necessary, taking appropriate action. However, for a shareholder in a large company such an analysis, even if it were possible, would be inappropriate as no action could be taken and the level of detail is too specific.

It is interesting to compare the balance sheets of Marks & Spencer Plc with those of Sainsbury. You can see from the balance sheets below that Sainsbury have net current liabilities and yet are one of the most successful food retailers in the country. Marks & Spencer Plc, because of the fact that they run an in-house credit account scheme for their customers, are not in the same position, even though most of their business is on a cash basis like Sainsbury.

CASE 14.1

LIQUIDITY

1991 Balance sheet of Sainsbury

	Note	Group 1991 £m	Group 1990 £m	Company 1991 £m	Company 1990 £m
Fixed assets					
Tangible assets	1	**3214.1**	2738.4	**2540.9**	2097.8
Investments	2	**19.0**	17.1	**478.9**	474.2
		3233.1	2755.5	**3019.8**	2572.0
Current assets					
Investment	5	**–**	29.4	**–**	19.0
Stocks		**360.7**	308.4	**236.2**	196.2
Debtors	6	**116.3**	94.9	**98.1**	72.8
ACT recoverable	7	**28.9**	27.3	**27.7**	22.0
Cash at bank and in hand		**110.5**	139.3	**50.8**	47.1
		616.4	599.3	**412.8**	357.1
Creditors: due within one year	8	**(1429.4)**	(1352.3)	**(1210.4)**	(1105.1)
Net current liabilities		**(813.0)**	(753.0)	**(797.6)**	(748.0)
Total assets less current liabilities		**2420.1**	2002.5	**2222.2**	1824.0
Creditors: due after one year	8	**(386.0)**	(431.8)	**(636.2)**	(493.0)
Deferred tax	10	**(3.6)**	(3.9)	**4.7**	2.0
Minority interest	11	**(210.9)**	(11.3)	**–**	–
		1819.6	1555.5	**1590.7**	1333.0
Capital and reserves					
Called up share capital	12	**382.0**	378.6	**382.0**	378.6
Share premium account	13	**218.0**	193.8	**218.0**	193.8
Revaluation reserve	14	**19.9**	20.3	**19.9**	20.3
Profit and loss account	15	**1052.4**	812.8	**970.8**	740.3
		1672.3	1405.5	**1590.7**	1333.0
5% Convertible capital bonds 2004	16	**147.3**	150.0	**–**	–
		1819.6	1555.5	**1590.7**	1333.0

Continued over page

Continued from previous page

1991 Balance sheet of Marks & Spencer Plc

	Notes	The Group 1991 £m	The Group 1990 £m (restated)	The Company 1991 £m	The Company 1990 £m
Fixed assets					
Tangible assets:					
Land and buildings		**2193.0**	2093.9	**2043.3**	1958.6
Fixtures, fittings and equipment		**357.8**	343.3	**307.1**	292.8
Assets in the course of construction		**61.8**	31.3	**51.4**	25.7
	13	**2612.6**	2468.5	**2401.8**	2277.1
Investments	14	**–**	–	**535.2**	433.4
		2612.6	2468.5	**2937.0**	2710.5
Current assets					
Stocks	15	**351.1**	374.3	**235.8**	268.7
Debtors	16	**617.7**	537.6	**663.9**	640.3
Investments	17	**28.8**	28.1	**12.4**	19.1
Cash at bank and in hand	18	**293.0**	266.6	**41.4**	33.4
		1290.6	1206.6	**953.5**	961.5
Current liabilities					
Creditors: amounts falling due within one year	19	**896.7**	925.0	**714.3**	751.2
Net current assets		**393.9**	281.6	**239.2**	210.3
Total assets less current liabilities		**3006.5**	2750.1	**3176.2**	2920.8
Creditors: amounts falling due after more than one year	20	**549.6**	565.2	**290.0**	290.0
Provisions for liabilities and charges	21	**19.1**	4.3	**16.0**	–
Net assets		**2437.8**	2180.6	**2870.2**	2630.8
Capital and reserves					
Called up share capital	22	**680.1**	675.0	**680.1**	675.0
Share premium account	23	**69.3**	50.0	**69.3**	50.0
Revaluation reserve	23	**459.7**	458.0	**470.8**	479.4
Profit and loss account	23	**1218.3**	991.6	**1650.0**	1426.4
Shareholders' funds	23	**2427.4**	2174.6	**2870.2**	2630.8
Minority interests		**10.4**	6.0	**–**	–
Total capital employed		**2437.8**	2180.6	**2870.2**	2630.8

Comparison of financial statements over time

With limited data a simple comparison of the rate and direction of change over time can be very useful. This can be done both in terms of absolute amount and in percentage terms. In fact both are normally required in order to reach any meaningful conclusions. For example, a 50 per cent change on £1000 is less significant than a 50 per cent change on £50 000. However, if you only have £1000 to start with a change of £500 may well

KEY CONCEPT 14.3

TREND ANALYSIS

In trend analysis the choice of the base year is vital. If the base year chosen is not typical the resultant analysis will at best be extremely difficult and at worst misleading.

be significant. Thus it is not only the absolute figure but also the amount relative to other figures that is important.

The period of time chosen is also worth considering. Too short a time period will not be very meaningful. This was the case with Broll where we could say that the profit had increased but had no idea about whether that was part of a trend or whether it was because last year was a particularly bad year. Conversely, too long a period may bring its own problems. For example, the nature of the business or the environment may have altered drastically. Finally, it must be borne in mind that there may be other changes which have affected the figures. For example, the business may have decided to depreciate its vehicles over three years instead of four with consequent distortions in profit trends. While keeping these warnings in mind, let us now look at how we could do the comparisons.

Trend analysis

This technique is normally used for time periods in excess of two to three years in order to make the results easier to understand and interpret. It involves choosing a base year and then plotting the trend in sales or profits or whatever from there on.

Example 14.2   ABC Ltd

ABC Ltd profit and loss summary

	1987 £000	1988 £000	1989 £000	1990 £000	1991 £000
Sales	12 371	13 209	16 843	14 441	13 226
Cost of sales	9 605	10 113	12 544	10 284	10 901
Gross profit	2 766	3 096	4 299	4 157	2 325
Distribution expenses	619	660	842	1 011	926
Administration expenses	1 052	1 123	1 432	1 300	1 190
Operating profit	1 095	1 313	2 025	1 846	209
Interest charges	215	252	460	768	676
Pre-tax profit	880	1 061	1 565	1 078	−467
Taxation	464	529	875	579	98
Profit after tax	416	532	690	499	−565
Extraordinary items	−18	132	−263	426	−11
	398	664	427	925	−576
Dividends	164	185	336	337	112
Retained profit	234	479	91	588	−688

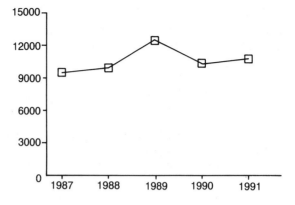

Figure 14.1 ABC Ltd: cost of sales.

If we take the cost of sales figure it is clear from a casual examination of the figures that it rises in 1987 and 1988 to a peak in 1989 after which it falls in 1990. If we plotted that on a graph it would look like Figure 14.1.

As you can see from the graph the information contained is fairly limited; it merely reflects what we have already found. To make any sensible comment we need to see how these costs are behaving in relation to something else. This could be in relation to another item in the profit and loss account such as sales or in relation to the costs in a comparable company. To do the latter comparison, however, we first have to find some common means of expression as the companies being compared are unlikely to be exactly the same size. One way of doing this is to use index numbers to express the figures we are looking at and the way in which they change from year to year.

Index number trends

As with other forms of trend analysis this technique is normally used for time periods in excess of two to three years. It is intended to make the results easier to understand and interpret. It does this by choosing a base year, setting that base year to 100 and expressing all other years in terms of that base year.

If, for example, we used 1987 as the base year and set that at 100 we would be able to calculate the sales trend as follows:

$$\frac{1988 \text{ Sales}}{1987 \text{ Sales}} \times 100 = \frac{13\,209}{12\,371} \times 100 = 107$$

For 1989 the calculation would be:

$$\frac{1989 \text{ Sales}}{1987 \text{ Sales}} \times 100 = \frac{16\,843}{12\,371} \times 100 = 136$$

Using the same formula we can find the index for each of the other years and we can then look at the trend. It this case the figures are:

1987, 100; 1988, 107; 1989, 136; 1990, 117; 1991, 107

We could do the same for the cost of sales and the profit figures and then these could be analysed. In the case of sales we can see that the sales peaked in 1989 and then declined to the same level as in 1988. This can

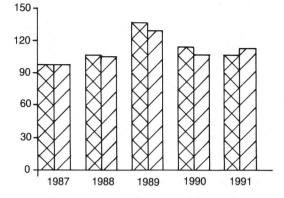

Figure 14.2 ABC Ltd: sales and cost of sales.

be seen more easily in Figure 14.2 which shows the sales in the left-hand blocks and the cost of sales in the right-hand blocks for each year.

This graph is much more informative than that in Figure 14.1 because it relates sales to cost of sales. In addition the use of index numbers (see the vertical axis) allows us to compare this company with another irrespective of size. The graph in this case shows that both sales and cost of sales peak in 1989. After that, however, we see that, although sales fall in both 1990 and 1991, the cost of sales rises again in 1991. This together with the other costs means that for 1991, although ABC Ltd makes an operating profit, this is not sufficient to cover the interest charges and a loss results.

Percentage changes

Another technique often used in trend analysis is to identify the percentage change from year to year and then examine the trends in this. For example, if we look at the sales we find that the change from 1987 to 1988 was 7 per cent, whilst that from 1988 to 1989 was 27 per cent. These figures are calculated using the following formula:

$$\frac{\text{This year's sales}}{\text{Last year's sales}} \times 100$$

$$\text{i.e. } \frac{13\,209}{12\,371} \times 100 = 107 \text{ or } 7\% \text{ up}$$

Once again it should be pointed out that these trends are of most use if they are compared with other trends, either in the business itself or in the industry. You should also bear in mind that these percentage increases are often illusory as they merely reflect the increase that would be expected as a result of the rate of inflation in the particular period and the particular country concerned.

Common size statements

A technique which can be used to turn the large numbers we often encounter in accounts into more digestible information is 'common size' statements. This technique, as the name implies, deals with the problem of comparisons of different size companies. It involves expressing the items in the balance sheet, for example, as percentages of the balance sheet total. Once again this is best illustrated by looking at ABC Ltd, the balance sheets of which are reproduced below. We can derive certain information and questions from just looking at the balance sheets but it is not easy to identify exactly what is happening. For example, why has the land and buildings gone up in 1989 by a greater amount than the other fixed assets? Where did the intangibles come from, and what are they? These questions can often be answered, in part at least, by using the detailed information contained in the notes to the accounts.

Example 14.2   ABC Ltd contd

ABC Ltd summary balance sheets

	1987	1988	1989	1990	1991
Fixed assets	£000	£000	£000	£000	£000
Land and buildings	639	660	682	1070	1103
Plant and equipment	875	849	959	863	767
Other fixed assets	450	554	486	663	683
Tangible fixed assets	1964	2063	2127	2596	2553
Intangibles			470	451	460
Current assets					
Stocks	3645	3952	3903	3289	3624
Debtors	2259	2389	3012	2776	2508
Cash	400	464	183	15	41
	6304	6805	7098	6080	6173
Creditors: amounts falling due in one year					
Creditors	3701	3706	4842	3311	4277
Taxation	110	415	196	44	48
Dividends	121	137	224	225	1
Bank overdraft	0	3	86	427	663
	3932	4261	5348	4007	4989
Net current assets	2372	2544	1750	2073	1184
Creditors: amounts due after one year					
Loans	297	148	0	427	92
Provisions for liabilities and charges					
Deferred tax	922	843	620	369	0
	3117	3616	3727	4324	4105
Financed by	£000	£000	£000	£000	£000
Share capital	1447	1459	1471	1476	1476
Share premium	137	145	153	157	157
Reserves	1533	2012	2103	2691	2472
	3117	3616	3727	4324	4105

The problem when looking at standard balance sheets is that the figures often disguise what is really happening. If, however, we convert the statements to some common measure the underlying trends become clearer. We could take the share capital for 1987, for example, and express it as a percentage of the balance sheet total. If we do this we find that it is 46 per cent in that year as compared to 40 per cent in 1988. To calculate this we simply divide the share capital figure by the balance sheet total and then multiply the result by 100. Thus for 1989 we would have:

$$\frac{\text{Share capital}}{\text{Total}} \times 100$$

$$\text{i.e.} \ \frac{1471}{3727} \times 100 = 40\%$$

Following this procedure for all items in the balance sheets produces common size statements as shown below:

ABC Ltd common size balance sheets

	1987	1988	1989	1990	1991
Fixed assets	%	%	%	%	%
Land and buildings	21	18	18	25	27
Plant and equipment	28	23	26	20	19
Other fixed assets	14	15	13	15	17
Tangible fixed assets	63	56	57	60	63
Intangibles			13	10	11
Current assets					
Stocks	117	109	104	76	88
Debtors	72	66	81	64	61
Cash	13	13	5	1	1
	202	188	190	141	150
Creditors: amounts falling due in one year					
Creditors	(117)	(102)	(130)	(76)	(105)
Taxation	(4)	(11)	(5)	(1)	(1)
Dividends	(4)	(4)	(6)	(5)	0
Bank overdraft	0	0	(2)	(10)	(16)
	(125)	(117)	(143)	(92)	(122)
Net current assets	77	71	47	49	28
Creditors: amounts due after one year					
Loans	(10)	(4)	0	(10)	(2)
Provisions for liabilities and charges					
Deferred tax	(30)	(23)	(17)	(9)	0
	100	100	100	100	100
Financed by	%	%	%	%	%
Share capital	46	40	40	34	36
Share premium	4	4	4	4	4
Reserves	50	56	56	62	60
	100	100	100	100	100

One of the things that we can see from an analysis of these statements is that the net current assets has shown a very marked decline over the period from 77 per cent of the balance sheet total in 1987 to only 28 per cent in 1991. We can also see that 1990 was in many ways an untypical year, e.g. the stock level and creditor level were out of line with other years. By 1991 the bank overdraft had risen to its highest level ever and stock and creditors were moving back towards the same level as 1989. It should be pointed out that with this technique the choice of the base year is just as important as it was with trend analysis. For example, any analysis of ABC Ltd that uses 1990 as a base year will produce results that are extremely difficult to interpret.

The technique of common size statements can be applied just as easily to the profit and loss account as to the balance sheet. In the case of the profit and loss account it is normal to express all items as a percentage of sales as illustrated below:

ABC Ltd common size profit and loss account

	1987 %	1988 %	1989 %	1990 %	1991 %
Sales	100	100	100	100	100
Cost of sales	78	77	74	71	82
Gross profit	22	23	26	29	18
Distribution expenses	5	5	5	7	7
Administration expenses	8	8	9	9	9
Operating profit	9	10	12	13	2
Interest charges	2	2	3	5	6
Pre-tax profit	7	8	9	7	−4
Taxation	4	4	5	4	1
Profit after tax	3	4	4	3	−4
Extraordinary items	0	1	−2	3	0
	3	5	3	6	−4
Dividends	1	1	2	2	1
Retained profit	2	4	1	4	−5

Apart from the rounding errors which result from working in whole numbers, such as those in 1989, the statement above is fairly self-explanatory. An item that is worth highlighting is that the increase in the cost of sales in 1991 has squeezed the operating profit down to only 2 per cent return on sales in a year when the interest charges are seen to be in excess of 5 per cent of sales. This illustrates the risk of high gearing which we referred to earlier in the chapter.

Common size statements and the other techniques we have examined so far have largely ignored the relationship between the balance sheet and the profit and loss account. The effect of this is that we have not been able to extract everything we could from the information available. Other techniques of analysis are available which look at the relationship between items in the balance sheet and items in the profit and loss account. The most common of these techniques is known as ratio analysis and this is explored more fully below.

A ratio R is quantity X divided by quantity Y: $$R = X/Y$$ In essence a ratio is merely a shorthand notation of the relationship between two or more things. It is the relationship that it is expressing that must be understood. Without that understanding the ratio, no matter how precisely calculated or sophisticated, is meaningless.	KEY CONCEPT 14.4 **RATIOS**

Ratio analysis

Although ratio analysis is seen in virtually every accounting textbook most students, whilst having little difficulty in calculating ratios, find extreme difficulty in understanding what they mean once they have been calculated. Because of this we shall not deal extensively with all the possible ratios that can be calculated but instead we shall try to concentrate on the relationships we are trying to express through the ratios we calculate. This approach will increase your understanding of the reasons for calculating these ratios and will therefore enable you to interpret the results from a sound basis of understanding. We shall discuss some ratios which express relationships between items in balance sheets, and then those based upon items in the profit and loss account. We shall then examine ratios which combine information from these two statements. Finally we shall consider how the cash flow statement and the information contained in it fits with the rest of our analysis.

Before doing that, we need to be understand exactly what a ratio is. This is defined in Key Concept 14.4.

Apart from understanding the relationship underpinning the ratio we also need to examine ratios in a wider context. For example, if we want to work out how many police we need to police a football match we could work on the basis of one policeman to a number of spectators. If we found that we needed two hundred police for a crowd of forty thousand spectators the ratio would be one to two hundred or 1:200.

Obviously this ratio is meaningless on its own as it does not tell us whether we are using the right number of police. To decide that we would need to establish whether there were still problems of violence or, if not, whether we could achieve the same result with fewer police. The former problem would require additional information whilst the latter could perhaps be judged, in part at least, by looking at what other football clubs do and what ratio of police to spectators they use. This simple example serves to illustrate the fact that the ratio on its own cannot tell us very much – it needs to be looked at in context of other information and experience.

Ratios based on the balance sheet

As we have already said, the important point to bear in mind is what the ratio is attempting to illustrate. For example, we could look at the balance sheet of ABC Ltd and calculate the ratio of plant and equipment to other fixed assets but this would be of little use unless we knew what the relationship meant and what we expected. Calculation of ratios is not an end in itself. We could waste hours calculating meaningless ratios. There are some relationships, however, that do mean something. For example, earlier in this chapter we discussed the need to find out about liquidity and financial risk. We said that financial risk was related to the amount of debt finance compared with equity finance. If we wanted to express this as a ratio, using ABC Ltd for example, we could take the loans in 1987 and compare them to the equity in that year. The figure for loans for that year was £297 000 and the equity figure was £3 117 000. The ratio could be calculated by dividing the equity figure by the loans figure as follows:

$$\frac{£3\,117\,000}{£297\,000} = 10.5 \text{ times} \quad \text{or} \quad 10.5:1$$

This tells us that for every £1 of loan finance there is £10.5 of equity finance, or that there is 10.5 times more equity than debt. If we compare that to 1990 we find that the ratio in that year is:

$$\frac{£4\,324\,000}{£427\,000} = 10.1 \text{ times} \quad \text{or} \quad 10.1:1$$

If we had calculated this ratio for all years we would find it goes up and down which is something we could have established by looking at the common size statements. We still do not know whether this is good or bad or why it is going up and down. To answer those questions we need to look at the environment, industry norms, and what else is happening in the particular business we are analysing.

To illustrate the latter point we can look in more detail at the balance sheets for the two years in question. We find that, on the face of it, the ratio we have just calculated would suggest that the business is more or less as reliant on debt in 1990 as it was in 1987. In fact this is not the case as the short-term debt, in the form of the bank overdraft, has gone from a position in 1987 of having £400 000 in cash and at the bank to having only £15 000 in cash and having an overdraft at the bank of £427 000 in 1990. This illustrates that the ratio we calculated only tells us part of the story as ABC Ltd is now relying on short-term as well as long-term borrowing.

One way to overcome this problem is to calculate more than one ratio to establish the relationship between debt and equity. We could, for example, also calculate the ratio of total debt to equity or the ratio of the total debt less cash balances to equity. All these ratios attempt to give some indication of financial risk involved.

Other balance sheet ratios that are commonly used relate to the relationship between current assets and current liabilities and to the relationship between current monetary assets, such as debtors and cash, and current liabilities. These relationships are used to express what is happening in relation to what is often referred to as 'short-term liquidity'. They are calculated by dividing, for example, the current assets figure by the current liabilities figure. Once again, on its own, the result of this calculation does not necessarily tell us much. We need to look at trends and take into account the nature of the business. For example, we would expect a high street greengrocer to be in a different situation with regard to the optimum level of stock held than, say, a car manufacturer. This is because the greengrocer's stock, being perishable goods, has a limited shelf-life. We also need to take into account the industry norms and the size of the business in our interpretation of the results.

We can calculate the liquidity ratios of ABC Ltd for the five years and see if the trend in these gives us any idea of what is happening. The first liquidity ratio is the current ratio. This is defined as

$$\text{Current ratio} = \frac{\text{Current assets}}{\text{Current liabilities}}$$

$$1987 = \frac{£6\,304\,000}{£3\,932\,000} = 1.6 \text{ times} \quad \text{or} \quad 1.6:1$$

The ratios for the other years are as follows:

1988, 1.6:1;   1989, 1.3:1;   1990, 1.5:1;   1991, 1.2:1

These show that the ratio is declining, but what does this mean? To answer that we need to think about the relationship being expressed, i.e. the relationship between those assets that will be turned into cash in the short term and the amounts we potentially have to pay out in the short term. If the ratio is going down it means that we have less cover and therefore there is more risk. If we find that the risk is increasing we may then wish to use a more sensitive measure to try to establish what is causing the increase in risk. One such measure simply excludes the stock from the current assets and compares the remaining current assets to the current liabilities. The reasoning behind the exclusion of stock is that it will first have to be sold and then the debtors will have to pay before we can use the cash to pay our creditors.

This ratio, i.e. the ratio of current assets, excluding stock, to current liabilities, is often referred to as the 'acid test' or 'quick ratio' and is defined as:

$$\text{Quick ratio} = \frac{\text{Current assets} - \text{Stock}}{\text{Current liabilities}}$$

Calculating this ratio for 1987 we obtain:

$$1987: \frac{£6\,304\,000 - £3\,645\,000}{£3\,932\,000} = 0.67 \text{ times} \quad \text{or} \quad 0.67:1$$

The fact that the ratio is less than one to one tells us that we could not pay our current debts if we were called upon to do so. Or to put it another way, the ratio tells us that we have 67p to pay each £1 of current liabilities. The question is: does this matter? ABC Ltd has after all stayed in business well after 1987.

The interpretation of the information obtained from calculating this ratio, as with all other ratios, only makes sense if it is judged by comparison to a set of industry norms. Even this is not as straightforward as it sounds as there are often different norms within an industry depending on the size and relative power of the firms in that sector. There is also the point that any norm based on a number of firms will actually be the average not the best and so care has to be exercised when looking at these norms and applying them to a particular firm. This all seems to imply that comparison with norms may not be meaningful in any case. This is certainly true if it is done without adequate attention to what constitutes the norm that the results are being compared to.

The question of the usefulness or otherwise of an industry norm does not apply in the case of ABC Ltd as we do not have that information. What we do have is the information base to calculate a trend and the trend in the quick ratio for ABC Ltd is shown below:

$$1988, 0.67:1; \quad 1989, 0.6:1; \quad 1990, 0.7:1; \quad 1991, 0.5:1$$

Once again the trend shows an overall decline with 1990 being the odd year out. As before we can conclude that the risk is increasing but can say very little about whether this is in line with what is happening generally because we are looking at the company in isolation. In reality we would know from our knowledge of what was happening in the economy generally whether credit was getting tight or easing off and this knowledge would help us in our interpretation of the trend shown above.

Having looked at some of the balance sheet ratios for measuring financial risk it is worth remembering that because the balance sheet represents the position at a point in time the ratios we calculate may not be typical of the position throughout the year. Because of this we would be better using the cash flow statement when attempting to judge the liquidity position of a firm. However, before we look at the cash flow statement let us turn our attention to the profit and loss account.

Ratios based on the profit and loss account

Most ratios that relate solely to the profit and loss account are really expressions of costs as a percentage of sales, for example the gross profit or net profit expressed as a percentage of sales. These relationships are also made apparent with common size statements, which we have already examined, therefore we shall not discuss them further here. There are some other ratios based on the figures in the profit and loss account that are required to meet the needs of the users which we identified earlier which are not related to sales. These are the interest cover and dividend cover. Both these ratios express the relationship between the profit available and the item in question. In the case of ABC Ltd it is hardly worth calculating the ratio of dividend cover as in 1991 there was no profit left after interest and tax to pay the dividend. We shall therefore concentrate on interest cover. This can be expressed as:

$$\text{Interest cover} = \frac{\text{Profit available before interest charge}}{\text{Interest charge}}$$

$$1987 = \frac{£1\,095\,000}{£215\,000} = 5.1 \text{ times}$$

The trend can also be calculated.

1988, 5.2 times;   1989 4.4 times;   1990, 2.4 times;   1991, 0.3 times

We can see a decline in this ratio from 1988 on. Clearly the fewer times interest is covered by profits the more at risk that interest is from the lender's point of view. From the point of view of the shareholders the lower the cover the more likely it is that all the profits will be absorbed by interest charges, especially if they rise. This then leaves no profits available for the payment of dividends.

We shall now consider some of the relationships between the profit and loss account and the balance sheet.

Profit and loss and balance sheet relationships

In many areas the balance sheet and the profit and loss account are directly related such that a movement in one will have a consequential effect on the other. For example, if we have an increase in sales we would expect our debtors to go up, we would probably have to buy more goods to sell so our creditors may rise and in all probability our level of stocks would also have to rise to cope with the increased demand. In the case of ABC Ltd the sales have risen as have the debtors. At this stage we are not sure whether the increase in debtors is solely due to the increase in sales or whether it is in part caused by the debtors taking longer to pay up. The use of a ratio that compares sales and debtors would provide answers to questions such as this.

When calculating ratios that relate balance sheet items to profit and loss account items we have to bear in mind that if prices are changing the relationship can be distorted. This is because the balance sheet represents prices at one point in time, whereas the profit and loss account represents the results of operations for a period. This can be shown diagrammatically as:

$$T_0 \qquad \text{Profit and loss account} \qquad T_1$$

$$\longleftarrow \qquad\qquad\qquad\qquad \longrightarrow$$

Opening   Closing
balance   balance
sheet   sheet

Thus the opening stock figure or debtors figure would be expressed in start-of-year prices, the profit and loss figures in average prices and the closing figures in end-of-year prices. Added to this problem of a changing price level is the fact that the volume will also change. For example, as sales increase so we need to hold more units of stock to provide the same service. Thus we have two problems, i.e. changes in prices and changes in volumes. One way to compensate for this is to use the average of the opening and closing balance sheet figures and compare that average figure for stocks, debtors, etc., to the figure from the profit and loss account which is already expressed in average prices. Thus to calculate the relationship between sales for 1991 and the debtors we would take the debtors at 1990 and at 1991 and take the average of the two figures. This would give us a better approximation of the true level of debtors required to sustain that volume of sales.

The relationship thus calculated can be expressed either as the turnover of the balance sheet figure, e.g. debtors turnover or as the number of days debtors take to repay. We shall use the latter for the purposes of illustration as experience shows that this is more readily understood.

To calculate this ratio the formula we require is:

$$\text{Debtor collection} = \frac{\text{Average debtors}}{\text{Sales}} \times 365$$

Thus for 1991 for ABC Ltd the debtor collection period is:

$$\frac{\frac{1}{2}(2776 + 2508)}{13\,226} \times 365 = 73 \text{ days}$$

Once again we cannot comment on whether this is good or bad without some reference point and some more information. For example, if the sales mix had changed and ABC Ltd had moved into overseas markets this may mean that it takes longer to collect money.

A number of other ratios of this type can be calculated, e.g. the number of days' stocks held or the period taken to pay creditors using cost of sales and purchases respectively. However, as this is an introductory text we shall not deal with these other ratios in depth. Instead we would encourage the reader to identify the relationships which will aid their understanding and derive their own ratios. If, having done that, readers are interested in looking at some of the more commonly used ratios they should make reference to one of the texts suggested at the end of this chapter.

The cash flow statement

We have talked about the use of balance sheet based ratios such as the current ratio and the quick ratio as measures of liquidity. The problem with these ratios is that they are based upon a static position statement and they can be manipulated by changing the timing of stock purchases etc. round the year end for example. A better guide to the liquidity position can be found in the cash flow statement which tells us what money is coming in, where it is coming from, and how it is being spent. The cash flow statement for ABC Ltd for 1991 is reproduced below.

Note: You should not try to reconcile this to the main statements as without the notes to the accounts you do not have sufficient information to do so successfully.

Cash flow statement of ABC Ltd for 1991

Net cash inflow from operating activities		1321
Returns on investments and servicing of finance		
Interest paid	(676)	
Dividends paid	(336)	
Net cash flow from returns on investment and servicing activities		(1012)
Taxation		
Corporation tax paid (including ACT)	(94)	
Net cash outflow from taxation		(94)
Investing activities		
Payment for redundancies	(11)	
Payment to acquire tangible fixed assets	(70)	
Payment to acquire intangible assets	(9)	
Net cash outflow from investing activity		(90)
Net cash outflow before financing		125
Financing		
Debenture loan repayment	(335)	
Net cash outflow from financing		(335)
Decrease in cash or cash equivalents		(210)

Notes to the cash flow statement

1. *Reconciliation of operating profit to net cash flow from operating activity*

Operating profit	209
Depreciation charges	213
Increase in stocks	(335)
Decrease in debtors	268
Increase in creditors	966
	1321

2. *Analysis of changes in cash and cash equivalents during the year*

Balance at 1990	(412)
Net cash inflow	(210)
Balance at 1991	(622)

3. *Analysis of the balances of cash and cash equivalents per the balance sheet*

	1991	*1990*	*Change*
Cash at bank and in hand	41	15	26
Bank overdrafts	(663)	(427)	(236)
	(622)	(412)	(210)

4. *Analysis of changes in financing during the year*

	Shares	*Loans*
Balance at 1990	1476	427
Cash outflow from financing	0	(335)
Balance at 1991	1476	92

The cash flow statement tells us that there is a net cash inflow from operating activities of £1 321 000 which would appear to be healthy until we look at note 1 where we find that most of this comes from the increases in creditors so increasing the reliance on short-term financing which is further evidenced by the increase in the overdraft level. This may on its own not be a problem especially as we can also see long-term loans being repaid. It does, however, raise the question of why the company is switching from long-term to short-term borrowing as the latter is generally more expensive.

Before leaving the subject of financial analysis and in particular ratio analysis it is worthwhile reminding ourselves of some of the points made in this chapter about putting the analysis into context and also reiterating the limitations of this sort of analysis.

Summary

There is no point in using sophisticated techniques for analysis without an understanding of the following.

☐ The wider context, i.e. the economic, social and political pressures, the type of industry and where the industry as a whole is going.

☐ The organization's environment, i.e. what type of organization are we are dealing with, is it a charity, does it have an American parent company, what business is it in? How are these factors affecting the information that is being presented and the way in which that information is presented, and how should they affect our analysis?

☐ The organization and its structure, i.e. what sort of organization are we dealing with, how big is the organization, is it a partnership, sole proprietorship or company and how does that affect the information provided, its presentation and our analysis?

☐ Who the analysis is for? As we have seen, different users have different needs in terms of analysis and, even when their needs appear to overlap, it is often the case that the emphasis is different from group to group.

☐ Any analysis will only be as good as the base data. Here we are dealing with analysis based upon historic cost accounts which assume prices do not change when in practice this is not the case. Even if we overcome that problem, there is the question of how up to date or out of date the information is. There are also issues of comparability because of different accounting policies being adopted, because of the effects of organizational size on the norms, and the question of what norms actually mean.

Finally we need to be clear on the purpose of the analysis. Are we providing the base for a decision about the future actions of a user of accounting information and, if so, what alternatives in terms of decisions is that user facing? Having identified in our case that ABC Ltd seems to have some problems we now need to identify what, if any, action can be taken to solve some of those problems. In general, the role of the outside user is probably limited to that of problem-identification as in most cases there is little that the outside user can do in terms of problem-solving. This is a task that should be carried out by the management of the company.

In order for management to be able to carry out this task, as we have already suggested, they will need more detailed information and often they will also require different forms of information. For example, the fact that the costs are rising does not help as they need to know which costs are actually rising. They also need to know whether the problem is due to the fact that at a lower level of sales they are losing economies of scale. Then they need to know the level of sales and costs they would expect in 1992 and thereafter so that they can take appropriate actions to improve the performance of their business. Whether such forecasts can be made from a base of historic cost information is questionable and we shall be examining some of the alternatives suggested in the next three chapters. However, before leaving the area of financial analysis it is important that we summarize some of the key features and limitations of financial statement analysis.

Key features

- ☐ Financial analysis has to be looked at in the wider context of the industry, the environment, etc.
- ☐ Financial analysis has to be targeted to meet the needs of the user of the analysis.
- ☐ Financial analysis is only as good as the base information that is being analysed.
- ☐ Financial analysis involves both inter-temporal and inter-firm comparisons and this imposes limitations.

The key features outlined above point to some limitations that have to be borne in mind when discussing financial analysis. These can be usefully summarized under three headings as follows.

Key limitations

Information problems
- ☐ The base information is often out of date, i.e. timeliness of information leads to problems of interpretation.
- ☐ Historic cost information may not be the most appropriate information for the decision for which the analysis is being undertaken.
- ☐ Information in published accounts is generally summarized information and detailed information may be needed.
- ☐ Analysis of accounting information only identifies symptoms not causes and thus is of limited use.

Comparison problems – inter-temporal
- ☐ Effects of price changes make comparisons difficult unless adjustments are made.
- ☐ Impacts of changes in technology on the price of assets, the likely return and the future markets.

☐ Impacts of a changing environment on the results reflected in the accounting information.
☐ Potential effects of changes in accounting policies on the reported results.
☐ Problems associated with establishing a normal base year to compare other years with.

Comparison problems – inter-firm
☐ Selection of industry norms and the usefulness of norms based on averages.
☐ Different firms having different financial and business risk profiles and the impact on analysis.
☐ Different firms using different accounting policies.
☐ Impacts of the size of the business and its comparators on risk, structure and returns.
☐ Impacts of different environments on results, e.g. different countries, home-based versus multinational firms.

Thus there are a number of issues that you need to bear in mind when carrying out your analysis. They should not, however, be used as a reason not to attempt the analysis but should be an integral part of your thinking when interpreting and reporting the results of your analysis.

Further reading

Lev, B. (1984) *Financial Statement Analysis – a New Approach*, Prentice Hall.

Review questions

1. Identify the main user groups and their common needs in terms of financial analysis.

2. How do the needs of long-term lenders differ from those of equity investors?

3. What factors do we need to take into account in order to put our analysis in context?

4. What sources of information outside the business are available to you and how would you use this information in your analysis?

5. What information would you derive from reading the chairman's statement?

6. What other parts of the annual report would you use in your analysis?

7. Explain briefly what the difference is between financial risk and business or commercial risk.

8. How would you measure financial risk in the short and long term?

9. What are the limitations of financial analysis that are inherent in the accounting data being used?

Problems for discussion and analysis

Belper

Given below are the summarized accounts of Belper Ltd for the past five years. These form the basis for the questions which follow.

Summarized profit and loss accounts of Belper Ltd

	1984 £000	1985 £000	1986 £000	1987 £000	1988 £000
Sales	93 930	116 232	259 470	278 340	372 753
Cost of sales	81 750	101 673	230 334	244 809	346 695
Trading profit	12 180	14 559	29 136	33 531	26 058
Depreciation	1 023	1 380	3 678	4 065	8 151
Interest	2 727	2 652	7 707	10 167	14 082
Net profit before tax	8 430	10 527	17 751	19 299	3 825
Taxation	2 517	1 746	9 270	7 833	2 601
Net profit after tax	5 913	8 781	8 481	11 466	1 224
Extraordinary items		(870)	(15)	4 989	489
	5 913	7 911	8 466	16 455	1 713
Dividends	801	1 812	3 339	3 738	3 672
Retained profits	5 112	6 099	5 127	12 717	−1 959
Retained at start of year	14 637	19 749	25 848	30 975	50 427
Retained at end of year	19 749	25 848	30 975	43 692	48 468

Notes

(i) During 1988 some of the freehold properties were revalued.

(ii) Loans amounting to £22 million were repaid during the year.

(iii) The extraordinary item shown in the profit and loss account in 1988 represents the damages received by the company from a libel action against a newspaper.

(iv) No fixed assets were disposed of during the year.

Summarized balance sheets of Belper Ltd

	1984 £000	1985 £000	1986 £000	1987 £000	1988 £000
Fixed assets					
Freehold land and buildings	14 058	14 571	20 559	20 598	29 721
Leasehold land and buildings	2 349	2 490	5 184	5 193	12 564
Plant and machinery	8 082	11 541	26 781	30 000	47 172
Total gross fixed assets	24 489	28 602	52 524	55 791	89 457
Depreciation freehold					597
Depreciation leasehold	117	147	345	774	858
Depreciation plant etc.	4 197	5 325	8 259	11 277	18 747
Total depreciation	4 314	5 472	8 604	12 051	20 202
Net fixed assets	20 175	23 130	43 920	43 740	69 255
Intangible fixed assets					
Goodwill	789	807	849	936	936
Investments	486	795	393	303	393
Patents and trade marks	3 972	3 618	6 063	8 730	9 345
Current assets					
Stock	20 031	23 034	53 091	74 823	99 606

	1984	1985	1986	1987	1988
Debtors	17 589	24 693	60 270	48 987	66 768
Bank and cash	4 698	6 801	7 839	3 273	9 747
	42 318	54 528	121 200	127 083	176 121
Current liabilities					
Creditors	16 197	24 588	55 659	41 130	72 831
Taxation	459	768	4 302	2 712	3 444
Dividends	801	1 812	3 339	3 738	3 672
Bank loans and overdraft	10 581	4 026	18 180	29 316	37 638
	28 038	31 194	81 480	76 896	117 585
Net current assets	14 280	23 334	39 720	50 187	58 536
	39 702	51 684	90 945	103 896	138 465
Financed by	£000	£000	£000	£000	£000
Ordinary share capital	2 229	2 829	3 396	6 792	7 077
Share premium account	2 931	7 530	14 598	11 247	12 387
Retained profits	19 749	25 848	30 975	50 427	48 468
Revaluation reserves			6 735	6 735	9 423
Total equity and reserves	24 909	36 207	55 704	75 201	77 355
Loans	14 793	15 477	35 241	28 695	61 110
	39 702	51 684	90 945	103 896	138 465

1. From a review of the information above identify the areas which you would concentrate on in your analysis of the position of Belper Ltd.

2. Produce common size profit and loss accounts for the five years and analyse these statements with particular reference to the profitability of Belper.

3. Calculate the trends in the Sales and Cost of sales and comment on the information disclosed by your analysis.

4. Using whatever form of analysis you consider appropriate comment on the financial risk profile of Belper Ltd for the five years under review.

5. Based on your analysis write a brief report for the bank advising them on whether to continue to provide finance for Belper Ltd.

6. Apart from the information arising from your analysis what other information would you advise the bank to consider when making its decision?

7. Discuss how your analysis would have been altered if you were carrying out the analysis on behalf of a prospective shareholder.

8. The summarized common size balance sheets for eight companies in different industries are given below. In addition, the areas of activity of the eight companies are listed. Discuss, which company is represented by which balance sheet giving reasons for your choices.

Areas of activity
A. General engineering
B. Investment in properties for rental
C. Estate development and house builders
D. Whisky distillers and blenders
E. Brewers
F. Retail stores
G. Conglomerate with diversified activities
H. Insurance brokers

Common size balance sheets

Number:	1	2	3	4	5	6	7	8
	%	%	%	%	%	%	%	%
Land and property	83	31	12	32	72	81	11	107
Other fixed assets	13	28	3	22	23	7	9	3
Stock and work in progress	8	43	111	45	0	11	75	0
Trade debtors	11	36	36	56	436	4	18	7
Cash/temporary investments	4	5	1	3	91	7	1	1
	119	143	163	158	622	110	114	118
Trade creditors	19	34	45	47	509	10	9	9
Bank overdraft	0	9	18	11	13	0	5	9
Net assets employed	100	100	100	100	100	100	100	100

15 Income concepts and valuation

We have now looked at the historic cost model of accounting in some detail and have pointed out its limitations and their effects on financial analysis. In this chapter, we shall return to a discussion of approaches to the measurement of profit that have evolved from economists' income measures. We shall look at present value systems and the problems associated with applying such systems in the real world. From here, we shall go on to propose a benchmark against which alternative accounting measures, such as historic cost, replacement cost, net realizable value, etc., can be evaluated. Finally, we shall evaluate the historic cost model against our benchmark, and then look at some of the alternatives available. In Chapters 16 and 17 we shall examine two of the alternatives in greater depth.

Economists' income measures

In Chapter 3, we discussed some of the measures of income which have been proposed by economists and adopted a definition of income derived from the writings of Sir John Hicks. Hicks' definition of an individuals income is reproduced as Key Concept 15.1.

The definition does not specify a point in time at which the measurement should be made. Should we measure wealth from a point at the start of the period, using forecasts of the future, or should we wait until the end of period and look backwards? In Chapter 3 we assumed that wealth should be measured at the end of the period. Thus, we took the wealth as measured at the end of the period and subtracted the wealth at the start of the period to produce a measure of income. This we showed as:

$$\text{Income} = \text{Wealth}_1 - \text{Wealth}_0$$

KEY CONCEPT 15.1	Income is that amount which an individual can consume and still be as well off at the end of the period as he or she was at the start of the period.
HICKS' DEFINITION OF INCOME	

> Ex-post income measures relate to measures made from a point in time at the end of the period. They are essentially backward looking.
>
> KEY CONCEPT 15.2
>
> **EX-POST INCOME**

> Ex-ante income measures relate to measures made from a point in time at the start of the period. They are essentially forward looking.
>
> KEY CONCEPT 15.3
>
> **EX-ANTE INCOME**

> The net present value is arrived at by estimating future cash flows and discounting them back to the present using an appropriate discount rate.
>
> KEY CONCEPT 15.4
>
> **NET PRESENT VALUE**

where Wealth$_1$ is the wealth at the end of the period and Wealth$_0$ is the wealth at the start of the period. This measure is known as an ex-post income measure, i.e. one based on measuring wealth at the end of the period.

An alternative measure that we could have used is to measure income and wealth from the start of the period, i.e. ex ante. This would involve estimation of future cash flows in order to estimate the wealth at the end of the period. Clearly, in terms of investment decisions, and consumption decisions, it would be better to know the income to be derived from an investment in advance.

Estimation of the ex-ante income can be done using forecasts of the future income streams and discounting them back to the present. The estimates are, of course, subject to estimation error and to changes in circumstances during the period. Having arrived at the estimates, they are discounted back to their present value using a discount rate that takes account of the fact that £1 now is worth more to most people than £1 in five years' time. This produces the net present value of the future cash flows and we shall now turn our attention to the technique that is used to arrive at the net present value.

Net present value

Net present value requires that the amounts, and timing, of the future cash flows associated with an investment are known, or can be estimated. It also requires that an appropriate discount rate is chosen. The discount rate would be arrived at by looking at the risk involved, the alternative opportunities available and such things as the certainty of the cash flows, their timing and the availability of finance. The way in which the net present value is calculated can best be illustrated with a simple example.

Example 15.1
Bert wishes to invest his money and to earn a 10 per cent return. He is offered an opportunity to invest in a project which will last for three years and generate the following cash flows at the end of each year.

	£
Year 1	3000
Year 2	3000
Year 3	4000

If we project the income that Bert should receive from the project, we can see that at the end of Year 1 there will be a net cash flow of £3000, the same at the end of Year 2 and at the end of Year 3, £4000. To find out the net present value of these cash flows, we have to take account of the timing of the cash flows and adjust the value to reflect the fact that £1 now is more valuable than £1 in a year's time. In this way we can measure the wealth at the start of Year 1, i.e. T_0. This we do as follows:

$$\text{Wealth } T_0 = \frac{3000}{1.1} + \frac{3000}{1.1^2} + \frac{4000}{1.1^3}$$
$$= 2727 + 2480 + 3005$$
$$= 8212$$

Thus, the project has a net present value of £8212. If Bert invests £8212 he will get a 10 per cent return on his money.

Ex-ante income

As we have said, ex-ante income is the projected income for a period based upon estimates of cash flows at the start of that period. We shall use an example to illustrate how it is calculated and then examine some of its properties.

Example 15.1 contd
Assume that Bert does invest £8212 in the project and that, after withdrawing the income he requires, Bert reinvests any surplus to obtain a 10 per cent return. What is Bert's projected, i.e. ex-ante, income for Year 1?

Income Year 1
We know the wealth at the start of Year 1 which is £8212. If we wish to establish the ex-ante income for Year 1, we also need to measure the wealth that we anticipate at the end of Year 1, i.e. T_1. At that point in time, the first £3000 will have been received, the second £3000 will be one year away, and the £4000 will be two years away. Thus, we can calculate the value of the wealth at time T_1 as follows. We shall use the notation T_1^0, to indicate that the measurement relates to T_1 and that it is taking place at the start of the period T_0.

$$\text{Wealth } T_1^0 = 3000 + \frac{3000}{1.1} + \frac{4000}{1.1^2}$$
$$= 3000 + 2727 + 3306$$
$$= 9033$$

We are now in a position to measure the income for Year 1 on an ex-ante basis, by using the formula:

$$\text{Income Year 1} = \text{Wealth } T_1^0 - \text{Wealth } T_0$$
$$= 9033 - 8212$$
$$= 821$$

You will note that the income for the year represents a 10 per cent return on the investment. This is, of course, what we would expect given that the net present value of the investment was calculated using a discount rate of 10 per cent. We can also show that the income for Year 2 will be the same as for Year 1 assuming that Bert only spends the income we calculated above and that he reinvests the remainder of the £3000 at 10 per cent.

Income Year 2
This is calculated using exactly the same approach as for Year 1. That is, we need to calculate the wealth at the end Year 2, and deduct from this the wealth at the start of Year 2. This we do as follows.

Wealth at the start of Year 2
This is the same as the wealth at the end of Year 1 after deducting the income that Bert withdrew:

$$\text{Wealth } T_1^0 = (3000 - 821) + \frac{3000}{1.1} + \frac{4000}{1.1^2}$$
$$= (3000 - 821) + 2727 + 3306$$
$$= (3000 - 821) + 6033$$
$$= 8212$$

As you can see, the wealth at the start of Year 2 is the same as it was at the start of Year 1. This is, of course, as it should be, because Bert has only taken out as income the amount that he can consume and stay as well off as he was at the start of the year.

Wealth at the end of Year 2
Here we are measuring the wealth at the end of Year 2 from a point at the start of Year 1. The calculation of the wealth at the end of Year 2 would be as follows:

$$\text{Wealth } T_2^0 = 3000 + \frac{4000}{1.1}$$
$$= 3000 + 3636$$
$$= 6636$$

To this wealth that is still tied up in the investment, we need to add the wealth that was released at the end of Year 1 and reinvested elsewhere.

This amounted to £2179, i.e. (3000 − 821). Thus Bert's wealth at the end of Year 2 will be:

$$\text{Wealth } T_1^0 = 6636 + 2179$$
$$= 8815$$

We can now calculate the ex-ante income for Year 2. This is done by taking the anticipated wealth at the end of Year 2 and subtracting that at the start of Year 2. However, we cannot stop there, because Bert also reinvested the £2179 to obtain a return of 10 per cent. So, we need to add to our calculation £218, the return on the reinvestment. The income calculation is therefore as follows:

$$\text{Income Year 2} = (\text{Wealth } T_2^0 - \text{Wealth } T_1^0) + 218$$
$$= (8815 - 8212) + 218$$
$$= 603 + 218$$
$$= 821$$

As you can see, Bert's income for Year 2 is the same as for Year 1. This, of course, is what we would expect given the assumptions we have made. These are listed below:

☐ that all cash flows are as predicted;
☐ that Bert only consumes the income for Year 1;
☐ that Bert is able to reinvest at a return of 10 per cent.

Given these assumptions, we can see that the ex-ante income measure provides us with a measure that allows us to predict what the income will be next year. It also allows us to identify how much can be consumed, or distributed, while still maintaining wealth intact. What the ex-ante measurement cannot do is to provide us with information for evaluation, since in order to evaluate we need to measure actual outcomes against our expectations. For this we need an ex-post measure, i.e. a measure taken at the end of the period in question. As we have indicated, in general, accounting models tend to concentrate on past events and as such they use ex-post income measures. Assuming that the estimates are correct and things turn out as planned, then, as we shall illustrate, this would make no difference to the income.

Ex-post income

Ex-post income is measured at the end of the period, i.e. after the events have taken place. Applying this to our example, we could recalculate the wealth at the end of Year 1. Here you will notice that the wealth at the end of Year 1 is denoted as Wealth T_1^1; this means that the Wealth at T_1 is being measured at the end of the period.

$$\text{Wealth } T_1^1 = 3000 + \frac{3000}{1.1} + \frac{4000}{1.1^2}$$
$$= 3000 + 2727 + 3306$$
$$= 9033$$

We are now in a position to measure the income for Year 1 on an ex-post basis by using the formula:

$$\text{Income Year 1} = \text{Wealth } T_1{}^1 - \text{Wealth } T_0$$
$$= 9033 - 8212$$
$$= 821$$

As you can see, the ex-post measure of income is exactly the same, in this case, as the ex-ante income measure. Thus, on the basis of this, it would appear that if we measure income ex-post we get a measure that can be used for prediction and for distribution decisions. This is because these were properties that the ex-ante income measure had, and here ex-post income equals ex-ante income. In addition, because we are now at the end of the period we can evaluate outcomes against expectations. Thus we have a measure that can be used for prediction, evaluation and distribution decisions.

However, this will only be the case if the estimated future cash flows are actually achieved. If the cash flows differ from those estimated, either in amount or timing, then the ex-post income and the ex-ante income will not be the same. Similarly, if the yield from alternative investments changes, then this will change the discount rate to be applied and the ex-post income will not be the same as the ex-ante income. We shall illustrate the effect of different cash flows by extending the example above and altering one of the outcomes.

Example 15.1 contd
The facts, at the start of the year, are the same as previously. However, due to changes in prices that occurred after the start of Year 1, the actual outcome for Year 1 is a cash flow of £3500 instead of £3000. For simplicity of exposition, we shall assume that the remaining cash flows are unaffected and that the discount rate is unaffected. We shall confine our discussion to Year 1, as that will enable us to illustrate the points we wish to make without unnecessary complications.

Ex-ante income – Year 1
The ex-ante income will not change as it is measured before the events that changed the actual cash flows were known. It is therefore based on the original estimates.

Ex-post income – Year 1
The ex-post income measure is calculated at the end of the period and, as such, will take into account the changes that have occurred in the period. The ex-post income calculation will be as follows:

$$\text{Wealth } T_1{}^1 = 3500 + \frac{3000}{1.1} + \frac{4000}{1.1^2}$$
$$= 3500 + 2727 + 3306$$
$$= 9533$$

We are now in a position to measure the income for Year 1 on an ex-post basis by using the formula:

$$\text{Income Year 1} = \text{Wealth } T_1{}^1 - \text{Wealth } T_0$$
$$= 9533 - 8212$$
$$= 1321$$

We can see that, because the conditions have changed during the year, the ex-post income measure of £1321, no longer equals the ex-ante measure of £821. Thus, although the ex-post measure allows us to evaluate the actual outcome against the projected outcome, or against alternative investments, it can no longer be used for prediction or distribution, as it no longer has the same properties as the ex-ante measure.

To sum up the above discussion, we have shown that ex-ante and ex-post income are the same under conditions of certainty about the timing of cash flows, the amount of cash flows, and the discount rate to be applied. However, if any of those conditions change then clearly the ex-ante measure is no longer helpful. If this is the case, the ex-post measure is no longer useful for prediction, and its usefulness for evaluation and distribution decisions has yet to be tested. If we look at the example, the ex-post income measure tells us that income is £1321, it does not tell us why it has increased, or whether this is a permanent change which will occur again next year. Part of the reason for this is that we are calculating wealth at the start of the year, based on one set of expectations and assumptions, and comparing that to wealth measured at the end of the year, using different expectations and assumptions.

This is, of course, very similar to what happens in reality where the prices of goods are rising and conditions of certainty do not exist. In practice, we take some assets expressed in terms of prices that exist in 1991, and add to it other assets expressed in prices that pertained at different times in the past, to arrive at our 1991 balance sheet. We then effectively subtract the wealth at the start of the year expressed in 1990 and pre-1990 prices to arrive at a profit for the year. In order to overcome this problem, i.e. that the two wealth measures are expressed in different terms, we need to revise our wealth at the start of the period and express it in the same terms as the wealth at the end of the period, i.e. in end-of-period terms.

Economists recognized this problem and devised a third measure of income which is an ex-post measure that revises the wealth at the start of the period before calculating the income.

Revised ex-post income – Year 1

The general formula for calculating the revised ex-post income can be expressed as follows:

$$\text{Income Year } 1^r = \text{Wealth } T_1{}^1 - \text{Wealth } T_0{}^r$$

This simply says that the revised ex-post income for Year 1, Income Year 1^r, can be calculated by taking the wealth at the end of the year as calculated at the end of the year, i.e. $T_1{}^1$, and deducting the wealth at the start of the year calculated on the basis of the revised conditions, depicted by r, existing at the end of the year, i.e. $T_0{}^r$.

Applying the above formulation to Example 15.1 we can recalculate the wealth at the start of the year and then the revised income for the year as follows:

$$\text{Wealth } T_0{}^r = \frac{3500}{1.1} + \frac{3000}{1.1^2} + \frac{4000}{1.1^3}$$
$$= 3182 + 2480 + 3005$$
$$= 8667$$

We have already calculated the wealth at the end of the year to be £9533 (see above), so we can now calculate the revised income figure as follows:

$$\text{Income Year } 1^r = \text{Wealth } T_1{}^1 - \text{Wealth } T_0{}^r$$
$$= 9533 - 8667$$
$$= 866$$

You will note that we have now returned to the situation we had when we originally calculated the ex-ante income for Year 1. That is to say, the revised ex-post income for the year of £866 represents a 10 per cent return on the wealth at the start of the year which was £8667. The economists argue that the difference between this revised ex-post income and the original ex-post income represents windfall gains or losses. The windfall gain or loss can be calculated by taking the revised wealth at the start of the year and deducting the original estimate of wealth at the start of the year, as follows:

$$\text{Windfall gain/loss} = \text{Wealth } T_0{}^r - \text{Wealth } T_0$$
$$= 8667 - 8212$$
$$= 455$$

The windfall gain of £455 is a capital gain. Because the capital gain occurred at the start of the year Bert earned additional income on the £455. This additional income amounts to £45, i.e. 10 per cent of £455. These figures together make up the additional cash flow of £500 caused by the change in prices.

To summarize the discussion so far, we have shown that ex-ante income is only useful under conditions of certainty and that, under those conditions, ex-post income equals ex-ante income. We have also seen that in this situation ex-post income has the same properties as ex-ante income in terms of usefulness for prediction, i.e. the income is 10 per cent of the capital or wealth. Under these conditions, ex-post income also provides a useful measure of the income available for distribution, at it is the same as the ex-ante measure. In addition, ex-post income provides a measure that is useful for evaluation of performance if there are no changes taking place.

However, in the real world, certainty does not exist and prices do change. This affects the measures of wealth and the measures of income. In this situation, ex-ante income is not necessarily useful. Ex-post income under this scenario cannot be useful for prediction or distribution. This is because the measure does not revise the capital value, and therefore the relationship of income being a 10 per cent return on capital no longer holds. It can also be argued that the ex-post income figure is no use for evaluation as, although the total income is known, there is no distinction between that part of it that will be repeated, i.e. maintainable income, and the one-off windfall gain.

Therefore, in conditions of change, the ex-post income figure has to be revised to identify the components of the total gain. The revised ex-post income figure, calculated under conditions of change, has the same properties as ex-ante income under static conditions, i.e. it shows a 10 per cent return on wealth. It can therefore be argued that the revised ex-post income measure is useful for prediction and distribution decisions. In addition, the revised ex-post income figure when combined with the windfall gain is the total gain split into its component parts. The decision-maker, with this knowledge, can evaluate performance better as he or she now knows which part of the total gain is a one-off gain and which can be maintained.

Economic measures and accounting income

The discussion above may seem to have been somewhat removed from accounting as we have seen it so far in this book. However, we said in Chapter 3 that all accounting does is to measure wealth at two points in time, and the difference is the profit for the year. Thus we can use the economic income measures set out above to evaluate the usefulness of any accounting model. As we have said accounting, particularly financial accounting, is mainly about ex-post measures. Thus, all we need to do is to see whether an accounting model is providing a revised ex-post measure or an unrevised ex-post measure. If it is providing a revised ex-post measure it is more likely to meet the needs of users as set out in the conceptual framework.

These needs, which were discussed in Chapter 1, included the provision of information that was useful in predicting future profits and dividends. This implies that there is a need for a profit or income measure that is useful for predicting future profits. The income measure should also provide information on the maximum amount that can be distributed, without endangering those future profits through the erosion of the wealth which produces those profits. Thus, in order to meet these needs, an accounting model has to have a profit measure that is useful for prediction and distribution decisions. We have shown that in real-world conditions, i.e. in a dynamic environment where change is taking place, the revised ex-post income is the only measure that has these qualities.

We also saw in Chapter 1 that users want information about the enterprise resources and the 'effects of transactions, events and other circumstances' that change those resources. They also need information that is useful for 'making rational investment, credit and other decisions'. Clearly, if the only information that is given is the total gains, and there is no indication of how they arose and whether they are maintainable, then these needs will not be met. In order to meet these needs, which we have called the need to evaluate, an income measure that shows the component parts of the total gain is needed. The only measure that does this, in a world where change exists, is the revised ex-post income measure.

Therefore in order to evaluate alternative accounting models we need to look at their usefulness for prediction, for evaluation and for distribution decisions. We can see that a useful accounting model should revise the opening wealth in times of rising prices and should split the total gains for the period between one-off gains and maintainable gains. These can be equated in accounting terminology with holding gains and operating gains respectively.

Evaluation of the historic cost model

The historic cost model defines capital as the nominal amount of the owners' equity. As such it is a model that takes a proprietary viewpoint, i.e. it is concerned with the owners' wealth rather than the enterprise wealth. It takes no account of changes in the value of the currency unit in which the assets, and claims on the assets, of the enterprise are expressed. Nor, in its pure form, does it take any account of any increase in prices or values of specific assets. In its modified form, i.e. the one in common use, it actually takes account of some changes in prices, e.g. through revaluations of land and buildings. However, the way in which revaluations are included is fairly *ad hoc* and it only applies to certain assets. The fact that it is a mix of historic cost, current value and last year's values may be one of the explanations why, as we saw in Chapter 10, it has problems in dealing with assets such as intangibles.

Returning to the subject of the usefulness of the model, if we take a simple example we can use that to illustrate how historic cost works in times of rising prices.

Example 15.2
George goes into business making hand-made leather sandals. He puts in £10 000 of his own money which he uses to purchase an industrial sewing machine at a cost of £3000 and to buy a stock of 1000 hides at a cost of £4.00 per hide. He also buys buckles and materials for soles at a cost of £2000. This he calculates is enough to make 6000 pairs of sandals.

During his first year the remainder of his transactions were as follows.

Under historic cost capital is defined as the nominal amount of the owners' equity.	KEY CONCEPT 15.5
	HISTORIC COST – DEFINITION OF CAPITAL

Sales	£30 000
Electricity	1 000
Rent	2 000
Advertising	1 000
Wages	12 000

At the end of the year he has sold all 6000 pairs of sandals. Before the year end he purchases 1000 hides for next year at a price of £4.50 per hide, and buckles and materials for soles for 6000 pairs of sandals for £2500. For the sake of simplicity we shall assume that all transactions occurred on a cash basis. The sewing machine has a life of three years and no residual value and over the three years the replacement price rises at £1000 per year. Thus, to replace it at the end of Year 3 will cost £6000.

George's opening and closing balance sheets follow the worksheet below.

Worksheet of George the sandal-maker

	Bank	Sewing machine	Leather	Buckles & soles	Owner's equity	Profit & loss
Equity	10 000				10 000	
Machine	−3 000	3000				
Leather	−4 000		4000			
Buckles	−2 000			2000		
Sales	30 000					30 000
Electricity	−1 000					−1 000
Rent	−2 000					−2 000
Advertising	−1 000					−1 000
Wages	−12 000					−12 000
Cost of sales			−4000	−2000		−6 000
Leather	−4 500		4500			
Buckles	−2 500			2500		
Depreciation		−1000				−1 000
Balances	8 000	2000	4500	2500	10 000	7 000

Balance sheets of George the sandal-maker

	Year 1	Year 0
Fixed assets		
Machine	2 000	3 000
Current assets		
Leather	4 500	4 000
Buckles etc.	2 500	2 000
Bank	8 000	1 000
	17 000	10 000
Owner's equity	10 000	10 000
Profit	7 000	
	17 000	10 000

We have used the conventional approach to calculate the profit for the year. However, we could have simply taken the definition of capital, as shown above in Key Concept 15.5, and calculated the profit using the formula:

$$\begin{aligned}
\text{Income Year 1} &= \text{Wealth } T_1^{\,1} - \text{Wealth } T_0^{\,0} \\
&= 17\,000 - 10\,000 \\
&= 7000
\end{aligned}$$

The fact that we come to the same answer this way shows that the historic cost model uses an ex-post income measure. The profit measure, if it were useful, would need to predict next year's profit and be useful for evaluation and distribution decisions. Based on the profit measure we have, George could withdraw £7000 from the business and be as well off as he was at the start of the year. If we assume that he does that, and that next year the business does the same as this year, the profit should be the same. However, if we project forward to the end of Year 2 we will find that the worksheet for Year 2 is as follows:

Worksheet of George the sandal-maker for Year 2

	Bank	Sewing machine	Leather	Buckles & soles	Owner's equity	Profit & loss
Balances	8 000	2000	4500	2500	17 000	0
Drawings	−7 000				−7 000	
Sales	30 000					30 000
Electricity	−1 000					−1 000
Rent	−2 000					−2 000
Advertising	−1 000					−1 000
Wages	−12 000					−12 000
Cost of sales			−4500	−2500		−7 000
Depreciation		−1000				−1 000
Balances	15 000	1000	0	0	10 000	6 000

You will have noticed that the new worksheet does not include replacing the stock of leather and buckles as we do not know what their price will be. However, that does not affect the profit for Year 2 under the historic cost model, which is what we are interested in. We find that the profit for Year 2 is in fact only £6000 compared to £7000 in Year 1. Thus we can see that the historic cost profit is not a good predictor in times of rising prices.

If we now take the example one stage further, assume that in Year 3 the price of hides rises to £5.00 each and the price of the buckles and other materials rises to £3000. All other costs and revenues stay the same and George takes out, as drawings, the full amount of the distributable income as he did in Year 1. The worksheet for Year 3 would be as follows:

Worksheet of George the sandal-maker for Year 3

	Bank	Sewing machine	Leather	Buckles & soles	Owner's equity	Profit & loss
Balances	15 000	1000	0	0	16 000	0
Drawings	−6 000				−6 000	
Leather	−5 000		5000			
Buckles	−3 000			3000		
Sales	30 000					30 000
Electricity	−1 000					−1 000

	Bank	Sewing machine	Leather	Buckles & soles	Owner's equity	Profit & loss
Rent	−2 000					−2 000
Advertising	−1 000					−1 000
Wages	−12 000					−12 000
Cost of sales			−5000	−3000		−8 000
Depreciation		−1 000				−1 000
Balances	15 000	0	0	0	10 000	5 000

From this we can see that the profit is now only £5000. If we were to evaluate the performance of George the sandal-maker over the three years we would find that he is less profitable each year, although the reasons are not necessarily apparent. If at the end of Year 3 George again withdrew his distributable income, which this year is £5000, he would be back where he started, i.e. he would have £10 000 in the bank. Thus we can see that the historic cost model has done what it set out to do and has maintained the nominal amount of the owner's equity.

Summary

What the example above has shown is that the historic cost model provides a profit figure based on an ex-post measure. The ex-post measure used is the unrevised ex-post measure. Therefore, in times of changing prices, it will not be useful for prediction. As regards evaluation, we have partial information only. We know, for example, that each year a profit is made. However, the historic cost model does not tell us that part of that profit is attributable to gains made by holding and using stocks of leather and buckles bought at a lower price than that ruling at the end of each year.

In terms of the usefulness of the profit measure for distribution decisions, George has maintained his original equity investment. However, if the value of the pound has dropped over the three years, which is likely, then in fact, although George may have maintained the nominal amount of his equity, he is worse off on a personal basis.

If he wishes to continue his business he will be unable to do so at the same level since to replace the machine would now cost £6000, and, even assuming no further rises in the price of leather and buckles, etc., he would need to pay £8000 to buy the quantities he started with three years ago. Thus to stay in business with the same capacity as three years ago George would require £14 000 and he only has £10 000 in the bank.

The discussion in the last two paragraphs on the subject of whether George has retained his wealth intact illustrates two alternative approaches to the definition of an enterprise's capital. The first of these is a proprietary approach which views capital as the owner's investment in an enterprise. This approach is used for the historic cost model and the current purchasing power model that we shall discuss in Chapter 16. The alternative approach adopts an entity viewpoint and sees the wealth or capital of the business as the earning capacity of its assets. An example of a model that adopts that approach is the replacement cost model which we consider in Chapter 17.

To find a model that provides a useful profit measure in times of change is extremely difficult and a number of alternatives have been suggested. Some of these look at the problem solely in relation to changes in general price levels. These affect the value of the currency unit. Some see the problem as relating to changes in the specific prices of the assets owned by the enterprise, while others see it as a combination of the two factors.

To compound the difficulty, there is also debate about whether one should start from input prices, whether those are historic cost, replacement cost or whatever. These are known as entry price models. An alternative is to start from output prices, such as net realizable value. These models are exit price models. There are, of course, models which combine both entry prices and exit prices and use whichever is appropriate to the particular circumstances. An example of such a model is the deprival value model which we shall discuss, albeit fairly briefly, at the end of Chapter 17.

References

Hicks, Sir John (1946) *Value and Capital*, Clarendon Press, Oxford.

Further reading

Arnold, J., Hope, J. and Southworth, A. (1985) *Financial Accounting*, Chapters 12 and 13, Prentice Hall International.
Lee, T.A. (1985) *Income and Value Measurement: Theory and Practice*, Van Nostrand Reinhold.
May, R.G., Mueller, G.G. and Williams, T.H. (1980) *A New Introduction to Financial Accounting*, Prentice Hall.
Sandilands Report (1975) *Report of the Inflation Accounting Committee*, HMSO, Cmnd Paper 6225.

Review questions

1. What is ex-ante income and what are its limitations?

2. What is ex-post income and what are its limitations?

3. How does revised ex-post income overcome the limitations of the other income measures?

4. What are the qualities that a profit measure should have in order to meet the needs of users?

5. What is the definition of capital adopted by the historic cost accounting model?

6. Describe the differences between an entity approach and a proprietary approach to defining capital.

7. What do the terms entry and exit values mean?

Problems for discussion and analysis

1. The proprietary and entity approaches to defining capital have radically different starting points. Based upon your knowledge of how businesses work, what do you think are the arguments in favour of, and against, each approach?

2. Given the following information calculate the ex-ante, ex-post and revised ex-post income for Maydon for Year 1.

   Maydon has decided to invest as much as is required in Project B to ensure a 10 per cent return on capital. The expected cash flows, which occur at the end of the year, are as follows:

Year 1	£5000
Year 2	6000
Year 3	7000
Year 4	7000

   As a result of changes in prices, the actual cash flow for Year 1 turned out to be £6000. It is anticipated that the cash flows for the remaining years will be as predicted.

3. Each of the income measures calculated above, it could be argued, meets some of the needs of users. Identify what needs each income measure meets, and discuss the extent to which those needs are met.

Price level changes 16

In this chapter, we shall consider the effects of changes in price levels on accounting information and examine the system known as current purchasing power accounting (CPP). The principles underlying the CPP model will be described. The model will then be illustrated using a simple example. We shall then look at some of the advantages claimed for the model and some of the criticisms of the model. Finally, we shall consider whether it provides information that is likely to be useful for making financial decisions.

Review of accounting for changing prices

Prior to discussing the model in detail, it is worth briefly recapping on the problem of accounting for changing prices. In most years since the Second World War the prices of goods and services have increased. This has meant that one of the basic assumptions needed to ensure that an accounting model based on historic costs was useful, i.e. that prices are stable, does not in fact hold. The accounting profession recognized this fact and it has made various announcements on this subject. In the UK these have varied from encouraging accountants to take inflation into account where appropriate, to full-blooded alternative systems of accounting. In the 1960s and early 1970s, the problem was seen in terms of dealing with the effects on the enterprise of the general rise in prices. By the mid 1970s, the accepted wisdom was that a system that dealt with the specific price changes that affected an enterprise's assets was what was needed. In fact, the nature of the problem that has to be dealt with encompasses both points of view. The effect of specific price changes such as the increase in car prices will have to be dealt with. However, just dealing with the effects of specific price changes does not fully account for the effects of price changes. This is because the value of £1 may also be changing, and this will have an effect on some or all of the items measured in monetary terms. This, of course, includes all the items in the annual accounts.

In this chapter, we shall be considering an accounting model which looks at the effect of general price changes and in Chapter 17 we shall consider a model that is based upon specific price changes. The model we shall consider here is one that adjusts historic cost accounts to take account of general changes in price levels. This system, known as current purchasing power accounting (CPP), was advocated in 1974 by the Accounting Standards Steering Committee who promulgated a provisional accounting standard on the subject under the title of *Accounting for Changes in the Purchasing Power of Money* (PSSAP 7). This was issued as a provisional standard, rather than a full standard, because at the time the government had set up a Royal Commission under the chairmanship of Sir Francis Sandilands to look at the question of 'inflation accounting'. In 1975, this group, having completed its work, published *The Report of the Inflation Accounting Committee*. This is more commonly referred to as 'The Sandilands Report'. The report specifically rejected the purchasing power approach in favour of an approach based upon deprival value, which we shall discuss in Chapter 17. As a result the provisional standard was withdrawn.

Current purchasing power accounting

However, although the standard relating to the CPP system has been withdrawn the CPP model is worth discussing for a number of reasons. These are set out below. First of all, it should be said that, to date, no other system has been introduced and accepted although a number of alternatives have been tried in the UK. Secondly, this system, or variants of it, is in use in countries suffering from hyper-inflation. In the USA the statement issued by the Financial Accounting Standards Board (FASB) on the subject of price level accounting (FASB 33) suggested that figures, adjusted for changes in the general price level, should be provided as well as historic cost and current cost figures. More importantly, any comprehensive system that is suggested will have to deal with the question of changes in general price levels and a study of this approach will be useful in understanding and judging the usefulness of alternatives. Finally, as is clear from its definition of capital in Key Concept 16.1, it is a good example of a model based upon a proprietary view of accounting. That is, it concentrates on maintaining the owners' capital rather than attempting to maintain the enterprise capital.

The definition of capital in Key Concept 16.1, is, as you will have noticed, very similar to that underlying the historic cost model. The difference between the two lies in the fact that the historic cost model is concerned with maintenance of the nominal amount of the owner's equity, whereas the CPP model is concerned with maintaining the purchasing power of that owner's equity. To put that simply, historic cost is happy if you start a year with £1 and at the end of the year have £1. The fact that at the start of the year you could buy a lot more with your

KEY CONCEPT 16.1	The wealth or capital that has to be maintained is the purchasing power of the owners' equity.
CPP DEFINITION OF CAPITAL	

£1 is not considered relevant. CPP on the other hand is concerned that you can buy the same amount of goods at the end of the year as you could at the start. The CPP model, in order to maintain the purchasing power of the owner's equity, needs to distinguish between monetary and non-monetary items for reasons we shall discuss below.

Monetary and non-monetary items

CPP accounting, or general price level accounting as it is called in the USA, assumes that all moneys invested in non-monetary assets, e.g. fixed assets and stock, keep level with the general rate of inflation as measured by the retail price index (RPI). It further assumes that moneys invested in monetary items do not. Therefore, the first stage in dealing with the model is to identify and distinguish between monetary and non-monetary items.

Although this looks easy, as to distinguish between cash or debtors and land and buildings is in fact straightforward, in reality it is not so easy. For example, do you classify investments as monetary or non-monetary, and what of other assets such as goodwill, etc.? The reason the distinction is important to the model is that, as monetary items are assumed not to keep up with changes in the RPI, monetary gains and losses arise from holding these items.

Monetary gains and losses

CPP assumes that if you hold monetary assets, e.g. debtors and money in the bank, you will lose purchasing power. In other words if you keep £100 in the bank for a year, at the end of the year you will be able to buy less with your £100 than you could have bought at the start of the year. This is a result of the effects of the rise in prices over a period and is called a monetary loss. By contrast, if you borrow money then you will make a monetary gain. This is because the money you pay back is worth less, in terms of its ability to purchase goods and services, than the same amount of money at the time you borrowed it.

The CPP system is based upon updating the balance sheet and the profit and loss account of an enterprise to express all items in terms of the current purchasing power at the balance sheet date. In order to understand the way in which the system works it is best to work through a simple example. For ease of exposition we shall use an example based upon a new business. This does not affect the principles involved but instead allows them to be explained without unnecessary complications.

Example 16.1
Highrisk commenced trading on 1 February 1991, with £5000 owners' equity and £10000 on a long-term interest-free loan. On that day, Highrisk purchased a printing machine for £12000 and a second-hand van for £2000. The rest of the transactions for the year to 31 January 1992 are summarized below:

Sales	£20000
Materials purchased	10000
Wages paid	6000
Van expenses	1500

On 31 January 1992, materials that cost £2000 were in stock. All transactions were for cash and took place evenly throughout the year unless otherwise stated. The machine is to be depreciated over five years and the van over four years. Both use the straight line method and neither has any residual value. The retail price index covering the period is given below:

		RPI
1 February 1991		130
31 July	1991	135
31 January	1992	142
Average for year		136

You will note that the retail price index starts at 130. This is because it is worked out from a base year when it is set at 100, in the same way as we illustrated when looking at index number trends in Chapter 14. You should also note that the average for the year is not necessarily the same as the index midway through the year. It is the average that is appropriate, in this case, because of the fact that all transactions took place evenly throughout the period.

Stage 1
The first stage is to produce the historic cost balance sheets and profit and loss account. These are reproduced below:

Balance sheet of Highrisk at 31 January 1992

	1992			1991
Fixed assets	£	£	£	£
Machine	12000		12000	
Depreciation	2400	9600	0	12000
Van	2000		2000	
Depreciation	500	1500	0	2000

		1992		1991
Current assets	£	£	£	£
Stocks		2 000		
Cash at bank		3 500		1 000
		16 600		15 000
		£		£
Owners' equity		5 000		5 000
Profit		1 600		0
Total equity		6 600		5 000
Loans		10 000		10 000
		16 600		15 000

**Profit and loss account of Highrisk
for the year ended 31 January 1992**

	£	£
Sales		20 000
Purchases	10 000	
Less: Stock	2 000	
Cost of sales		8 000
Gross profit		12 000
Wages	6 000	
Van expenses	1 500	
Depreciation:		
Machine	2 400	
Van	500	10 400
Net profit		1 600

Stage 2

The next stage is to apply the retail price index to the figures. However, before we can do that it is necessary to identify the monetary assets and liabilities and separate them from the non-monetary items. As we have said, the reason for doing this is that the model assumes that non-monetary assets retain their purchasing power. However, they are currently expressed in the balance sheet in terms of units of purchasing power that existed when they were purchased. This therefore has to be updated to current purchasing power. This is done using the general formula.

$$\text{Historic cost} \times \frac{\text{Index ruling at the balance sheet date}}{\text{Index ruling at the transaction date}} = \text{£CPP}$$

Monetary assets and liabilities, on the other hand, are already expressed in current purchasing power and, as such, they need no adjustment.

Having identified the non-monetary items, i.e. the machine, the van, the stock and the owners' equity, we can now start to produce accounts in current purchasing power terms. We shall start by updating the balance sheet working from the top down. In Highrisk's case, all the fixed assets were purchased when the RPI stood at 130. At 31 January 1992, the balance sheet date, the RPI stands at 142. Therefore to express these amounts in current purchasing power terms we need to apply the formula above as follows:

$$\text{Historic cost of the fixed asset} \times \frac{142}{130} = \text{£CPP}$$

The depreciation, which is also a non-monetary item, is updated in the same way as the fixed assets to which they relate, i.e. using the index at the time the asset was purchased and that ruling at the end of the period.

As the stock was bought evenly throughout the period, it is expressed in average purchasing power at present. We need to express it in terms of purchasing power units at 31 January 1992. Thus, in this case, we divide the amount by the average RPI, 136, and multiply it by the RPI at the balance sheet date, i.e.

$$\text{Historic cost of stock} \times \frac{142}{136} = \text{£CPP}$$

The cash is a monetary item so it does not need adjusting. It is already expressed in terms of its current purchasing power. This means that we have now dealt with the assets.

On the other half of the balance sheet, we have the owners' equity and the loan. The loan is clearly a monetary liability and Highrisk will pay back £10000 in cash. On the other hand, the owners' equity will not, in theory, be paid back assuming the enterprise is a going concern. It is therefore classified as a non-monetary item. We therefore update this to purchasing power at 31 January 1992 in the same way as the fixed assets, i.e. by 142/130:

$$\text{Historic amount of the owners' equity} \times \frac{142}{130} = \text{£CPP}$$

The only figure that we have not dealt with is the retained profit which we shall return to shortly. However, at this stage we can produce a partial balance sheet in current purchasing power units (£CPP) at 31 January 1992, as shown below:

Partial current purchasing power balance sheet
of Highrisk at 31 January 1992

	Historic cost			Current purchasing power	
	£	1992 £	Index	£CPP	1992 £CPP
Fixed assets					
Machine	12 000		142/130	13 108	
Depreciation	2 400	9 600	142/130	2 622	10 486
Van	2 000		142/130	2 185	
Depreciation	500	1 500	142/130	546	1 639
Current assets					
Stocks		2 000	142/136		2 088
Cash at bank		3 500			3 500
		16 600			17 713

			£CPP
Owners' equity	5 000	142/130	5 462
Profit	1 600		??
Total equity	6 600		7 713
Loans	10 000		10 000
	16 600		17 713

You will note that we have filled in all figures except the CPP profit figure. By a process of elimination we can work out that the missing figure is £CPP 2251. However, for reasons that will become apparent, we have not inserted this figure. Before explaining those reasons, let us look at the profit and loss account and see if the figure we arrive at for the CPP profit is £CPP 2251.

Stage 3

For the profit and loss account to be expressed in purchasing power units at 31 January 1992 we need to upgrade every item by the end-of-year index, i.e. 142, divided by the index ruling at the date the transaction took place. In our example, for all items except the depreciation the appropriate index is the average index for the year, i.e. 136. Thus for all these items we use:

$$\text{Historic cost amount} \times \frac{142}{136} = \text{£CPP}$$

In the case of the depreciation, the index that we need is the index ruling at the date the asset to which the depreciation relates was purchased. In this case, that is the index at the start of the accounting year, i.e. 130. Thus, the index we use for the depreciation here is:

$$\text{Historic cost amount} \times \frac{142}{130} = \text{£CPP}$$

In reality, of course, the fixed assets will normally have been purchased on many different dates. The principle that we apply remains the same no matter how many assets are involved or when they were purchased – it just requires a lot more calculations.

Applying the formulae above, our CPP profit and loss account will be as follows:

**Current purchasing power profit and loss account
of Highrisk for the year ended 31 January 1992**

	Historic cost		**Current purchasing power**		
		1992			*1992*
	£	£	*Index*	£CPP	£CPP
Sales		20 000	142/136		20 882
Purchases	10 000		142/136	10 441	
Less: Stock	2 000		142/136	2 088	
Cost of sales		8 000			8 353
Gross profit		12 000			12 529
Wages	6 000		142/136	6 265	

	1992				1992
	£	£	Index	£CPP	£CPP
Van expenses	1 500		142/136	1 566	
Depreciation					
Machine	2 400		142/130	2 622	
Van	500	10 400	142/130	546	10 999
Net profit		1 600			1 531

As you can see, the profit figure is £CPP 1531. This is less than we need if our balance sheet is going to balance. The reason the two figures do not match, i.e. £CPP 2251 and £CPP 1531, is because of gains and losses on monetary items. As we pointed out, the assumption is that if you hold monetary items, then although the face value in cash terms may remain the same over time, in times of rising prices the amount of purchasing power that the money represents is falling. Thus the argument is that you make a loss by holding money and a gain by borrowing money. In the latter case the amount you will eventually pay back will be the same face value but will have less purchasing power. Therefore, it is argued, the lender has made a loss and you have made a gain.

Stage 4

To calculate the monetary gains and losses we need to identify the monetary items and to work out how long we have held them. In our example, we have two monetary items, i.e. the money in the bank and the loan. In the case of the loan we have had this loan from the start of the year so the calculation is straightforward. We need to work out how many £ sterling we would need on 31 January 1992 to have the same purchasing power as our £10 000 loan had on 1 February 1991. If the amount is greater than £10 000 then the difference is the amount of monetary gain. The calculation is shown below.

Monetary gains

Loan of £10 000 expressed in end of year £CPP units:

$$\pounds 10\,000 \times \frac{142}{130} \qquad 10\,922$$

| Less: Actual liability | 10 000 |
| Monetary gain | 922 |

Monetary losses

These arise as a result of holding money. In our case we have held £1000 (see opening balance sheet) from the start of the year and the additional £2500 has come in evenly during the year as a result of trading. The losses on these amounts are different as we have held the money for different time periods. In the first case, the index we use as the denominator is that ruling at 1 February 1991, i.e. 130, and in the second case it is the average index for the year, i.e. 136. The calculation of the monetary loss is as follows:

Cash of £1000 expressed in end of year £CPP units:

$$£1000 \times \frac{142}{130} \qquad\qquad 1092$$

Cash of £2500 expressed in end of year £CPP units:

$$£2500 \times \frac{142}{136} \qquad\qquad 2610$$

	3702
Less: Actual cash balance	3500
Monetary loss	202

The net monetary gains therefore are £CPP 720, i.e. the monetary gain of £CPP 922 less the monetary loss of £CPP 202. The stages we have gone through to calculate monetary gains and losses are:

1. Update the monetary item to purchasing power at the balance sheet date.
2. Deduct the amount of the monetary item expressed in £ sterling.

Having identified the effects of monetary items, a monetary gain in this case, we can now complete our CPP balance sheet and this is shown below:

**Current purchasing power balance sheet
of Highrisk at 31 January 1992**

		1992		1991
Fixed assets	£CPP	£CPP	£CPP	£CPP
Machine	13 108		12 000	
Depreciation	2 622	10 486	0	12 000
Van	2 185		2 000	
Depreciation	546	1 639	0	2 000
Current assets				
Stocks		2 088		0
Cash at bank		3 500		1 000
		17 713		15 000
		£CPP		£CPP
Owners' equity		5 462		5 000
Profit		1 531		0
Monetary gains		720		0
Total equity		7 713		5 000
Loans		10 000		10 000
		17 713		15 000

You can see, by looking at the balance sheet above and the original historic cost balance sheet, that the comparatives for 1991 are the same as the historic cost accounts at the start of the year. This is because they are expressed in 1991 £CPP which at that time was what Highrisk used to purchase its assets etc. This makes comparisons difficult as the two balance sheets are now expressed in different units of measurement. Of course this could be overcome by updating the 1991 accounts to 1992 £CPP.

We shall now move on to a discussion of some of the arguments in favour of and against CPP accounting. If you are not clear on how the CPP system works from reading through the example you should go over it again. There are more examples for you to work through yourself in the questions for discussion and analysis at the end of the chapter.

Arguments in favour of the CPP model

Those who supported the CPP model – and there were many accountants who did support the CPP approach – argued that the model was more objective than other models which relied on assessing the specific prices of assets. At the nub of this argument is that, whereas there is a standard general index of price movements, there is not necessarily one for every asset an enterprise could conceivably own. Thus, if you try to update the price of assets to take account of changes in prices that affect those specific assets you will have to be more subjective. How strong this argument is you can judge for yourselves by looking at how much subjectivity already exists in the historic cost figures that are being converted, e.g. depreciation, goodwill, research and development, stock, etc.

Another argument put forward in favour of CPP was that it overcame the problem of an unstable currency unit. It was further argued that by expressing the accounts in £CPP it increased the comparability of the accounts. This argument was disputed in the Sandilands report on the grounds that the unit of measurement, i.e. the £CPP, changes from one month end to the next. Thus, the £CPP at the end of March is a different unit from the £CPP at the end of May. It is therefore difficult to sustain an argument that it overcomes the problems of an unstable monetary unit or that it increases comparability. Additionally, in the case of comparisons between enterprises, unless they had the same year end, one or other sets of accounts would have to be changed so that the two were expressed in the same £CPPs.

It was also suggested that as people are familiar with the idea of purchasing power, i.e. they are faced with it on a daily basis, they would therefore find the model easy to understand. This, of course, assumes that the purchasing power with which the users are familiar is that used in the model. Clearly in the case of overseas investors and creditors this is unlikely to be the case. Even in terms of users in the UK, it is extremely doubtful that those on low incomes in the north-west of England face the same price changes in terms of how they spend their money as a prosperous stockbroker in the south-east.

Other supporters of CPP asserted that it was a simple model to produce and that it was easy to understand. The first assertion is probably true in comparison to most alternative models. However, it does raise the question of whether accounts should be simple or whether they should be useful, a discussion we shall be returning to later in this chapter. In terms of the assertion that users would find them easy to understand, this was never tested empirically and as such it is merely one possible outcome.

The final argument put forward in favour of CPP that we are going to consider relates to the identification by the model of monetary gains and losses. As we have seen, the argument is that if we hold money or monetary assets when the value of the £ sterling is falling we will make a loss. The corollary is that if we owe money we will make a gain because what we pay back is worth less. This argument is intuitively appealing as it takes some account of the changes in the general level of prices. Indeed, variants on this theme have been apparent in many of the alternative models suggested. We shall return to the question of monetary gains and losses as we look at some of the main arguments against the model.

Arguments against the CPP model

The first point to make is that this model is a proprietary-based model, i.e. it views the wealth of the enterprise in terms of the owners' equity (see Key Concept 16.1). In this it is similar to the historic cost model. The difference is that under historic cost the wealth is defined in nominal terms whereas under CPP it is expressed in purchasing power terms. The fact that it is proprietary based is one reason for criticizing the model since, it is argued, we should be accounting for the performance of the economic entity not that of the owners' equity. This fundamental difference in viewpoint is at the base of a number of the criticisms of CPP which follow.

The first of these concerns the index that is used. The RPI is based upon consumer spending on a basket of household goods, and those that criticize the CPP model argue that the movements in the price of eggs, butter, cheese, etc., do not relate to the changes in the prices affecting the assets of a business. Therefore, to express BP's oil refineries in these terms is totally irrelevant. This criticism is valid if you believe that accounting should be reporting on the performance of the entity. If, however, you believe it is about reporting to the owners on their equity, then, as we have seen, you can argue that owners buy goods every day and therefore they understand purchasing power as expressed by the RPI.

The second criticism relates to the profit measure and what it means. It does not represent what has happened in the year as it is expressed in end-of-year £CPP. Thus it could be confusing as the sales, for example, will be shown as greater under CPP than the actual sales. There are also some questions regarding the amount of profit that can be distributed. We shall return to consider some of these questions from another perspective in the next section on the usefulness of the profit measure. The issue we wish to deal with here is whether monetary gains are realized and whether they can be distributed. Some argue that the monetary gains are real gains and therefore could be distributed. They cite how much better off people are by borrowing money to buy a house which they then sell for much more than it cost them, and as the mortgage is fixed in amount they therefore increase their equity. For example, if you had bought a house in 1981 for £30 000 having put in £6000 of your own money and borrowed the rest, then in 1991 you sold that house for £120 000, you would have turned your £6000 into £96 000 after paying back your mortgage of £24 000. Thus, it is suggested, that you would have made a monetary gain amounting to £90 000 from having borrowed money.

The problem with the argument is that two things are getting confused. One is the act of borrowing money and the other is that of using the money. The gains come from the latter. For example, if instead of buying a house in 1981 with the £24 000 you had borrowed you had simply put the money under the bed, then in 1991 you would have £30 000 and you would owe £24 000 so you would be no better off as your monetary gains would equal your monetary losses. The reason this point is important is because, if the gains are made from holding assets, as we have shown, then it is difficult to see how they can be distributed. This is because while the assets are still held the gains would not be realized, therefore we would, in effect, be distributing unrealized gains. However, the CPP model does not make any distinction between realized and unrealized monetary gains and all monetary gains are distributable. This means that unrealized gains, as well as realized gains, can be distributed and wealth will still be maintained.

Another source of criticism that relates to the gains and losses on monetary items is that these can lead to misleading results that may be difficult for the less sophisticated user to interpret. This argument is based upon the fact that the more you borrow the greater are your monetary gains, therefore the better your results appear to be. In reality, the more you borrow the greater the risk and this is especially true in times of high inflation. It is the high risk that leads to high gains and this could potentially be misleading to the unsophisticated user as the CPP model highlights the gains but not the risks.

Finally, there is the problem of comparisons with previous performance and comparisons with others. As we pointed out earlier, comparisons between two enterprises with different year ends requires that the accounts be converted to the same CPP units. Similarly, to compare this year's results with previous years' results would require the results of the previous years to be converted into the same £CPP units as this year.

CPP profit as a useful measure

In Chapter 1, and again in Chapter 15, we suggested that in order to be useful an accounting model needed to provide information that was useful for the prediction of future profits and the evaluation of past performance. We also suggested, in Chapter 15, that there was a need to provide information about distributable profits. We shall now examine the CPP model in terms of its usefulness against these three criteria.

We shall start this discussion by looking at the distributable profit measure. To find out the distributable profit, we first need to define the capital that we are trying to maintain. As we stated in Key Concept 16.1, the definition of capital is the purchasing power of the owners' equity. Thus, in Example 16.1, we find that the capital we have to maintain is the £5000 that was contributed at the start of the year. We can see that the purchasing power required at the end of the year to maintain that capital is £CPP 5462. Thus we can distribute £CPP 2251, i.e. the total equity of £CPP 7713 less the purchasing power of the owners' equity of £CPP 5462, and stay as well off as we were at the start of the year. We can now see that the distributable profit measure includes the operating gains of £CPP 1531 and the monetary gains of £CPP 720. This brings us back to the question of whether these gains are realized when the assets on which the gains arose are still held. There is, of course, also a question about whether these gains exist in reality, as they are based on the assumption that the prices of the specific assets are rising in line with the RPI. This, as we have already discussed, is an assumption that is unlikely to hold in reality, and if it does it would only be by chance. Therefore, we have to conclude that the CPP profit measure is unlikely to be useful for making judgements about the distributable profit.

On the question of the CPP profit and its usefulness for the purposes of evaluation, a number of criticisms are levelled. One of these is that you cannot compare the performance of a firm with a December year end with one with a June year end. This is because one is accounted for in December purchasing power units and the other in June purchasing power units. Another criticism relates to comparisons over time and uses a similar line of reasoning. There is, of course, the question of which profit should be used for evaluation as, in the case of CPP, we have two profits, i.e. that including monetary gains and that excluding monetary gains. In fact, as we have seen when discussing economists' income models, in order to evaluate the performance the user would have to look at both sets of gains. This then raises the problems of interpretation that we referred to earlier. From this discussion we can conclude that CPP is unlikely to be very useful for evaluation.

Finally, we shall look at the question of the usefulness of the profit for prediction. In order for the profit figure for 1991/2 to be useful for predicting 1992/3 we would have to assume the same level of activities and price rises. Clearly, if we include the monetary gains and losses in our definition of profit this is a nonsense. We do not, for example, start 1992/3 with £1000 in the bank as we did 1991/2 therefore the same monetary gains and losses are unlikely to arise. Even if the monetary gains or losses are excluded, the fact that we have to assume the same level of price rises makes the usefulness of the profit figure for prediction dubious. In fact, some of the empirical testing on the usefulness of profit figures referred to in Chapter 1 showed that price level adjusted models were no better than historic cost for this.

Thus it would seem that, despite the fact that the CPP model could be seen as utilizing a revised ex-post income measure which we said in Chapter 15 was the basis of a useful model, the profit is not useful for prediction, evaluation or distribution decisions. This is hardly surprising since, if profits arise from the use of the enterprise's assets, it is vital that the definition of capital relates to the enterprise's assets. The argument for defining capital in terms of productive assets rather than in terms of owners' equity appears to be very strong. It is the assets, together with the labour, that produce the goods or services which are sold, and it is that process that produces profit. Thus to expect a profit figure derived from a capital definition that is not based on assets to be useful for prediction is perhaps naive. Whether the model arrives at an ex-post or revised ex-post profit measure is irrelevant if the capital definition is inadequate.

Summary

We have looked at the CPP model which was initially proposed to deal with the problem of an unstable monetary unit as a model in its own right. From this, we have seen that, whilst recognizing that there is a need to deal with the effects of general price changes, the CPP model is not an appropriate model for measuring enterprise profit. We have looked at the workings of the model, some of the arguments advanced in its favour and some of the criticisms of the model. Finally we have looked at its performance measure in terms of its usefulness for prediction, evaluation and distribution, and found it to be poor in these areas. This we have suggested arises in the main from an inappropriate definition of capital.

The confusion surrounding monetary gains, how they arise and when they are realized exacerbates the problems arising from the definition of capital. This, we have said, is a definition of capital that comes from a proprietary viewpoint whereby the focus of concentration is the owners' equity. In Chapter 17 we shall look at a model that takes the physical assets as the base of its definition of capital – in other words one that approaches the problem from an entity perspective.

References

Provisional Statement of Standard Accounting Practice No. 7, (1974) *Accounting for Changes in the Purchasing Power of Money*, Accounting Standards Committee.
Sandilands Report (1975) *Report of the Inflation Accounting Committee*, HMSO, Cmnd Paper 6225.

Further reading

Sandilands Report (1975) *Report of the Inflation Accounting Committee*, HMSO, Cmnd Paper 6225.
For further discussion on the treatment of monetary gains, see M. Bourne, (1976) 'The "gain" on borrowing', *Journal of Business Finance and Accounting*, **3**, 167–83. R.S. Gynther, *Accounting for Price Level Changes: Theory and Procedures* (Pergamon, 1966), and J. Arnold, T. Hope and A. Southworth, *Financial Accounting*, Chapters 12 and 13 (Prentice Hall International, 1985).

Review questions

1. Explain the difference between an entity and proprietary view of the enterprise and identify which view the CPP model adopts.

2. In your own words define CPP capital.

3. What is a monetary and a non-monetary item and why is the distinction important under CPP?

4. Explain how monetary gains and losses arise.

5. Identify the arguments in favour of the CPP model.

6. Identify the criticisms of the CPP model.

7. Explain why the CPP profit is not useful as a measure of distributable profit.

8. Explain the limitations of CPP profit for the purposes of prediction and evaluation.

Problems for discussion and analysis

The information below relates to questions 1 to 5 below.

Printalot commenced trading on 1 April 1991 with £12 000 owners' equity and £3000 on a long-term interest-free loan. On that day they purchased a printing machine for £12 400 and a second-hand van for £2000. The rest of the transactions for the year to 31 March 1992 are summarized below:

	£
Sales	20 000
Materials purchased	10 000
Wages paid	6 000
Van expenses	1 500

At 31 March 1992 there were £2000 worth of materials in stock. All transactions were for cash and we shall assume that they took place evenly throughout the year unless otherwise stated. The machine is to be depreciated over five years and the van over four years. Both will use the straight line method and neither will have any residual value. The retail price index covering the period is given below.

1 April 1991	132
31 August 1991	139
31 March 1992	144
Average for year	138

1. Produce the historic cost and CPP accounts for the year to 31 March 1992.

2. Comment on the performance of Printalot as shown by the two sets of accounts you have produced.

3. Compare the performance of Printalot in its first year to that of Highrisk (the example in the chapter) and identify which appears to be a better investment.

4. From your answers to questions 1 to 3 comment on any problems that are apparent with the CPP model.

5. If the current interest rate was 15 per cent and the loans were not interest free would your choice of investment change from that identified in your answer to question 3?

17 Replacement cost accounting

In Chapter 16 we considered current purchasing power accounting. That system was based upon a proprietary view of accounting where the definition of capital was the purchasing power of the owners' equity. It attempted to deal with the issue of accounting for changes in price levels by looking at the problem from the perspective of changes in general price levels. In this chapter, we shall be considering replacement cost accounting which takes an entity perspective and attempts to deal with changes in the prices of the specific assets of the entity.

Replacement cost accounting is one of a number of entity-based alternatives to historic cost and current purchasing power accounting which are the main proprietary-based models. Other models that have been proposed are based upon net realizable value and deprival value. We discussed net realizable value as a basis for arriving at accounting profit in Chapter 3 so you are already familiar with that model at a basic level. We shall return to consider deprival value at the end of this chapter. Prior to that, we shall examine replacement cost in more detail.

The replacement cost model defines capital in terms of the physical assets of the entity. It is argued that to use a general price index, such as the RPI which relates to domestic consumption, to arrive at a figure for the assets is not sensible as the resultant figure is meaningless. It does not reflect what the asset cost, what it could be sold at, what it would cost to replace or how much the enterprise could potentially earn from the asset. What it tells you is what it would have cost in today's £ sterling to buy the asset assuming that the price of the asset has risen in line with the RPI. The underlying assumption that the price would rise in line with the rise in general prices reflected by the RPI has been questioned on the basis of the RPI being an average of price rises and therefore not reflecting the rise in the individual prices of the goods included in the RPI. It has also been questioned on the basis that the assets of business entities are not included in the index in any case. The replacement cost model tries to answer these criticisms by using price changes that relate to the specific assets.

We shall follow a similar pattern to the previous chapter and start by describing the principles of the replacement cost model and illustrating it using a simple example. We shall then look at the arguments in favour of the model and the criticisms of the model. Finally we shall judge the model's profit measure against the criteria of usefulness for prediction, evaluation and distribution decisions.

Capital is defined as the physical assets of the enterprise at the start of the period.

KEY CONCEPT 17.1

REPLACEMENT COST – CAPITAL

Replacement cost accounting

Definition of capital

The replacement cost model is based on an entity view of the firm. The definition of capital underlying the model is that the capital to be maintained is the physical assets of the enterprise. This definition of capital assumes that it is the assets that produce the goods or services from which profits are ultimately derived. Therefore, if they are not maintained, then the same level of output cannot be maintained and profits will suffer accordingly.

Holding and operating gains

The replacement cost model suggests that there are two types of gains that occur in times of rising prices. These are operating gains and holding gains. Operating gains arise, as the name implies, from the operations of the enterprise. Thus if the enterprise operates at the same level next year, other things being equal, the same level of operating gains will arise. Holding gains, on the other hand, arise from holding assets where the price of those assets has increased over the period. The difference between operating and holding gains can best be illustrated with a simple example.

Example 17.1

Two jewellers each buy an ingot of gold for £5000 at the start of the year. Jeweller A makes the gold into jewellery at a cost of £4000 and sells the jewellery for £15 000. Jeweller B simply puts the gold into the safe and keeps it there. At the end of the year the price of an ingot of gold has doubled to £10 000.

If we take the case of Jeweller A first, under historic cost a profit of £6000, i.e. £15 000 less costs of £5000 and £4000, has been made. Jeweller A could distribute the profit of £6000 and be as well off as at the start of the year, i.e. the owners' equity of £5000 at the start of the year would have been maintained in money terms. However, under replacement cost there is a need to maintain the physical asset of an ingot of gold. At the end of the year this would cost £10 000, so under replacement cost Jeweller A will make a profit of £1000, i.e. £15 000 less costs of £4000 and the replacement cost of the gold sold £10 000. He will also have made a holding gain of £5000, i.e. the price of an ingot of gold has risen from £5000 to £10 000. This holding gain has been realized by selling the jewellery. Thus under replacement cost the total gain, i.e. the holding

<table>
<tr><td>KEY CONCEPT 17.2

**REPLACEMENT COST
– HOLDING AND
OPERATING GAINS**</td><td>Replacement cost separates holding gains, i.e. those that arise as a result of holding assets, from operating gains, i.e. those that arise as a result of trading operations.</td></tr>
</table>

gain and the operating profit, is £6000, the same as the historic cost profit. All replacement cost has done is to split the gain into its component parts.

If we turn now to Jeweller B, he had an ingot that cost £5000 at the start of the year and he now has an ingot that would cost £10000 to replace. Therefore, he has made a gain of £5000 simply by holding the ingot. If we compare the two holding gains the amount of the holding gain is exactly the same which is what we would expect. The only difference – and it is an important one – is that in the case of Jeweller B the gain is an unrealized holding gain and in the case of Jeweller A it is a realized holding gain.

From this simple example we can draw out a number of points about the replacement cost model. The first is that it splits the total realized gains for the year between those that arise from operating and those that arise as a result of holding assets. This is important because these two types of gain arise as a result of different pressures. Therefore, in order for them to be useful for prediction or evaluation they need to be considered separately. The second point is that some of the gains made as a result of holding assets are unrealized gains. The final point to emerge is, the distributable profit is only arrived at after taking out the effects of holding gains. This is because the distribution of holding gains would not maintain the physical capital, the gold ingot in our example.

Having set out some of the basic ideas and principles involved we shall now use an example to illustrate how the model works. We shall use the same example as the one we used in Chapter 16, this time including specific price changes. Using the same example has the advantage that you are already familiar with it and the historic cost and CPP accounts have already been completed. You can therefore use them for comparison.

Example 17.2

Highrisk commenced trading on 1 February 1991, with £5000 owners' equity and £10000 on a long-term interest-free loan. On that day, Highrisk purchased a printing machine for £12000 and a second-hand van for £2000. The rest of the transactions for the year to 31 January 1992 are summarized below:

	£
Sales	20000
Materials purchased	10000

Wages paid	6 000
Van expenses	1 500

On 31 January 1992, there were materials in stock that had cost £2000. All transactions were for cash and they took place evenly throughout the year unless otherwise stated. The machine is to be depreciated over five years and the van over four years. Both use the straight line method and neither has any residual value. On 31 January 1992, the replacement cost of the stock held, obtained from suppliers' price lists, is £2500. A van the same age as that owned by Highrisk currently retails at £2400. Unfortunately, as the machine was partially custom-built, a current price is not readily available. However, the movements in prices of similar machines is covered by the machinery price index below:

		Machinery prices
1 February 1991		120
31 July	1991	125
31 January	1992	130
Average for year		125

Stage 1
In this case, we can draw up a replacement cost balance sheet from the information given with very little additional workings. The only amount we need to calculate is the replacement cost for the machine using the index above. We also have to leave the total equity as a balancing figure, at this stage, as without the profit and loss and some other workings, which we shall explain shortly, we do not know its exact composition. We do, however, know that the contributed capital was £5000 so that can be included without any change.

Working 1 – Replacement cost of machine
This is arrived at in a similar way to the application of the general price index in the previous chapter, i.e.

$$\text{Actual cost at 1 February 1991} \times \frac{\text{Index at balance sheet date}}{\text{Index at transaction date}}$$

$$£12\,000 \times \frac{130}{120} = £13\,000$$

We can now produce a partial balance sheet as shown below.

**Partial balance sheet of Highrisk at 31 January 1992
using the replacement cost model**

	1992			1991
Fixed assets	£	£	£	£
Machine	13 000		12 000	
Depreciation	2 600	10 400	0	12 000
Van	2 400		2 000	
Depreciation	600	1 800	0	2 000

	£	1992 £	£	1991 £
Current assets				
Stocks		2 500		
Cash at bank		3 500		1 000
		18 200		15 000
		£		£
Owners' equity		5 000		5 000
Profit		?		0
Total equity		8 200		5 000
Loans		10 000		10 000
		18 200		15 000

It is worth noting that all we have done is to show the replacement cost of all the physical assets and calculated the depreciation based upon the replacement cost at the end of the year. The balance sheet shows that there is an increase in the total equity of £3200 but we do not, as yet, know how that is made up.

Stage 2

We can now draw up the profit and loss account. As this covers the period of the year we need to express the items in the profit and loss account at the replacement cost ruling at the date the transaction took place. In our example, the transactions took place evenly throughout the year and are therefore already at average replacement cost. In situations where there is stock held at the start of the year or where the transactions do not take place evenly throughout the year then these figures would have to be adjusted to average prices for the year. The only exception to this rule of expressing items at their replacement cost at the time they were used relates to the depreciation charges. These we have expressed in end-of-year prices. The problem with depreciation is that the balance sheet requires depreciation to be charged at end-of-year prices in order to be able to maintain the physical capital. The profit and loss, on the other hand, if we were to apply the matching concept, requires depreciation based on average prices. Thus one or the other will be wrong. However, if we are to apply the idea of maintaining the physical fixed assets then this can only be done by charging the depreciation based on end-of-year costs. This is the approach we have adopted. We shall consider what would happen if average replacement costs were used in Example 17.3 later in this chapter.

**Profit and loss account of Highrisk for the year
ended 31 January 1992
using the replacement cost model**

	£	£
Sales		20 000
Purchases	10 000	
Less: Stock	2 000	
Cost of sales		8 000
Gross profit		12 000
Wages	6 000	
Van expenses	1 500	
Depreciation		
Machine	2 600	
Van	600	10 700
Net profit		1 300

We can see that the profit is £1300, which only partially explains the increase in total equity of £3200. This is what we would expect as we have not yet taken account of holding gains. We shall now examine these gains which we can split into realized holding gains and unrealized holding gains.

Stage 3   Realized holding gains

In the context of an enterprise, realized holding gains can arise in two ways. The first is by selling an asset, the most common example of this is the sale of the goods held in stock at the start of the year. If, for example, you had 100 units in stock at the start of the year that had cost £2 each and when you came to sell them at £3 per unit the replacement cost of those units had risen to £2.40, then there is a realized gain of 40p as a result of holding those goods. This holding gain has to be separated from the operating gain of 60p if we are to replace our stock of units. In our example, as we have no stock at the start of the year, this type of holding gain does not present a problem.

The other type of realized holding gain arises from the charging of additional depreciation or amortization on fixed assets. In these cases, the gain is realized by reducing the profit available for distribution by that amount. Once again, it is important to understand the reason why this has to be separated from operating gains. This is because, unless the money represented by the full replacement cost depreciation charge is retained in the business, then when the time comes to replace the asset there will not be sufficient funds retained in the business to do so.

Working 2 – Realized holding gains

In our example, we have realized holding gains on the fixed assets. To calculate the amounts involved, we need to calculate the depreciation based on the historic cost and the depreciation based upon the replacement cost. The difference between these two figures is the amount of the holding gain that has been realized by being charged against the profit for the year. The depreciation charges under replacement cost can be obtained from the profit and loss account which we have just completed.

The historic cost depreciation can be obtained from the historic cost accounts in Chapter 16. The calculation of the realized holding gains can then be done, as shown below:

	Replacement cost	Historic cost	Realized holding gains
	£	£	£
Machine	2600	2400	200
Van	600	500	100
Total realized holding gains			300

Unrealized holding gains

As we have pointed out, these gains arise on assets that were held for all or part of the year and are still held by the enterprise at the balance sheet date. They arise as a result of increases in the prices of the specific assets. Common examples relate to fixed assets and stock held at the end of the year. In the case of fixed assets, the unrealized gain is that part of the total gain that has not been realized by being charged through the profit and loss account in the form of extra depreciation. In the case of stock, it is the difference between the replacement cost of the goods in stock at the end of the year and the cost when the stock was acquired.

Working 3 – Unrealized holding gains

In Example 17.2, these arise on the machine, the van and the stocks held on 31 January 1992. In the case of the van and the machine, we need to calculate the total holding gain and deduct the realized holding gains calculated in Working 2 above. The total holding gain is calculated by taking the replacement cost at the end of the year and deducting the original cost to the business. This applies equally to the fixed assets and the stock, the only difference is that in the latter case no further calculation is needed.

	£	£
Stock at replacement cost 31 January 1992	2500	
Original cost of stock	2000	
Unrealized holding gain on stock		500
Machine at replacement cost 31 January 1992	13000	
Original cost of machine	12000	
Total holding gain on machine	1000	
Less: Realized holding gain on machine	200	
Unrealized holding gain on machine		800
Van at replacement cost 31 January 1992	2400	
Original cost of van	2000	
Total holding gain on van	400	
Less: Realized holding gain on van	100	
Unrealized holding gain on van		300
Total unrealized holding gains		1600

We can now complete the replacement cost balance sheet of Highrisk:

**Balance sheet of Highrisk at 31 January 1992
using the replacement cost model**

	1992			1991
Fixed assets	£	£	£	£
Machine	13 000		12 000	
Depreciation	2 600	10 400	0	12 000
Van	2 400		2 000	
Depreciation	600	1 800	0	2 000
Current assets				
Stocks		2 500		
Cash at bank		3 500		1 000
		18 200		15 000
		£		£
Owners' equity		5 000		5 000
Profit		1 300		0
Realized gains		300		
Unrealized gains		1 600		
Total equity		8 200		5 000
Loans		10 000		10 000
		18 200		15 000

As can be seen, the total gain is split between the profits, the realized holding gains and the unrealized holding gains. You will also have noted that the 1991 replacement cost balance sheet is the same as the historic cost balance sheet and the 1991 CPP balance sheet. This will always be the case at the point when the assets etc. are acquired as the replacement cost at that point in time is equal to the transaction cost, i.e. the historic cost, and of course the money spent reflects the purchasing power of £1 at that point in time. You may also have worked out that the replacement cost profit plus the realized holding gains equals the historic cost profit. This is because replacement cost divides the realized gains into those that arise as a result of operating, i.e. operating profits, and those that arise as a result of specific price changes, i.e. holding gains.

Having looked at the way the model operates, and the resultant balance sheet and profit and loss account, we can now move on to a consideration of some of the arguments in favour of the replacement cost model and some of the criticisms of the model. However, prior to that we shall use Example 17.3 to illustrate why the depreciation charge had to be based on the end-of-year replacement cost rather than the average replacement cost.

Example 17.3
Paul starts a business selling ice cream. He puts in £10 000 and buys a van for £8000 and uses the other £2000 for working capital and buying stock as and when he needs it. At the end of the first year he has no stock, has made sales of £12 000 and incurred costs including buying ice cream of £6000. We shall assume for the sake of simplicity that the van will last two years and have no residual value.

In the second year his results are exactly the same as for the first year.

The replacement cost of a van at the end of the first year is £11 000 and, due to a slump in the commercial vehicle market, it is the same at the end of the second year.

Paul withdraws all of the operating profit from the business at the end of each year.

Solution – based on end-of-year replacement costs
If we were to draw up the profit and loss and balance sheets using replacement costs at the end of the year for depreciation, the resultant accounts would be:

Replacement cost profit and loss accounts of Paul's business – version 1

	Year 1	Year 2
Sales	12 000	12 000
Cost of sales	6 000	6 000
Gross profit	6 000	6 000
Depreciation	5 500	5 500
Operating profit	500	500

Replacement cost balance sheets of Paul's business – version 2

Fixed asset	Year 0		Year 1		Year 2	
Van	8 000		11 000		11 000	
Depreciation	0	8 000	5 500	5 500	11 000	0
Current asset						
Cash		2 000		7 500		13 000
		10 000		13 000		13 000
Owner's equity		10 000		10 000		10 000
Profit for year			500		500	
Less: Drawings			500	0	500	0
Holding gains						
– Realized		0		1 500		3 000
– Unrealized		0		1 500		0
		10 000		13 000		13 000

As can be seen, at the end of the second year Paul has retained enough profits to replace the van and still have £2000 for working capital and to buy ice cream when he needs it.

Solution – based on average replacement costs
If depreciation was based on the average replacement cost the profit and loss accounts and balance sheets would be:

Replacement cost profit and loss accounts of Paul's business – version 2

	Year 1	Year 2
Sales	12 000	12 000
Cost of sales	6 000	6 000
Gross profit	6 000	6 000
Depreciation	4 750	4 750
Operating profit	1 250	1 250

Replacement cost balance sheets of Paul's business – version 2

Fixed asset	Year 0		Year 1		Year 2	
Van	8 000		11 000		11 000	
Depreciation	0	8 000	4 750	6 250	9 500	1 500
Current asset						
Cash		2 000		6 750		11 500
		10 000		13 000		13 000
Owner's equity		10 000		10 000		10 000
Profit for year			1 250		1 250	
Less: Drawings			1 250	0	1 250	0
Holding gains						
– Realized		0		750		1 500
– Unrealized		0		2 250		1 500
		10 000		13 000		13 000

As you can see, at the end of year 2, Paul only has £11 500 in cash which will not allow him to replace the van for £11 000 and still use £2000 for working capital and for buying ice cream. You can also see that, at the end of the second year, the asset is shown at £1500 when in fact under our assumptions it is worthless. Thus if we are to follow the matching principle we will not have full capital maintenance; conversely, if we use end-of-year depreciation, then our costs and revenues are no longer matched.

Obviously if we apply the same assumptions and use the historic cost model then Paul will only have £10 000, i.e. his original equity, at the end of year 2, and unless he could obtain additional finance he would have to cease trading.

It is worth noting that the problem of not retaining enough funds through using average replacement costs for depreciation would also apply to the use of end-of-year replacement costs if the price of the van rose again in the second year. This is because the funds retained in respect of its use in the first year would have been based upon the replacement cost at that time. This is, in fact, a general problem with any model in times of rising prices and is commonly referred to as 'backlog depreciation'. Thus, although it is a fault with the replacement cost model, it is applicable to other models and, as such, we shall not specifically refer to it under the criticisms of the replacement cost model which follow the next section.

Arguments in favour of the replacement cost model

The replacement cost model, in contrast to the historic cost and the CPP model, is entity based. Its supporters would argue that this is more appropriate as it maintains the income-generating assets of the entity, not the owners' equity. It does this by adopting a definition of capital based on the physical assets. The fact that it aims to maintain physical assets also means that it has to use specific price changes which, it is argued, are more relevant to an enterprise than general price changes.

It is also claimed that, as it expresses the accounting numbers in £ sterling, it is more easily understood than CPP. Those in favour of the model also argue that, unlike many of the other models suggested, replacement cost has proved to be a practical model and cite the use of the model since 1959 by Philips as evidence of this.

A major argument in favour of the replacement cost model is that it separates out operating gains from holding gains. This allows the user to predict what will happen to these separately and to evaluate management in terms of those gains over which the user thinks they have control. Similarly the fact that the unrealized holding gains are identified provides the user with more information on the changes in the enterprise over the period in question.

Arguments against the replacement cost model

Perhaps the most commonly heard, but by no means the most important, of the arguments against the use of replacement costs is that they are subjective. Whilst there is some substance in this argument, it has to be weighed against the fact that all models, in practice, have degrees of subjectivity in them. For example, the version of historic cost that we use allows for revaluation of buildings, for depreciation, for amortization, for stock valued at net realizable value, etc. Thus whilst the criticism is valid, it needs to be put into perspective and judged against the criteria of relevance, as we showed in Figure 1.1 in Chapter 1. That diagram, you will recall, shows the qualitative characteristics of information and the trade-off between relevance and reliability.

A second area of criticism which is more fundamental relates to the problems of finding the replacement cost of an equivalent asset if the asset the enterprise is using is no longer made. For example, if we have out-of-date computers, what is the equivalent of those in today's terms? The answer, in a number of cases, is that there is no equivalent – there are only better, more powerful machines. Allied to this point, and in some ways an extension of it, is the question of whether the asset would, in fact, be replaced. The model within its definition of capital assumes that physical assets would be replaced. This is alright in a static world, but in a world of changing tastes, fashions and technology it is highly suspect.

Also related to the definition of capital are arguments which question whether maintaining physical assets is sufficient. These suggest that profits arise out of operating and not just out of production. Thus, if changes in prices affect the amount needed to finance debtors and the amount of credit taken, then the effects of those price changes must also be taken into account if we are to arrive at a profit that can be maintained in the future.

Finally, there are those who argue that whilst replacement cost deals with the effects of specific price changes it ignores the effects of general price changes on the monetary items. Thus they argue that what is needed is a model that deals with both types of price change, i.e. a real value model.

Replacement cost profit as a useful measure

Any evaluation of the usefulness of the replacement cost model profit must be put in the context of some of the criticisms of the model set out above, in particular the fact that the model is a static model and that the definition of capital may be somewhat narrow in that it excludes working capital requirements from consideration. We also need to include in our consideration not only the replacement cost operating profit but also the holding gains as these are an integral part of the model.

Bearing the above remarks in mind, we can see that as far as distribution is concerned the profit measure is superior to that under historic cost and CPP. In the case of historic cost the profit includes realized holding gains which are not separately identified. Thus, they could be distributed even though they need to be retained for the continuation of the business. The fact that replacement cost identifies the amounts involved as realized holding gains allows a decision to be made about whether they should be retained or distributed, the latter course of action perhaps being appropriate when the particular physical asset is not going to be replaced. In contrast to CPP, the replacement cost profit does distinguish between realized and unrealized gains and thus unrealized gains will not be distributed as a result of a lack of information.

In terms of evaluation, the fact that the user is given information about the total gains made and how each of the components of those total gains arose improves the usefulness of the information to the user. It allows the user to evaluate management in terms of their performance in achieving operating gains and, if appropriate, to evaluate management in terms of their performance in respect of holding gains. It also allows the user to compare alternative investments without the distorting effects of price changes on the operating results. However, there is a trade-off in terms of the costs of producing the information and the reliability of the information.

Finally in terms of prediction, the fact that operating gains and holding gains are separated will lead to improved predictive ability because each of these are likely to be driven by different forces. However, in terms of prediction there are severe limitations imposed by the model assuming replacement of physical assets, especially in a rapidly changing environment. This assumption imposes a severe limitation on the usefulness of the profit measure if assets are not to be replaced.

The replacement cost model, by the fact that it separates holding gains from operating gains, can be seen to be using a revised ex-post profit measure. It also uses an entity approach to the definition of capital. Thus, overall, it would seem reasonable to conclude that replacement cost is probably a better measure of performance than historic cost or CPP. However, it does suffer from a major limitation in that it is a static model and therefore is unlikely to fully reflect economic reality in a dynamic environment. To answer this particular problem the Sandilands report suggested the use of the deprival value model on which models such as current cost accounting are based. We shall briefly introduce deprival value but will not consider it or the other models in detail as they are outside the scope of this introductory text.

	£80		£60		£40	Deprival value
1.	NRV	>	PV	>	RC	RC
2.	NRV	>	RC	>	PV	RC
3.	PV	>	NRV	>	RC	RC
4.	PV	>	RC	>	NRV	RC
5.	RC	>	PV	>	NRV	PV
6.	RC	>	NRV	>	PV	NRV

Figure 17.1 Basis of deprival value.

Deprival value

The concept of deprival value, or value to the business as it is often referred to, is derived from the work of Bonbright in 1937. He defined what he called opportunity value as 'The value of a property to its owner is identical in amount with the adverse value of the entire loss, direct and indirect, that the owner might expect to suffer if he were deprived of the property.'

This value is not based on a single measure such as replacement cost but on a combination of possible values which are replacement cost (RC), net realizable value (NRV) and the present value (PV) of potential earnings. The Sandilands report identifies six possible hypothetical combinations of these values. These are shown in Figure 17.1 together with the correct basis for arriving at the deprival value and some hypothetical figures which we shall use in our explanation.

In case 1, the enterprise would be better off selling the asset than using it, as the net realizable value is greater than the potential future earnings, i.e. the present value. If the enterprise sold the asset it could earn £80. However, if it lost the asset it could replace the asset for £40 and either use it to earn £60 or sell it for £80. Therefore the maximum loss that the enterprise would suffer, if it was deprived of the asset, would be £40, i.e. the replacement cost.

In case 2, a similar argument applies except, in this case, there would be no point in replacing the asset for use in the business as the replacement cost is more than the present value. What would happen here is that the asset would be replaced and sold. This is because the net realizable value is £80 and it can be replaced for £60. So, in this case, the deprival value is again the replacement cost.

In case 3, the asset would again be replaced for £40 if the enterprise was deprived of it. It could either be resold for £60 or used in the business to earn £80. Thus, once again, the deprival value is equal to the replacement cost.

KEY CONCEPT 17.3 **VALUE TO THE BUSINESS**	The value of an asset or a liability to a business is equivalent to the maximum loss it would suffer if it were to be deprived of that asset or liability.

In case 4, the asset would be replaced for £60 because by doing so the enterprise could earn £80 through using the asset in the business. Thus, once again, the deprival value is equal to the replacement cost.

In case 5, the asset would not be replaced if the enterprise was deprived of it because it would cost £80 to replace, whereas the maximum that can be earned through using it or from selling it is £60, i.e. the present value. So, in this case, the maximum loss that would be suffered is £60 and deprival value is equal to the present value.

In case 6, once again the asset would not be replaced if the enterprise was deprived of it. This is because it would cost £80 to replace whereas the maximum that can be earned through using it or from selling it is £60, i.e. the net realizable value. So, in this case, the maximum loss that would be suffered is £60 and deprival value is equal to the net realizable value.

From this we can see that the concept of deprival value or value to the business overcomes the problems of the static nature of the replacement cost model. In other words, where the asset would not be replaced, for whatever reason, an alternative figure to the replacement cost is the appropriate value to use. We can also derive from the discussion above a rule relating to deprival value or value to the business as follows:

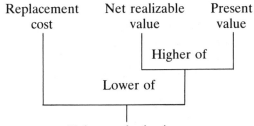

Summary

In this chapter we have introduced an entity-based model in the form of replacement cost accounting. This model, unlike the CPP model, is based on specific price changes rather than general price changes. We have illustrated how the model works and looked at some of the arguments in favour of and against the model. We have then evaluated the model against the criteria for a useful profit measure set up in Chapter 15. Overall we have seen that although the model is a considerable improvement on historic cost it does not address two issues. The first is that the model is static and is therefore limited in its usefulness in a dynamic world. This can be overcome to some extent by the adoption of a hybrid model such as that based upon deprival value. The second area of weakness is that it fails to deal with general price changes which will affect the enterprise. To deal with general as well as specific price changes needs an accounting model that encompasses what is known as a real value system and consideration of such a model has to be left to your further studies. Similarly, consideration of alternative systems based on a

CASE 17.1

EXAMPLES OF ALTERNATIVE ACCOUNTING MODELS

Although the accounting standard relating to current cost accounting has been withdrawn the accounts of ex-nationalized industries are still prepared using a current cost model. Below is an extract from the accounting policies statement of British Gas Plc explaining how value to the business is arrived at in respect of tangible fixed assets. It is followed by the current cost profit and loss account and the historic cost profit and loss account for 1991 of British Gas Plc. An alternative way of presenting such information is provided by the extract from the notes to the 1990 accounts of BAT Industries.

Extract from the notes to the accounts of British Gas Plc

Tangible fixed assets

a) Tangible fixed assets are included in the balance sheets at their value to the business. The value to the business has been assessed on the following bases:

Current replacement cost

i) land and buildings – periodic valuation by the Group's qualified internal valuers determined on the basis of open market value for existing use, excepting specialised properties for which depreciated replacement cost is used;

ii) regional distribution mains, services, meters and gas storage – application of calculated average unit replacement costs to the physical lengths or quantities in use;

iii) national transmission system and regional transmission mains – replacement cost estimated by the Group's engineers as at 1 April and indexed to 31 March using appropriate indices; and

iv) exploration and production tangible assets and other tangible fixed assets – indexation of historical costs using appropriate indices.

The assessment of value to the business involves certain estimates being made which are subject to continuing revision.

Additions represent extensions to, or significant increases in, the capacity of tangible fixed assets; expenditure on the replacement of certain categories of UK tangible fixed assets (mains, services and meters) is charged as a trading cost. Contributions received towards the cost of tangible fixed assets are included in creditors as deferred income and credited to the profit and loss account over the life of the assets. Previously these contributions were included in revaluations. This represents a change in accounting policy; comparative figures have been restated.

Regulatory book values

v) the tangible fixed assets of the regulated operations of Consumers' are recorded at historical cost, being amounts recoverable through revenues in future periods under the regulatory environment.

Current cost profit and loss account of
British Gas Plc
for the year ended 31 March 1991

	Notes	1991 £M	1990 £M (as restated)
Turnover	1	**9491**	7983
Cost of sales		**(4717)**	(4111)
Gross profit		**4774**	3872
Distribution costs		**(2051)**	(1843)
Administrative expenses		**(1068)**	(922)
Current cost operating profit	1 and 2	**1655**	1107
Gearing adjustment		**41**	29
Net interest	4	**(140)**	(73)
Current cost profit before taxation		**1556**	1063
Taxation	5	**(640)**	(368)
Current cost profit after taxation		**916**	695
Minority shareholders' interest		**2**	(3)
Current cost profit attributable to British Gas Shareholders		**918**	692
Dividends	6	**(533)**	(447)
Current cost profit retained	22	**385**	245
Current cost earnings per ordinary share	7	**21.5p**	16.2p

Historic cost profit and loss account of British Gas Plc
I. Group historical cost profit and loss account

For the year ended 31 March 1991	Notes	1991 £M	1990 £M
Turnover	a	**9491**	7983
Cost of sales		**(4586)**	(4039)
Gross profit		**4905**	3944
Distribution costs		**(1875)**	(1698)
Administrative expenses		**(1041)**	(876)
Historical cost operating profit	a	**1989**	1370
Net interest		**(140)**	(73)
Historical cost profit before taxation		**1849**	1297
Taxation		**(640)**	(368)
Historical cost profit after taxation		**1209**	929
Minority shareholders' interest		**2**	(3)
Historical cost profit attributable to British Gas shareholders		**1211**	926
Dividends		**(533)**	(447)
Historical cost profit retained		**678**	479
Historical cost earnings per ordinary share	b	**28.4p**	21.7p

Continued over page

Continued from previous page

Extract from the notes to the accounts of BAT Industries

12. Accounting for inflation

	1990 £M	1989 £M
Commercial activities		
Cost of sales adjustment	**211**	250
Depreciation adjustment	**61**	47
Monetary working capital adjustment	**(110)**	(123)
	162	174
Gearing adjustment – net other monetary items	**(9)**	28
	153	202
Associated companies	**1**	3
	154	205
Attributable to minority shareholders	**(61)**	(73)
Required inflation retention	**93**	132
Net tangible fixed assets	**1289**	1445
Current replacement cost of stocks	**1336**	1570

The figures shown above have been calculated as follows:

(a) Cost of sales adjustment represents the difference between the cost of sales charged in the profit and loss account on page 35 and their replacement cost at the time of sale.

(b) Depreciation adjustment is the excess of the depreciation charge based on the current cost of fixed assets over the depreciation charge on their costs as shown in note 14 on page 47.

(c) Monetary working capital adjustment represents that part of the inflation adjustments which is not borne by the business as a result of the financing benefit derived from the excess of trade creditors over trade debtors.

(d) Gearing adjustment is calculated by reference to price indices on monetary items not included in the monetary working capital adjustment.

wider definition of capital than that adopted by the replacement cost model will have to be something to look forward to. The intention in the last three chapters – and indeed the whole of this book – has been to provide an introduction to areas of interest and hopefully to whet the appetite for more.

References

Bonbright, J.C. (1975) *The Valuation of Property*, McGraw-Hill.
Sandilands Report (1975) *Report of the Inflation Accounting Committee*, HMSO, Cmnd Paper 6225.

Further reading

Gee, K.P. and Peasnell, K.V. (1976) A pragmatic defence of replacement cost accounting, *Accounting and Business Research*, Autumn.

Gynther, R.S. (1966) *Accounting for Price Level Changes: Theory and Procedures*, Pergamon.

May, R.G., Mueller, G.G. and Williams, T.H. (1980) *A New Introduction to Financial Accounting*, Prentice Hall.

Sandilands Report (1975) *Report of the Inflation Accounting Committee*, HMSO, Cmnd Paper 6225.

Review questions

1. What is the definition of capital adopted by the replacement cost model?

2. Explain the difference between operating gains and holding gains.

3. Explain why it is important for users to have operating gains and realized holding gains separately identified.

4. For what purpose could users use the information about unrealized holding gains?

5. What are the major criticisms of the replacement cost model?

6. In terms of the usefulness of the profit measure what are the major caveats that have to be borne in mind?

7. Define deprival value in your own words and explain why it could be seen as an improvement on the replacement cost model.

8. In what circumstances would deprival value be something other than replacement cost? Provide examples applicable to a business enterprise.

Problems for discussion and analysis

The information below relates to questions 1 to 3 below.

Printalot commenced trading on 1 April 1991 with £12 000 owners' equity and £3000 on a long-term interest-free loan. On that day they purchased a printing machine for £12 400 and a second-hand van for £2000. The rest of the transactions for the year to 31 March 1992 are summarized below:

	£
Sales	20 000
Materials purchased	10 000
Wages paid	6 000
Van expenses	1 500

At 31 March 1992 there were materials in stock which had cost £2000. All transactions were for cash and they took place evenly throughout the year unless otherwise stated. The machine is to be depreciated over five years and the van over four years. Both use the straight line method and neither has any residual value. The specific price indexes for machines and commercial vehicles are given below:

	Machines	Commercial vehicles
1 April 1991	124	200
31 August 1991	130	224
31 March 1992	138	250
Average for year	131	225

The replacement cost of the goods in stock at 31 March 1992 was £2600.

1. Produce the replacement cost accounts for the year to 31 March 1992.

2. Comment on the performance of Printalot as shown by the set of accounts you have produced.

3. Of the three sets of accounts that you have produced for Printalot, i.e. historic cost, current purchasing power and replacement cost, which do you consider would be more useful to shareholders and what are your reasons for your answer?

Index

Absorption costing 162
Accounting
 definition 2, 3
 limitations 17
 uses 3
 policies statement 300
 Standards Committee 10, 17
 theory 17
Accrual accounting 92–4, 147
 see also Matching principle
Accruals 136–43
 definition 137
Acid test 317–8
Altman, E. 21
American
 Accounting Association 17
 Accounting Principles Board 3
 Institute of Certified Public
  Accountants 2
Amounts
 payable 137
 receivable 129
Annual reports 7
Arnold, J.
 Hope, T. and Southworth, A.J.
  23, 61, 240, 341, 356
 and Moizer, P. 20

Assets
 circulating 69
 current 69
 definition 66
 fixed 68
 indeterminate 70
 intangible 204–18
 tangible 175–94
Auditors' report 301
Average cost 161

Bad debts 132–3
 See also Debtors
Balance sheet 300
 definition 64
 equation 72–5, 111

format 77–84
 importance of 65
 purpose 65, 77–8
Bank
 loans 226
 overdrafts 225–6
 (*see also* Short- and Medium-term
  finance)
B.A.T. Industries 146, 374
Baxter W.T. 195
Bentalls Plc 168, 188, 261, 284, 288
Berry A.J., Citron D., Jarvis R.W.
  9, 20, 44, 77, 84, 88, 106,
  225, 267
Blake J. 147, 262
Body Shop International Plc 76–7
Bonbright, J.C. 370, 374
Bonds 199
Book-keeping
 traditional approach 243–8
Bourne, M. 356
Brands 204–8
Brighton Cooperative Society 40, 41
Brittania Building Society 37
British
 Airways Plc 5, 19, 42, 145, 230–1
 Coal 11
 Gas Plc 49, 188, 210, 372–3
 Petroleum Plc 59, 95, 169, 211
Building societies 36–7
Bull, R.J. 70, 84
Business entity principle 64, 68

Cadbury Schweppes 208, 214
Capital redemption reserve 236
Carsberg, B. and Page, M. 44, 79,
  84
Carsberg, B. and Noke, C. 92, 106
Cash flow statements 268–85
 cash and cash equivalents 271
 financing activities 282–3
 financial analysis 301, 320–2
 investing activities 282

net cash flow from operating
  activities 280–1
 returns on investments and
  servicing 281
 taxation 281–2
Chairman's report 300
Charges, fixed and floating 225
CIPFA 36
Companies
 act formats 83–4, 103
 guarantee 256
 limited 256–60
 listed 256
 size 43
Consistency principle 209
Consolidated accounts
 entity approach 216–7
 minority interest 217–8
 parent company method 217–8
 proprietary approach 215–6
Contingent liabilities
Co-operatives 40
Coopers & Lybrand 263
Corporate report 6, 285
Cost of goods sold 154–5
Cost, types of
 average 161
 current 208
 historic 52
 original 52
 plus pricing 153
 replacement 53, 208
 written down 53
Creditors 137–43
 amounts falling due within one
  year 83
 amounts falling due after one year
  83
 definition 137
Credits and debits 243–4
Cum div 203
Current assets 69
 definition 70

net 82
purchasing power
    accounting model 344–52
    arguments against 353–4
    arguments for 352
    definition of capital 344
    evaluation of model 354–6
    monetary and non-monetary
        items 345
    monetary gains and losses 345
Current ratio 317
Cyert, R.M. and Ijiri, Y. 26, 44

Databases 299
Debentures 199
Debits and credits 243–4
Debt finance
    debt to equity ratio 236–40
    long-term 229–32
    medium-term 226–9
    short-term 223–6
    total debt 316
Debtors 130–1
    aged 133
    bad debts 132–3
    collection period 320–1
    doubtful debts 133
    provision 133
    turnover 320–1
Department of Employment 106
Department of Trade and Industry
    106
Depreciation
    definition 181
    methods 185–9
    purpose 181–5
    rates 186–8
    reducing balance method 186
    straight line method 185–6
Deprival value 370–1
Directors' report 300
Dividends 234
    cover 318–9
Double entry book-keeping 111–18
    incorrect entries 116
    single entry 116
Drawings 96
Duality principle 75, 111

Earnings process 92–4
Economic value 54
Edwards, E.O. and Bell, P.W. 17
Egginton, D. 267, 289
Employee reports 288
End-of-period adjustments 246–7

Entity
    accounting 64
    approach or view 260, 287
    business 64, 68
    legal 64
    tax 64
Equity finance 234–6
    see also Shares
Errors
    incorrect double entry 116
    single entry 116
    transposition 117
European community 20
Ex ante income 329, 330–2
Ex post income 329, 332–6
    revised 334–6
Ex div 203
Expenses 92–8
    definition 95
Exceptional items 143–4
Exposure drafts 204
    ED 47 213
    ED 52 204
Extraordinary items 143–4

Factoring 224–5
Final accounts 248–9
    effects of organizational forms
        249–60
Financial
    accounting 4, 7
    Accounting Standards Board
        (FASB) 14
        Statement of Financial
            Accounting Concepts No. 1
            15, 286
        Statement of Financial
            Accounting Concepts No. 2
            16
    analysis
        basis of 297
        business risk 298
        cash flow statements 320–2
        context 297–302
        effects of size 297–8
        environmental, social and
            political factors 298
        key features 323
        key limitations 323–4
        industrial trends 298
        price changes 298
        sources of information 299–302
        techniques 307–23
            common size statements
            311–4

importance of base year 314
index number trends 310
percentage change 311
ratios 315–20
trend analysis 309–11
press 299
reporting
    Standard No. 1 39, 267–72
Finished goods 167–9
First-in, first-out 160
Fisher, I. 55, 60
Fixed assets
    cost 177–80
    definition 69
    disposal 191–4
    net book value 185
    residual value 180
    revaluation 189–90
    sale 191–4
    transportation costs 177–8
    useful life 180
    written down value 185
Friends Provident 38
Future benefits 66, 114, 130, 158

Gearing 236–9
Gee, K.P. and Peasnell, K.V. 375
Generally accepted accounting
        practice (GAAP) 42
Goodwill 212–3
    definition 212
    on consolidation 213–4
Government statistics 299
GKN Plc 168
Gray, R.H. 23, 219
Gray, R.H., Owen, D.J. and
        Maunders, K.T. 289
Gray, S.J. and Maunders, K.T. 287,
        289
Guinness Plc 168–9, 194, 207
Gynther, R.S. 219, 356, 375

Henley, D., Holtham, C.,
        Likierman, A. and Perrin, J.
        48
Hicks, Sir John 47, 176, 328
Hire purchase 178–80, 226–7
Historic cost 52
    definition of capital 337
    model generally 337–40
    evaluation of 337–41
Hussey, R. 21

Income
    definition 47

distribution, use for 337
evaluation, use for 337
ex ante 329, 331–2
ex post 332–6
maintainable 336
revised ex post 334–6
prediction, use for 337
Indeterminate assets 70
Inflation accounting 10
Institute of Chartered Accountants
    in England and Wales 6
Intangible assets 204–5
Interest cover 318–9
Interim reports 9
International accounting standards
    number 18 90, 106
Investments 199–204
    equity 203–4
    fixed interest 200–3

Just-in-time 150–1, 170

Kaldor, N. 55, 60

Lall, R.M. 66, 175
Last-in, first-out 160–1
Laughlin, R. and Gray, R. 44, 267,
    289
Leases 179, 227–8
    finance 228
    operating 228
Lee, G.A. 195, 263
Lee, T.A. 219, 289, 341
    and Tweedie, D.P. 20
Legal ownership 67
Lev, B. 324
Liabilities 65, 70–1
    contingent 145
    current 71
    definitions 71
    net current 82
Limitations of accounting
    information 17–19, 323–4
Limited companies
    guarantee companies 256
    legal status 256
    listed companies 256
Limmack, R.J. 263
Liquidity 65, 305–6
    measures 317
    short term 317–8
Loan stock 199, 232
Long-term contracts 166–7
Long-term finance 229–36
    loans 229–30

Lotus 1, 2, 3 111

McIllhattan, R.A. 170
Macve, R. 10
Management accounting 4, 6
Manufacturing process 153
Marginal costing 162
Marks and Spencer Plc 308
Matching principle 92–4, 147,
    365–7
Materiality 144
May, R., Mueller, G. and
    Williams, T. 60, 341, 375
Medium-term finance 226–9
Meyer, P.E. 289
Modified accounts 43
Moonitz, M. 17
Morley, M.F. 289
Myers, J.H. 106

Needle, D. 170
Net present value 54, 329–30
Net realizable value 55, 158
    definition 158
    forced sale 55
    open market 55
Notes to the accounts 301

Objectives of accounting 14
Opportunity cost 151
Original cost 52
Organizations
    forms 31–8
    goals 35–40
    size 39, 79–80, 103
    types 79–80, 102
Ownership, legal title 67
Owners' equity 71–2
    definition 72

Page, M. 23
Par value of shares 233–4
Partnerships 233, 250–6
    agreements, basis of 250–6
    capital accounts 250
    current accounts 250
    drawings 248–62
    final accounts 254–5
    interest on capital 252
    liability of partners 250
    salaries and bonuses 253
    share of profits 251, 253
Pizzey, A. 147, 195, 240
Prepaid expenses 98
Prepayments 97, 130–2

Price changes
    effects on stock 159–62
Pricing, cost plus 153
Prior year adjustments 143–4
    See also SSAP 6
Profit
    definition 48
    gross 101
    net 101
    retained 223–4
Profit and loss account 98–104, 300
    determinants of format 102–4
    importance of 89
    purpose of 300
Profitability 302–4
    future 299
Proprietary approach or view 260,
    286, 337, 344
Provident and Friendly Societies 36,
    38
Prudence 95, 119, 124, 133, 159, 210

Qualitative characteristics 16
Quick ratio 317–8

Rank Hovis McDougall Plc 206, 239
Ratio analysis 315–20
    balance sheet ratios 316–8
    combined statement ratios
    319–20
    profit and loss account ratios
    318–9
Realization principle 92
Receivables 91, 129
Regulatory framework 80, 103–4
Replacement cost 53
    accounting
    arguments against 368
    arguments for 367–8
    backlog depreciation 365–6
    evaluation of model 369–70
    holding gains and operating
    gains 359–60
    holding gains, realized 363–4
    holding gains, unrealized 364–5
    model 359–70
    model, definition of capital 359
Research and development 209–12
Reserves
    revaluation of assets 189
Retail price index 345
Revaluation 189–90
Revenue
    definition 90
    recognition 92–4

Risk
  business 223
  financial 223, 236–9, 305–6

SSAP
  see Statements of Standard
    Accounting Practice
Sainsbury 307
Sandilands report 266, 341, 344,
    370, 374
Shares
  bonus issue 235–6
  full price issues 234–5
  issue of shares 234–6
  ordinary 233
  premium account 234
  preference 236
  rights issue 235
  voting rights 257
Sherer, M. 21
Short-term finance 223–6
Single entry error 116
Sole proprietorships 232–3, 250
Solvency 316–8
Source and application of funds
    statements 276–7
Sources of information
  external 299
  internal 300–2
Specialist agencies 299
Spreadsheets 111
Statements of Standard Accounting
    Practice
  number 1 203
  number 2 17, 92, 106, 209
  number 3 39
  number 6 13–14, 192, 193, 259
  number 7 344
  number 8 258
  number 9 161–2, 260
  number 10 266, 267

  number 12 181, 190
  number 13 209, 260
  number 14 203
  number 15 258
  number 18 145
  number 21 39, 179, 227
  number 22 212, 260
Stock 151
  cost determination 154–7, 162–5
  count 155, 156
  disclosure requirements 167–8
  levels 155
  valuation 157–8
Stock and work in progress
  definition 151
  finished goods 152
  long term contracts 167
  work in progress 152
Stock Exchange 7, 9
Stock valuation
  cost, establishment of 154–7
  effects of price changes 159–60
  effects of technological change
    158–9
  effects of type of business 152–4
  methods
    average cost 162–3
    first-in, first-out 161–2
    last-in, first-out 162–3
  valuation rule 158–9

T accounts 243–6
Taffler, R.J. 21
Taxation
  deferred 258
Time value of money 54
Timeliness of information 323
Tottenham Hotspur FC 18
Trade
  credit 223–4

  journals 299
Transposition errors 117
Trend analysis 309–11
Trial balance 246
  extended 247
Trueblood Committee 6

Underdown, B. and Taylor, P. 16,
    17
Users and their needs 80, 104
  auditors 296
  common needs 297, 302–6
  customers 9
  employees 9, 296
  financial analysis 294–7
  government 10
  internal 4
  investors 293–4
  lenders 8, 295–6
  management 296
  preference shareholders 294–5
  public 10
  shareholders 7
  stockbrokers 8
  suppliers 9

Value added statements 285–8
  advantages 286–7
Value of money 49
Value to the business 370

Watts, R. and Leftwich, R. 21
Wealth
  definition of 47
  maintenance of 46–7
  measurement 46–58
Work in progress 152
  See also Stock
  valuation 152–4
Worksheet 110–20

Level of measurement of dependent variable	Group Comparisons: Number of groups (the independent variable)				Correlational analyses (To examine relationship strength)
	2 Groups		3+ Groups		
	Independent Groups Tests	Dependent Groups Tests	Independent Groups Tests	Dependent Groups Tests	
Nominal (Categorical)	χ^2 p. 401 (or Fisher's exact test) p. 402	McNemar"s test p. 402	χ^2 p. 401	Cochran's Q	Phi coefficient (dichotomous) or Cramér's V (not restricted to dichotomous) p. 403
Ordinal (Rank)	Mann-Whitney Test p. 396	Wilcoxon signed ranks test p. 396	Kruskal-Wallis H test p. 400	Friedman's test p. 400	Spearman's rho (or Kendall's tau) pp. 403
Interval or Ratio (Continuous)*	Independent group t test pp. 394-395	Paired t test p. 396	ANOVA pp. 396-399	RM-ANOVA pp. 400	Pearson's r p. 402
	Multifactor ANOVA for 2+ independent variables p. 398				
	RM-ANOVA for 2+ groups x 2+ measurements over time p. 424				

*For distributions that are markedly nonnormal or samples that are small, the nonparametric tests in the row above (for ordinal measures) may be needed.